Turning Points

Turning Points

35 Visionaries in Education
Tell Their Own Stories

Edited by Jerry Mintz & Carlo Ricci
Associate Editors: Isaac Graves & Jessica Graves

Turning Points: 35 Visionaries in Education Tell Their Own Stories

Foreword copyright © 2010 by Alfie Kohn
Transforming Society copyright © 2010 by Riane Eisler
My Green River copyright © 2010 by John Taylor Gatto
Democratic Education copyright © 2010 by Yaacov Hecht
Some Thoughts On My Education and My Work copyright © 2010 by Herbert Kohl
What I've Learned copyright © 2010 by Deborah Meier.

Alternative Education Resource Organization
417 Roslyn Road
Roslyn Heights, NY 11577

Cover: Black Dog Design
Layout: Isaac Graves

Photo Credits: Herb Snitzer by Carol Dameron, Yaacov Hecht by Richard Loveszy, Herbert Kohl by Jose Arenas, Basir Mchawi by Kaleah Mchawi, and Mary Leue by Emmanuel Bernstein.

Printed in the United States of America

Library of Congress Control Number: 2010904113
ISBN: 978-0-9745252-5-9

To visionaries in education past, present, and future.

Acknowledgements

We would like to thank this marvelous group of authors who contributed to this project without hesitation. We are pleased to be able to offer their insights to our readers. We are also grateful to Alfie Kohn who kindly accepted our request to write the foreword.

We would like to give a special thanks to Connie Shaw whose keen eye and editing skills have helped us complete this year and a half long project.

Contents

Preface

This book is a collection of stories about education from those who have dared to do things in different ways. The common theme behind all of the contributors' stories is that mainstream schooling needs to be transformed—how we think about and implement education, learning, and teaching needs to change. Moving forward, the assumptions that mainstream schooling makes about children, learning, and education no longer serve us, and we believe never did.

We speak to a lot of educators, parents, and people in the community at large. In sharing with others that there are other ways of educating, we often get similar responses. Far too many, including those most deeply and intimately committed to education, are unaware of what other possibilities are available. In addition, for the most part, mainstream society does not support and allow for these educational alternatives to exist. Mainstream schooling is set up in such a way that it ensures that anyone who tries to challenge its dominance and assumptions, anyone who tries to do things differently, is either pressured to fail or even forced to shut down.

Accordingly, when we tell people about our vision, they usually say that although it sounds utopian and great in theory, and is ethically the right thing to do, it is impossible to realize. Fortunately, the contributors to this book give all of us ostensible, working examples of how educating in different ways is not only theoretically possible, but practically happening. This book is an attempt to show the world not only what other people are saying about how education should change, but what other people have done and are doing to successfully transform education. In other words, it's happening. Despite the pressures, obstacles, and lack of mainstream support, it's happening.

When we were deciding whom we should ask to contribute, we did not want to limit ourselves to a particular tradition. Instead, we wanted to ask those whom we believe have made, or are starting to make, a difference in transforming education, regardless of their organizational affiliation. We were interested in people who had the courage to create their own paths. The contributors, therefore, are a powerful mix of those who are at the beginning of their advocacy career and those who have been at it for quite some time.

As a general guideline, we asked them to focus primarily around the following questions:

• What was your schooling like?
• When did you realize that there is a need for an alternative approach?
• What have you done since to help realize that vision?
• What are you doing now?

Ultimately, we gave them the freedom to deviate in any way they desired, and in the end, we could not be happier with the powerful narratives that we received. Inevitably, each person who has contributed—whether it's an article, an opinion, an idea, or the organizational tools that were needed to bring this book together—has individual commitments and philosophical beliefs. This book is about celebrating and understanding the diversity of possibilities in the hopes that people will be inspired to act. It's about showing what can be done. By bringing together a wide range of alternative mainstream schoolers, homeschoolers/unschoolers/life learners, free and democratic schoolers, Montessori and Waldorf schoolers, we hope that we can learn from each other, and that you as readers will be inspired enough to join in, in whatever ways you feel will make the greatest difference within your context. In *A Life Worth Living: Selected Letters of John Holt*, edited by Susannah Sheffer, Holt writes that, "true social change begins when people change their lives, not just their political ideas or parties" (p. 226). Even if all we do is transform ourselves, a huge gain is made in transforming the world. This book is a call for social change, a call to help us move toward hope and history and away from determinism. We trust that the conversation will continue.

Jerry Mintz & Carlo Ricci

Foreword

Having just spent a delightful few hours with the essays in this book and their refreshingly idiosyncratic blends of philosophy, history (of particular schools), and autobiography, my head is now buzzing with questions. What, for example, would each contributor say about the schools or movements created by the others? How vague would a statement of principles have to be in order for all of them to sign it? Why do so many interesting schools end up imploding or remaining perpetually in the institutional equivalent of intensive care, and why has alternative schooling more generally been in such a precarious state for so many decades? (It is deeply discouraging to hear even Debbie Meier confess that the recipe for "sustainability"—ensuring that a school will survive and remain true to its founder's vision after the founder leaves—has eluded her.)

Many more questions suggest themselves, but the one I'd like to play with—and invite you to think about as you make your way through these essays—concerns the relationship between the people who wrote them and the things they've done. Let's set aside the *why* questions: the rationale for pursuing an education that's child-centered, democratic, or progressive, as well as the relative merits of each variant of alternative education. And let's also put off the *how* questions that concern the developments (some carefully planned, some wholly serendipitous) and the decisions (some wise, some not) that comprise the founding of a school, a magazine, a movement.

Instead, let's ask *who* questions. How is it that certain individuals, and not others, find themselves attracted to these ways of thinking about education and children? What kinds of schools did *they* attend, these people with a stubborn attachment to an unpopular vision? Did most of the thirty-five contributors to this book spend their early days in alternative schools, love them, and resolve to keep the flame burning when they grew up—or did they go to traditional schools, hate them, and decide to devote their lives to creating for other children something that they themselves never had?

I've already read the book so I'll reveal the answer. (I assume no one will mind my doing so in light of the fact that I came up with the question.) Based on what they've written here, only one contributor (Seldin) falls squarely in the first camp, which, come to think of it, probably shouldn't be surprising given the scarcity of alternative education options. But that doesn't mean everyone else represented in this anthology is in the second camp. As is often the case, things become more complicated when you look more closely.

To start, we have to remember that elementary school might have been very different than high school for someone, which in turn might have been unlike college. Also, the academic and nonacademic aspects of schooling aren't always comparable. The former can be boring even when the latter is generally enjoyable, or the former can be reasonably satisfying while the latter is downright oppressive. Then, too, as these chapters make clear, merely knowing whether someone has a hippocampus packed with painful memories doesn't allow us to infer anything about how *successful* he or she was at school—or vice versa. Some people were impressive as hell—high-performing, maybe even popular, students—who were absolutely miserable.

And now comes the critical complication: Just because someone attended traditional schools and then became a nontraditional educator doesn't mean the two are causally related. Sometimes, yes, there's a clear connection: "My own schooling [was] boring, deadening, dull, dry, monotonous, repetitive, rote, uninspiring, irrelevant... [and] nobody apparently thought there was a problem with that"—an experience that eventually prompted the realization that "much of what kids needed was to be given their own lives back" (Llewellyn). And, more succinctly: In "starting a school...I wanted to avoid the mistakes made in my education" (M. Jacobs).

However, most of these writers describe their schooling as "unremarkable," "uneventful," "pretty standard," "a game, an irritation." A few actually enjoyed their years in traditional schools, and even some of those who have nothing positive to say on the subject seem disinclined to connect those early experiences to their subsequent interest in alternative education. (For some, that interest instead grew out of their commitment to social justice or their work in a related field such as humanistic psychology.)

But even this complication turns out to be, well, complicated. For many of these contributors, the search for, or desire to create, an alternative to traditional schooling represented a kind of rebellion after all, even if it wasn't against what had happened to them long ago. Rather, once they were grown, they may have been disturbed by their experiences as novice teachers (e.g., Montgomery) or by what they noticed when their own children started school (e.g., Leue, Hughes, Caldwell—all women, interestingly). At one point or another, then, most of these educators became dissatisfied, even angry, with what happens in conventional classrooms, and they decided to do something about it.

*****

I can certainly relate to these reactions. Some lowlights of my own years in traditional schools:

In third grade, it was easy for me to overlook the lack of intellectual stimulation given my status as a budding star. I had been selected to narrate the (public) school's Christmas Around the World pageant—which included a segment on "Christmas in Israel, which is called Hanukkah" —and, as if that were not a sufficient honor, I was then chosen to represent my class on the school's student council, a body charged with such weighty responsibilities as deciding what color crepe paper should be used to decorate the cafeteria for the sixth-grade dance. My political career came to an unceremonious end, however, when my teacher rescinded the appointment because I "failed to respect school property" —meaning that I had a habit of sitting with one leg tucked under my butt. (I still sit like that, and, perhaps not coincidentally, I have yet to be elected to public office.)

In fifth grade, there came a morning when, having been given yet another pointless assignment, I neatly headed a piece of notebook paper with my name, the date, and the word "Busywork." Very soon after handing it in, I was called up to the teacher's desk, where, remarkably, she neither congratulated me for my dry wit nor thanked me for inviting her to reflect on the value of her curriculum.

In sixth grade, which coincided with the peak of the U.S. invasion of Vietnam, much of music class was taken up with practicing a medley of military songs—"From the Halls of Montezuma. . . " "Off we go into the wild blue yonder...." "Anchors aweigh, my boys...." "Then it's hi! hi! hee! in the field artillery. . ."—that was to be the highlight of our program at a school concert. I refused to participate, defiantly sealing my lips during these numbers. When I explained my reasons to my classmates, some of them decided to join my protest—until the music teacher stared hard at them, at which point they immediately resumed singing. (I learned a lesson then about the limits of solidarity and commitment that has helped me to understand, among other things, why so many educators comply with accountability mandates that they know to be absurd and even harmful.)

In twelfth grade, having finally lived down the shame of being recalled from office nine years earlier, I was elected vice president of my high school's student council. I was happy to perform all of my constitutional duties, which included presiding over the student senate, meeting with cabinet officers charged with decorating the gym for dances, and standing by to assume the presidency in case Billy Blechman suddenly became incapacitated. But there was one exception. I refused to hop on stage as VPs had done in past years and lead those pre-game pep rallies that, in 1974, bore a striking resemblance to the Two Minutes Hate sessions that Orwell had described in *1984*—except that they lasted a lot longer and the vitriol was trained not on enemies of The Party but on another high school. In the name of "school spirit," the student body was whipped into a deafening frenzy as they prematurely celebrated the humiliating defeat of whatever school our football team would be playing against that Friday.

The administration (and Billy) indulged my aversion to a ritual that no one else seemed to mind and I was assigned a different responsibility in its place: delivering the morning announcements over the public address system. I took every opportunity to satirize the rituals of high school life—something I was also doing in my regular humor column for the school paper—and test the tolerance of the adults. The better part of at least one faculty meeting was devoted to me—specifically, to discussing whether I should be censured and silenced. I believe the last straw for some teachers took place on a day when the sequence of class periods had been shuffled due to an all-school assembly and, after reading the revised schedule into the microphone—"Third period first, then second, then homeroom, then fourth . . ."—I added helpfully, "Let me repeat that for those of you on drugs. . . ."

Mostly I spent my years as a student inwardly rolling my eyes at the absurdity of what we were made to do, but doing it anyway. I prepared a lavishly illustrated report on "My Community" in second grade. I memorized the angle-side-angle theorem in ninth grade. And neither passive voice nor the first person was used by me in twelfth grade because of an honors English teacher who seemed determined to make us as fussy and unimaginative as he was—slashing away at our essays with a purple Flair pen, and deducting points for any violations of his lengthy list of rigid restrictions.

I gritted my teeth and tried to figure out how to be in the school without being of the school, although I wouldn't have put it that way back then. I played by most of the rules while somehow holding on to my critical sensibilities so that I could shake off all that nonsense like an ill-fitting suit of clothes the moment I was able to leave.

*****

To tell the story of one's schooling is to tell the story of oneself, perhaps more than one intends. To read others' eerily familiar accounts, meanwhile, offers not only fascination but relief because we realize that our misery had plenty of company. Perhaps we were all drilled in basic math skills so that we'd be able to accurately tabulate the number of victims of traditional education, those who were "wounded by school," as Kirsten Olson puts it. Likewise, it's liberating—but perhaps also a bit depressing—to come across research that shows how everything from homework to grammar instruction rarely provides any benefit even in terms of conventional achievement, never mind the effects on one's interest in learning. Imagine: there are good data to show that the "bunch o' facts" curriculum to which we were subjected, with its lectures and worksheets, grades and quizzes, rewards for obedience and punishments for deviance, may have been exactly as worthless as we suspected it was at the time. And for those who harbored no such suspicions, an epiphany may have arrived later: "I am not the problem . . . schools are" (Ricci)—or at least certain kinds of schools are.

Some of us grumbled more than others did about the uselessness of what we were being made to do. We may even have cried out in pain at some of the cruelties. But at the same time, being children, we tended to accept it all as so many facts of life: the schedule, the curriculum, the rules. We may not have liked them, just as we didn't much care for unpleasant weather, but hey, whatcha gonna do? Once we grew up, we would acquire a sense of perspective, a recognition that Things Could Have Been Otherwise, along with the attendant outrage—or at least indignation.

That, at any rate, is the theory. The sad truth, however, is that some people never correct that posture of passive acceptance, never come to see school policies as contingent, man-made, opposable. It doesn't occur to them to question the premise that when kids do something bad, something bad must be done to them. They never think to ask whether it's necessary, or even sensible, to make children begin a second shift of academic tasks at home after having spent a full day in school. They take on faith that a child's learning must be reduced to a letter or number rating, and that most time in school should be spent listening instead of doing. Many people grow up and subject their own children to the same kind of schooling that they themselves endured. Some of these parents do so with enthusiasm (and flash cards), which is alarming; others just sigh and resign themselves to the inevitability of watching their kids act out an excruciating slow-motion exercise in déjà vu, which is even worse. Apparently the mantra is: "It was bad enough for me, it's bad enough for my kids."

Yet there are remarkable people—and you're going to read the testimonies of some of them when I finally wrap this up—who emerge from these experiences with an understanding that this kind of education is unhealthy for children and other living things, *and* with some insight about why that's true (and what might make more sense instead), *and* with a commitment to show the rest of us a better way.

Who does that? And how did they get here from there?

What we're talking about is, at least in part, something that might be called "negative learning," in which people treat a bad situation as a chance to figure out what *not* to do. They sit in awful classrooms and pay careful attention because they know they're being exposed to an enormously useful anti-model. They say to themselves, "Here is someone who has a hell of a lot to teach me about how not to be with children." Some people perfect the art of negative learning while they're still in these environments; others do it retrospectively, questioning what was done to them earlier even if they never thought—or were unable—to do so before. Some people do it on their own; others need someone to lend them the lens that will help them look at things that way.

Of course, a mind-numbing, spirit-killing school experience doesn't reliably launch people into self-actualization, intellectual curiosity, and maybe even a career in alternative education. If it did, we'd want everyone to live through that. But it doesn't, so we don't. The contributors to this book had to beat the odds, and they've designed options to make those odds better for children, options where the learning doesn't have to be by negative example.

If I were helping to prepare new teachers, I'd want them to see progressive education at its best. I'd want them to spend as much time as possible in a place where they can watch seasoned educators work *with* children rather than doing things *to* them, watch them help students make sense of ideas and laugh with delight at a marvelous turn of phrase or an unexpected solution to a problem, watch them as they do their best to shield students from moronic mandates handed down from on high. It's hard enough to walk into a classroom on wobbly legs and face a roomful of students for the first time; if at all possible, you want to have had a few role models who take children, and thinking, seriously.

But if student teachers find themselves in a place where test scores drive the instruction and children are bullied into doing whatever they're told, then someone has to introduce them to the idea of negative learning so they can say to themselves, "What a striking display of lousy pedagogy and disrespect for children in all its putrid particulars! I need to take careful notes so I can do *exactly the opposite* when I have my own classroom!" Or when I start my own school.

I really don't know how some people, including more than a few of the contributors to this book, managed to adopt this mental set while other people just ended up feeling lousy about themselves and about learning. I suspect it reflects an interesting confluence of environment and personality. Maybe the environment has to be really dreadful, as opposed to merely dull, in order to shake people up—but at the same time it must include a glimpse of something better so it's clear what's missing. Someone has to know from experience that schools, or teachers, or parents don't have to be like this.

The personality part, meanwhile, probably should include equal measures of assertiveness (including a contrarian spirit and a dash of up-yours rebelliousness) and empathy. The role of the former is obvious, but the latter is no less important. Some people suffer through the indignity or even brutality of being a newbie somewhere—a fraternity, a medical internship, whatever—and then, once they've attained a little seniority, turn around and abuse the new arrivals. "I got through it and so will they." They may even convince themselves that being treated like dirt was somehow good for them. They may derive pleasure from watching others take their turn at suffering.

What we're looking for are the people who instead say, "I want to work to change this system so others will be spared what was done to me." These are the people with compassion and the courage to shake up the status quo and denounce cruel traditions, who have mastered the art of negative learning and developed a commitment to making the world a better place than they found it.

To see how that sensibility might play out in the field of education, keep reading.

Alfie Kohn

Alfie Kohn writes and speaks widely on human behavior, education, and parenting. His eleven books include *Punished by Rewards* (1993), *Beyond Discipline: From Compliance to Community* (1996), *The Schools Our Children Deserve* (1999), *The Case Against Standardized Testing* (2000), *Unconditional Parenting* (2005), and *The Homework Myth* (2006).

Kohn has been described by Time magazine as "perhaps the country's most outspoken critic of education's fixation on grades [and] test scores." His criticisms of competition and rewards have helped to shape the thinking of educators–as well as parents and managers–across the country and abroad. He has appeared on numerous TV and radio programs, including the "Today" show and two appearances on "Oprah." He lectures widely at universities and to school faculties, parent groups, and corporations, as
well as speaking at staff development seminars and keynoting national education conferences. Kohn lives (actually) in the Boston area and (virtually) at www.alfiekohn.org.

Author Bios

Lynson Moore Beaulieu is currently working as an independent education consultant, and as a life and professional coach, with a focus on supporting leaders of color working in the non-profit sector. Her career spans early childhood and K-12 public education and over twenty-five years of effort. She spent more than a decade working on federal education policy in Washington, DC, and the same amount of time working on the ground with community-based organizations in the West, Midwest, Mid-Atlantic, and Northeast regions. Most recently, she spent time as a grant-maker, supporting grassroots education organizing efforts, and as a governor-appointed state education leader in Massachusetts. Throughout her career, Beaulieu's work has focused on low-income ethnic and culturally diverse children, youth, families, and communities; and on creating, promoting, and ensuring high quality early childhood and public elementary and secondary education experiences for all. Beaulieu is published on topics including early language and literacy development, the achievement of African American and other under-served students, early childhood educator preparation and professional development, family involvement, social movement building, and ethnic, cultural, and language diversity in child development and elementary and secondary education contexts.

Sharon Caldwell is the founder of Nahoon Montessori School, the world's first—and possibly only—democratic Montessori school. She is currently Editor of Montessori Leadership Online and Co-editor of Montessori Leadership. She lives in East London, South Africa, with her husband, Denver, and unschooled sons Christopher and Nicholas.

Lisa D. Delpit is the Executive Director/Eminent Scholar for the Center for Urban Education & Innovation at Florida International University in Miami, Florida. Delpit is a nationally and internationally known speaker and writer whose work has focused on the education of children of color and the perspectives, aspirations, and pedagogy of teachers of color. Delpit's work on school-community relations and cross-cultural communication was cited as a contributor to her receiving a MacArthur "Genius" Award in 1990; and she has used her training in ethnographic research to spark dialogues between educators on issues that impact students typically least well-served by the educational system.

Recently, Delpit has assisted national programs in school restructuring efforts, established projects serving South Florida children, such as the Family Literacy and Arts Project (FLAP) and Project Urban Success, and developed urban leadership programs for teachers and school district central office staff.

Her books include *The Real Ebonics Debate: Power, Language, and the Education of African-American Children, The Skin That We Speak: Thoughts on Language and Culture in the Classroom*, and *Other People's Children*, which received the American Educational Studies Association's "Book Critic Award." She is currently working on a book on creating excellence in urban educational settings.

Dr. Riane Eisler is an eminent social scientist, attorney, and author, sought after to keynote conferences worldwide. She is a consultant to business and government on applications of the partnership model introduced in her work, and is President of the Center for Partnership Studies (www.partnershipway.org).

Perhaps most well-known for her bestselling *The Chalice and The Blade: Our History, Our Future*, Eisler has a new book, *The Real Wealth of Nations: Creating a Caring Economics*, hailed by Archbishop Desmond Tutu as "a template for the better world we have been so urgently seeking." The book offers a road map to a new way of economics that gives visibility and value to the most essential human work: caring for people and the planet.

Other books include the award-winning *The Power of Partnership* and *Tomorrow's Children: A Blueprint for Partnership Education in the 21st Century; Sacred Pleasure*, a daring reexamination of sexuality and spirituality; and *Women, Men, and the Global Quality of Life*, which documents the key role of women's status in a nation's general quality of life.

She has received many honors and is included in *Great Peacemakers*, along with Mahatma Gandhi, Mother Teresa, and Martin Luther King, as one of twenty leaders for world peace. To learn more about Dr. Eisler and her work, please visit www.rianeeisler.com.

Gustavo Esteva is an independent writer and grassroots activist. A prominent voice within the "deprofessionalized" segment of the Southern intellectual community, he has been a key figure in founding several Mexican, Latin American, and international NGOs and coalitions. Esteva is the author of more than thirty books, as well as scores of articles that have made significant contributions to economics, cultural anthropology, philosophy, and education. He writes regularly in *La Jornada* and other leading Mexican newspapers. He is an advisor to the Zapatistas in their negotiations with the government and a strong advocate of Zapatismo. As a participant in the Popular Assembly of the Peoples of Oaxaca, Esteva has chronicled the people's uprising and struggles for a radical transformation. In Oaxaca, he participates in the activities of the Centro de Encuentros y Diálogos Interculturales and Universidad de la Tierra en Oaxaca, of which he is a founding member. His recent books include *Grassroots Postmodernism*, with Madhu S. Prakash, and *Celebration of Zapatism*.

John Taylor Gatto taught for thirty years in public schools before resigning dramatically in 1991, on the op-ed pages of the *Wall Street Journal*, claiming he was no longer willing to hurt children. He had recently been named New York State's official "Teacher of the Year" for the third time.

Later that year, he was the subject of a show at Carnegie Hall called "An Evening with John Taylor Gatto," which launched a career of public speaking that has now taken him around the world and nearly three million miles.

In 1992, he was named Secretary of Education in the Libertarian Party Shadow Cabinet and has been included in *Who's Who in America* since 1996. In 1997, he received the Alexis de Tocqueville Award for contributions to liberty, and in 2004, the QuaQua Award for service to humanity. He gave the keynote speech for Australia's Leadership Convention in 2005, and for South Korea's Alternative Education Convention in 2006. He has been on the Board of Advisers for National TV Turnoff Week since its inception.

His books include *Dumbing Us Down: The Hidden Curriculum of Compulsory Schooling*; *The Exhausted School*; *A Different Kind of Teacher*; *The Underground History Of American Education*; and *Weapons of Mass Instruction*.

Arnold Greenberg graduated from Temple University and taught fifth and sixth grade at the Miquon School, one of the earliest progressive schools in the country, and upon seeing the need for a similar high school, founded Miquon Upper School, now known as Crefeld School. He founded Deep Run School of Homesteading and Community—a one year post-high-school program to teach self-sufficiency—in York, Pennsylvania; and later taught at Shoreham-Wading River Middle School, integrating the school's farm into daily curriculum. He owned bakeries and cafés in New Jersey and Maine before returning to school life when he and his son Joe co-founded Liberty School—a Democratic Learning Community—in 1996. His book, *Adventures on Arnold's Island*, which describes a year in which students created a country within their classroom, was published in 1992. He now lives off the grid, in a cabin in the woods, where he writes poetry, short stories, and novels.

David Gribble was born in London in 1932. He was educated at Eton and Cambridge, taught for three years at Repton School, and then at Dartington Hall School from 1963 until it was closed in 1987. With a group of children and two other staff members, he set up Sands School, which is still flourishing. After retiring from Sands in 1992, Gribble played a prominent role in the early development of the International Democratic Education Conferences. He has visited many examples of free education around the world and has written books about what he learned from them. To learn more about Gribble and his work, please visit www.davidgribble.co.uk.

Yaacov Hecht is an internationally distinguished leader and visionary in democratic education, learning theory, and societal change. As president of the Institute for Democratic Education in Israel (IDE), and a sought after speaker and consultant, Hecht plays an essential role in the movement for democratic educational change in Israel and around the world. In 1987, he founded the Democratic School of Hadera, the first Israeli democratic school. When the waiting list for the school soared to over three thousand students, Hecht founded IDE to support the development of other democratic schools. Currently, IDE networks twenty-five democratic schools in Israel, operates democratization programs in schools and municipalities around the country, runs an academic training program for teachers and principals, and supports international projects in democratic education. Hecht has been an education advisor to two Israeli Ministers of Education, and in 2006, was chosen by the Israeli newspaper *Ha'aretz* as one of the fifty most influential educators in Israel.

Helen Hegener left school in the late sixties, at the age of fourteen, to continue her learning at home in Eagle River, Alaska. Her parents wisely understood the concept of unschooling, even then, and over forty years later, Hegener's large extended Alaskan family is still unschooling. Hegener's always-unschooled children have built their own businesses and their own homes, and are now unschooling her grandchildren. Hegener and her husband taught themselves skills with which they have run their own publishing business, *Home Education Magazine*, for thirty years.

They are still active in the greater homeschooling community, but these days also produce books and videos about Alaska. Hegener and her family enjoy canoeing, fishing, gardening, hiking, and much more during the long Alaskan summers, and following long distance dog sled races during the winter for their production company, Northern Light Media.

Matt Hern lives and works in East Vancouver, with his partner and daughters, where he founded the Purple Thistle Centre and Car-Free Vancouver Day. His writing has been published on all six continents and translated into ten languages, and he continues to lecture widely.

He holds a Ph.D. in Urban Studies and teaches at Simon Fraser University and the University of British Columbia.

His books include *Watch Yourself: Why Safer Isn't Always Better*; *Everywhere, All the Time*; and *Common Ground in a Liquid City: Essays in Defense of an Urban Future*.

Helen Hughes was born in 1939 in the beautiful Kootenay Mountains of British Columbia, and has since spent most of her life on the West Coast doing the counter-culture thing. After teaching for five years in the traditional public system, and three years in a Parent Participation Preschool, Hughes started a small alternative school for her children in her home on Windsor Road. She liked the parent participation idea, and preferred the preschool teaching methods to those of the traditional elementary school.

In thirty years, Windsor House Democratic School grew from fifteen students to two hundred. After Hughes retired, it devolved down to one hundred, and is now on the verge of a whole new paradigm. There is a resurgence of energy, and a very versatile, fascinating learning community is emerging.

Although Hughes is retired, she is still very active in the school and within the community. She is clear that in order to practice profound respect, you must be conscious that you personally do not have all the answers and do not know what is best and what is right for others.

Don "Four Arrows" Jacobs is a professor at Fielding Graduate University and author of sixteen books, including *The Authentic Dissertation: Alternative Ways of Knowing, Research and Representation*, and *Unlearning the Language of Conquest*. He has also contributed chapters to *Education as Enforcement: The Militarization and Corporatization of Schools* and *Battleground Schools*. He has doctorates in both health psychology and in curriculum and instruction, with a specialization in indigenous worldviews.

Mark Jacobs is co-founder and co-director of Longview School located in Cortlandt Manor, New York (www.longviewschool.org). He was a regional coordinator for the Kidsave Summer Miracles program, which helps older international orphans find permanent families. Jacobs is a social and political activist who has worked for freedom of speech in Peekskill, and a range of social, political, and environmental causes both as a volunteer and as the former director of WESPAC (www.wespac.org). He is co-founder of the Westchester Citizens Awareness Network and the Indian Point Safe Energy Coalition, two groups dedicated to the closing of the Indian Point nuclear power plants. In 2000, he ran for Congress with the Green Party. He lives in Garrison, New York with his wife, Elena, to whom he has been ecstatically married for fourteen years. He has two children, Jessica and Ben, who never cease to amaze and delight him.

Shilpa Jain spent the last ten years as a learning activist with Shikshantar: The Peoples' Institute for Rethinking Education and Development, based in Udaipur, India. While there, Jain researched, wrote books and articles, facilitated workshops, and hosted gatherings on topics such as globalization, creative expressions, ecology, democratic living, innovative learning, and unlearning. Jain is currently working with Other Worlds Are Possible, a multi-media collaborative focused on grassroots alternatives, and with YES! (based in Santa Cruz, CA) as coordinator of the Global Youth Leadership Collaborative and of the Leveraging Privilege for Social Change Jam. All of her work seeks to uncover ways for people to free themselves from dominating, soul-crushing institutions, and to live in greater alignment with their hearts and deepest values, their local communities, and with nature. She is excited about growing new roots and new possibilities in the United States after many years away.

Herbert Kohl is the author of more than forty books, including the bestselling classic *36 Children*. A recipient of the National Book Award and the Robert F. Kennedy Book Award, he was founder and first director of the Teachers & Writers Collaborative in New York City, and established the PEN West Center in San Francisco, where he lives.

Arnie Langberg has just begun his second half-century as an educator. He discovered the need for alternatives while an undergraduate at MIT and has helped to start four public alternative schools: The Iota Society (Lynbrook, NY, 1957), Great Neck Village School (Great Neck,

NY, 1970), Mountain Open High (Evergreen, CO, 1975), and High School Redirection (Denver, CO, 1988). Two of these schools are still in operation, Great Neck Village School beginning its fortieth year, and Jefferson County Open School (formerly Mountain Open High) entering its thirty-fifth.

Langberg is currently working on the Harmony Project, which provides professional artists as partners for teachers in under-served schools. He is on the board of a number of educational projects and teaches an action research course at the University of Denver. Langberg has consulted in Siberia and taught philosophy in a university in China.

Mary Leue, at ninety years old, is a mother of five, grandmother of fourteen, great-grandmother of eight. She has been a Maine farmer, registered nurse, teacher, civil rights and anti-war activist, lay midwife, school founder, leader in both alternative education and natural childbirth movements, therapist, community organizer, editor, writer, desktop publisher and bookseller. She has published a number of articles in national and international journals of education and psychotherapy, including the *Journal of Orgonomy*, *Energy and Character,* and *Holistic Education Review.* She has contributed writings to *SKOLE; the Journal of Alternative Education*, which she created and edited from 1985 to 1998, and *The Journal of Family Life*, which she co-created in 1995 and co-edited until her retirement in 1998. As a publisher at Down-to-Earth Books, Leue has produced twenty-seven books—ten as author, five as contributing author, and the remaining seventeen as editor, eight of them on the topic of education.

In 1969, Mary founded The Free School in Albany, NY, which has since inspired the creation of countless schools worldwide.

Dennis Littky is the co-founder and co-director of Big Picture Learning and the Met Center in Providence, Rhode Island. He is nationally known for his forty years of extensive work in secondary education in urban, suburban, and rural settings. As an educator, Littky has a reputation for working against convention and turning tradition on its head to deliver concrete results. Presently, his focus has been the expansion of the Big Picture Learning design to include college-level accreditation through

College Unbound, where student have the opportunity to earn a B.A. and advanced certifications through a critically challenging, real-world based, and entrepreneurial course of study.

Littky holds a double Ph.D. in psychology and education from the University of Michigan. In 2003, Littky was recognized as a leader in the small schools movement and awarded the Harold W. McGraw Jr. Prize in Education. In 2004, he and Samantha Grabelle published a book about the Big Picture Learning design, *The Big Picture: Education is Everyone's Business*, which won the Association of Educational Publishers' top award for nonfiction in 2005. *Fast Company* ranked Littky number four among the top fifty innovators of 2004, and the George Lucas Educational Foundation recently selected Littky as part of the Daring Dozen—the Twenty Most Daring Educators in the World.

Grace Llewellyn is the founder and director of Not Back to School Camp, a gathering held in Oregon and Vermont that draws over 250 unschooled teenagers each year. She's the author of *The Teenage Liberation Handbook: how to quit school and get a real life and education*, and the editor and co-author of three other books on unschooling. A former school teacher, Llewellyn has been involved in the homeschooling movement in many ways since 1990—always with the goal of supporting people in engaging more deeply and intentionally with their learning. In her other life, Llewellyn loves to dance. She is particularly smitten with Argentine tango (as a devoted amateur), bellydance (performs weekly in a Moroccan restaurant), and ecstatic dance (learning to teach a practice called Soul Motion).

Basir Mchawi has woven a distinguished career as an educator, activist, and communicator. Mchawi has taught and administrated in both public and independent Black schools. As a special assistant to New York's first African American Public Schools Chancellor, Mchawi voiced the concerns of communities of color in the central bureaucracy; and as chief architect of Ujamaa Institute/Freedom Academy, he enabled the development of smaller schools around New York City. Mchawi currently teaches English and African American Studies at

The City University of New York (CUNY), and serves as chairman of the International African Arts Festival.

Mchawi was editor and publisher of *Black News*, the innovative news magazine of Brooklyn's EAST organization, and helped transform New York talk radio as producer and host of the public affairs program, *View from the EAST.* Currently, he hosts and produces the award-winning *Education at the Crossroads,* heard on New York's Pacifica radio station WBAI, where he brings important educational and community issues to the attention of a broader audience.

Basir Mchawi continues to "agitate, educate and organize"; as Amilcar Cabral, soul of the liberation movement in Africa's Guinea-Bissau, said, he is "A Luta continua." The struggle continues.

Deborah Meier has spent more than four decades working in public education as a teacher, principal, director, founder, coalition builder, writer, board member, and public advocate.

Meier began her teaching career as a kindergarten and Head Start teacher in Chicago, Philadelphia, and New York City schools, before moving on to be the founder and teacher-director of a network of highly successful public elementary schools in East Harlem. In 1985, she founded Central Park East Secondary School, a New York City public high school in which more than 90 percent of the entering students went on to college. Serving predominantly low-income African American and Latino students, the schools Meier has helped to create are highly regarded exemplars of educational reform. She is currently on the faculty of New York University's Steinhardt School of Education.

Meier's books include: *The Power of Their Ideas: Lessons to America from a Small School in Harlem*; *Will Standards Save Public Education?*; *In Schools We Trust*; *Keeping School,* with Ted and Nancy Sizer; and *Many Children Left Behind.*

Chris Mercogliano recently concluded a thirty-five-year career at The Free School (Albany), the oldest inner-city alternative school in the United States. His essays, commentaries, and reviews have appeared in numerous newspapers, journals, and magazines, as well as in six anthologies.

Mercogliano's books include: *Making It Up as We Go Along, the Story of the Albany Free School*; *Teaching the Restless, One School's Remarkable No-Ritalin Approach to Helping Children Learn and Succeed*; *How to Grow a School: Starting and Sustaining Schools That Work*; and *In Defense of Childhood: Protecting Kids' Inner Wildness*.

Ron Miller is the editor of *Education Revolution*, the magazine of the Alternative Education Resource Organization. He has written or edited nine books, most recently *The Self-Organizing Revolution: Common Principles of the Educational Alternatives Movement*. He has helped start two alternative schools in the Burlington, Vermont area and at times was involved in homeschooling with his own three sons. Ron currently teaches at Champlain College in Burlington. Many of his writings are posted at www.pathsoflearning.net.

Jerry Mintz has been a leading voice in the alternative school movement for over thirty years. He was a public school teacher and principal, and, for seventeen years, an independent alternative school principal. In 1989, he founded the Alternative Education Resource Organization and has helped found dozens of alternative schools and organizations. He has been on National Public Radio and the major TV networks, and in *The New York Times*, *Newsday*, and many other publications. He was Editor-in-Chief for the *Handbook of Alternative Education*, and the *Almanac of Education Choices*. He is the author of *No Homework and Recess All Day: How to Have Freedom and Democracy in Education* and is managing editor of *Education Revolution* magazine. He continues to lecture and consult around the world.

Pat Montgomery is a first-generation Irish American whose parents, from Connemara and Limerick, met at Kennywood Park, an amusement park near Pittsburgh, Pennsylvania. She is the seventh of eight children. Montgomery is a career educator, beginning at the age of eighteen when she taught in St. Norbert's School as a Sister of Divine Providence. She and her late husband, Jim, founded Clonlara School in Ann Arbor. It is both a campus, day school, and a program for home educating families. Clonlara is known in virtually every part of the world and actively assists learners in many places.

Currently, Montgomery is devoting the bulk of her time to caring for her grandchildren, who live just blocks from her, and searches for time to write a book. In this latter venture, she is having considerably less success than she had in other educational pursuits. "It's hard to write things down when they are still taking place before my eyes," she says. "I feel the need to see how it all ends before telling the story."

Susan Ohanian is a longtime teacher, who has spent most of her teaching years in upstate New York. A prolific writer, she is the author of twenty-five books, the latest three being *When Childhood Collides with NCLB*, *Why Is Corporate America Bashing Our Public Schools*, and *The Great Word Catalogue: FUNdamental Activities for Building Vocabulary*. These titles reflect her interest in political forces impacting education and the need for a lively curriculum that interests students.

With a husband and three cats, Ohanian moved to Vermont to be near Lake Champlain, and for the past seven years has maintained a website in opposition to No Child Left Behind and high stakes testing. Education policies of the new administration have given her no reason to take down the website. In fact, with the U. S. Secretary of Education barnstorming the country in favor of the Business Roundtable plan for National Standards, Ohanian would remind people that, ten years ago, she wrote a book covering this very subject, *One Size Fits Few: The Folly of Educational Standards*.

Kirsten Olson (www.kirstenolson.org) is principal of Old Sow Consulting, which works with many public, charter, and alternative schools to create more engaging learning environments for children and adults. She is also a Visiting Assistant Professor at Wheaton College in Norton, Massachusetts.

After working in New York City publishing for over a decade, Olson started a cooperative school when her own four children were in preschool. She then went to the Harvard Graduate School of Education to learn more about the history of education. Her dissertation, on the radical school critics of the 1960s, became *Schools as Colonizers*, and is an analysis of the writings of John Holt, Jonathan Kozol, George Dennison, Herbert Kohl, Paul Goodman, and Ivan Ilich.

Based on a decade of autobiographical interviews with over one hundred "ordinary" students, teachers, and parents, her new book is *Wounded By School: Recapturing the Pleasure in Learning and Standing Up To Old School Culture.*

Olson is interested in finding ways for alternative and radical educators and critics to join together to form politically influential coalitions to affect educational policy change, and in supporting and energizing grassroots activism and consciousness raising around harmful school practices.

Wendy Priesnitz is an author, journalist, editor, former broadcaster, and mother of two adult daughters who lives in Toronto, Canada. She is the owner of Life Media (www.LifeMedia.ca), which she co-founded with her husband, Rolf, in 1976 to publish books and magazines. She founded the Canadian homeschooling movement, with the creation of the Canadian Alliance of Homeschoolers in 1979, and is also recognized as a pioneer in independent publishing, environmentally sustainable business practices, home-based business, and green politics. Her work is rooted in her experience of motherhood, which taught her about the emotional, social, cultural, economic, educational, and environmental responsibilities involved with bringing a child into this world. A prolific writer who has penned thousands of articles and radio and television scripts, in addition to nine books (three of which are about home-based education), Wendy is a poet, editor of *Natural Life* magazine, and a web blogger at www.wendypriesnitz.com. She is currently trying to find time to finish writing a collection of memoir-style essays about learning, mothering, and daughtering, entitled *It Hasn't Shut Me Up.*

Carlo Ricci currently teaches at Nipissing University, and he founded and edits the online *Journal of Unschooling and Alternative Learning* (JUAL). He tries to incorporate the spirit of unschooling, democratic, and learner-centered principles in all of his classes. He has taught in elementary and high school, as well as in undergraduate, teacher education programs, and graduate programs.

Ricci is part of a growing movement that advocates learner-centered, democratic approaches to education. Along these lines, his research interests include unschooling, homeschooling, free schooling, alternative schooling, and technology and education. His works appear in academic, traditional, non-academic, and non-traditional places and spaces. Ricci believes that children are the last acceptably oppressed group in the world we live in and that this injustice needs to stop. He believes the path to a more democratic world needs to begin with more democratic child rearing practices.

Tim Seldin is the President of the Montessori Foundation and Chair of the International Montessori Council. His almost forty years of experience in Montessori education includes twenty-two years as Headmaster of the Barrie School in Silver Spring, Maryland, his own alma mater. He has served as the Director of the Institute for Advanced Montessori Studies and as Head of the New Gate School in Sarasota, Florida. He earned a B.A. in History and Philosophy from Georgetown University, an M.Ed. in Educational Administration and Supervision from The American University, and his Montessori certification from the American Montessori Society. He is the father of three former Montessori students (Marc, Michelle, and Caitlin), stepfather to two former Montessori students (Robin and Chelsea), and grandfather of a present Montessori student (Hollis). He lives on a small vineyard north of Sarasota, Florida, with his wife, Joyce St. Giermaine, their three horses, twenty-five dogs, and two Sphinx cats.

Seldin's books on Montessori Education include: *How to Raise An Amazing Child*; *The Montessori Way* with Dr. Paul Epstein; *Building a World-class Montessori School*; *Finding the Perfect Match—Recruit and Retain Your Ideal Enrollment*; *Master Teachers-Model Programs*; *Starting a New Montessori School*; *Celebrations of Life*; and *The World in the Palm of Her Hand*.

Herb Snitzer's career covers fifty years of image making and he is the author of five books; a co-founder of a freedom school, which he directed for twelve years; and a husband, father, and grandfather. He is a former member of the executive committee of the St. Petersburg branch of the NAACP, and a former third vice-president. His commitment to racial and social justice is a matter of public record. As a photo-journalist, early in his career he worked for *Life, Look, Saturday Evening Post, Fortune, Time* and many other magazines and newspapers, such as *The New York Times*, and *London Sunday Times*. His images are also on over two hundred fifty CD and record covers. He moved to St. Petersburg in 1992, establishing a studio at Salt Creek Artworks.

Len Solo has been an educator for most of his professional work life. He has been a public high school teacher of English, math, and social studies; founder of a small, private alternative school in Atlantic City (Atlantic County New School); founder and department chairperson of the Teacher Drop-Out Center at Stockton State College, Pomona, New Jersey; principal for twenty-seven years at Graham & Parks Alternative Public School in Cambridge, Massachusetts; and is currently an education consultant. He is also a painter, writer, and poet.

Len's books include: *Landscape of the Misty Eye*, with Steve Weitzman; *Rooted in Place*; *Making an Extraordinary School: The Work of Ordinary People*; and *The Magic of Light*.

Lynn Stoddard served for thirty-six years as a public elementary school teacher and principal. He is thankful for a beautiful wife, twelve children, forty-nine grandchildren, and thirty-one great grandchildren. He is the author of three books on improving public education, and is now working with a growing group of distinguished educators, parents, and researchers to develop and field-test a framework for redesigning public education called "Educating for Human Greatness." He can be reached at: lstrd@yahoo.com.

Zoe Weil is the co-founder and president of the Institute for Humane Education (www.humaneeducation.org), where she created the first Master of Education program in humane education and Humane Education Certificate Program. The Institute for Humane Education also offers workshops, on-line courses, and more than a hundred activities for educators, available to download free. Weil (www.zoeweil.com) speaks widely on humane education and humane living, and is recognized as a pioneer in the comprehensive humane education movement. She received a Master of Theological Studies from Harvard Divinity School and a Master of Arts from the University of Pennsylvania.

Weil is the author of *Most Good, Least Harm: A Simple Principle for a Better World and Meaningful Life*; *The Power and Promise of Humane Education*; *Above All, Be Kind: Raising a Humane Child in Challenging Times* (New Society, 2003); and *Claude and Medea*. *Claude and Media* is the Moonbeam gold medal award winner for juvenile fiction, about twelve-year-old activists inspired by their eccentric substitute teacher.

A Lifetime of Work to Bring Quality Public Education to All of America's Children

Lynson Moore Beaulieu

My Schooling

I am a huge proponent of quality public schools. The lion's share of America's children participates in our public system, and thus, my efforts to reform education have been focused there. I was very well educated in public schools in working class and middle-income communities, and in the 80s, 90s, and early 2000s, so were my four children. My youngest currently attends one of California's public universities, and I have great faith that good public schools are possible. However, a lot of my early learning and development went on at home and in my community, and sometimes, in places farther away. Family and community resources are critical for enabling children to access the social, cultural, and extracurricular activities outside of school that, when combined with their school-based learning, lead to a much more complete formative developmental and educational experience. In the absence of well-resourced communities, there is much that schools can and should do to ensure that children have access to high quality educational experiences, but they cannot do it alone. The education of children requires the commitment and resources of the entire village, and the entire society.

From the time I began elementary school in the 1950s until I graduated high school in 1970, my family was able to access quality educational experiences for me through the Los Angeles Unified School District. I was lucky to live in Los Angeles and have access to a exceptional public education right in my own neighborhood. My schools had great, caring teachers who loved their work, and were well-resourced for offering challenging, interesting, and valuable learning experiences. In the early sixties, the War on Poverty and new federal education programs like Title I and Head Start infused important educational resources into low-income communities and their schools. Unfortunately, passage of Proposition 13 in California in 1978, and its limits on increasing property taxes, spelled the end of high quality education in California as state resources began to decline. I graduated ready for college, but most of today's students of color do not.

My first memories of learning were of my grandmother, Ethel, singing me to sleep for one of our lazy afternoon naps at her house. She sang many wonderful songs, but the song I remember most clearly was about a little red school house. Indeed, the idea of learning excited me early on. To top it off, there was actually a little red schoolhouse in Los Angeles—I think in Hollywood somewhere—that we would occasionally pass. What I understood from that song was that there was something in that schoolhouse that was valuable, and valued by my grandmother; school was a special place to be.

During my childhood, my family lived in working class communities of color around Los Angeles, first on the East Side where the people were largely Latino and the Mexican food was the best, and then in a couple of neighborhoods in South Central where the people in my immediate neighborhoods were predominantly African American. When I was a teen, we moved further west into neighborhoods more ethnically mixed, that included Whites, Chinese, Japanese, and Koreans. During all of those years, I had access to parents and other family members who loved and supported me, outstanding public schools, and a wealth of community resources to supplement and help bring meaning to my education.

My mother worked during some of the months and years of my early childhood, and my two siblings (one older, one younger) and I shared a few babysitters during that time. I don't remember those experiences, but I do have memories of spending quality time with my mother doing fun things. In particular, we attended a basket making class for children in a local park; I was so excited that I had made a basket. Perhaps this was the beginning of my love for creating beautiful things with my hands.

I also spent time in the basement of a neighborhood church along with other little children. In black communities in those years, churches were often centers of child caring and learning, just as many are today. From that place, I remember the freedom of being a child, being comfortable as myself, music, and some learning. Though I wasn't reading yet, I seem to remember an introduction to the alphabet— probably through songs and games. In those early family and child care experiences, I was learning the many things that would help me arrive at that place in my development where all of the sounds and sights of language and stories seen, heard, and told would come together in the act of reading. There was no pressure to learn something faster than the experiences of my life naturally allowed me to learn, but I ran to keep up with life because it was so exciting!

Then, kindergarten. A half-day program with what I now know were master, veteran teachers. Warm milk and graham crackers. Making friends, playing inside and outside, and learning the routines of learning and going to school. It was exhilarating! And I was a sponge, soaking it all in.

My elementary school was special. Although it was a community school, it was also a lab school for the University of Southern California and all of our teachers were master teachers. We had art and music, science and math, and field trips galore. We sang in the school chorus, learned to play instruments in the school band and orchestra, attended plays and ballets, and heard live symphony orchestras! We had a very enriched learning program, and an on site before and after school care (rare for the late fifties), and being in child care was special. They had their own little house on campus and were situated near a side gate for easy access. I wanted to be a part of that special group and place.

We also had a school romance between two young teachers whom

I now know met and fell in love while laboring over us with their love of teaching. Some students caught them kissing and everyone was all a-twitter over it! Eventually they got married and we serenaded the lady teacher; "Miss Monahan's getting married in the morning...ding dong the bells are going to chime..." or something close to that. The other teachers taught us the song and we sang for her and gave her flowers on the eve of her wedding. What could have been a scandal instead taught the children about very human and responsible behavior—how the love of their teachers, as expressed through that clandestine kiss, turned into a wedding and a marriage.

Menlo Avenue School was not my neighborhood school and my mother had to secure a special permit for us to attend there. I'm not sure how she did it, but I benefited greatly from that very full and high quality public elementary school education. My mother says, as we talk about this essay, that she believed that culture was very important in her children's education, and she made sure that we had access to music and the arts both in and out of school. She believes this is one of the most important roles a parent can, and should, play in their children's lives. My mother was present at all of my performances, open houses, and other key school events. She shuttled me and sometimes other children and our instruments around to different performance locations in the city, in a large old hot rod of a car. My father was involved in my school affairs much less frequently.

We walked the ten blocks to and from school almost daily, up and down Hoover Street. We didn't have backpacks then and had to carry our books and notebooks in our arms. On music days, I also carried first my ukulele (which my father purchased for me for the then exorbitant sum of $10.00 at a local pawn shop—more incredible excitement!), and then by third grade, my violin. I also sang in the chorus. While my teacher thought I was most appropriately a second soprano, I insisted that I was a first and always sang that part. She reluctantly allowed me to sing where my voice and heart sent me because I could actually sing well. I was musically inclined, and music has always been a large part of my life.

I played the violin through eighth grade, and battled over first chair with my closest competitor in my junior high school orchestra, which consistently ranked in the top school orchestras in junior and senior high schools in Los Angeles. We were better than many high schools and consistently earned 1's (Outstanding) in the district-wide public school orchestra competitions, playing very complicated pieces of music by well-known classical composers.

At Foshay Junior High School—an inner city public school—we had a fabulous music program under the tutelage of three very incredible, totally serious music teachers: Mrs. Bicknell, Mrs. Fowler, and Mr. Dale, a young African American man who was an accomplished musician in his own right. All of the children worked hard with our three great teachers to create a classically trained orchestra, and among our peers, ours was one of the very best. Mrs. Bicknell conducted the full orchestra and trained the band; Mrs. Fowler (who was actually a math teacher) assisted with the band; and Mr. Dale trained us string players. When the band and the strings came together as the orchestra, Holy Moses, could we kick some butt! There is nothing quite as thrilling as when all of the instruments fuse as an orchestra in full bloom. Every child on stage dressed in their white top and blue or black bottom—girls in skirts, boys in trousers—and bubbled with excitement and nervousness until the first note. How glorious as a child to experience that particular miracle! I am left with a deep love and appreciation for the many beautiful faces of music and its deep connection to places in the heart and soul.

Aside from music, my middle school learning experience included sewing and cooking—which afforded me the first C of my educational career. Up to that point, it was mostly A's, an occasional B, but the pineapple upside down cake did me in. My team was unable to get the pineapple safely out of the pan with the cake attached. That experience taught me an important lesson about grades. Having already cooked dinner regularly for my family solo for at least a year with pretty good results, receiving this C felt like a double injustice, but I had to face it like an adult because there was no remedy. I couldn't change it, and it would be there forever. This was one of my earliest encounters with an injustice, and it helped me to be able to identify the concept with the way an experience made me feel. This event triggered an understanding of humility, that there were some things outside of my control, and that getting a C was not a life or death situation. Although my pride was wounded, the grade obviously did not correctly define my cooking capability and somehow, I eventually understood that. Many years later, I overheard my youngest son say to someone, "my mom sure is a good cooker!" and I continue to love to cook to this day, finding it an important outlet for creativity and a necessary ingredient for achieving and maintaining good health.

Sewing went much better. Our class project was the gym bag, machine embroidered with our names. I wish I still had that bag, but by then, I was already sewing entire dresses for my school wardrobe at home under the guidance of my mother. My mother taught me to sew and my grandmother taught me how to knit and crochet, which I continue to do along with other arts and crafts to this day. About ten years ago, after feeling the urge for decades, while raising my children, I finally picked up paint and brush and found the joy of acrylic painting. Although I did not learn these particular skills in school, the cooking and sewing classes provided the opportunity for interesting intersections between schooling and my real life that promoted even higher order thinking and learning.

I loved earning good grades and getting the answers right. I don't know that I ever really thought about the rewards of learning as a young student, but I enjoyed the ease with which I learned new things and the opportunities for exciting learning that came my way. And I just plain loved to learn. I liked the way A's looked on my report card and I liked the sense of self-satisfaction I experienced for a job well done. The intrinsic reward that comes with being a successful learner is what keeps you in love with learning. When there is no joy associated with learning, and learning is a succession of failures and disconnects, how does one possibly imagine oneself successfully in that role? I think that having learning as its own reward was important for my becoming a successful life-long learner.

I attended two different public high schools, both known for exceptional academics. I attended Susan Miller Dorsey High School in Los Angeles' View Park/Crenshaw/Baldwin Hills area for two years, then spent my final year at Alexander Hamilton High School in West Los Angeles. By the time I arrived at Dorsey, I was no longer an active musician, but very much into academic learning.

I continued to study the French language, algebra and geometry, and fell in love with the biological sciences. I studied biology and physiology with great teachers, one of whom I had many years later as a professor at Los Angeles Trade Technical College, when I returned to school to begin a course of study for nursing. I also enjoyed my English classes where my teachers in separate classes were this very hip husband and wife team of educators who both taught language arts. She was an African American woman from Gary, Indiana, and he was a White man from upstate New York. They were dynamite educators who hung out with students and took groups to Europe for study tours. My parents couldn't afford to send me, but I sure would have loved to go.

Summer school and other summer programs were always available to any child who wanted to go. I always went, and in high school, always took the maximum of two classes. It was during one of these summer school sessions that I took a social studies elective where I prepared my first expansive, research-based paper on the world's religions, filled with lots of paraphrasing, I'm sure. The paper came out of my continuing interest in religion and spirituality, as I sought to understand more about people and their relationship to God and other important figures in religious history and teachings.

My last year of high school at Hamilton passed in a blur. I took my first and only formal typing class during the summer school between my junior and senior years. We were on to electric typewriters by then, at the dawn of word processing. I continued my French classes and took up German (eventually adding Spanish and Russian to my foreign language repertoire in college). Fluency always eluded me but I have a great appreciation for people who can think and speak in multiple languages. Because I had regularly attended summer school, I had enough credits to only attend half a day of school, so I got my first real job, with a company that sold social studies materials to teachers and schools all over the country, in the neighboring town of Culver City. I was hooked on the working world and a pay check; at sixteen years old, I worked about four hours a day in addition to my four morning classes. It was a very special place to work. We were making really valuable learning materials available to educators and their students everywhere. My work ethic, learned in the scrappy backyard of my grandmother's home and honed over the years in various ways, came in handy, and I worked there happily for over three years.

When they hired me, I was the youngest member of the team and worked with a small staff of administrators that included the partner/ owners and an office manager, and a number of other students who were attending local colleges and universities. I had access to a warehouse full of outstanding and beautifully presented multicultural learning materials, covering the social studies for students from kindergarten through high school. I worked my way up from filing the order cards in zip code order, to being a buyer in the warehouse. It was here that I had my first encounter with a personal computer. Those who know me will probably chuckle at this one, but I led the office protest against the use of computers—my first real protest of a perceived social and economic injustice. I was certain that we would soon lose our jobs and no longer be needed as workers, because those were the messages being given to us about computers. I remember how emotional it all was for me, and I'm sure others too who lived through the technological transition when large desktop computers entered the workplace to do work that we had previously done for ourselves.

Luckily, those fears never materialized, and if anything, computers ushered in heavier workloads. On the other hand, in ways I couldn't possibly have imagined, they have given us access to an incredible amount of information and data that is being gathered, examined, processed, reported on, and shared. We have the capability to communicate with large numbers of diverse people instantly, and are able to more effectively organize, participate in deliberations and decision-making, and advocate and protest for the adoption of education, related policies, programs and practices that lead to better outcomes for America's most educationally under-served children, especially our low-income children of color.

It Takes a Village to Raise a Child—The Community as School

I had so many mothers as a child—in my family and in the neighborhood. Our block was full of single family homes and families—a few of them large, many with children, and all had mothers and fathers. Every child's mother was every child's mother; fathers played a more silent role—they were seen but not often heard, and most worked. All of the mothers and grandmothers were kind and tolerant, you respected and listened to them all, and they did not hesitate to keep you, along with their own children, in line.

There were at least twenty children (I can still recall most of their names) on my immediate block—a rainbow of African Americans, one Chinese family, and a Chicano family at the end of the block—and many were available to play games at any given time. Most of us lived on the same side of the block, and we didn't often venture outside of that territory, even though we traversed the ten blocks to school daily, and went to the park in the summer. On the back side of the church at the corner was a vacant lot where we played rip roaring games of baseball, boys and girls, young children and older ones together. My sister was always better than me—she was light and limber, and I was heavy and a little clumsy—but I have a lasting memory of my first home run ever. I was usually one of the last kids chosen for a team and mostly struck out or got walked. But one day, there was a perfect connection between bat and ball. What an incredible feeling to hear that crack and see the ball soar over everyone's heads to the other side of the street, and then to be cheered home for the run.

The church was Missionary Baptist Church, and I attended during the years we lived on that block. At church, I learned about unconditional love. I can't imagine what the people of this congregation thought about a little girl showing up regularly with no parents in tow, but the mothers and grandmothers there made me feel like I belonged. Although my parents were agnostic, and didn't encourage or discourage our personal searches to find and understand God, the urge toward spirituality was strong in me. I used to get up early to shine my little black patent leather shoes with Vaseline, don my Sunday best, and head off to Sunday school and church, which followed. Staying for church was essential. That's when we got to see what it meant to get touched by the Holy Spirit.

The pastor opened that beautiful, old style brick sanctuary with incredible stained glass windows to the children of the neighborhood and community. The light streaming through the windows on Sunday morning was glorious. We were allowed to be everywhere in that church and we knew every nook and cranny. I attended Bible School each summer and our meals were provided in the church's basement, where the mothers of the church would cook and serve food, including celebratory meals. Being in the basement was special. The basement was the church community's gathering place, the place for more fellowship and rejoicing. For us children, these times were always happy, joyful and fun. I am so thankful for my experiences in that church.

These experiences whetted my hunger for the spiritual side of life. I visited many different churches during my childhood until I finally found, as a young adult, a set of teachings and a church that met my intellectual tests and resonated with my spirit and soul. While my spiritual development continues to be a work in progress, what was set in motion, I think, was an understanding that there was a power greater than myself and that I needed to trust it in all aspects of my life, including my professional life. Eventually, I came to understand my work in education as deeply connected to my life's purpose and my soul's journey, and as such, that I was doing it for and because of that greater power, and for a much greater good than myself or my own children.

More Important Community Resources

My family and I were big users of our neighborhood public libraries. While computers were in their infancy—gigantic and complicated, and the internet was not even a gleam in anyone's eye—books were the medium of information, communication and imagination, and I was a voracious reader. As a family, we could never have afforded to buy the amount of books I read as a young person—one summer I read ten every two weeks! I read through the children's section and went looking hungrily for material on the grownup side of the library. My mom even took me to a different library not too far away, to see if they had anything I hadn't read. At some point, my family acquired a *World Britannica* encyclopedia, which served as the basis of many a report during my elementary and middle school years. The encyclopedia was a wealth of information at my fingertips in the dawning days of the information age.

My family and I were also big users of our local museums. I grew up within walking distance of Exposition Park, with its Olympic Swimming Stadium and network of world class museums—Natural History, Science and Industry, and the Air and Space Museum. In the summers, my sister and I would pack lunches for ourselves and our little brother, and spend the day swimming and exploring the museums. I learned about the animals of the United States and dinosaurs, about infinity and the mobius and the law of averages from the dropping ping-pong balls. I learned how chicks grow in their shells and peck their way out of their shells at birth—all by themselves. The sights, sounds, smells, and information I found in those museums tantalized my brain and my senses, leaving an indelible mark forever in my memory and in my life.

The Importance of Family

My family was an important part of my education. I think that they expected the schools we attended to do their job, which was to educate us in a holistic fashion. They expected that we would be challenged academically, have opportunities to access and use our creativity, and in general, gain a positive influence on our development and learning. I think there was an assumption that I would be prepared for college when I graduated high school, and that minimally, we would all be ready for at least junior college (which later became community college). But as I mentioned earlier, my family life contributed significantly to my education, especially around issues of social justice.

I had two parents present for the majority of my childhood and two sets of grandparents into adulthood. My oldest children knew all four of their great-grandparents. In one regard, my grandparents were as different as night and day—my paternal grandparents were African American and my maternal grandparents were Jewish, my grandmother being Lithuanian and my grandfather Polish. My father's family came from Texas and my mother's from New York and New Jersey. On the other hand, they shared very similar family, social, and political values. Both sets of grandparents were political progressives, and my parents met as young people doing political work—advocating progressive political values and engaging in organizing, civil disobedience, and political protests as an expression of their beliefs. The lessons that come along with being a child of mixed ethnic and cultural heritage are too many to list, but they were all powerful forces for justice in my life.

We celebrated Christmas and Hanukah, some years as one big happy family. I don't know how much education my grandparents had—I don't know if any of them graduated from college, but I'm pretty sure some of them attended. They were all very intelligent.

My African American grandmother was a pre-med student at the University of Southern California before she married my grandfather, who was a union organizer in Texas and Los Angeles, where he was general manager of the Los Angeles public employees union. I don't know his level of formal education, but he was a brilliant and respected leader. He ran for Congress in the state of California in the forties and counted among his colleagues Martin Luther King, Jr., Thomas Bradley (eventually mayor of Los Angeles), and many other political notables of his time. He was also a very religious and spiritual man, and he and my grandmother were founding members of an African Methodist Episcopal Church (AME) in Los Angeles that has borne their names in a list of founders on its cornerstone since it was built. He valued education and once implored me to become a teacher—what he considered the noblest of professions. How prophetic he was.

My Jewish grandparents were not religious, and some of the most interesting conversations I remember were during our family celebrations of the Jewish High Holy days—they had to do with the existence of God. My grandmother worked for a number of newspapers and was a wiz on a manual typewriter. She was also a professional knitter, and did many of the hand crafts—crochet, cross-stitch, and beading. My grandfather was an electronics engineer and during my childhood owned a series of electronics stores. He was also an accomplished trumpet player and a master chess player.

We gathered as a family frequently, sometimes with one set of grandparents, or the other. We also spent lots of time visiting with aunts and uncles and cousins. Both sides of the family were vociferous debaters and I became aware early on of serious conversations about God and religion, politics, and social conditions. I remember one such gathering at my paternal grandparents' home, where it was an accepted cultural practice that children should be seen but not heard, especially during adult conversation. While all of the other children scrambled outside as soon as they were allowed, I hung back wanting to be with the adults. I remember getting the nod from my stern uncle and was allowed to sit quietly with them while they conducted their conversation, but I was not to interrupt, and I didn't. I remember standing at the knee of my mother listening intently to the conversation and knowing that it was special that I had been allowed to stay. From my grandparents, I learned to be respectful of my elders, to value their counsel, and to be a good listener. I was not inclined to have to learn life's lessons the hard way. I was satisfied even then to learn many of those lessons from the wisdom of my elders.

The Need for Alternatives

I graduated college with a degree in child development and used the knowledge I gained in that multidisciplinary major to be a better mother. I have always been interested in the growth and development of human beings, and my goal was to be the best mother I could possibly be. My four children, whom I would learn were four incredibly unique individuals and learners with varied interests and talents, taught me how important it is to have an education available for every student that supports their intrinsic potential for greatness.

During the three years in which my last three children were born, I began my work in education as a volunteer natural childbirth educator and midwife assistant in a clinic where we did home, center, and hospital births with mothers interested in more humane birthing experiences. I worked with mothers and their children and did home visits and one-on-one childbirth and parenting education work with them. I also coached their labors, working closely with the midwife.

In 1983, soon after my last son was born, I took a very part-time position with a local child care resource and referral agency in Los Angeles. I administered a respite care program that provided child care for children who had been identified as at risk of abuse and/or neglect. The program also provided support to their families to decrease their general isolation and ensure that they had access to the services and resources they needed to improve home conditions and the lives of their children. I tailored the children's child care arrangements to meet the needs of the children and families and worked with some programs that provided extraordinary services to meet their individual needs.

I also subcontracted for services to a Los Angeles non-profit organization providing therapeutic services to children and families. After two years on this small budget project that only lasted six months of each year, I joined the organization in a full-time capacity to manage the contracts and payment processing activities for a very large child care subsidy program. California was an early leader in subsidizing the early childhood education of low-income children with state funding, and took full advantage of federal support for early childhood programming. I continued operating both programs for three more years. I got my first glimpse of human services policy and early care and education system building when I joined a couple of statewide professional organizations linked to the child care subsidy programs.

My early years in this work kept me close to families and providers of services, including child care and early education workers. My efforts as a parent of four young children and working closely with families and providers in a professional capacity helped me to see the need to customize services so that they met the individual needs of the providers and children and families I engaged with. I raised my children with my eyes open to healthy development and my children's dreams for their own futures. When I look back, I realize that I was always inclined to work within the system, rather than start a new program or school outside of the public system. My upbringing kept me focused on access to quality, affordable services and programs as a social justice issue—a concern of the masses because it affected so many low-income families. My involvement inside the social services and early education systems sparked my interest in policy linked to programs, services, the early childhood workforce, and families. Once I went to Washington, DC, and became fully enmeshed in early childhood and K-12 education policy, working with states on state education system building efforts, I knew that we needed an alternative system, not just an alternative program. My journey has taken me to places and into the kind of work that supports change for children and families on a large scale—at the community, state, and federal levels.

Realizing the Vision

My work in public education has been my vocation, connected to the lives, values, and work of my ancestors. I have done this work with a deep sense of purpose and mission and a spiritual connectedness to the communities that I serve. The body of my work in the last twenty-five years has been focused on two things: first, helping to conceptualize the meaning of high quality, publicly funded early childhood and K-12 education—education that is meaningful, challenging, and fully resourced, engages families, and is liberating for low income children and communities of color. Second, working in and with organizations and communities of people at the local, state, regional, and federal levels to identify, develop, implement, and advocate for policies and programs that reflect what is desired by, and works in, those communities for those children.

A school community is comprised of the people directly affected by the school program and its outcomes—students, families, teachers, administrators, and other interested community members—and it is that community, that diverse array of stakeholders, who should exercise a large amount of control through informed decision-making about the educational programs in their schools. School communities must exercise their right to use the broad array of research, information, data and accountability tools available to them to create an informed base of knowledge and understanding from which decisions should be made. Stakeholders have a right to a voice in decisions about such things as curricula and student support services, teacher hiring practices, student discipline policies, funding, standards, data collection and management, graduation requirements and the awarding of diplomas, and accountability systems at the local, state, and federal levels.

Over these many years, I have been presented with many opportunities to impact public policy. I sat at tables where important decisions were made, decisions that had a direct impact on the children, families, educators, and communities whom I care deeply about. In these policy circles, I was frequently one of very few people of color, and one of the few with the knowledge, growing experience, and passion to ensure that important issues were raised and included in the discussions and decisions. My work had both immediate and long-term impact and I was frequently successful at introducing new ways of thinking that helped to move policy in directions that were equitable and more responsive to underrepresented communities.

When I arrived in Washington, DC, in 1994 to work, Goals 2000 was the federal policy initiative underway and I had a chance to work on the early childhood goal: all children will enter school ready to learn by having access to health care (as will their mothers), access to high quality early childhood education, and parenting education for families. Goals 2000 was this country's first real commitment to setting national goals for public education, including early childhood. Of course, 2000 came and went and I don't think we ever achieved any of the goals we set out to, but since then, we have continued to try to identify goals for the education of public school students and to create standards for teaching and learning and state accountability systems that meaningfully measure student achievement and other student outcomes. Although we have been disaggregating data for a number of years, we are just now beginning to bring nation-wide attention to our failure to educate large numbers of America's children, especially its African American boys. African American girls are not faring much better, and large numbers of children of Latino descent who are non- or limited-English speaking are also doing poorly. Dropout rates, as everyone now knows, are horrendous, creating an incredible financial drain on the nation, ruining the lives of millions of our children, youth, their families and communities, as well as representing a bigger threat to national safety than anything outside could possibly muster. The cradle to prison pipeline has been clearly identified and in many places the entire school community—along with local, state and national political leaders—is organizing for changes that will stem the tide.

While in DC, I worked in national and regional education organizations and with various offices in the U.S. Department of Education on family engagement, after-school, early childhood, and K-12 education policy. I wrote background papers and recommendations for federal involvement in early childhood education for the ESEA reauthorization of that time, and worked with a team to develop the parent information resource centers. With one of the organizations, I conducted a national survey of state family involvement policies, programs, and practices and gathered surveys and samples of materials from thirty-eight states, which with the help of two summer interns, I put into a huge report. Many states were making substantial investments in the engagement of families in education matters during the 1990s. During that era, Education Secretary Riley launched the America Goes Back to School Campaign and I worked on that steering committee and on the Department's Town Hall meetings.

As we moved into the new millennium, I also worked with the Office for Civil Rights (OCR) and the U.S. Department of Justice on school discrimination complaints as a part of my work in an equity-based organization. This new work brought me face to face with communities and school districts as they worked to resolve complaints of discrimination in school practices, policies, and outcomes that placed an unfair burden and disadvantage on children of color. The OCR was virtually powerless to institute any real sanctions on school districts for practices deemed discriminatory or resulting in racial disparities, but the Department of Justice was great at teaching me how to stay safe when I worked on the plantation, so to speak, and I took their wise counsel very seriously.

At some point, my journey began to gain a focus on issues of diversity among the leadership in education decision-making circles. The lack of diversity and the marginalization of the few people of color present in the circles was intolerable and a constant reminder of why we couldn't get our remedies right—of why over and over again, inappropriate and ineffective policies were being initiated. Addressing this issue was urgent, and I was presented with an opportunity to work with a national organization on a leadership development initiative that sought out mid-career professionals in early care and education so that we could link them to policy experiences and mentoring by nationally recognized leaders in national organizations. We also sought to build cross-cultural partnerships in selected communities around the country with local leaders to facilitate better early care and education system building efforts in those communities. We held meetings in Los Angeles, Miami, and New Jersey that brought together diverse groups of leaders to talk about race and cultural issues in their programs and systems so that they could work together across cultures for the benefit of all of the community's children.

For about fourteen months, I went to live and work in Milwaukee, WI. While there, I completed an application for a charter school for a community-based organization and successfully presented the school's dual-language development design and the organization's qualifications to operate the three million dollar school. We were awarded the charter school contract and I had an opportunity to work side-by-side with a highly successful, veteran school principal who came out of retirement to run the school. She was an amazing woman who had spent ten years of her life in a convent as a nun and was famous in Milwaukee for her advocacy work on behalf of Milwaukee's poorest children. Together with other key staff, we organized, furnished, and launched a preK-8 school serving some of Milwaukee's lowest income children, most of whom were recent arrivals and native Spanish speakers with very limited English language skills. The goal was for all children to learn to speak, read, and write English and Spanish at academic skill levels. For the first time in my life, I was the language minority person on the team. It was a humbling experience and I worked hard to ensure that the school met all state and federal regulations and that all of our required plans and documents were successfully submitted. This experience was one of the most powerful of my career.

Upon my return to DC, I worked for a second time with a national organization, this one focused on African American children. While there, I conducted research with a small group of early childhood educators—African American and Latina—and their participation in professional development activities. The research helped to highlight the challenges of providing quality educational experiences for early childhood educators, and resulted in improved practices and child outcomes. I also completed a policy brief with the help of leaders in New Jersey on the impact of the Abbott ruling on diversity in the early childhood workforce.

In 2006, I went to work for a progressive education-focused foundation in Cambridge, Massachusetts. I provided grants and my education leadership expertise to non-profit organizations, primarily in Boston and Cambridge, who were working on efforts to improve public education through increases in state funding, strategic policy change, the development of new leaders of color—including youth— and community organizing. I worked in partnership with other funders to build collaboratives for organizing work, and worked with grantees to strengthen their partnership efforts for better outcomes in their advocacy work. My efforts as a grant-maker helped to increase the participation of people of color in efforts to improve education public policy in Massachusetts schools. I continued funding for a leadership development program that supported mid-career early care and education professionals, with a focus on increasing the numbers of leaders of color involved in public policy decision-making in early care and education. With grants to support community organizing, my work was effective in mobilizing communities of color around Massachusetts to vote down a ballot in the past presidential election to prevent efforts by a conservative tax group to eliminate the state income tax.

I was also able to continue to support research conducted by researchers of color focused on children of color. With grants I supported research efforts to highlight the impact of legislation that eliminated bilingual education for English language learning students in Massachusetts. I also funded a research effort that I conceptualized and advised, which looked at the state of early care and education data gathering and systems in Massachusetts and New York, with a particular eye toward how these systems were serving low-income preschoolers of color. I recently served seventeen months as a board member of the State Board of Early Education and Care in Massachusetts, the nation's first such state board, appointed by Governor Deval Patrick. We had to undergo the painful exercise of deciding on and implementing major budget cuts resulting in significant and devastating reductions in levels of service to young and school-age children and their families.

Today

This essay provides only a brief overview of the ways that I have been involved in efforts to provide alternative educational experiences for our children in public schools. Over the course of my career, I have served as an advocate and leader in many efforts to reform and transform local, state, and national policy, programs, and practices. Some of the initiatives that I continue to be involved in are: the Broader, Bolder Approach—an effort to offer a new, more progressive vision of quality public education; the National Council on Educating Black Children's Black Male Student Initiative—a statewide initiative in Indiana involving twenty communities; Project 2025: Black Men and Boys Initiative—a national initiative focused on improving outcomes for Black men and boys in education, health, employment and wealth, fatherhood and family formation, and in the criminal justice system; Spirit in Action's Education Circle of Change—a gathering of education organizing leaders and advocates of alternative education opportunities; and the Boston Learning Center—a Boston-based organization that provides tutoring and other culturally-based youth development opportunities to students attending schools across Massachusetts.

I just recently relocated to the Southern California community of Irvine and completed an almost year-long training program to become a certified life and professional coach. I applied for and received a scholarship that was provided through a project funded by a group of forward looking foundations who came together with the goal of increasing the numbers of coaches of color available to coach professionals of color engaged in social justice work. I plan to use what I have learned in my work in public education, and the skills that I have developed as a coach, to support the growth and development of professionals, especially young professionals, as they work to grow into their leadership capacity. I'd like to help them solve challenges they face in their work and personal lives so that they can be more effective at what they do professionally and live more fulfilled, content, and happier lives.

Conclusion

Not currently connected to any particular organization, I'm not sure at this point what direction my continuing work in public education will take, but as I have my whole life, I will rely on the power of Spirit to lead me there. For certain, I will be working with my grandchildren on their education and on some of the initiatives I identified above, including establishing a successful coaching practice. But the "what else for public education" will remain a mystery until it is eventually revealed, which I'm sure will be soon. Although I am enjoying this period of semi-retirement, I am most definitely looking forward to the next installment in my exciting and fulfilling career to bring high quality public education to all of America's children.

Finding What Matters
Sharon Caldwell

My first introduction to schooling was somewhat dramatic. After attending for only a few days, I was expelled from preschool for biting another child. I lived in an apartment block in an inner city area in Johannesburg, South Africa, and had little opportunity to play with other children because I was not allowed out on my own. I suppose my mother felt that sending me to the school would get me out of my grandmother's hair. Lacking any social skills left me significantly unprepared to deal with the boys, who felt that I should be playing house with the girls when my own fantasies revolved around being a knight from the Prince Valiant comics I read with my father.

Apparently I was a difficult child. I don't know much about my own early history other than the fact that my mother boasts that she taught me not to touch things by pricking my hands with pins—a discipline technique that has left a lasting legacy in my tendency to put my hands behind my back when I enter someone else's home, or a shop. Apparently I somehow taught myself to read and my mother, with the support of the family doctor, convinced the local school to allow me to start first grade shortly after my fifth birthday. There were no recurrences of violence on my part (or none that I recall) and barring two instances I was never in trouble in primary school. My handwriting was awful and because the newly introduced ball-point pens were thought to be a contributing factor, I was required to write with a dip-pen. Academically I did reasonably well, probably due more to weekends spent with my father when we visited the planetarium, museums, and art galleries, rather than to the efforts of the teachers. For the most part school was just boring, and I held on to the hope that come high school, things would get more interesting. We would start to learn "real stuff."

Two events in primary school do, however, stand out as being pivotal in forming my view of myself, and thus in influencing my understanding of the institution of school. One of my earliest memories is of first grade. We were set a series of sums to do, and being totally bored at doings sums—sums that I had been able to do on my first day—I decided to decorate the numerals with little flowers and leaves to show how much I really loved arithmetic. I was awarded 0 out of a possible 10 points for my efforts and felt profoundly ashamed. In seventh grade (in South Africa, primary school—our version of US elementary school—goes to the equivalent of grade seven) a friend and I decided to publish a school magazine and obtained permission to do so, subject to each edition being checked by our class teacher. My mother's employer donated an old hand operated copying machine that used wax sheets and methylated spirits in its operation. I had a small manual typewriter on which I typed our copy. We were immensely excited. We obtained some sponsorship for a prize for our crossword competition, and our first edition was completely sold out. Our second edition was double the size, and my mother helped to type the wax sheets. This time we sold some advertising space to a local toy shop, which donated a board game as a prize for our crossword competition. We were so excited that we forgot to get everything approved and arrived at school with the entire run of our second edition. When our teacher checked it, he noticed that there was no punctuation on a poem that had been written by my friend. Maybe I forgot the punctuation, or maybe it was my mother, I don't remember, but what I do remember was that my teacher said that this was the kind of sloppiness he expected from me, and that I must insert all the correct punctuation by hand in any issue we sold. Again, we sold out. It was the last issue of *Jaunty Jalopy*, and the last time I did anything innovative in school.

Needless to say, high school proved to be as boring as primary. I kept my head down and managed to stay out of trouble. I graduated with a stunning D average, and because I had been assured by my teachers that I was not "university material," I got myself enrolled in a secretarial course, and learned touch typing, speed writing, and accounting. When I shared my hopes of one day being able to study English at university I was again advised—this time by my speedwriting instructor—that with my poor spelling I really was not "university material." I got a job as a secretary and was again very bored.

I did, however, manage to enroll myself in the University of South Africa and obtain an honors degree in history (by means of distance learning), while working as an internal auditor's assistant. I decided to begin a commerce degree, with the aim of becoming an auditor, but luckily, realized after one year that it was not for me. When I was asked to teach accounting at a local high school I jumped at the chance, and after two years enrolled to do a teaching diploma by distance education.

Fast forward to 1994. With a teaching diploma and six years of high school teaching experience, I was now a mom of two very active boys. My oldest son, Christopher, was exceptionally bored and lonely. All his play date friends were attending preschools and I began to explore options—more for the opportunity for him to be with other children than for any educational reasons.

While I was teaching at the high school I had encountered David Gribble's book, *Considering Children*, and while the concepts espoused had interested me, I had assumed that the schools he mentioned either no longer existed, or were irrelevant, unrealistic ideals. So, while the notions of democratic learning did not influence me directly at that time, they did lead me to respond positively when I first encountered Montessori. In my search to find a place for my son, I visited a large number of nursery schools and other preschool establishments— and was determined that I wanted something else for my children. Ultimately, I enrolled him in a small local school and though he was relatively happy, I was not. I eventually found a Montessori school and began to explore the philosophy, finding it to resonate with what I wanted for my children. I was particularly attracted to the notion of freedom for the child to develop according to his or her own interests and aptitudes. My father somehow scraped together money to lend me to enroll for a distance Montessori training and buy some basic equipment, and I started a very small (eight children) school at my home.

Scroll forward again. My son is five years old and will begin "proper" school the following year. There were limited choices in the town where we lived. Most of Chris's friends were due to enroll in an all-boys school that stood for everything I held in contempt—rigid discipline (the staff still vociferously opposed the recent banning of corporal punishment in schools), a focus on sport and competition, and a very conservative approach all round. We moved town for him to attend a somewhat more liberal, more innovative, co-ed school in East London. After a brief stint working at a local Montessori school I decided to do things my way, and started a small school from home. This time my school grew to thirty children. It was pretty much a regular Montessori three-to-six group, with the children all moving to first grade at the local government primary. At that stage I had no intention of extending this to a Montessori Primary School and did not consider home-schooling as an option. In my heart of hearts, I knew that I wanted my children to have the benefits of a Montessori education right up to high school level, but did not feel capable of doing this myself. At any rate, I had only a Montessori three-to-six diploma and saw no way of acquiring the further training I felt I would need.

Within a few months, however, I began to see changes in my child, and slowly came to realize that traditional school was (to use the words of John Taylor Gatto) "dumbing him down." I am not going to include the litany of school problems that we encountered, but suffice it to say that it took four and one-half years to reach the crisis that precipitated my search for alternatives. In the interim, I had visited a number of Montessori Primary Schools in South Africa, but was not at all impressed by what I saw there. With one notable exception, I encountered children being compelled to perform the same type of busywork tasks that one expects in regular schools, together with time-tables and testing. Despite mixed-age classes, children were placed in graded groups for mathematics and reading lessons. Some schools were using strictly managed control systems, or outside programs such as Kumon Maths. Freedom for individual choice and development was being subverted in pursuit of measurable academic success to comply with external bureaucratic and market demands. I enrolled for a six-to-twelve correspondence training course and received the training materials. I was not impressed with either the level of the materials contained in the manuals or the general level of competence, or knowledge, of the instructor. The material seemed incomplete, with very little reference to research or any recognition of viewpoints or interpretations other than that of the person who drew up the course. I decided that if that was what Montessori was about, it was not what I was looking for—for myself or for my children.

I remembered that book I had read so long ago and wondered if similar schools still existed.

Now I began the search anew, this time with the benefit of the internet. I stumbled across AERO (Alternative Education Resource Organization), which introduced me to an Aladdin's cave of educational variety. I found that Summerhill is not only still in existence, but is thriving after winning a major court victory against the British Education Department. I learned about Sudbury Valley, free schools, and the hundreds of schools worldwide where children are not compelled by adults to do anything against their will. This notion of freedom for children, based on the integrity and inalienable rights of the individual, was what had drawn me to Montessori in the first place.

I wondered if my assessment of Montessori in South Africa was true for other countries as well, and also wanted to learn more about other alternatives to regular schooling. Australia offered both a large number of Montessori schools and a diverse cross section of independent alternatives fairly close together, as well as a fairly favorable exchange rate against the SA Rand. I visited seven schools in and around Brisbane and Melbourne in March 2001. These included Montessori schools and independent community schools. Not all of the independent schools could be termed democratic, but they all deviated from both the traditional school model and Montessori. It is not possible in this article to fully explore the diversity of workable alternatives I encountered. At all the schools, however, my overriding impression was that they would all gain from the insights of Montessori. On the other hand, it was clear that the Montessori schools had a great deal they could learn from the "alternatives," especially in regard to individual liberty, respect, and creativity.

It was at the last school I visited, Booroobin Sudbury School, at Maleny near Brisbane, that I had to confront a large number of my own preconceptions. What I saw was children and teenagers, aged between five and eighteen years of age, working, learning, and playing in freedom. I was astonished by the confidence and responsible attitude of the teenagers at Booroobin. This impression has been confirmed over the years by teenagers I have met from other Sudbury schools, as well as those who have attended similar schools.

I returned to re-examine Montessori literature in the context of more recent work on learning styles, multiple intelligence, and brain development. I discovered a world-wide ground-swell opposition to conventional and compulsory schooling. It seemed that the so-called democratic or free schools are more in keeping with the principles of Montessori than most of the schools that use the name. Maria Montessori was, however, one of the first educators to suggest that children should have a choice in what they learn, to put individual freedom at the heart of her educational method. How did it come to be that schools bearing her name were employing many of the control and testing mechanisms developed to comply with the aims of conventional schooling?

I read everything I could find on democratic and free schools. It occurred to me that Montessori, as well as other approaches based on individual liberty, could find common ground, and it surprised me that gatherings such as the International Democratic Education Conference did not draw much interest from Montessori circles. (The only other Montessori school represented at the 2003 IDEC in Albany, NY, was Abacus Montessori School from Chennai, India, which subsequently opted to become a democratic Montessori School at the 2004 IDEC in India.)

Upon my return from Australia, we had a number of meetings to decide what to do. Eventually, we determined to establish Nahoon Montessori School Primary section as a democratic school, but to retain both the Montessori name and the Montessori concepts of the prepared environment, didactic materials, and methods. This is what made our school new and different from anything else in South Africa, and possibly in the world.

The school differed from the more traditional concept of Montessori, and from regular schools, in a number of ways. We were based, first and foremost, on the principles of individual liberty within a democratic structure. Every person in our school had equal rights, whether aged three or fifty. We had no externally imposed timetable; no child was compelled to do any activity at all if that was not what he or she wished to do. We interpreted work, learning, and playing as integral and indivisible parts of the same concept—growing. Our children played a lot more than one would see in a more conventional Montessori school, but did more formal, academic learning than one normally encounters in a free school.

Nahoon Montessori was in existence for ten years. In that time we evolved from a Montessori three-to-six environment that differed little from other Montessori schools around the globe to a place where people aged two-and-a-half to forty-five spent their days learning and playing and laughing and crying together.

Every time an adult solves a problem for a child, the child is deprived of an opportunity to learn. Every time an adult fails to observe the recurring miracle of the child, that adult dies a little. It is one of the myths of conventional schooling that people (adults and children alike) need to be taught in order to learn. Our staff was required to spend a lot of time simply observing—something stressed by Dr. Montessori but sadly lacking in the Montessori schools I had visited. In fact, we use this as a sort of barometer of whether we are interfering too much. A minimum amount of time was spent in direct teaching. This does not imply that the adult is redundant, or that the children are left entirely to their own devices. We often just did things ourselves, like crafts, or cooking, or reading, or working in the common space we shared with the children.

In keeping with Maria Montessori's view of the role of the adult, it was also incumbent on the staff to ensure that the environment was maintained in a way that encouraged and supported the natural needs of the children.

While we asserted the equal rights of adults and children, we did acknowledge the Montessori concept of planes of development and sensitive periods. This is an understanding that children differ significantly from adults in the way they learn, and that at different stages their needs and the way they seek to satisfy them change. These different needs are met through the prepared environment, a concept that I regarded as lacking in the free schools I visited.

Maria Montessori declared that we could not speak of the liberty of the child without providing an environment that would facilitate that freedom. Thus we had a room set up for the two-and-one-half- to six-year-olds where everything is child-sized and conformed to what one would expect in any Montessori environment. It was very orderly and structured. The second room was set up for the older children, but in this case the children themselves played a more active role in the environment. This room has evolved somewhat over the years in response to the needs of the children. In addition to a selection of regular Montessori materials, we also had a sewing machine, a computer, various toys, a library, a science and technology workbench, musical instruments, radio, Dacta kits, lots of art and craft materials, and anything else the children wish to bring to school themselves. We also built a kitchen. Interestingly, as time passed this room developed a more academic flavor than it had intially, and most of the toys fell into disuse.

The democracy of our school was found in the structures by which the children regulated the day to day running of the school. We adopted a constitution that effectively changed the legal structure of our school from a sole proprietorship (that is, an individually owned business) to a corporation governed by constitution. Our constitution was designed to make parents, staff, and children co-owners of the school, each with rights and responsibilities. All decisions that affected the children were made in our weekly meeting, run by the children. All rules were proposed and voted on in these meetings. Each member had one vote. The staff had no veto rights and parents had no vote in this process. The assembly, a general meeting of all members of the community, dealt with such issues as tuition and fund-raising. Although all children were entitled to attend and vote at these meetings, the matters dealt with were generally of little interest to all but the oldest students—in effect, this was a parent/staff body. A third body, the management committee, was responsible for the actual running of the school, and was required to put into effect decisions taken by the assembly and school meeting. Students were nominated to stand for the management committee, as were staff and parents. The children under six years of age did not display much interest in the meeting or in other processes unless they had a specific problem. Generally, matters involving the under-sixes were brought to the meeting by the directress, but we did have occasions where younger children attended, and voted, at meetings.

Everything about Nahoon Montessori School was in a constant state of evolution. When we started the primary group, we had no clear ideas of how we were going to work. Sometimes when we hit a snag the children would ask me how things were done at the schools I visited in Australia. We found that initially we tended to opt for adaptations of the Sudbury approach, or the ideas and principles espoused by The New School, a liberty-based school in Delaware, USA. In the last two years of NMS we began to explore the principles of sociocracy.

Initially, I discussed ideas of democracy, and human rights and responsibilities, with the children. We formulated some ground rules that outlined the type of system the children wanted. As about half of our primary group had come from regular school, there was a heavy emphasis on preventing bullying and violence. We soon found, however, that the children began to debate the meaning of these rules, and it became necessary to formulate more specific rules to deal with particular situations. Even the rules for running the meetings came under discussion.

We had no mechanism for dealing with infringements of rules, due in part to my own aversion to punishment, which was also heavily supported by the children. After a few months we were faced with some problems that did not appear to be able to be resolved by our normal methods of mediation or discussion in meeting, and it was decided to try out the Sudbury-type method of judicial committee (JC), which I had seen in action at Booroobin. Our JC was never as successful as it appears to be in other schools, and this could be for a number of reasons. We began to understand that it was not the efficacy of the system that is important to us, but the process by which it was established, through which, we grappled with improving it. One of the notable features of our rules was their flexibility and the way in which the children used them to maintain the type of learning environment they wanted. They came to see rules as a tool by which free people can regulate their environment, not a way of controlling and manipulating others. Eventually we abandoned the concept of JC as the students just did not use it, and we noticed that the children showed less and less interest in the rule-making process, in favor of exploring a variety of conflict resolution and problem solving processes.

Our journey was not without pitfalls. We had to constantly work at helping parents, the Education Department, and the general public understand our approach. We had to guard against being sucked into a cycle of either defending what we did or compromising to accommodate the contradictory demands placed upon us. We nonetheless feel that we were steadily moving towards our goal of being a fully democratic school, with the complete support of both the parents and the community at large.

Human beings generally resist anything that is forced upon them. The fight for individual autonomy is a human trait, which exists forever in tension with the opposing desire to live in harmony with a group or tribe of some sort. So far, the best solution humans have been able to come up with to answer these conflicting needs is a political system called democracy.

Around the world, as in South Africa, children are rejecting imposed schooling, but without a clear understanding of either what they are rejecting, or of what, if any, alternatives are available to them. They resort to vandalism and violence in extreme cases, or sink into despair and depression in others. My research over the past few years, backed by the experience at Nahoon Montessori School, has convinced me that the traditional schooling system is long past its sell-by date. Tinkering with curriculum (both in terms of delivery methods and content) cannot significantly change a system that was intentionally designed to destroy individual thought and suppress personal liberty. Montessori had a vision of something different, and she spent her life trying to develop a method or system to transform that vision into a reality. Since their inception, Montessori's discoveries and ideals have been adapted to conform to the agenda of the traditional notion of schooling. My goal was to liberate Montessori's vision from the paradigm of compulsory mass schooling and move into the realm of educating the human potential.

One of the biggest problems faced over the years has been the inability to find staff who are Montessori trained, dedicated to working in a fully democratic environment, and willing to work for the pittance of a salary we were able to pay. At this point I must acknowledge Matthew Rich, who arrived at the school at a pivotal time and helped me in no small way to refine my own ideas on education and democracy. Ultimately, it was a decision taken by Matthew and I that we both needed to move on that led us first to try to find a way of helping the school survive without us personally. It became clear that there was no way the school could continue financially, and two years of searching showed that we would not find suitable staff to work in this type of school in this town.

It became evident to the existing staff and the core group of students and parents who were there at the beginning and were still with us at the end, that NMS would need to change or it could not survive. We took the decision when we ratified our constitution that the school would dissolve rather than compromise our fundamental principles. We realized that in order to promote the ideas and principles that NMS had evolved, we would need to move on. As a result of a unanimous vote by parents, students, and staff, Nahoon Montessori School Assembly met on October 3, 2007 to formally dissolve school meeting, and the school closed its doors on November 30.

Nahoon Montessori School was, for its brief existence, both a true Montessori school and a democratic school. I would argue that you cannot really be Montessori without being democratic (in the sense that those who are governed also do the governing) and that a school that is democratic without being Montessori is depriving its students of a myriad of wonderful opportunities for self-directed, individualized learning.

The lessons learned continue to flavor the work and play of the students and staff who were an integral part of this experiment, and will be carried on to the projects we are planning for the future. I hope that through my writing I can influence both Montessori and democratic schools to see the value in the other approach. I cherish the dream of somehow contributing to a program that will help prepare adults to work in environments that can bring together not only the ideals of Montessori and democratic education, but also principles of ecoliteracy and non-violent communication, and the integration of life and learning into a continuum that transcends the notions of school and home as separate places. The story will continue.

Turning to My Mother
Lisa Delpit

I'm sitting in my 94-year-old mother's house, surrounded by decades of history. On every bookshelf, baby pictures of nieces and nephews, who are now solidly situated in middle age, are still proudly displayed. There are three sets of encyclopedias from the sixties, seventies, and eighties, whose pages are marked by grape juice stains and doodles of generations of family children who came to "Mimi's house" seeking help for school projects.

While I sit filling storage bins in an attempt to make space for my daughter and I, now that Mimi can no longer live on her own, I'm slowed to a snail's pace as I contemplate the mementos of my, my daughter's, my siblings', my nieces' and nephews', and great nieces' and nephews' lives stuffed into drawers. I'm also moved to see the professional archives of a woman who was a remarkable high school mathematics teacher for over forty years, and who continued teaching even after retirement, when she learned—at age seventy-four—to manipulate computers in order to teach computer literacy "to the elderly" at the local community center.

Stacked away in the backs of cabinets are lesson plans she wrote, lesson plans her student teachers wrote, and lesson plans to teach the student teachers. The faded pages still bubble with the excitement, creativity, and commitment embodied in finding a new way to teach a geometry proof or binomial equations. Lesson plans from earlier decades include teaching solid geometry by having students (all low-income African Americans) construct Christmas ornaments, which were often too expensive to buy; and teaching plane geometry by designing and fabricating a baby quilt for a classmate who had left high school in her senior year to get married and bear a son. Bursting out of the hand-written words and slightly blurry (by laser printer standards) manually-typed pages are an excitement about teaching and learning, high expectations, a connection to family and community, and a love for the ability to share knowledge.

This book's title, *Turning Points*, is apropos for me right now as I try to find a firm footing in the education system of today. I look back to my own history, and now my mother's, and I find it very hard, in our current educational era, to feel the excitement about learning, the desire to connect to children and their families, and the thrill of exploring and finding new teaching strategies to reach our students. In his recent doctoral dissertation, one of my students interviewed young children about school. All said that the purpose of school was to pass the state test; they couldn't imagine what a school day could consist of if the mandated test-taking drills were eliminated. Another graduate student, and practicing teacher, bemoaned the fact that after fifteen years of teaching she could now find little joy in her days. Before, she said, all of her extended family knew her students because she couldn't stop talking about them. Now, no family member can name one of the children she teaches because her time with them is spent not bonding or connecting, but documenting how state standards were covered and insuring that other required paperwork was completed.

Yet I still maintain a passion for children and teachers. I can think of no day better spent than in the company of children. Perhaps my passion for education came from being born into a teaching family. Whether it was in the genes or because I was surrounded by the tools of my mother's trade, I began my teaching career early on—almost as soon as I could talk. Before I ever entered formal schooling, I set up "classes" with my dolls, and later, with the children in my neighborhood, to instruct them in anything I had recently learned. By the time I was in fourth grade, I had instituted dance classes at recess for my classmates, teaching them whatever new moves I had learned at my own dance class the previous Saturday. I even sent notes home requesting that my "students" have a certain kind of shoes, and am amazed that some parents provided them—I still wonder who they thought I was!

Perhaps sensing my destiny, the principal or teachers of younger children would call me into the classrooms of first or second graders to "take over the class" when the teacher had to be away for an hour or two. I can only marvel now at how a ten-year-old could be left in charge of a full classroom, but at the time, it seemed absolutely appropriate.

My elementary school years, spent in a small African American Catholic school, were built upon a model of community connection. Teachers and students were known both inside and outside the classroom. In our segregated black communities, students would see teachers at church, at the grocery store, in doctors' offices, in restaurants, and in every venue of our everyday lives. Many students were actually related to each other, and to the lay teachers, and to the African American teaching nuns. There was a seamlessness between school and community living. Parents and teachers carried on conversations comfortably in and out of school. Although we were very aware of the racism surrounding us, we were protected, for the most part, in a safe community bubble.

The bubble burst, however, when Catholic diocese desegregation orders hit, well after the public schools had already erupted in racial strife around integration. I was in eighth grade when I found out I would be going to a then all-white Catholic school for girls. The community could no longer be a buffer for us in that ninth grade year, as African American students were confronted by angry white parents and sometimes angry teachers. I will never forget one red-faced nun screaming at a group of students to "stop acting like niggers!" We weren't able to be on the basketball team because other schools wouldn't play us if there were black team members; we weren't allowed to participate in choral competitions for the same reason. But the biggest loss wasn't these activities, it was a sense of belonging, a sense of community, a sense of being known and valued, a sense of safety.

That loss has led me to believe that we must do things differently in our schools. Although my college education at a historically white, liberal institution focused on creative instruction, it did nothing to speak to belonging. Recapturing lost community and revitalizing my mother's sense of educational joy have informed my own career choices and paths.

When I began my "official" teaching career in inner-city Philadelphia in my early twenties, I spent hours creating beyond-the-book games, activities, songs and dances designed to teach the required curriculum. My first and second graders and I would close the door, put Carol King's *Simply Rosie* on the old turntable, and transform the entire classroom into a giant portrayal of Maurice Sendak's *Chicken Soup with Rice* or *Alligators All Around.* We read the texts together as we sang the songs, we found all of the "b" words or all the words that rhymed, and we created new verses with familiar names and places.

With the encouragement and company of a remarkable lead teacher, I also made attempts to get to know parents and the community by making visits to the local housing projects. I sent letters to parents asking them to help me know what their first graders already knew and what, as parents, they were most interested in their children learning. I learned new teaching strategies from the young innovative white teachers at the school, but I also learned from the older, more traditional black teachers who had taught in, and attended, elementary schools similar to my own. Through them and my mother's earlier example, I learned to connect to my students' home and community experiences, and out-of-school lives. Although I wasn't from Philadelphia and didn't have the deep connections that my own teachers had within our community, I did try—and was encouraged by the school culture—to connect in as many ways as my young teacher-self could imagine.

Today's young teachers—lost in a morass of test drills—seem neither encouraged, taught, nor *allowed* to connect with the community or create their own exciting teaching ideas. Instead, they are often tied to scripted curricula that include no music, art, dance, or joy. I don't know what to do about it. I'm just as beaten down and discouraged as many of the young teachers I teach on weekday evenings. These young teachers, rather than see their students' communities as a potential resource, seem to view them as the enemy. I was encouraged to look beyond the poverty, crime, or single parent families to the community strengths—the church programs, the extended families, the lively households, the cooking, the music, the family celebrations, and even the candy store and the popular television shows—in order to both connect to students and use community knowledge to create meaningful curricula. Today's teachers are frequently taught to consider these community realities a part of the *reason* for school failure.

Though I question what impact I might have in changing the current ethos, I continue to try. For most of my career in higher education I have focused on getting pre-service and practicing teachers to connect with their students, their students' interests, and their students' communities; to get to know parents and give them the opportunity to teach educators about their children; and to find spaces within the day to touch upon the real joy of teaching and learning. In years past, teachers became excited about these ideas and created inspired classrooms to implement them. But in more recent days, they've just become tired. I hear over and over again, "We don't have time. We have to do the test prep and follow the mandated curriculum." I've had little success in convincing teachers and principals that the test scores would improve if we focused on connections, creative teaching, high standards, and joy.

Master teacher Carrie Secret, whose low income students in one of the poorest areas of Oakland, California, always score at the top of the district on state-mandated tests—outscoring children from much more affluent areas—says she never teaches to the test, never does the test drills, never makes a big deal of the testing time. She knows her children well, connects with their parents (and they with her), helps them to figure out what they might be able to do to improve their community, and develops creative, multidimensional experiences for every day in the classroom. Carrie reads, or has her elementary students read, adult-level texts often related to the children's cultures. They study the difficult vocabulary and the complex sentence structures until they are fully fluent with the texts. Using these texts as a starting point, they create and perform dramatic readings, original songs and dances. They invite other schools, parents, and members of the community to watch and learn from their performances.

Most recently, I've wondered if my colleagues at universities and I should spend our time solely helping teachers develop a "post-test curriculum." Once the tests are over in March, maybe instead of everyone breathing a collective sigh of relief and settling in to just counting the days until the end of school, we could spend the next few months teaching what really matters. We could develop exciting lessons using real literature, dance, music and art; we could connect with children and their community.

In writing all of this, I wonder if it might seem like a departure from my previously well-publicized positions on explicit instruction. In fact, it is a nuanced position I am trying to forge here. Decontextualized drills are not explicit, they are only the constant repetition of meaningless bits. I am suggesting that when we know our students, their culture, and their communities, we can access *meaningful* aspects of their lives to create instruction that *explicitly* teaches specific elements of the required curriculum.

I don't know where I will end up in my quest to reshape what we are doing to our children and our teachers. I don't know if I will be able to remain connected to institutions that seem so bereft of what I want education to be. For the moment I am still working at it, one class, one teacher, one principal at a time. If nothing else, I can make my mother proud.

Transforming Society: A Partnership Educational Agenda
Riane Eisler

Educational debates have largely centered on standards, testing, and other procedural reforms. Unfortunately this debate ignores not only children's individual needs and capacities but also the role education plays in forming children's views about what is normal or abnormal, possible or impossible, right or wrong. In short, the conventional conversation about education ignores the critical matter of whether children grow up to accept an unjust status quo or understand they can play a role in social transformation.

My interest in education as a means for social transformation is rooted in my early life experiences. On November 10, 1938—later known as Crystal Night because so much glass was shattered in Jewish stores, homes, and synagogues—a gang of Nazis came for my father, shoved him down the stairs, and dragged him off. Miraculously, my mother obtained his release, and my parents and I fled my native Vienna and eventually got to Cuba. Had we remained in Europe, we would almost certainly have been killed.

These early childhood experiences led to burning questions. Why is there so much cruelty, destructiveness, and hate in the world? Is this our inevitable lot? Or can we create a more peaceful, just, and caring world?

It was only much later that I began to systematically look for answers to these questions. For much of my childhood, adolescence, and early womanhood, I was too involved in simply trying to make it through what was at first a harsh and lonely environment in Cuba and then struggling to adapt to what was socially expected of me. It was only when it was clear that these expectations were wrong for me that I embarked on the road that eventually led to my research and writing— including my writings on transformative education.

My Early Life

The Nazis confiscated (that is, officially stole) my parent's business, bank accounts, and most of their other possessions. We fled with just a few pieces of luggage, and arrived in Cuba almost destitute. I grew up in the industrial slums of Havana, where we remained even after my parents started a new business. But already before then, they scrimped and saved to do what Jews often consider most important: providing their children with the best possible education.

What this meant for my parents was sending me to the best private schools. So first I went to a bilingual Methodist school (where among other things I was constantly importuned to raise my hand and say I believed in Jesus Christ, a terrible burden on a little girl trying to do what was expected both at home and school—which were miles apart). Then, I was sent to a British school in the suburbs (attended by the scions of Cuba's extraordinarily rich café society elites), commuting every day by streetcar from the industrial slums to where the rich lived (a kind of daily culture shock).

And so I received a classical education. It was rigorous and I will always be grateful for it, as it included not only a focus on classics but also Latin and other subjects that are not part of the U.S. curriculum. In fact, when I came to the U.S. at the age of fourteen (my parents always saw Cuba as just an antecedent to finally obtaining a U.S. visa), my high school classes were so boring I can honestly say I learned almost nothing of use there. The same was true of my first two years at UCLA, even though that was a step up.

However, since early childhood I had been an avid reader, so that much of my education came from books from outside school. Though my parents were rather strict and overprotective (in typical European fashion), for some strange reason they hardly paid any attention to what I read. So my readings were wide-ranging, from French novels I only understood much later (I started reading those when I was ten) to intermittent excursions into philosophy and science, including Plato and later Marx.

I should say, however, that when I came to the U.S. as an adolescent, having been a stranger in a strange land for seven years in Cuba, I was, above all, hungry to belong. So much of my energy went into trying at last to belong that I did not really care that much that I was bored silly in my classes. Moreover, my parents, as was the norm at that time, saw my going to university as mainly a way to get a Mrs. degree—that is, to marry a professional man and assume my womanly life roles as wife and mother.

Even though I was a brilliant student (Phi Beta Kappa, etc.), it never seemed to occur to any of my professors, or anyone else, that I should be encouraged to pursue a career of my own—much less that I should be groomed to make a significant intellectual contribution. So it was only gradually that I began to awaken to these possibilities.

My Middle Years

My first job after graduating from UCLA was as a social scientist at the Systems Development Corporation, an offshoot of the Rand Corporation. I did not like the work, because my employers were only interested in military systems. But I learned a basic principle of systems thinking: that looking at how different parts of a system interact makes it possible to see more than just the sum of its parts.

I wasn't aware at that time that studying social systems would become my life's work. That was in the 1950s, and many things happened before I returned to the fundamental questions of my childhood. By the time I did it was the 1970s, and I had become aware of something I had been completely unconscious of: that while being a Jew and an immigrant had obviously, and critically, affected my life, so also had being born female. Indeed, I realized that if I felt like an outsider it was not only because I was an immigrant and a Jew, but because hardly any of what I was taught as "important knowledge and truth" was about or by those who were female. This new consciousness not only led me to take a leadership role in the 1960's women's movement; it also profoundly affected my approach to the study of human societies.

By that time I had married and had given birth to two daughters. Like many of us, I saw that the global crises that futurists then called the *world problematique* can't be solved by the system that created them. I saw that a grim future awaits my children—and all of us—if we don't make transformative social changes.

The question was: transformation to what? And that in turn led me back to the questions of my childhood, questions about whether injustice and violence are inevitable or whether we can construct a social system that supports more just, sustainable, and peaceful relationships.

From Conventional Categories to Holistic Frameworks

When I embarked on my transdisciplinary, crosscultural, historical analysis of human societies, I developed a new approach: the *study of relational dynamics*. This is a method of inquiry that differs markedly from traditional studies. To begin with, it draws from a much wider data base. While most social studies, including most so-called systems studies, focus primarily on the so-called public sphere of political and economic relations, the study of relational dynamics looks at the whole of our lives—including our family and other intimate relations. Unlike the majority of studies (often aptly called "the study of man"), it takes into account the whole of humanity—both its female and male halves. And rather than examining one period at a time, it looks at the whole span of history—including the long period before written records called prehistory.

A basic principle of systems theory is that if we don't look at the whole of a system, we can't see the connections between its various components—just like if we look at only part of a picture we can't see the relationship between its different parts. Using this larger data base made it possible to see connections between different parts of social systems that are not visible otherwise. It was now possible to see patterns or configurations repeating themselves cross-culturally and historically. Since there were no names for these social configurations, I called one the *domination system* and the other the *partnership system*.

Conventional categories, such as ancient/modern, Eastern/

Western, religious/secular, rightist/leftist, technologically developed/
undeveloped, and capitalist/communist only describe certain aspects
of social systems. They do not take into account the totality of the
institutions, assumptions, beliefs, relationships, and activities that
constitute a culture. They pay hardly any attention to the cultural
construction of the formative childhood relations and the relations
between the male and female halves of humanity—even though
these primary human relations are foundational to what people learn
to consider normal or abnormal, possible or impossible, moral or
immoral.

By contrast, the domination system and the partnership system
describe interactions that establish and maintain two very different
types of relations—from intimate to international. One type is based
on rigid rankings of domination ultimately backed up by fear and force.
The other type is based on mutual respect, mutual accountability, and
mutual benefit.

Two Human Possibilities: Domination or Partnership

No society orients completely to either the domination or
partnership continuum. But the degree to which it does profoundly
affects which of our large repertoire of human traits and behaviors—
from caring and sensitivity to cruelty and insensitivity—are culturally
reinforced or inhibited.

Some of the most brutally violent, repressive societies of the
twentieth century were Hitler's Germany (a technologically advanced,
Western, rightist society), Stalin's USSR (a secular leftist society),
Khomeini's Iran (an Eastern religious society), and Idi Amin's Uganda
(a tribalist society). There are obvious differences between them. But
they all share the core configuration of the domination system.

The first component of this configuration is a structure of rigid
top-down rankings: hierarchies of domination maintained through
physical, psychological, and economic control. This structure is found
in both the family and the state or tribe, and is the template or mold for
all social institutions.

The second core component is the rigid ranking of one half of
humanity over the other half. Theoretically, this could be the female
half over the male half. But in practice, it has been the ranking of the

male half over the female half. Along with this, we see the high valuing of "hard" qualities and behaviors, such as "heroic" violence and "manly" conquest and control. I want to emphasize that these are not qualities inherent in men but rather qualities stereotypically associated with "real masculinity" in dominator ideology.

The third core component of domination systems is culturally accepted abuse and violence, from child- and wife-beating to chronic warfare. Every society has some abuse and violence. But in cultures orienting to the domination system, we find the institutionalization and idealization of abuse and violence to maintain hierarchies of domination—man over woman, man over man, race over race, and nation over nation.

The fourth core component consists of beliefs that dominator relations are inevitable, even moral. In cultures and subcultures that orient closely to the domination model, we find teachings and stories that say it's honorable and moral to kill and enslave neighboring nations or tribes, stone women to death, stand by while "inferior" races are put in ovens and gassed, or beat children to impose one's will. In this belief system, there are only two options. You either dominate or you are dominated. Therefore, both war and the "war of the sexes" are inevitable. The guiding belief is that there is no other alternative.

The partnership system has a very different core configuration, also consisting of four interactive, mutually supporting components.

The first core component is a democratic and egalitarian structure. This structure is found in both the family and the state or tribe, and is the template for other institutions. That is not to say that there are no rankings. But they are what I call *hierarchies of actualization* rather than *hierarchies of domination*. These are more flexible hierarchies in which power is viewed not as power *over* but as power *to* and power *with*: the kind of power described in the progressive management literature today as inspiring and supporting, rather than controlling, others.

The second core component is equal partnership between women and men. With this comes a high valuing, in *both* women and men, of qualities and behaviors such as nonviolence, nurturance, and caregiving, denigrated as "soft," feminine," and "unmanly" in domination systems.

The third core component of the partnership system is that abuse and violence aren't culturally accepted. This doesn't mean that there is no abuse or violence. But they aren't institutionalized or idealized, because they're not needed to maintain rigid rankings of domination.

The fourth core component consists of beliefs about human nature that support empathic and mutually respectful relations. Although cruelty and violence are recognized as human possibilities, they're not considered inevitable, much less moral.

Cultures that orient to the partnership end of the partnership/ domination continuum also transcend conventional categories such as religious or secular, Eastern or Western, industrial, pre-industrial, or post-industrial. Among the Teduray, a technologically primitive tribal society in the Philippines, as anthropologist Stuart Schlegel writes, family and social structure were egalitarian and social relations unranked and peaceful. Decision-making was typically participatory; softer, stereotypically "feminine" virtues were valued; and nature and the human body were given great respect. Similarly, among the agrarian Minagkabau of Sumatra, women play major social roles, violence is not part of childraising, and stereotypically feminine values such as caring and nurturing are valued—not only in women but also in men.

Orientation to the partnership core configuration can also be seen in the highly technologically developed, industrialized Nordic societies. These are not ideal societies. But they are democratic cultures where there aren't huge gaps between haves and have-nots, where women have higher status, and where nurturance and nonviolence are considered appropriate behavior for men as well as women and are supported by fiscal policy.

Nordic countries such as Sweden, Norway, Finland, and Iceland built societies with both political and economic democracy and succeeded in creating a generally good living standard for all. This success has sometimes been attributed to the fact that they are relatively small and homogeneous. But smaller and even more homogeneous societies, such as some of the oil-rich nations of the Middle East where there are large gaps between haves and have-nots, orient closely to the domination system. So to understand why the Nordic nations developed a more caring and equitable economics we have to look at other factors. And one such factor is that women in the Nordic world have held the highest political offices, and a larger proportion of legislators (over 40%) are female than anywhere else in the world.

As among the Teduray and Minagkabau, the higher status of women in the Nordic world has important consequences for how men define masculinity. As the status of women rises, so also does the status of traits and activities that in domination-oriented cultures are unacceptable in men because they are stereotypically associated with "inferior" femininity. These traits become more highly valued in, and by, both men and women. So along with the higher status of women in the Nordic world, came fiscal priorities that support more stereotypically "feminine" values and activities.

As I detail in my book *The Real Wealth of Nations: Creating a Caring Economics,* these more partnership-oriented nations pioneered caregiving policies such as government-supported childcare, universal health care, and paid parental leave. As a result of these more stereotypically "feminine" caregiving policies, these countries, which earlier suffered from extreme poverty—including severe famines that led to waves of immigration to the United States—became prosperous. This contradicts still another reason sometimes given for more humane Nordic social policies: that these policies were due to greater prosperity. In reality, these policies were the cause, not effect, of greater prosperity.

Nordic nations also pioneered laws prohibiting violence against children in families. They have a strong men's movement against male violence toward women. They pioneered nonviolent conflict resolution and established the first peace studies programs. They pioneered environmentally sound manufacturing approaches; for example, the "Natural Step," where materials are recycled even after they reach the consumer to avoid pollution and waste. And their educational systems give children far more individual attention and freedom—accounting in large part for the fact that their high school students regularly score high in international achievement tests.

These are *not* coincidental developments. They are all outcomes of the fact that the core configuration of the Nordic world orients much more to the partnership side of the partnership-domination continuum.

Partnership Education

Obviously, education for domination systems and partnership systems is very different. So in my book *Tomorrow's Children: A*

Blueprint for Partnership Education in the 21ˢᵗ Century I set out to apply my findings to education.

As educators know, there are three primary elements in education: process (how we learn and teach), structure (the learning environment), and content or curriculum (what we learn and teach).

Partnership process is about *how* we learn and teach. It applies the guiding template of the partnership model to educational *methods* and *techniques*. Are young people treated with caring and respect? Do teachers act as primarily lesson-dispensers and controllers, or more as mentors and facilitators? Are young people learning to work together or must they continuously compete with each other? Are they offered the opportunity for self-directed learning? In short, is education merely a matter of teachers inserting "information" into young people's minds, or are students and teachers partners in a meaningful adventure of exploration and learning?

Partnership structure is about *where* learning and teaching take place: what kind of *learning environment* we construct. Is the structure of a school, classroom, and/or home school one of top-down authoritarian rankings, or is it a more democratic one? Do students, teachers, and other staff participate in school decision-making and rule-setting? Diagramed on an organizational chart, would decisions flow only from the top down and accountability only from the bottom up, or would there be interactive feedback loops? In short, is the learning environment organized in terms of hierarchies of domination ultimately backed up by fear, or is it a combination of horizontal linkings and hierarchies of actualization where power is not used to disempower but to empower?

Partnership content is *what* we learn and teach. It is the *educational curriculum*. Does the curriculum effectively teach students not only basic academic and vocational skills but also the life-skills they need to be competent and caring citizens, workers, parents, and community members? Are we telling young people to be responsible, kind, and nonviolent at the same time that the curriculum content still celebrates male violence and conveys environmentally unsustainable and socially irresponsible messages? Does it present science in holistic, relevant ways? Does what is taught as important knowledge and truth include—not just as an add-on, but as integral to what is learned—

both the female and male halves of humanity as well as children of various races and ethnicities? Does it teach young people the difference between the partnership and domination systems as two basic human possibilities and the feasibility of creating a partnership way of life? Or, both overtly and covertly, is this presented as unrealistic in "the real world"? In short, what kind of view of ourselves, our world, and our roles and responsibilities in it are young people taking away from their schooling?

Much of progressive education has focused primarily on process, and to some degree on structure. This is very important. But partnership education is not only a matter of more self-directed learning, peer teaching, cooperative learning, more individualized assessment tools, and other partnership pedagogies. Nor is it only a matter of a more democratic and participatory structure. It emphasizes the importance of narratives, and very specifically what kinds of behaviors and values are presented as valuable in curriculum narratives.

One of the goals of progressive education is to give young people more choices. Yet even in many progressive schools the curriculum offers few alternative narratives. At best it does so in bits and pieces, mostly as add-ons to conventional narratives we inherited from earlier more domination-oriented times. So all too often there is a conflict between the worldviews and values progressive educators talk about and try to model, and the implicit, and even explicit, messages of the narratives or stories that both consciously and unconsciously mold what people consider normal and desirable. For this reason, attention to narratives is a major component of partnership education.

On all sides young people see and hear stories that portray us as bad, cruel, violent, and selfish. Video games and action adventure movies and TV shows present violence as the way to solve problems. Situation comedies make insensitivity, rudeness, and cruelty seem funny. Cartoons present violence as exciting, funny, and without real consequences. As in the journalistic motto of "if it bleeds, it leads," even the stories that make top headlines focus on the infliction and/or suffering of pain as the most significant and newsworthy human events.

Rather than correcting this false image of what it means to be human, much of what children still learn in schools reinforce it. Not only do history curricula still emphasize battles and wars, but classics such as Homer's *Iliad* and Shakespeare's kings trilogy romanticize "heroic violence." And scientific stories tell children that we are the puppets of "selfish genes" ruthlessly competing on the evolutionary stage.

If we are inherently violent, bad, and selfish, we have to be strictly controlled. This is why stories that claim this is "human nature" are central to an education for a domination system. They are, however, inappropriate if young people are to learn to live in a democratic, peaceful, equitable, and Earth-honoring way.

This is why I included in *Tomorrow's Children* a panoply of curriculum components. These components are woven into a coherent curriculum loom and learning tapestry for those who want a whole-systems approach. But they are also intended for teaching in all kinds of settings, providing materials that can be integrated into existing curricula.

A major focus throughout *Tomorrow's Children* is a more gender-balanced curriculum. Most of what children are taught is still extremely male-centered, from textbook illustrations of primate and human evolution with only male figures to how the canon in just about every field (from art to science) primarily features males. This marginalization, and often invisibility, of the female half of humanity perpetuates domination systems. A male-superior/female-inferior model of our species is a template for learning to associate difference— beginning with the most basic difference between male and female— with superiority or inferiority, dominating or being dominated, being served or serving. This is a template that can then be applied to different races, religions, ethnicities, and so forth—which is why, for example, regressive regimes or would-be regimes (such as so-called religious fundamentalists) focus so heavily on getting women back into their traditional or subservient place.

A major theme running through partnership education is providing young people the analytical lenses of the partnership-domination continuum to make sense of what otherwise seems random and disconnected. For instance, all the progressive modern social movements have challenged traditions of domination—from the "rights of man," feminist, abolitionist, and economic justice movements of the 18th and 19th centuries, to the 20th century peace, environmental, and women's rights movements, to the continuing struggle for human rights, including the rights of women and children. As young people understand these connections, they too can make a difference in promoting the cultural transformation from domination to partnership.

My hope, and goal, is that adapted for different regions and cultures, partnership education can be a blueprint for refocusing, reframing, and redesigning education to help children grow up to be active agents of social transformation. We must use education to show our children that a partnership future is not a *utopia* or no place, but a *pragmatopia*, a possible place—and we must teach them the knowledge and skills they need to build partnership cultures worldwide.

Escaping Education?
Gustavo Esteva

I learn slowly. Only later in my life did I discover the real meaning and impact of education, when indigenous peoples revealed them to me. My path was rather convoluted, full of bends and unexpected turns and surprises.

The point of departure

I got a very conventional education, which seemed to fascinate me. I asked anxiously for it, when I was three years old and my older brother started his school. I wanted to do everything he was doing, and in aping him, I soon learned to read and write. This ability made possible my acceptance in primary school before my sixth birthday, the minimum required in those times.

From the very beginning I added homework to the work prescribed, to accumulate points allowing me to be the first in my group, every week, and to, at the end of the year, receive the Award of Excellence. Getting the highest possible grade became an obsession.

Most activities in the school fascinated me and I followed religiously all its norms. No critique to the system ever came to my mind, in those years, even when I suffered the consequences of an absurd discipline—when, for example, I was forced to pee in my pants in the classroom because I was not allowed to go to the bathroom, and I remained in my seat, full of shame, at the end of the class.

I was sixteen years old when my father died, and I was forced to work for the sustenance of my family. I then made the foolish decision of adding to that the studies in two universities, in two different professions. I abandoned the first after a couple of years of delirious effort and concluded the second with Summa cum Laude: I was still trapped in the norms.

Apparently, I had no reason to criticize the educational system. Had it prepared me for life and work, as it promised? No doubt! From the very first day in a job I was an obedient, disciplined, hard-working and competitive employee. I soon started to get the reward for my efforts; I was the youngest executive ever in IBM in Mexico; I was Personnel Manager in Procter & Gamble before I was twenty. I also succeeded in Mexican corporations and my own professional bureau. It seemed that the promise of equality offered by education was, in my case, fulfilled. I soon enjoyed "social mobility." I had been in schools well above my socio-economic level, but once in the business world I advanced quickly, and began to be part of the privileged minority. I did not notice, at that time, the new form of discrimination created by education. My education certificates opened many doors for me, while closing them on those without diplomas. Education had no noticeable impact on my rich classmates, who could fail in it without consequences, but those of my same social class, or of one inferior, who were unable to get good results in the school, or, even worse, who were forced to abandon it for whatever reason, often suffered for the rest of their lives the discrimination usually practiced against drop-outs. But far from providing a motive to criticize education, this experience seemed to confirm its value. In the name of justice good education should be extended to everyone, in order to offer equal opportunities to all.

First signs

In the late 1950s, my country and my region were in turmoil. I witnessed great social mobilizations and brutal repression while Che Guevara was awakening us politically, and forging in many of us the moral obligation to attempt revolution in our own social contexts. I started the path of autonomous learning, through conversations with friends and frequent incursions into secondhand bookshops—where

I had the fortune of finding, for pocket change, books that defined my political and theoretical path for many years.

Challenging the system seemed to have no relationship with my education. I was fired from both IBM and Procter & Gamble because I refused to do things that appeared unjust and indecent. In fact, in spite of my professional and economic success, I abandoned my profession before I was twenty-five years old. It seemed that to live a decent and dignified life, I could no longer work for private corporations or apply what I had learned. Thus, I began one of the most difficult tasks of my life: to de-learn what I had been taught. However, this still did not seem to represent a critique to education itself, only to its orientation, imposed by the dominant economic and political regime. The latter was the evil, not education, and once we were able to change its nature and direction, there would be no reason to worry about it: we would get the proper education for everyone and thus equity and justice.

In the sixties, when my first daughter became school age, I looked around for a good public or private school, an institution to which I could entrust my beloved child. I could not find any in Mexico City, and since other friends were in the same predicament, we invented one. We mixed up a marvelous cocktail, with our own creativity—a lot of Freinet, some Montessori, a little bit of Steiner and the Waldorf Schools, some Summerhill, and more. It was really beautiful. In the first bulletin of the school, quickly improvised by the children and their parents, our intention became explicit: "A link between the useless traditional education and the privilege of raising children in freedom, able to love their own lives." Every year we added a grade, for my daughter to continue her studies. She enjoyed the experience, however, when she finished high school, we closed the school. Both my daughter and her parents knew by that time that the problem was not the quality of the school, but the school itself. No matter how much we redesigned the classroom and the curriculum, no matter how free our school was, how beautiful the trees and the garden that substituted for a classroom, how open and creative the teachers, our school was still a school. My daughter did not follow university studies and I was forced to begin my exploration of alternative paths.[1]

In the late seventies, I began to live and work in autonomous niches at the grassroots level. Through a series of NGOs, a group of friends and I attempted to work directly with the people—with peasants in the countryside and marginals in the cities, with all the usual "untouchables." We learned far more with the "untouchables" than with the experts and the rulers, and with them, we began enjoying a different kind of freedom and autonomy. Increasingly, however, I found myself confused and puzzled. With all the formal categories of my education, I could not make any sense of my daily experience. For some time, I assumed I needed to study more, to do more extensive academic research. So at a furious pace, I studied the latest theories of economics, sociology, anthropology, and political science, and my confusion grew. There were times, I must confess, when I even assumed that the problem was not with the theoretical models that fascinated me, but that reality needed to change in order to fit into all the beautiful, neat, academic, theoretical categories of the brilliant experts of Development and Education!

Then one day, in spite of myself and my education, my lenses of development just fell off. Dazzled, blind, mute, I groped for words, for different doors of perception, of thought. The lenses of development—whether tinted Left or Right, Republican or Democrat, Marxist or Fascist, capitalist or socialist—could not help me see or understand the complex worlds of real people living real lives.

Then two things happened. First, I started to remember. When I was a child I had asked to be sent to Oaxaca, with my Zapotec grandmother, to enjoy my holidays with her. Remembering what she taught me by her very being, in the market where she tended a stall, I began the slow, very slow, path of re-membering my own people.
Second, I met Ivan Illich.

CIDOC was just forty miles from my place in Mexico City. Ivan, internationally renowned and infamous, drawing brilliant intellectuals and activists from all over the world, did not draw us from Mexico's Left. For us, he was just a reactionary priest; his fields—education, health, transportation—were irrelevant, mere services we would deal with once we were in power, after eliminating capitalist exploitation. Looking from the Left, we were convinced that Illich's focus on education or health was a mistake or a rightist trick[2].

In 1983 I was invited to a seminar in Mexico City on the social construction of energy with Wolfgang Sachs. Ivan was there. I was mesmerized. That very night, I embarked on my Illich studium. A little later, I started to collaborate with him. Still later, slowly, we became friends.

My fascination with Ivan was born out of the fact that his ideas, his words, and his writings were a brilliant intellectual presentation of ordinary people's common discourse. He was describing ways of living and being that I encountered all the time; in my grandmother's world, the world of other indigenous peoples, the world of *campesinos* or *marginales*. "Vernacular" and "convivial," two words that are central to Ivan's work, were magnificent symbols for my people's worlds. I heard them there first, in all those pre-Illich years, when I felt and sensed and smelled and touched and experienced those words and what they symbolized, in the villages, at the grassroots.

Ivan once said that "people can see what scientists and administrators can't." And he said something more: that the people in our countries, rather than the dissident elite in the advanced ones, were the ones implementing the political inversion he conceived in *Tools for Conviviality* (1973)[3]. People are *"just using their brains and trusting their senses"* and that was exactly my experience. Using Ivan's terminology and concepts I was able to see very clearly what ordinary, common people were doing.

What to do?

I joined up with several friends in the 1980s and launched a public campaign asking for a legislation that would punish, with ten years of prison, any person producing any diploma or asking another person for any kind of certification of studies, to apply for a job or for whatever. I had no hope of getting my legislation passed, but I wanted public debate and I got it. Most people said: If we pass your stupid legislation 99% of the children will abandon school, whatever grade they are in. That sentiment revealed what I wanted to make evident, that in Mexico, at least, people go to school or parents send their children to it only to get the diploma. Most people know that the school is not an appropriate place to learn; it is a place to get an institutional certification, a kind of visa, which allows you to circulate in modern society. Even our magnificent school was not a good place to learn. And it was even less of a good place for children to live and flourish.

Years later, I attempted the other extreme: to give diplomas to everyone.[4] We still have political campaigns, for example against compulsory education. But we are not using too much time or resources in such campaigns. We are, rather, dedicated to implementing our own initiatives.

Reclaiming our freedom to learn

The impact of the Zapatista uprising in 1994 was immense in Oaxaca, the state where I live and the only state in Mexico where the majority of the population is indigenous, one of the poorest according to conventional indicators, and the richest in terms of natural and cultural diversity—sixteen indigenous peoples coexist there, and among them the *mestizos*. Their struggle forced the government to enact laws, in 1995, to acknowledge their own system of government and their autonomy. A little later, those peoples created a public forum to articulate their voices and give to them appropriate visibility.

In 1997 this forum offered a public declaration, after long reflection and debate, denouncing school as the main tool of the state to destroy indigenous cultures. The scandal produced with this manifesto was compounded with the discovery that some communities were closing the schools. Very few were acquainted with the findings of a young anthropologist who, after applying the proper tests, discovered that the unschooled children were better prepared than the schooled ones in all but one aspect: the latter knew how to sing the national anthem (Maldonado 1998).

People from those communities later shared with me their concern that their young men and women, after learning all they could from the immediate community, would not be able to continue their studies because they had no institutional certification. We thus created, with them and for them, Universidad de la Tierra en Oaxaca, a space where those young indigenous men and women will be able to learn whatever they want to learn without previous schooling or any documentation. This space has evolved a lot in its first years of life. We have learned a lot. We currently define the experience as a space dedicated to learning, study, reflection and action. Our efforts are focused on actions of social transformation aimed at rooting, strengthening and expanding the convivial way of life and radical democracy.

Unitierra practices and enriches intercultural dialogue through learning stays in which people from different communities, cultures, and countries interact and reflect together.

Our learning style emphasizes practice. We learn by doing what we want to learn with the people who are practicing it in the field. The members of Unitierra follow their self-directed path of learning, at their own pace, and in the field of learning they choose. The fields of learning define spheres of common interest. They can be theoretical: social movements, the nature of the current crisis, the challenges of democracy; or practical: video production, appropriate technology, alternative therapies, and urban agriculture, among others.

Those who wish to learn at Unitierra can begin to do so at any time, without any preconditions. They do not need to demonstrate certification of prior studies.

We classify our practical initiatives as the expression of specific struggles: for cultural regeneration; food sovereignty; free, autonomous interaction; and reclaiming tools. The main fields of learning that exist in Unitierra include the theoretical and practical aspects of a convivial way of life and learning how to live it, facing together the challenges that it represents and sharing our practical experiences on eating, healing, learning, settling, intertwining and others. In the area of tools, by designing, creating, reproducing and employing tools that expand our capabilities in daily life; and in the area of autonomous media, to conceive, construct, organize and operate means of interaction with other people and groups. Reflection In Action is the name we give to all the documented, disciplined, rigorous, public, and critical activities that allow us to reflect on the reality in which we are immersed, on our own activities, and on the experiences of other people and groups.

And friendship?

At the end of *Deschooling Society,* where he elaborates on his not very smart proposals, Ivan wrote:

> What characterizes the true master-disciple relationship is its
> priceless character. Aristotle speaks of it as a "moral type of
> friendship, which is not in fixed terms: it makes a gift, or does
> whatever it does, as to a friend." Thomas Aquinas says of this kind

of teaching that inevitably it is an act of love and mercy. This kind of teaching is always a luxury for the teacher and a form of leisure (in Greek, *"schole"*) for him and his pupil: an activity meaningful for both, having no ulterior purpose. (1970b, p.101).

That is the main point in friendship. Gratis. Not only because there is no economic exchange involved, but because you are doing what you are doing for the joy of it, having no ulterior purpose. Gratis. Learning together is not a means towards an end, but an end in itself, for the joy of it. It is a pleasure to do it with friends, as an expression of friendship. The "students" coming to Unitierra are not our friends. When we put them in contact with a person doing what they want to learn, they are not friends. We know very well that you cannot create friendship, you cannot force it. Furthermore, you cannot befriend everybody. There is always a personal element of mutual attraction for friendship to be possible.

Austerity has been a key element in the creation of a social environment in which friendship emerges and flourishes. Austerity, as Aquinas clarified, is a virtue that does not exclude our delight. It does not exclude wine and women. It only excludes those delights degrading personal relationship. Austerity often includes techno fasting, renouncing anything that can be an obstacle for friendship, excluding any tool or technology that can create a distance between friends. Austerity, as a virtue, wrote Ivan thirty years ago, "is part of another virtue which is more fragile and embraces and overcomes it; joy, eutrapelia, friendship" (1973, México: Posada, 1978, p.16).

We are not, in Unitierra, a community of friends. Notwithstanding, friendship is always at the very center of our activities. Friendship flourishes in every corner. If one of our friends does not feel he is comfortable with an apprentice or thinks he cannot befriend him or her, he may call us to ask for a change. Any "student" can do the same. We need such flexibility and openness to walk our own path. While creating a situation in which no condition for learning is scarce, our challenge becomes how to deal with the affluence of joy and friendship which may overwhelm us. And there, more and more, we discover ourselves, who we are, in the eyes of our friends.

Escaping education?

Are we escaping education[5]?

We don't know exactly what we are doing, but we nourish the hope that we are creating and dis-covering alternatives to education. Yes, we are coming back from the future, living in the present, living in our own places, not in search of any kind of mobility which will take us to the centers of power of the global economy.

Like John Holt, I don't like the word *education*. I am convinced that we can abandon it. Escaping education has become, for many of us, a very profound path of liberation.

Ivan Illich often celebrated the master-pupil relationship. What he opposed was trapping such a relationship inside a curriculum, a program, a teaching, an ideology, a plan, a goal. The master is not trying to transfer certain knowledge or skills to the pupil. He or she has no educational goals for the student, is not interested in transforming the student into something. The master loves their student with a caring love, no strings attached, and while he or she may nourish hopes about the pupil, does not hold onto expectations.

"True learning," Ivan once said, "can only be the leisurely practice of free people." In the consumer society, he also said, we are either prisoners of addiction or prisoners of envy. Only without addiction or envy, only without educational goals, in freedom, can we enjoy true learning.

Our audacity, our playfulness, our non-suicidal Luddite-ism, our creative ways of swimming against the modern current in order to enjoy regenerating our traditions—all of these help to explain our recent adventures, like Unitierra. Yes, we can do everything we are doing without it, without the institution, but playing with the symbols of the system is not only an expression of humor, it is also a kind of protection. What we are doing is highly subversive. In a sense, we are subverting all and every institution of the modern, economic society. The expanding dignity of every one of us, every one of our relationships necessarily challenges existing systems (Illich 1970a, p.19). In packaging our activities as one of the most respected sacred cows of modernity—education—we protect our freedom from the attacks of the system. We don't want to be accused of being terrorists!

In my place, every I is a We. And thus we live together, in our living present, rooted in our social and cultural soil, nourishing hopes at a time in which all of us, inspired by the Zapatistas, are creating a whole new world.

Notes

1. For full disclosure, I must say that my second daughter, six years younger than the first, was basically educated by her mother, a professional educator, after our divorce when she was only one year old. She was loyal to school and got a college degree.

2. Ivan described our attitude in 1970: "We are used to considering schools as a variable, dependent on the political and economic structure. If we can change the style of political leadership, or promote the interest of one class or another, or switch from private to public ownership of the means of production, we assume the school system will change as well" (Illich 1970b, p.73). But we did not read him then.

3. "In the last words of that book"—Ivan commented to David Cayley—"I said that I knew in which direction things would happen but not what would bring them to that point. At that time I believed in some big, symbolic event, in something similar to the Wall Street crash. Instead of that, it is hundreds of millions of people just using their brains and trusting their senses. We now live in a world in which most of those things that industry and government do are misused by people for their own purposes." (Cayley 1992, p.117).

4. At one point, on our local TV station in Oaxaca, we were talking about the horrendous damage produced by sewage and how the flush toilet was spoiling our lives. In discussing the politics of shit, we were examining the advantages of an ecological dry toilet, designed by a friend. It was fantastic, not only because it helped you to dispose responsibly of your own shit, radically canceling out very dirty shitwork, but also to disconnect your stomach from any public or private centralized bureaucracy. Because of the extended requests for dry toilets, we organized intensive five-day courses through which all kinds of people learned everything about that trade. At the end of every course, we gave every participant a magnificent diploma, with golden letters, recognizing them as "Experts in alternative sanitation, with a specialization in dry toilets." This approach helped implement the construction of 100,000 dry toilets in Oaxaca, Mexico. Knowing about these courses, the TV station asked us if they could be present for the last day of one of them, to interview some of the participants. We saw later, on TV, a conversation between two of them:

> I don't understand this world... I am an architect. I have been unable to find a job since I graduated, three years ago, after twenty years of studies. And now, after only five days of enjoying myself in this fascinating workshop, I have three very good job proposals, in a very dignified position, and my family is telling me: "You finally learned something really useful!"

Another example. We had many traditional healers in Oaxaca. We thought it was a good idea to gather them for an exchange of the experiences of their forty-eight different healing practices. There they were, enjoying themselves. After three days of the workshop, we gave them beautiful diplomas certifying their attendance. We repeated the experience the next year. A little later, I was visiting a friend in the middle of the jungle of the Chimalapas. Upon entering his hut, I discovered on the wall, very well framed, the two diplomas. This healer was also enjoying his mirthful mimicry of medical doctors who cover their walls with official diplomas and certificates of every stripe.

5.   As I wrote in a book with M. Prakash, 1998.

References

Cayley, D. 1992. *Ivan Illich in conversation,* Concord: House of Anansi Press.

Illich, I. 1970a. *Celebration of awareness.* New York: Doubleday.

_____. 1970b. *Deschooling society.* New York: Harper & Row.

_____. 1973. *Tools for conviviality.* New York: Harper & Row.

_____. 1978. *La convivencialidad.* México: Editorial Posada.

Maldonado, B. 1988. La escuela indígena como camino hacia la ignorancia. Paper presented at the second reunion for Exchange of Educational Experiences in the Indigenous Environment, Oaxaca, México.

Prakash, M. and G. Esteva. 1998. *Escaping education.* New York: Lang.

My Green River
John Taylor Gatto

As a schoolteacher I operated out of the assumption that a special state called "childhood" could not exist in a healthy society much past the age of seven, and certainly was over for everyone sane by the age of twelve. I drew this understanding in the first place from coming to consciousness in a gritty steelworkers/coal miners town in the Monongahela Valley of western Pennsylvania near Pittsburgh where pride in the ability to pull your weight existed like oxygen in the air: everywhere. My strongest memories as a little boy were about doing grown-up things, and actually doing them. The idea of extending childhood would have disgusted me and the crowd I ran with.

The Character of a Village

Before I went to first grade I could add, subtract, and multiply in my head. I knew my times tables not as work but as games Dad played on drives around Pittsburgh. Learning anything was easy when you felt like it. My father taught me that.

When I went to first grade I could read fluently. I loved to read grown-up books I selected from the three-level glass-enclosed bookcase behind the front door in Swissvale. It held hundreds. I knew if I kept reading, things would eventually come. My mother taught me that and she was right. I remember taking down *The Decameron* time after time, only to find its deceptively simple language concealing meanings

I couldn't fathom. Each time I put the book back I made a mental note to try again next month. And sure enough, one month it happened. I was ten.

My father was a cookie salesman. Mother called him that anyway when she was angry, which was often. He had gone to work as a teenager to help support my widowed grandmother and to help brother Frank, the smart one, through the University of Pittsburgh. Dad never got to college, but he was a genius just the same. Mother went for one year; she was a genius, too. They were the kind of people who expose the malice of bell curves and rankings for what it is. I miss them both and think of them often with love and gratitude.

Mother I called "Bootie" most of the time because that's what I heard her own mother say. Bootie read fairy tales to me in the cradle, she recited poems, she filled my ears and eyes with language even though she had little else in the way of things to give. One day she bought a set of encyclopedias from a door-to-door salesman that cost more than we could afford. I know because she and dad fought when he got home. From then on mother read from the encyclopedia every day. We read all the newspapers, too. In those days they only cost a couple of cents. I liked the Hearst *Sun-Telegraph* best because it used violent layout, and on the upper corner of the Sunday edition, a little boy dressed like a fop called "Puck" said in a speech balloon, "What fools these mortals be." I didn't know what that meant, but I said the words out loud often to punctuate adult conversation and always got a smile when I did.

As far as I can figure, any success I had as a schoolteacher came from what my mother, my father, my family, friends, and town taught, not from a single thing I remember about Cornell and Columbia, my two colleges, not from any findings of institutes of child study or directives from departments of education. If I'm correct, then this insight is more significant than it may appear. The immense edifice of teacher instruction and schooling in general rests on the shaky hypothesis that expert intervention in childhood produces better people than might otherwise occur. I've come to doubt that.

A gigantic social investment rides on this hypothesis, one which might otherwise be spent on reducing stress on family life, which interferes with happiness and the growth of intelligence. Had the small fortune spent on my own schooling been placed instead in my people and my place directly, I have a hunch I would have turned out better. Whatever the truth of this complex proposition, as long as you've paid your money and time to hear what I have to say, you have a right to know something about the fountainhead of my school-teaching practice, my growing up time on the green river Monongahela.

I feel grateful for the luck to be been born in a tiny city with the character of a village on the river Monongahela in western Pennsylvania. People cared for each other there. Even the town wastrels had a history. But we minded our own business in Mon City, too. Both are important. Everyone seemed to understand that within broad limits there is no one best way to grow up. Rich or poor doesn't matter much if you know what's important. *Poverty can't make you miserable; only a bad character and a weak spirit can do that.*

In Monongahela, people seemed to know that children have a remarkable power to survive unfavorable environments as long as they have a part in a vital community. In the years I grew up, in the place I grew up, tales of social workers breaking up families "in the best interests of the child" weren't common, although on several occasions I heard Uncle Bud threaten to punch out this man's lights or that one's if the person didn't start treating his wife better. Or his kids. Bud was always punching someone in the interest of justice.

Over the years any number of students found a way to tell me that what they appreciated most about my classes was that I didn't waste their time. I think I learned how not to do that through a bit of good luck—being born in Monongahela during the Depression when money was tight and people were forced to continue older traditions of making their own meanings instead of buying them. And they learned how many very different ways there were to grow strong. What the vast industry of professional child-rearing has told you about the right way to grow up matters less than you've been led to believe. Until you know that, you remain caught like a fly in the web of the great therapeutic community of modern life. That will make you sick quicker than anything.

Singing and Fishing Were Free

I went Christmas caroling long before I knew how to read or even what Christmas was about. I was three. The carolers stood on a corner diagonally across from my grandfather's printing office where their voices filled an informal amphitheater made by the slope of Second Street just before it met Main, the principal intersection of the town. If I had to guess where I learned to love rhythmical language it would be on that corner at the foot of Second Street hill.

In Monongahela I fished for carp and catfish made inedible by river acids leaching out of the mines and waste put there by the mills. I fished them out with homemade dough balls whipped together in grandmother Mossie's kitchen. In Monongahela I waited weekly for the changing of Binks McGregor's haberdashery window or Bill Pulaski's hardware display as eagerly as a theatergoer might wait to be refreshed by a new scenery change.

Mother's family, the Zimmers, and the branch of Gattos my father represented, were poor by modern big city standards, but not really poor for that time and place. It was only in late middle age that I suddenly realized that sleeping three to a bed—as mother, sister, and I did—is almost an operational definition of poverty, or its close cousin. But it never occurred to me to think of myself as poor. Not once. Not ever. Even later on at Uniontown High School when we moved to a town with sharp social class gradations and a formal social calendar, I had little awareness of any unbridgeable gulf between myself and those people who invited me to country club parties and to homes grander than my own. Nor did they, I believe. A year at Cornell, however, made certain my innocence would come to an end.

Mother was not so lucky. Although she never spoke openly of it, I know now she was ashamed of having less than those she grew up with. Once she had had much more before Pappy, my granddad, was wiped out in the 1929 crash. She wasn't envious, mind you, she was ashamed, and this shame constrained her open nature. It made her sad and wistful when she was alone. It caused her to hide away from former friends and the world. She yearned for dignity, for the days when her clothes were made in Paris. So in the calculus of human misery she exercised her frustration on dad. Their many separations and his long absences from home on business even when they lived together are likely to have originated in this immaculate tension.

The great irony is that mother did beautifully well *without* money. She was resourceful, imaginative, generally optimistic, a woman with greater power to make something from nothing—totem poles from thread spools, an award-winning Halloween costume from scrap paper and cloth, a walk through the hills turned into high quality adventure—than anyone. She had no extravagant appetites, didn't drink, didn't crave exotic food, glamorous places, or the latest gadgets. She set her own hair and it was always lovely. And she kept the cleanest house imaginable, full of pretty objects that she gathered watchfully and with superb taste on her journey through life. As if to compound the irony of her discontent, Mon City was hardly a place to be rich. There wasn't much to buy there.

The Greatest Fun Was Watching People Work

I shouldn't say nobody had money in Monongahela, but it's accurate to say nothing was expensive. Beer was the town passion, more a religion with the men, and a big glass cost only a nickel, the same price as twelve ounces of buttermilk or a candy bar three times heavier than the modern sort. Bones to make soup were free. Beyond movies—twelve cents for kids—commercial entertainment hardly existed, a few bowling alleys at a nickel a frame, Redd's Beach (a pool at least ten miles away where swimming was a dime) and a roller-skating rink I never went to.

Where society thrived was in hundreds of ethnic social clubs and fraternal organizations up and down the Valley: the Moose, the Elks, the Oddfellows, Mystic Knights, Sons of Slovenia, the Polish-American Society, the Russian-American Club. These were places for men to drink and talk cheaply except on Saturday night when ladies could drink and talk too, alongside their men, and have a dance. Sometimes with even a live band to give snap to the joint.

No kid in Mon City reached for the "Events and Activities" page of the papers, because there wasn't one or any special kid places that people of all ages didn't frequent. When the men weren't playing *boccie* at the Italian Club, kids were allowed, passing first through a barroom reeking of unpasteurized stale beer. No special life was arranged for kids. Yet there was always a full menu, just spying on the adult world, watching people work, and setting out on expeditions to explore filled whatever time you wanted to spare. Until I got to Cornell, I can't recall anyone I ever knew saying, "I'm bored." And yet when I got to New York

City, hardly a day passed without crying loud and long about ennui. Perhaps this indicates some important marker we've missed in our modern search to make private worlds for children—the constituents of meaning have been stripped away from these overspecialized places. Why a child would want to associate exclusively with children in a narrow age or social class range defies understanding. Why adults would impose such a fate on kids strikes me as an act of madness.

The greatest fun was watching work at construction sites, watching freight trains unload or coal up, studying lumberyards at work, seeing gas pumped, hoods lifted, metal welded, tires vulcanized, watching Johnny Nami cut hair, Vito fill chocolates. Best of all was trailing Charlie Bigerton, the cop, on his rounds without his catching on. When kids around town pooled data about Charlie we could recreate the police patrol schedule accurately enough that violating wartime curfew was like taking candy from a baby.

Sitting in the Dark

At 213 Second Street we lived over the printing office Granddad owned, the Zimmer Printing Company. "Since 1898," his swinging sign read. It was located only a block and a half from the green river west of the streetcar tracks on Main. In between river and streetcars was the Pennsylvania Railroad right of way and tracks that followed the river down to Pittsburgh. Our second floor bay window hung over the town's main intersection where trolleys from Charleroi and Donora passed constantly, clanging and hissing, all lit up in the dark night.

An incredible vision, these things, orange metal animals with people in their stomachs, throwing illuminated reflections in color onto the ceiling of our living room by an optical process I often thought to have explained to me but never did. Bright sparks flew from their wheels and fell from the air around the overhead power lines, burning sharp holes in dark places.

From our perch, we could also see long freight trains roaring along the river sending an orchestra of clanks and whistle shrieks into the sky. We could watch great paddle-wheel steamers plying the river in both directions, filling the air with columns of white steam.

From early till late, Grandmother Mossie sat rocking. She sat at the window facing the river, quietly observing this mechanical show of riverboat, train, and streetcar—four tiers of movement if you count the stream of auto traffic, five if you include the pedestrians, our neighbors, flowing north and south on Main far into the night hours. Though she seldom ventured to the street from our apartment after her great disgrace of fifteen years earlier, when lack of money forced her to move abruptly one day from a large home with marble fireplaces. (She never spoke to my grandfather, not a word, after that, though they ate two meals a day at the same small table.) The telephone supplied sufficient new data about neighbors, enough so she could chart the transit of the civilization she had once known face to face.

Sitting with Moss in the darkness was always magic. Keeping track of the mechanisms out there, each with its own personality, rolling and gliding this way or that on mysterious errands, watching grandmother smoke Chesterfield after Chesterfield with which she would write glowing words in the air for me to read, beginning with my name, "Jackie." Words became something exciting seen that way. I couldn't get enough of them. Imagine the two of us sitting there year after year, never holding a recognizable conversation yet never tiring of each other's company. Sometimes Moss would ask me to find numbers in the inspired graphics of an eccentric comic strip, "Toonerville Trolley," so she could gamble two cents with the barber across the street, who ran numbers between clipping hair.

Although we really didn't hold conversations in any customary fashion, Moss would comment out loud on a wide range of matters, often making allusions beyond my ken. Was she speaking to herself? I would react or not. Sometimes I asked a question. After a smoke-filled interval, she *might* answer. Sometimes she would teach me nonsense riddles like "A titimus, a tatimus, it took two 't's to tie two 't's to two small trees, How many 't's are in all that?" Or tongue twisters like "rubber baby buggy bumpers" or "she sells sea shells by the sea shore," which I was supposed to say ten times in a row as fast as I could.

Sometimes the verses would sound ugly to modern ears as in "God made a nigger, He made him in the night; God made a nigger but forgot to make him white." Yet I have good reason to believe Moss never actually met or spoke with a black person in her entire life nor harbored any ill-will towards them. It was just a word game.

On the subject of race, we all officially learned to sing about black people in third grade: "Darktown Strutters Ball," "Old Black Joe," and others. No discussion of race preceded or followed; they were just songs. Before you conclude that Mon City must have been a bigoted place, you need to know that its tiny population contained the broadest diversity of ethnic groups living together in harmony. Ninety years earlier it had been a regular stop on the Underground Railroad. The barn of the Anawalt house was used for that purpose all through the 1850s.

If Vico's notion in *The New Science* is correct, we encounter the world in ways first implicit in ourselves. There can be no filling of blank slates in education, no pouring of wisdom into empty children; if Vico is correct, the Monongahela I bring dripping to you from the bottom of my river memory is a private city, revealing the interior of my own mind. Whether you believe the Fall is real or only a metaphor for the feeling we get when by losing our home, we find ourselves cut off from our creative source, who I am and why I taught the way I did is long ago and far away in that town, those people and that green river.

I Hung Around a Lot in Monongahela

The great destructive myth of the twentieth century was the aggressive contention that a child couldn't grow up correctly in the unique circumstances of his own family. In order to avoid having you finish this essay with the feeling that it might have been all right for *my* family to influence my growth so intensely, but for many children with worse families that just wouldn't do, fix your attention a minute on the less savory aspects of my people, as they might be seen through social-service eyes. Both sets of grandparents and my mother and father were seriously alienated from one another, the men from the women and vice versa.

On the Zimmer side, heavy drinking and German/Irish tempers led to one violent conflict after another, conflicts to which my sister and I were fully exposed. We grew like weeds as children, with full run of the town, including its most dangerous places, had no effective curfew, and tended to excess in everything. Did I forget to mention the constant profanity? By up-to-the-minute big-city standards my family skirted the boundary of court-ordered family dissolution more than once.

Since a substantial number of the families I worked with

productively as a schoolteacher had similar rap sheets to my own by social hygiene standards, I want to offer you my Monongahela years as a case study of how a less than ideal family by social work standards can still teach courage, love, duty, self-reliance; can awaken curiosity and wonder; can be a laboratory for independent thought, well-rooted identity, and communitarian feelings; and can grow in memory as a beloved companion even when it is composed of ghosts.

The city of Monongahela itself is offered as a case study of a different sort, showing the power of common places to return loyalty by animating the tiniest details of existence. The town is a main character in my personal story, a *genius loci* interacting with my development as a schoolteacher. The extreme effort I invested in the physical presence of my classrooms when I taught was done, I think, because the physical presence of my town never left me even after I was far removed from it. I wanted that same sort of ally for my kids.

Gary Snyder once said, "Of all memberships we identify ourselves by, the one most forgotten that has greatest potential for healing is place." The quiet rage I felt at bearing the last name of a then socially devalued minority, the multiple grievances I felt off and on against my parents for being a house divided, at my sister for making herself a stranger to me, at my dad for staying away so I grew up with only a distant acquaintanceship between us, the bewilderment I felt from having to sit nightly at dinner with grandparents who hadn't spoken to one another for fifteen years and for whom I was required to act as go-between, the compounding of this bewilderment when I discovered my Italian grandfather had been buried in an unmarked grave, perhaps for taking a mistress, the utter divide geographically and culturally between mother's family and father's—the fantastic gulf between the expressive idiom of the Germans, who treated rage and violence as if they were normal, and dad's people, the quintessence of decorous rationality, the absolute inability of mother to face the full demands of her maturity, yet her inspiring courage when her principles were challenged—all these made for an exciting, troubled, and even dangerous childhood. Would I have been better off in foster care, do you think? Are others? Are you insane?

What allowed me to make sense of things against the kaleidoscope of these personal dynamics was that town and its river, two constants

I depended upon. They were enough. I survived, even came to thrive because of my membership in Monongahela, the irreducible, unclassifiable, asystematic village of my boyhood. So different from the neo-villages of social work.

All the town's denizens played a part: the iridescent river dragonflies, the burbling streetcars, the prehistoric freight trains, the grandeur of the paddle-wheel boats, the unpackaged cookies and uncut-in-advance-of-purchase cheese and meat, women in faded cotton housedresses who carried themselves with bearing and dignity in spite of everything, men who swore constantly and spit huge green and yellow globs of phlegm on the sidewalks, steelworkers who took every insult as mortal and mussed a little boy's hair because he was "Zim's nephew."

I hung around a lot in Monongahela looking at things and people, trying them on for size. Much is learned by being lazy. I learned to fish that way, to defend myself, to take risks by going down in the abandoned coal mine across the river full of strange machinery and black water—a primitive world with nobody around to tell me to be careful. I learned to take knocks without running away, to watch hard men and women reveal themselves through their choices. I cleaned Pappy's printing office after closing for a silver St. Gaudens walking Liberty fifty-cent piece weekly, the most beautiful piece of American money ever made. I sold *Sun-Telegraphs* and *Post-Gazettes* on the corner of Second and Main for one cent a paper profit. I had a Kool-Aid stand on Main and Fourth on hot summer days.

Shouldn't you ask why your boy or girl needs to know anything about Iraq or about computer language before they can tell you the name of every tree, plant, and bird outside your window? What will happen to them with their high standardized test scores when they discover they can't fry an egg, sew a button, join things, build a house, sail a boat, ride a horse, gut a fish, pound a nail, or bring forth life and nurture it? Do you believe having those things done for you is the same? You fool, then. Why do you cooperate in the game of compulsion schooling when it makes children useless to themselves as adults, hardly able to tie their own shoes?

I learned to enjoy my own company in Monongahela, to feel at ease with anyone, to put my trust in personal qualities rather than statistical gradations. Anything else? Well, I learned to love there.

Just across the river bridge and over the river hill was open farm country, anyone could walk there in thirty minutes. Everyone was welcome, kids included. The farmers never complained. Mother would walk Joanie and I there in the early morning as mist was rising from the river. When she was seventy-two, I wrote to her trying to explain what I'm trying to explain now, how her town had given me underpinnings to erect a life upon:

Dear Mom,

I think what finally straightened me out was memory of those early morning walks you used to take with me up River Hill, with mist rising from the green river and trees, the open pits of abandoned coalmines producing their own kind of strange beauty in the soft silence of the new day. Coming out of the grit and rust of Monongahela, crossing the clean architecture of the old bridge with its dizzy view to the river below through the wide-set slats underfoot, that was a worthy introduction to the hills on the far shore. Going up those hills with you we startled many a rabbit to flight. I know you remember that, too. I was amazed that wild things lived so close to town. Then at the top we could see Monongahela in the valley the way birds must but when we turned away, everything was barns and cornland. You gave me our town. What a gift it was!

My best teachers in Monongahela were Frank Pizzica, the high-rolling car dealer; old Mr. Marcus, the druggist wiser than a doctor; Binks McGregor, psychological haberdasher; and Bill Pulaski, the fun-loving mayor. All would understand my belief that we need to be hiring different kinds of people to teach us, people who've proven themselves in life by bearing its pain like free spirits. *Nobody should be allowed to teach until they get to be forty.* No one who hasn't known grief, challenge, success, failure, or sadness should be allowed anywhere near kids.

We ought to be asking men and women who've raised families to teach, older men and women who know the way things are and why. Millions of retired people would make fine teachers; college degrees aren't a good way to hire anybody to do anything. Getting to teach should be a reward for proving over a long stretch of time that you understand and have command of your mind and heart.

And you should have to live near the school you teach at. I had some eccentric teachers in Monongahela, but not a single one didn't live close to me as a neighbor. All existed as characters with a history profiled in a hundred informal mental libraries, like the library of her neighbors my grandmother kept.

Shooting Birds

On the way up Third Street hill to Waverly school each morning to discover what song Miss Wible was going to have kids memorize that day, I would pass a shack made of age-blackened hemlock, the kind you see on old barns long gone in disrepair. This shack perched at the edge of an otherwise empty double lot grown wild in burdock, wild hollyhock, and briar. I knew the old woman who lived there as Moll Miner because boys tormented her by shouting that name as they passed in the daily processional headed for school. I never actually saw her until one Saturday morning when, for want of anything better to do, I went to shoot birds.

I had a Red Ryder BB rifle, Moll Miner's lot had birds, and so lying on my belly as if birds were wild Indians, I shot one. As it flopped around dying, the old woman ran shrieking from her shack to the fallen bird, raised it to her bosom and fled shouting, "I know who you are. You're the printer's boy. Why did you kill it? What harm did it do to you?" Then overcome with sobs, she disappeared into her shack.

Her wild white hair and old cotton housedress, light grey with faded pink roses, lingered in my vision after I went home. Who could answer such a question at eight or at twenty-eight? But being asked made me ask it of myself. I killed because I wanted to. I killed for fun. Who cared about birds? There were plenty of birds. But then, what did it mean, this crazy old lady taking the downed bird into her home? She said she knew me; how was that possible? It was all very puzzling. I found myself hoping the BB hadn't really killed the bird but only shocked it. I felt stupid and tried to put the incident out of my mind. A week or so later I got rid of my BB gun, trading it for an entrenching tool and some marbles. I told myself I was tired of it; it wasn't a real gun anyway. Around Halloween some kids were planning a prank on the old lady. I protested, saying we should pick on someone who could fight back and chase us. "We shouldn't pick on weak people," I said. "Anyway, that lady's not crazy, she's very kind."

That winter, without asking, I shoveled the snow around her house. It was a business I usually did for pocket money, and I was good at it, but I didn't even ask permission. I just shoveled the sidewalk without asking for money. She watched me from her window without saying a word. Whether she recognized I was the boy who shot the bird, I wish I could tell you, but that's all there is. Not a sparrow falls, they say. That was the way I learned to care about moral values in Monongahela— by rubbing shoulders with men and women who cared about things other than what money bought, although they cared about money, too. I watched them. They talked to me. Have you noticed nobody talks to children in schools? I mean *nobody*. All verbal exchanges in school are instrumental. Person-to-person stuff is contrary to policy. That's why popular teachers are disliked and fired. They *talk* to kids. It's unacceptable.

On Punishment

There was a time when hamburger pretty much described Alpha and Omega in my limited food sensibility. My grandparents didn't much care, and in the realm of monitored eating, Bootie was a pushover, but not the new girl on Second Street, Bud's wife, brought home from Cincinnati after WWII. Well I remember the evening Helen prepared Chinese food, hardly a daring thing anywhere now, but in those long gone days around Pittsburgh, radical cuisine. I shut my nine-year-old mouth and flatly refused to eat it.

"You will eat it," said Helen, "if you have to sit there all night." She was right. At midnight I did eat it. By then it tasted awful. But soon after the indignity, I discovered that miraculously I had developed a universal palate. I could eat and enjoy anything.

At ten and eleven, I still made occasional assaults on my sister's sexual dignity. She was older, bigger, and stronger than me so there was little chance my vague tropisms could have caused any harm, but even that slight chance ended one afternoon, when on hearing one of these overtures, Pappy grabbed me abruptly behind the neck and back of a shoulder and proceeded to kick me like a football, painful step by painful step, up the staircase to our apartment.

On theft: having discovered where the printing office stock of petty cash was kept, I acquired a dollar without asking. How Pap knew it was me I never found out, but when he burst through the apartment calling my name in an angry bellow, I knew I had been nailed and fled to the bathroom, the only door inside the apartment with a lock. Ignoring his demands to come out, with the greatest relief I heard his footsteps grow faint and the front door slam. But no sooner had I relaxed than he was back, this time with a house-wrecking bar. He pried the bathroom door off, hinge by hinge. I still remember the ripping sound it made. But nothing else.

Almost every classroom in my junior high school and my high school had a wooden paddle hung prominently over the classroom door, and these weren't merely decorative. I was personally struck about a dozen times in my school career; it always hurt. But it's also fair to say that unlike the assaults on my spirit I endured from time to time for bearing an Italian name at Cornell, none of these physical assaults caused any resentment to linger—in each instance, I deserved some sort of retribution for one malicious barbarism or another. I forgot the blows soon after they were administered. On the other hand, I harbor a significant amount of ill feeling for those teachers who humiliated me verbally; those I have no difficulty recalling.

It might seem from examples I've given that I believe some simple relation between pain and self-improvement exists. But it isn't simple—with the single exception of a teenage boy whose pleasure came from terrifying girls, I never struck a single kid in three decades in the classroom. What I'm really trying to call your attention to is that simplistic codebook of rules passed down to us from academic psychology and enshrined as sacred text. Punishment played an important and positive role in shaping me. It has in the shaping of everyone I've known as a friend. Punishment has also ruined its share of victims, I know. The difference may reside in whether it arises from legitimate human grievances or from the bloodless discipline of a bureaucracy. It's a question nobody should regard as closed.

Separations

For the first three years of my life I lived in Monongahela; then we moved to a tiny brick house in Swissvale, an urban village despite its bucolic name, a gritty part of industrial Pittsburgh. We lived near Union Switch and Signal Corporation, a favorite goal of exploratory probes among the street urchins on Calumet to which I quickly pledged my loyalty.

On rainy days I would stand on the porch watching raindrops. It was next best to my lost river, I suppose. Sometimes on the porch of the next house, two enchanting little girls, Marilyn and Beverly, played. Because our porch was somewhat higher than theirs I could watch them unobserved (at least they pretended not to see me). Thus it was that I fell in love.

Marilyn was a year older than me, already in first grade. Even in 1939 that placed her impossibly beyond me in every regard. Still, as my next door neighbor, she spoke to me from time to time in that friendly but distant fashion grand ladies adopt with gardeners and chauffeurs. You would have to see how humble both our homes were to realize the peculiarity of my analogy.

Beverly, her sister, was a year younger. By the invisible code of the young in well-schooled areas she might well not have existed. Her presence on the social periphery merited the same attention you might give a barking puppy, but at the age of four I found myself helplessly in love with her older sister in the pure fashion the spiritual side of nature reserves as a sign, I think, that materiality isn't the whole or even the most important part.

The next year, when I matriculated at McKelvy elementary, first graders and second were kept rigidly separated from each other even on the playground. The first heartbreak of my life, and the most profound, was the blinding epiphany I experienced as I hung on the heavy wire fence separating the first grade compound from the combined second/third grade play area. From the metal mesh I peered through astigmatically, I could see Marilyn laughing and playing with strange older boys, oblivious to my yearning. Each sound she made tore at my insides. The sobs I choked back were as deep at five as ever again I felt in grief, their traces etched in my mind six decades later.

So this was what being a year younger had to mean? My sister was two years older and she hardly ever spoke to me. Why should Marilyn? I slunk around to avoid being near her ever again after that horrible sight seared my little soul. I mention this epiphany of age-grading because of the striking contradiction to it Monongahela posed, presenting a universe where all ages commingled, cross-fertilizing each other in a dynamic fashion I suddenly recognized one day was very like the colonial world described by Benjamin Franklin in his *Autobiography*.

Swissvale taught me also that mother and father were at war with each other—a sorry lesson to learn at five. That the battles were over differences of culture that have no rational solution I couldn't know. Each couple who tries to merge strong traditions as my parents did must accept the challenge as vast, one not to be undertaken lightly or quit on easily. The voices of timeless generations are permanently merged in offspring; marriage is a legal fiction, but marriage in one's children is not. There is no way to divorce inside the kid's cells. When parents war on each other, they set the child to warring against himself, a contest which can never be won. It places an implacable enemy deep inside that can't be killed or exorcised, and from whose revenge there is no escape.

I thank God my parents chose the middle road, the endless dialectic. Dad, the liberal thinker (even though his party affiliation was Republican and his attitude conservative) always willing to concede the opposition some points; Mom, the arch conservative even though her voice was always liberal Democrat, full of prickly principles she was prepared to fight for, like Beau Geste, to the bitter end.

For all the hardly bearable stresses this endless combat generated, their choice to fight it out for fifty years saved me from even harsher grief. I love them both for struggling so hard without quitting. I know it was better for sister and me that way; it gave us a chance to understand both sides of our own nature, to make some accurate guesses about the gifts we possessed. It prepared us to be comfortable with ourselves. I think *they* were better for the fifty-year war, too. Better than each would have been alone.

I remember FDR on the radio in our postage-stamp living room announcing Pearl Harbor, eight days before my sixth birthday. I remember the uneasy feeling I harbored for a long time at war reports from the Far East that played out of the old Philco; I thought the

Japanese would cut off my hands because the war news said that's what Japs did to prisoners.

The high point of the Swissvale years for me wasn't the war or the phenomenal array of wax lips, sugar dot licorice, Fleers Dubble Bubble, and other penny candies, which seemed to vanish all at once just a short time after the war ended, like dinosaurs. It wasn't leaping from a high wall with a Green Hornet cape streaming behind as I fell like a stone, scarring my knees for eternity. It wasn't even Marilyn herself. The hinge in all my years, separating what went before from all that followed, was the night sister and I awakened to the shrieking contralto of Mother's voice and the quieter second tenor of Father's, intermingling in the downstairs entrance hall.

I remember crawling to the upstairs landing bathed in shadows to find sister already there. The next five minutes was the closest we ever came to each other emotionally, the most important experience we ever shared. Bootie was threatening to leave Andy if something important wasn't done. She was so upset that efforts to calm her down (so the neighbors wouldn't hear) only fanned the flames higher. With the hindsight of better than a half century, I'm able to conclude now that they were arguing over an abortion for what would have been her third child, my never-to-be brother or sister.

Mother was tired of being poor and didn't want to be any poorer. She was tired of constant work when she had grown up with servants. She was overwhelmed by the unfairness of being confined with children, day in, day out, when her husband drove off to the outside world in a suit and tie, often to be gone for days at a time, living in hotels, seeing exciting things. She would have implied (because I was to hear the insinuation many times in their marriage) that he was living the life of Riley while she slaved.

Bootie wanted an abortion, and the angry words that went back and forth discussing what was then a crime wafted up the stairwell to where two little children sat huddled in uncomprehending disbelief. It was the end of our childhood. I was seven, Joan was nine. Finally Mother shouted, "I'm leaving!" and ran out the front door, slamming it so hard it made my ears hurt and the glass ring. "If that's the way you want it, I'm locking the door," my father said with a trace of humor in his voice, trying to defuse mother's anger, I think.

A few seconds of silence, then a pounding and pounding upon the locked door commenced. "Open the door! Open the door! Open the door or I'll break it down!" An instant later her fist and entire arm smashed through the glass panes in the front door. I saw bright arterial blood flying everywhere and bathing that disembodied hand and arm. I would rather be dead than see such a sight again. Indeed as I write I see Mother's bleeding arm in front of my eyes.

Do such things happen to nice people? Of course, and much more often than we acknowledge in our sanitized, wildly unrealistic human relations courses. It was the end of the world. Without waiting to see the next development, I ran back to bed and pulled the pillow tightly over my ears. If I had known what was coming next, I would have hid in the cellar and prayed.

A week later, Swissvale was gone for good. Just like that, without any warning—like the blinking light of fireflies in our long, narrow, weed-overgrown backyard stopped abruptly on a secret firefly signal—on a secret tragic signal, Marilyn and Tinker, penny candy, McKelvy school and contact with my Italian relatives stopped for the next six years. With those familiar things gone, my parents, went too. I never allowed myself to have parents again. Without any good-byes they shipped us off to Catholic boarding school in the mountains near Latrobe, placed us in the hands of Ursaline nuns who accepted the old road to wisdom and maturity, a road reached through pain long and strong.

There was no explanation, none at least that I could understand for this catastrophe. In my fiftieth year Mother told me offhandedly in an unguarded moment about the abortion. She wasn't apologetic, only in a rare mood of candor glad to be unburdened of this weight on her spirit at last. "I couldn't take another child," she said. We stopped for a hamburger and the subject changed, but I knew a part of the mystery of my own spirit had been unlocked.

The contrast presented to my former life was stark and harsh. I had never made a bed in my life. Now I was forced to make one every morning, and the made bed was inspected! Used to the privacy of my own room, now I slept in a dormitory with fifteen other boys, some of whom would cry far into the night, every night. Sometimes I cried with them. Shortly after arrival, I was assigned a part in an assembly about roasting in Hell, complete with stage sets where we dressed up like flames. As the sinner unrepentant was tormented by devils, I jumped up and down to make it hot for the reprobate. I can hear my own reedy falsetto squeezing out these parentless verses:

Know ye not the burning anguish,
Of thee-eese souls, they-er heart's dee-zire?

I don't want to beat up on the sisters as if I were Fellini in *Juliet of the Spirits*. This was all kosher according to their lights, and it made a certain amount of sense to me, too. By that point in time, although nominally Roman Catholic, I probably hadn't been to church more than ten times counting Baptism and First Communion. Just walking around, though, is enough to make a kid conscious of good and evil, conscious, too, of the arbitrary nature of human justice. Even a little boy sees rottenness rewarded and good people smacked down. Unctuous rationalizations of this by otherwise sensible adults disgust little children. The sisters had a story that gave satisfying human sense to these matters. For all the things I hated about Xavier Acadamy, I actually *liked* being a flame and many other aspects of the religious narrative. They felt right somehow in a way the dead universe of Newton, Darwin, or Marx never did.

I carried the status of exile around morning, noon, and night, the question never out of mind—what had I done to be sent here? Only a small part of me actually showed up in class or playground or dining hall each day, the rest of my being taking up residence in the lost Oz of Monongahela, even though Swissvale should have logically been the more proximate yearning since it was where we lived when I was sent away.   Joan was there, too, but we were in separate dormitories. In the year we spent at Xavier I can't remember holding a single conversation with my sister. Like soldiers whose unit has broken apart in dangerous terrain, we struggled alone looking for some personal way out of the homelessness. It couldn't have helped that my sister was two years older. By that time she had been carefully indoctrinated, as I had been, that every age hangs separately. Sticks to its own class. You see how the trick is done?

At Xavier Academy, scarcely a week passed without a beating. I was publicly whipped for wetting the bed, whipped for mispronouncing French verbs, whipped for hiding beets inside my apple pie (hated beets, but the house rule was that vegetables had to be eaten, dessert did not). Some telltale beet corner where a brown apple should have been must have given me away to a sharp-eyed stoolie—the kapo who bussed away dessert. I was nabbed at exactly the moment dining hall loudspeakers blared the wartime hit, "Coming in on a wing and a prayer. With one motor gone we can still carry on, coming in on a wing and a prayer." Most dramatic of all the beatings I endured, however, was the one following my apprehension by the Latrobe police.

The spirit that entered mother when she broke glass must have revived in me to set the stage for that whipping. One night after bed check, I set out to get home to my river. I felt sure my grandparents wouldn't turn me away. The break had been planned for weeks, nobody taken into my confidence. I had a dozen bags of salted peanuts from the commissary, a thin wool blanket and a pillow, and the leather football Uncle Bud gave me when he went away to war.

Most of the first night I walked, hiding in the tall grass away from the road all the next day, eating peanuts. I had gotten away full of determination. I would make it home, I knew, if I could only figure out what direction Monongahela was in! But by mid-afternoon the following day, I made a fatal mistake. Tired of walking and hiding, I decided to hitch a ride as I had once seen Clark Gable do in a famous movie with Claudette Colbert. I was picked up by two matronly ladies whom I regaled deceitfully with a story of my falling out of the back of granddad's pickup truck where dog Nappy and I had been riding on the way back to Mon City. "He didn't notice I was gone and he probably thinks I jumped out when we got home and went to play."

I hadn't calculated the fatal football. As a precaution against theft (so they said) the Ursalines stamped "St. Xavier" many times on every possession. My football hadn't escaped the accusatory stencil. As we chatted like old comrades about how wonderful it was to be going to Monongahela, a town out of legend we all agreed, the nice ladies took me directly to the Latrobe police, who took me directly—heedless of my hot tears and promises to even let them have my football—back to the ladies in black.

The whole school assembled to see my disgrace. Boys and girls arranged in a long gauntlet through which I was forced on hands and knees to crawl the length of the administration building to where

Mother Superior stood exhorting the throng to avoid my sorry example. When I arrived she slapped my face. I suppose my sister must have been there watching, too. Sister and I never discussed Xavier, not once, then or afterwards.

The intellectual program at Xavier, influenced heavily by a Jesuit college nearby, constituted a massive refutation of the watery brain diet of government schooling. I learned so much in a single year I was nearly in high school before I had to think very hard about any particular idea or procedure presented in public school. I learned how to separate pertinent stuff from dross, I learned what the difference between primary and secondary data was, and the significance of each, I learned how to evaluate separate witnesses to an event; I learned how to reach conclusions a half-dozen ways and what distortions the different dynamics of these methods threatened. I don't mean to imply at all that I became a professional thinker. I remained very much a seven- and eight-year-old boy. But I moved far enough in that year to become comfortable with matters of mind and intellect.

Unlike the harsh treatment of our bodies at Xavier, even the worst boy there was assumed to have dignity, free will, and a power to choose right over wrong. Materialistic schooling (which is all public schooling—even at the best—can ever hope to be) operates as if personality changes are properly caused externally—by applications of theory and by a skillful balancing of rewards and punishments. This agenda mutilates personal sovereignty. The idea that individuals have free will that supersedes any social programming is anathema to the very concept of forced schooling.[1] Was the Xavier year valuable or damaging? If the Ursalines and Jesuits hadn't forced me to see the gulf between intelligence and intellect, between thinking and disciplined thinking, who *would* have taken that responsibility?

The greatest intellectual event of my life occurred early in third grade before I was yanked out of Xavier and deposited back in Monongahela. From time to time a Jesuit brother from St. Vincent's College would cross the road to give a class at Xavier. The coming of a Jesuit to Xavier was always considered a big-time event even though there was constant tension between the Ursaline ladies and the Jesuit men. One lesson I received at the visiting brother's hands altered my consciousness forever.[2] By contemporary standards, the class might seem impossibly advanced in concept for third grade, but if you keep in mind the global war claiming major attention at that moment, then the fact that Brother Michael came to discuss causes of WWI as a prelude to its continuation in WWII is not so far-fetched.[3] After a brief lecture on each combatant and its cultural and historical characteristics, an outline of incitements to conflict was chalked on the board.

"Who will volunteer to face the back of the room and tell us the causes of World War One?"

"I will, Brother Michael," I said. And I did.

"Why did you say what you did?"

"Because that's what you wrote."

"Do you accept my explanation as correct?"

"Yes, sir." I expected a compliment would soon follow, as it did with our regular teacher.

"Then you must be a fool, Mr. Gatto. I lied to you. Those are not the causes at all." It was like being flattened by a steamroller. I had the sensation of being struck and losing the power of speech. Nothing remotely similar had ever happened to me.

"Listen carefully, Mr. Gatto, and I shall show you the true causes of the war, which men of bad character try to hide," and so saying he rapidly erased the board and in swift fashion another list of reasons appeared. As each was written, a short, clear explanation followed in a scholarly tone of voice.

"Now do you see, Mr. Gatto, why you must be careful when you accept the explanation of another? Don't these new reasons make much more sense?"

"Yes, sir."

"And could you now face the back of the room and repeat what you just learned?"

"I could, sir." And I knew I could because I had a strong memory, but he never gave me that chance.

"Why are you so gullible? Why do you believe my lies? Is it because I wear clothing you associate with men of God? I despair you are so easy to fool. What will happen to you if you let others do your thinking for you?"

You see, like a great magician he had shifted that commonplace school lesson we would have forgotten by the next morning into a formidable challenge to the entire contents of our private minds, raising the important question, "Who can we believe?" At eight, while public school children were reading stories about talking animals, we had been escorted to the eggshell-thin foundation upon which authoritarian vanity rests and asked to inspect it.

There are many reasons to lie to children, the Jesuit said, and these seem good reasons to older men. Some truth you will know by divine intuition, he told us, but for the rest you must learn what tests to apply. Even then you should be cautious because it is not hard to fool even these tests.

Later I told the nun in charge of my dorm what had happened because my head was swimming and I needed a second opinion from someone older. "Jesuits!" she snapped, shaking her head, but would say no more.

Now that Xavier is reduced to a historical marker on Route 30 near Latrobe, I go back to it in imagination trying to determine how much of the panic I felt there was caused by the school itself, how much by the chemical fallout from my parents' troubled marriage, how much from the aftershock of exile. In wrestling with this, one thing comes clear: those nuns were the only people who ever tried to make me think seriously about questions of religion. Had it not been for Xavier, I might have passed my years as a kind of freethinker by default, vaguely aware an overwhelming percentage of the entire human race did and said things about a God I couldn't fathom. How can I reconcile that the worst year of my life left behind a dimension I should certainly have been poorer to have missed?

One day it was over. The night before it happened, Mother Superior told me to pack; I would be leaving the next morning. Strong, silent, unsentimental Pappy showed up the next day, threw my bag into the car, and drove me back to Monongahela. It was over, just like that.

Back home I went as if I'd never left. Mother was waiting, friendly and smiling as I had last seen her. We were installed, the three of us, in a double bed in a back room over the printing office. Our room was reached through the kitchen and had another door opening onto an angled tarpaper roof from which on clear nights the stars could be seen, the green river scented. It was the happiest day of my life.

Where father was, nobody ever told me, and I never asked. This indifference wasn't entirely generated by anger, but from a distinct sense that time was rapidly passing while I was still ignorant of important lessons I had to learn.

Principles

Five days a week the town turned its children out in the morning to march up the hill to Waverly or down to the end of town to high school. There was no school bus. Waverly was frozen midway between the one-room schoolhouse tradition of transferring responsibility to children—we fought to fill the inkwells, clean the pen nibs, sweep the floor, serve in the lunchroom, clean the erasers, help our slower classmates in arithmetic and reading—and the specialized procedures and curriculum of the slowly dawning corporate age of schooling. While this latter style had been sold as more "socially efficient" ever since 1905, the realities of town life were such that nothing passed muster at Waverly that didn't first pass muster with parents and the elders of the town.

School was something you took like medicine. You did it because your mother had done it and your grandmother. It was supposed to be good for you. Nobody believed it was decisively so. Looking back, I might agree this daily exercise with neighbors suddenly transformed into grammarians, historians, and mathematicians might well have been, as Mother said, "good for me." One thing is certain, these part-time specialists cared a great deal about mother's opinion of what they were doing, just as she cared about theirs in regard to her parenting.

The schoolteachers I remember are few but bear noting: Peg Hill who spoke to me exactly the way she did to the principal and won my heart for treating me as a peer; Miss Wible who taught me to sing and memorize song lyrics so ferociously my vocabulary of words and dramatic situations increased geometrically (even if we did whisper to each other that she was reading "love books" at her desk as we copied the day's words); old Miss McCullough, who played "American Patrol" every single day for an entire school year on a *hand-cranked* phonograph: "You must be vigilant, you must be diligent, American Patrol!" Her expressionless face and brutally stark manner stifled any inclination to satire. If we have to have schoolteachers, let some be this kind.

At Waverly I learned about principle when Miss Hill read from Gibbon's *Decline and Fall of the Roman Empire*. She read of the courageous death of Blandina the slave, a teenage convert to Christianity who was offered her life to repudiate her faith and a cruel death if she refused. She refused. I learned that all the management savvy of the most powerful empire of history couldn't overwhelm the principles of a teenage slave.

Principles were a daily part of every study at Waverly. In latter days, schools replaced principles with an advanced form of pragmatism called "situational ethics" where principles were shown to be variable according to the demands of the moment. During the 1970s, forcing this study on children became an important part of the school religion. People with flexible principles reserve the right to betray their covenants. It's that simple. The misery of modern life can be graphed in the rising incidence of people who exercise the right to betray each other, whether business associates, friends, or even family. Pragmatists like to keep their options open. When you live by principles, whatever semantic ambiguity they involve you in, there are clear boundaries to what you will allow, even when nobody is watching.

The Sovereign Zimmer Nation

Frances "Bootie" Zimmer was born on Halloween in 1911 at Monongahela General Hospital, three years before the country had an income tax or a Federal Reserve Bank, in the first flush moments of scientific pedagogy practically realized. She was five years younger than dad, two inches taller, born in a country on the gold standard where common citizens carried precious metal in their pockets as money.

She was three when WWI began, six when the Gary Plan riots struck New York City schools. In the postwar years, her father, son of a German immigrant from the Palatinate, became prosperous by working around the clock as a print shop proprietor and sometime investor in movies, carnivals, newspapers, and real estate. His grandchildren are still in the printing business in Bethel Park near Pittsburgh one hundred years later.

Bootie graduated from Monongahela High, where she was a cheerleader, in 1929 a few months before the market crash. Besides losing money, some other great catastrophe must have happened to the

Zimmers then, but I've only been able to unearth a few shards of its nature. Whatever its full dimension, it included the sudden eviction of Grandmother Moss from her home, the incarceration of great grandfather Frederick in an old-age institution far away, the flight of great grandmother Isabelle to Detroit at the age of seventy-nine, at a time when Detroit and the moon were equally distant, and the severing of ties between granddad and his brothers to the extent that though they lived cheek by jowl with us in the tiny city, I was not aware of their existence nor did they once say hello. Ach!

In the great breakup, Bud ran to Chicago without a penny and without graduating from high school; mother, too, ran off in dramatic fashion, telling her best friend as she boarded a train for Pittsburgh that she would wave a handkerchief at the window if she intended to return. She didn't wave. And though she did return, she hid ever after, never speaking to any of her childhood friends again. I discovered all this when I advertised in the local paper after Bootie's death, asking to speak to anyone who had known her as a girl.

Mother was bone-thin with large blue eyes and hair gone white at thirty, just as my own did. She lived on a razor's edge between a need to avoid shame and an almost equally desperate need to find a way to express her considerable talents, a goal that conventional assessment would say eluded her forever. Yet everything she turned her hand to was marked by electrifying energy. Our Christmas trees were an art form. Our home was cleaner and neater than a hospital operating room. Beauty and good taste flowed from her fingertips. But the shame, which she would rather have died than acknowledge, always defeated her in the end and made her melancholy when she thought no one was looking.

I think mother tried to force her fierce spirit into dad and live through him. When that failed, she pinned her hopes on me. This, I think, caused the original breach in the marriage. Compared to the driven Germans she knew best, dad must have provided a lifelong frustration. And though we never went hungry or lacked a roof, the absence of extra money represented decisive evidence to her of damnation, permanent exile from the fairyland of her youth.

And yet the exquisite irony bedevils me like a fury—never have I met anyone able to make such magic out of nothing. When, to her great surprise, she came into a considerable amount of money after father's death, like Midas' wish, it offered her nothing she really needed. Nor was she able to spend any of it to buy her heart's desire, an avenue for her talent and some dignity.

In 1932 Frances Zimmer went off alone on her frightening adventure, marrying into a magnificent Italian family which had pulled itself out of the immigrant stew while the patriarch was alive, only to plummet back into the soup after his death. She married all alone, without a father or mother there to give her away.

Giovanni Gatto, my grandfather, had been an enlightened *publicista* in Italy, an unheard of *Presbyterian* Italian who swept a contessa off her feet in Calabria in the elopement that resulted in her disinheritance. Together Giovanni and Lucrezia came to America with their young children and set up house in Pittsburgh.

Giovanni is another family ghost I worked to discover. After a short time in this country, he was hired (personally) by Andrew Mellon to be manager of the Foreign Exchange Department of Mellon Bank. He was a man for whom restaurants kept a personalized champagne bucket, a man who commissioned stone sculptures for his garden. Grandfather Gatto was also leader of the Freemasons of Pittsburgh, the Grand Venerable. He was Caruso's host when the immortal tenor came on tour to Pittsburgh and Caruso stayed in Giovanni's home. An old news clipping I have reported his death in thirty-five column inches with three headlines and a dignified picture. The obituary called him "leader of the Italian colony of Pittsburgh," continuing, "fifty-eight cars, each carrying eight persons, were required to convey friends of the deceased to the cemetery and back home again."

His death produced a shock for the living. No assets survived Giovanni. Only a hasty sale of the home for much less than its value kept the family out of immediate poverty. The children scrambled to find a toehold in the working world and by a stoic acceptance of reduced circumstances managed to keep the family together and to support Lucrezia, who spoke little English. It was a pulling together the Zimmers had not been able to manage.

Ten years later, mother was drawn into this family orbit, she holding tight to her secrets, dad doing the same with his own. What the merger should have conferred on Joan and I was a striking band of distinctive individuals: big-hearted Laura, elegant Josephine, witty caustic Virginia, crotchety Achilles, (renamed Kelly), the humanist Nick, a genuine world-class intellect in Frank, the contessa Lucrezia. But instead our private hurts kept us separated as surely as the same force divided my sister and I.

Mother found subtle ways to discourage fraternization with the sociable Gattos, dad eventually taking the hint. Until I was fully grown and well into mid-life, the Gattos were a palimpsest for me; what cousins that family held, I was strictly partitioned from. When occasionally I was taken to visit Frank or Laura or Josephine, or all together, we were formal with each other, in Old World style. Each extended courtesy to me, complete with those little flourishes of etiquette that give significance to the best encounters of children with grownups—a quality once common and now rare, which transferred naturally into my schoolteaching.

Walking Around Monongahela

We're back in Monongahela now, a town of strong principles even if some of them are wacky or plain wrong. Pragmatism is a secondary theme here, scorned by most unless it keeps to its place, a bittersweet oddity because practicality is the town's lingua franca. The phenomenon of open scorn for the lower orders isn't seen in my Valley, never to the degree I experienced it later in Ithaca, Cambridge, and Manhattan. The oppressed are insufficiently docile in Monongahela to revile openly. So the Pinkerton detectives found out when they went to do Andrew Carnegie's dirty work at Homestead during the steel strike of 1893. There is only one restaurant in the town proper, "Peters." It's a place where the country club set drinks coffee alongside rubber jockeys from the tire vulcanizing shop across the street.

Several nights a week, long after dark when house lights were blazing, Mother would gather sister and me for long quiet walks up Second Street hill to the very top, then along the streets on the ridge line parallel to the river. From these and the morning walks on River Hill I learned to listen to my senses and see that town as a creature in itself instead of a background for my activity.

We would walk this way for hours, whispering to each other, looking in windows, and as we walked, Bootie would deliver an only partially intelligible stream of biographical lore about the families within; I realize now that she must have been talking to herself. It was like having a private Boswell to the Dr. Johnson of town society. When she had some money, which was now and then, we would buy candy at the little grocery at the top of the hill and share it together, sometimes two candy bars for the three of us or in flush times a whole bar each— and in the weeks following Christmas when there was holiday money, two each. On two-candy nights the atmosphere seemed so filled with chocolate perfume that I could hardly sleep.

When my granddad was a boy in Monongahela he watched John Blythe, a planing mill operator, rebuild large sections of the town in the Italianate style. Blythe had no degree, and the religion of professional licensing was still in infancy, so he just did it without asking anyone's permission. Whole sections of the town are now handsome beyond any reasonable right to be because nobody stopped him. If you see a keystone over a window molding, it's likely to be one of John's.

When my granddad was a boy in Monongahela he used to sit in Mounds Park, site of two ancient burial mounds left there by the Adena people three thousand years ago. In 1886, the Smithsonian robbed those graves and took the contents to Washington where they still sit in crates. The government built a baseball field where the mounds had been to compensate the town. When my granddad was a boy, school was voluntary. Some went, but most not for long. It was a free will choice based on what you valued, not a government hustle to stabilize social classes.

The College of Zimmer and Hegel

The most important study I ever had wasn't at Cornell or Columbia, but in the windowless basement of the Zimmer Printing Company, a block and a half from the railroad tracks that paralleled the mysterious dark green river with its thick ice sheet near the banks in winter, its iridescent dragonflies in summer, and its always breathtaking sternwheelers pounding the river UP AND DOWN, BAM! BAM! BAM! going to places unknown, on a river without beginning or end for me.

Before he went to Germany to beat up the Nazis, my warrior Uncle Bud worked on a riverboat that went down the Mississippi to New

Orleans, on what mission I can't say, then on other boats that went up and down smaller local rivers. When I was five, he once threw an orange to me from a riverboat galley while it passed through a lock. A right fielder's strong throwing arm sent that orange two hundred feet out of the watery trench into my hands, I didn't even have to move.

In the basement of the printing office, Bud's father ("the General" as Moss called him behind his back) moved strong hands in and out of a printing press. Those presses are gone, but my grandfather's hands will never be gone; they remain on my shoulder as I write this. I would sit on the steps into his subterranean world, watching closely hour after hour as those rough hands fed sheets of paper into the steam-driven clamshell press. It went BAM! (feed) BAM! (feed) BAM! (feed) like the riverboats and bit by bit the job piled up on the table next to the press.

It was a classroom without bells or tests. I never got bored, never got out of line. In school I was thrown out of class frequently for troublemaking, but Pappy wouldn't stand for nonsense. Not a scrap of it. He was all purpose. I never saw a man concentrate as he did, as long as it took, whatever was called for. I transferred that model unconsciously to my teaching. While my colleagues were ruled by start-up times, bell schedules, lunch hour, loud-speaker announcements, and dismissal, I was oblivious to those. I was ruled by the job to be done, kid by kid, until it was over, whatever that meant, kid by kid.

No baseball or football, no fishing, no shopping, no romantic adventure could possibly match the fascination I felt watching that tough old man in his tough old town work his hand-fed press in a naked light bulb lit cellar, without any supervisor to tell him what to do or how to feel about it. He knew how to design, to do layout, set type, buy paper, ink presses and repair them, clean up, negotiate with customers, price jobs, and keep the whole ensemble interacting. How did he learn this without school?

He worked as naturally as he breathed, a perfect hero to me—I wonder if he understood that. On some secret level it was Pappy who held our family together, regardless of his position as pariah to his wife and his estranged brothers, regardless of an ambivalent relationship of few words with his daughter and son, granddaughter and grandson, and with his remaining brother, Will, the one who still spoke to him and worked alongside him at the presses. I say "spoke" when the best I can personally attest to is only association. They worked side by side but I never actually heard a single conversation between them. Will never entered our apartment above the shop. He slept on the press table in the basement. Yet Pappy kept the family faith. He knew his duty. When Bud brought his elegant wife home from the war, she would sit in Pappy's room talking to him hour after hour, the two snorting and laughing thick as thieves. It was only his bloodline he had lost the key of conversation with.

I realize today that if Pappy couldn't count on himself he was out of business and the rest of us in the poorhouse. If he didn't like himself he would have gone crazy alone with those heavy metal rhythms in the eternal gloom of the printing office basement. As I watched him he never said a word, didn't throw a glance in my direction. I had to supply my own incentive, welcome to stay or go, yet I sense he appreciated my presence. Perhaps he did understand how I loved him. Sometimes when the job was finished he would lecture me a little about politics I didn't understand.

In the craft tradition, printers are independent, even dangerous men. Ben Franklin was a printer like my German grandfather, himself preoccupied with things German at times. Movable type itself is German. Pappy was a serious student of the Prussian philosopher Hegel. I would hear Hegel's name in his conversations with Bud's wife, Helen. Late in his own life he began to speak to my father again. And sometimes even to me in my middle teens. I remember references to Hegel from those times, too.

Hegel was philosopher in residence at the University of Berlin during the years Prussia was committing itself to forced schooling. It's not farfetched to regard Hegel as the most influential thinker in modern history. Virtually everyone who made political footprints in the past two centuries, school people included, was Hegelian, or anti-Hegelian. Even today many knowledgeable people have no idea how important Hegel has been to deliberations of important men as they debated our common future.

Hegel was important wherever strict social control was an issue. Ambitious states couldn't let a single child escape, said Hegel. Hegel believed nothing happened by accident; he thought history was headed somewhere and that its direction could be controlled. "Men as gods" was Hegel's theme before H.G. Wells.' Hegel believed when battle cannon roared, it was God talking to himself, working out his own nature dialectically. It's a formidable concept. No wonder it appealed to men who didn't labor, yet disdained easeful luxury. It engaged a printer's attention, and a little boy's, too.

When I began to teach, I took the lessons of Monongahela and my two families to heart. The harder I struggled to understand myself, the better luck I had with other people's kids. A person has to know where his dead are buried and what his duty is before you can trust him. Whatever I had to teach children is locked up in the words you just read, as is the genesis of my critique of forced schooling.

In September of 1987, upon my return from a year long medical leave of absence granted by Community School District 3 in Manhattan, to recover from injuries suffered in a head-on collision outside Monterrey, Mexico, I learned that my teaching license had been terminated without notice for "abandoning your post." No trace of the approved leave papers could be found, not in my school, not in the school district, and not at the medical office at the central board of education in Brooklyn. The notice of termination which my district was legally required to send so that the accused might mount a defense had been sent to an address where I had once lived twenty years earlier—it was returned to the board marked "addressee unknown at this address."

On March 5, 2004, I traveled to Highland High School in Rockland County, at the invitation of the school board to address graduating seniors. It was very visibly a school whose student body was prosperous and conventional, in the customary sense that SAT scores and GPA and faculty recommendations were primary motivations. I decided to lecture on the myth that neither standardized tests or grades counted for much in gaining admittance to elite universities like Harvard and Stanford—and what actually did count most at these places, real accomplishment, adding other things like that. In the middle of my lecture, a few minutes after listing some names from the very large number of accomplished adults who hadn't wasted time acquiring a college degree, names like Bill Gates, Steven Jobs, Michael Dell, Warren Avis, and Ted Turner, and the mediocre school records of presidents like Franklin Roosevelt, John Kennedy, and George

Bush, local police entered the auditorium with bullhorns, dismissed the students, and ordered me to leave "at once!"

In November 2008, the organizer of a lecture I was to give at Five Towns College on Long Island called to tell me that she had been ordered to cancel—with the warning "to watch where she stepped!"

Notes

1.   In her best seller of the 1990s, *It Takes a Village*, Hillary Clinton expressed puzzlement over the fact that Western conservative thought emphasizes innate qualities of individual children in contrast to Oriental concepts that stress the efficacy of correct *procedure*. There are a number of paths that led to this vital difference between West and East, but Western spiritual tradition, which insists that salvation is a personal matter and that personal responsibility must be accepted, is the most important influence by far. See the chapter "Absolute Absolution."

2.   Traditions of intellectual refinement have long been associated with Jesuit orders. Jesuits were school-masters to the elites of Europe well before "school" was a common notion. Not long ago it was discovered that the rules of conduct George Washington carried with him were actually an English translation of a Jesuit manual, *Decency Among the Conversations of Men*, compiled by French Jesuits in 1595.

3.   It's almost impossible these days to chart the enormous gulf between schooling of the past and that of the present, in intellectual terms, but a good way to get a quick measure of what might be missing is to read two autobiographies: the first that of John Stuart Mill, covering a nineteenth-century home education of a philosopher, the second by Norbert Wiener, father of cybernetics, dealing with the home education of a scientist. When you read what an eight-year-old's mind is capable of you will find my account pretty weak tea.

My Education:
An Adventure Story
Arnold Greenberg

The first words I remember reading: "Hitler is Dead!" I had just turned six years old and didn't know who Hitler was; reflecting now, I don't remember learning to read, just as I don't remember learning how to talk. I remember the Dick, Jane, Spot books I was given in school, but I believe I gradually began learning to read from the comic books we had in our little corner grocery store at Second and Flower Streets in Chester, Pennsylvania. The only thing I remember of first grade was coming home on September 2nd—my first day—to see my new baby brother lying on my mother's lap. I remember nothing about the school.

Following my first grade year, we moved to Roxborough, a neighborhood in Philadelphia where my parents bought a dress store—The Style Shop—on Ridge Avenue. We lived above the shop, and I was enrolled in second grade at the Levering Elementary School, two blocks away. Nearby, there were two movie theaters—The Roxy, and directly across from it, The Boro. I spent countless Saturday afternoons in those movie theaters watching double features, serials, cartoons, and shorts like *The Three Stooges* and the *News of the Week*. I absorbed the world according to Hollywood—a view that had a tremendous impact on my life. Those movies taught us so much about how to be—what was masculine, feminine, strong, weak, funny. War movies taught patriotism; westerns and gangster flicks taught good over evil. They inspired romance, showed us how we should look, act, hold a cigarette, kiss, fall in love and live the "American Dream of rags to riches." At that time, the line between illusion and reality was not apparent.

I went obediently to school, and other than standing in line and following instructions, remember very little. I do, however, remember my scowling fifth grade teacher, Miss Fleming, who humiliated me on a number of occasions. Once, when I yawned while a boy was giving a report, and she made me stand up and apologize to the whole class. She also frightened me by the way she taught arithmetic, emphasizing drilling as if she were a sergeant, scowling if I made a mistake, and often making cruel remarks about my inability to learn the subject. But her definition of learning was memorizing how to do things with the numbers as if they were recipes, and though I could recite the multiplication tables, though I could manipulate them, still they made no sense.

That same year I started taking tap dancing lessons from Mrs. Bauer, a friend of my mother's who was just starting a dance studio. Her son, Freddie, my brother, Jerry, and I were her first students. I was reluctant, convinced that "only sissies take dance lessons," but we went every Saturday morning. It takes a long while before the heavy stomping of a beginner's tap dancing looks like what you see in the movies, but gradually, my brother and Freddie and I became quite good. Two years later, we were a dance trio called "The Rhythm Boys," performing at local events—fashion shows, dinners at the Lion's Club, church suppers, and school assemblies.

This was the beginning of a long period of performances, awards, and prizes—when I was twelve we won first prize on the *Paul Whiteman TV Teen Club*; we won the New Faces contest on a weekly radio and TV show called *The Children's Hour*. We joined a USO troupe and performed two Saturday nights a month at Fort Dix and other military facilities. In our teens, we became popular in Philadelphia because we were young with a very professional, polished act. We had several agents who booked us for banquets and other events. We practiced every day after school, perfecting our precision and continued our tap lessons, always learning new routines.

When I was sixteen and had my driver's license, we booked The William Penn Civic Club, an after hours private club where we did not go on until two in the morning. We shared a small dressing room with a strip tease dancer, and changed into our tuxedos behind our held up raincoats while she sat with her long legs up on the table, drinking from a bottle of gin. We were getting an education that our high school could not compete with.

My parents worked hard in their grocery store from six in the morning until eleven at night, seven days a week, and many long hours in their dress business. I became the stock boy when I was twelve, and it was my job to open all of the boxes of merchandise, check the invoices, make the price tickets for the dresses, coats, skirts, and blouses, and put the clothes on the racks and shelves. I was being trusted with a big responsibility, and though I was learning about the family business, there was nothing in my growing up that would have introduced the world of literature into my life. I became passionate about writing at a young age, encouraged by an assignment in fourth grade from a substitute teacher, and from there my interest in books, art, and composition evolved. It was a slow, unconscious unfolding that later, as a teacher, helped form a lot of my ideas about educating young people. By the time I was in tenth grade, I spent much of my time outside of school writing poetry and stories. This fever for writing never seemed to overlap with my school curriculum in a meaningful way, until my class was assigned the task of completing a traditional book report. I was inspired, and decided to do something different by writing about my favorite baseball book, *The Kid from Tomkinsville*, as a poem. I worked harder than I had ever worked on a school assignment before, and wrote over thirty verses in rhyme, and five pages of poetry that I loved, and I couldn't wait to hear what my teacher, Mr. Townsend, thought. My poem was handed back to me with an F written in red ink and the words, "This is plagiarized. I don't believe you wrote this." I was stunned. I didn't even know what the word plagiarized meant. I had never received an F before. Instead of explaining why he had instructed that the report be written a specific way, he demeaned my creative effort. I felt completely discouraged and rejected.

I went into a tailspin. I tuned out. I was numb. I went from A's and B's to failing all of my subjects. Though I was quiet and obedient, I wouldn't do any homework. The counselor said I was lazy and that I had better start working harder. We didn't have the words for depression or alienation back then, and I had no vocabulary for expressing what I was going through. I drew pictures of leaping trout or trees or fields and wrote stories and poems; I stared out the window. I walked in a fog from class to class.

I then did something that surprised everyone: I signed up for the U. S. Navy. I was seventeen and saw this as my way out. At the rate I was going I would have been in tenth grade for the rest of my life, and since I was not yet eighteen, I convinced my parents to sign the papers. I dropped out of high school, broke up our dance trio, and went off to boot camp.

It was overwhelming and scary; I was now out in the world and far away from home. But an important part of my education began. I met people from all over the country, I was drilled and ordered, and learned again how cruel people can be. After boot camp I went to school to become a teletype operator and learned how to run a post office. I was then assigned to a destroyer, the USS Caperton out of Newport, Rhode Island, and eventually became the ship's postal clerk.

On the Caperton, I had time to read books that were freely chosen— books on religion, psychology, philosophy, mystery, science fiction. I traveled to over thirty countries, going to ports throughout the Mediterranean—Gibraltar, Portugal, Spain, the French and Italian Riviera, Greece, Turkey, Lebanon. Being the postal clerk enabled me to leave the ship in the morning, and while the ship went out for exercises, I traveled the countryside, sat in cafes, and explored. I was able to tour Greece, where I fell in love with reading the myths, seeing the Elysian Fields, the Parthenon, the temples at Delphi.

While in the navy I got my GED, the equivalent of a high school diploma, and began thinking of college. Because I did not have enough knowledge of algebra to pass the SATS, or the requirements on a transcript to be admitted to a university, I attended Brown Prep—a private preparatory school in Philadelphia—and eventually got accepted to Temple University.

I wanted to be a writer, and I hoped that college would prepare me for that, but I was wrong. My freshman courses felt like high school— dull assignments, lectures, tests, classes I had to take to fulfill the university's requirements. I decided to get a job on a freighter instead, and go back to sea to have the kinds of life experiences I needed to be a writer. I found out about the Scandinavian Seaman's Union offices in Brooklyn, where I would have to hang out to find a job on a ship. It took two weeks of going there twice a day, sitting with sailors of all ages from many countries, to check the bulletin board announcing openings on ships. I wanted a freighter that would take me to Europe, where I could sign off and wend my way to Paris, where my literary heroes from the twenties lived.

I finally signed on as a galley boy on a freighter going to Lisbon. I joined the Norwegians Seaman's Union and was on the ship by five that afternoon. I had twenty dollars to my name. When the ship left the harbor, I saw the Statue of Liberty, with the torch that welcomed immigrants, fading behind me as I sailed away searching for my new life somewhere else. For the Norwegian equivalent of $50.00 a month, I peeled sixty pounds of potatoes every day, washed all the pots and pans, scrubbed the floors, hauled sides of beef, lamb, and swordfish from the freezer, and dumped the garbage overboard. We traveled to Port Said, Egypt, and many ports in Arabia and Yemen, and up the Tigress River to Iran and Iraq, where I saw date fields, boys throwing nets out into the water for fish, long small boats moved along the river by a man standing with a pole. At night, I walked through the dirt streets of backwater towns, my eyes seeing images that could have been from two thousand years ago.

I left the ship in Alicante, Spain, with a hundred dollars and meandered my way to Paris and then on to Copenhagen, where I arrived one cold December morning with a dollar to my name. I was fortunate to find an old woman who gave me a room and said I could pay her when I got a job. I then went to a fine restaurant and spent my dollar on a steak dinner; if I was going to be broke, let it be today and not tomorrow.

After several months in Copenhagen, hanging out at the ABC Cafeteria, meeting fellow travelers and making friends, I returned to the United States by working on a coal ship out of Hamburg, Germany. We hit a huge storm in the North Atlantic and a trip that should have taken eleven days took eighteen, but I made it home with my food-stained raincoat, a suitcase filled with books, and very long hair.

All of these experiences—dropping out of high school, joining the Navy, and having the opportunity to read what I wanted, travel, be out in the world with little money and my own resourcefulness—shaped my views on education. One day, while sitting on the deck after writing a poem, I suddenly thought of myself as a poet, and realized that if I wanted have the skill to express myself, I would have to master the craft. So I read a wide variety of poets, criticism, and biographies, and practiced writing different forms. I consciously became a student, aware that the two most important ingredients in being a learner are passion and choice.

If a person is not fully engaged and wanting to learn something, it may or may not be remembered. Passion is essential for real learning to take place. I realized that the state of most schools, where students are captives—forced there by law—and the curriculum is imposed on them, is ultimately immoral. A student must be allowed the freedom to choose what to learn, and be actively excited and engaged with a teacher or a subject.

The sudden notion of what a school could be inspired me to write and describe my vision. Among many other books about education, I read A. S. Neil's *Summerhill*, and over the next few years wrote what became the brochure for Miquon Upper School. I had heard about an experimental elementary school called Miquon School, just outside of Philadelphia. I didn't know much about it, except that there were ducks and that kids played in a creek, and I wanted to go and see it. The school was started in 1932, on what was once an old farm, and inspired by the philosophy of John Dewey. When I drove up, I felt I had entered a wonderland. I saw happy kids playing and learning in a relaxed way. I went to an all-school meeting, made up of the students from kindergarten to sixth grade, and when I witnessed the children participating in a discussion on an issue pertinent to the school, I knew instantly that I had to teach there.

It is impossible for me to describe fully the adventure in education that began when I became a teacher at Miquon. I was twenty-five, recently married and the father of an infant—my first born of four—and was given the opportunity to try different things, to evolve as a teacher. The good fortune of having ideas about a school and the opportunity to experiment with my fifth and sixth grade students was something that would impact the rest of my life as an educator.

In 1968, at the beginning of my fourth year at the Miquon School, the students arrived on the first day to a completely empty classroom— nothing to sit on but the floor, nothing on the walls, nothing in the room but me, and in my hand, a small piece of chalk. I announced that I was very wealthy because I had fifty pounds of peanuts. I said that I would share my wealth through an economic system created by the class, where they would get paid in the money we invented. The peanuts would back up the economy, just as gold once did in America. Along with this system of money, I proposed we create our own country and whatever laws we needed by creating a government. After a lot of skepticism and questions, the kids all agreed to try it and they named it Arnold's Island[1].

A few students went off to create a money system and came back with the idea that a quarter of an ounce of peanuts was a mill, half an ounce was a moola, three quarters was a moke, and a pound was called a rupee. Students would get paid one mill for each learning exercise they completed, which could be several different types of work—writing a story, doing a page of mathematical word problems, dictionary exercises looking at etymology, and many other activities. Students signed a contract that determined deadlines and what they would be paid, minus taxes and other penalties for late work. We created the laws of Arnold's Island and various students created businesses to help our struggling economy. Someone started a bank where students could deposit their checks from fulfilling a contract, get cash if they needed it. But it didn't take long to see we were running out of money and had to decide what to do—raise taxes or print more money. We did both, but learned that by printing more money, we were also devaluing the currency, causing inflation. In short, we learned a great deal about economics by having a real economic system.

Arnold's Island was a huge success as a way of teaching social studies in a real way, and as a way of allowing students to structure their own day. They could work where and when they wanted, as long as their contracts were fulfilled on time. Students also proposed and enacted their own ideas; they could do school work and get my help, if needed, or they could work on the various businesses they started in order to earn more mills and moolas. For instance, a business two students created was a Pencil Insurance Company, issuing policies for a certain amount of money that ensured that a student who lost a pencil or just didn't have one could get a pencil from the insurance company. Of course, their rates went up or their policy was canceled if they lost too many pencils.

While teaching fifth and sixth grade, I had many conversations about the high school I wanted to start. I shared what I had written with many parents and board members, and talked to the students to get their reactions. Miquon School ended in sixth grade and the question of high school was always a dilemma.

In December of 1969 I held meetings with parents and students to talk about the possibility of a high school. Although lots of questions and concerns emerged, there was great enthusiasm for the school I was describing, and later, I began getting calls from the students asking me to talk to their parents; teachers called to say they were interested in working with me. I spent a lot of time visiting homes, talking to students, searching for a place, getting the Miquon Board to approve of the idea, and forming an ad hoc committee to work with me. I produced a brochure, and after some dramatic twists in finding a building, our school began in the fall of 1970 with 112 students, far more than the 70 I had hoped for.

As teachers of the Miquon Upper School, we made a commitment to have high expectations of the students, and made this clear to all applicants. We were licensed by the state and obligated to meet the state's requirements for a high school diploma. To do this, we offered exciting courses that students could choose or not choose, and we encouraged them to do independent work if they wanted. Students were required to do something, anything, that was meaningful to them, and many students designed their own courses. We were not a free school in the way many alternative schools were, we weren't a hangout for those who just didn't want to be in school—we were a learning community first and a social place second. We operated with a credit or no-credit system, and were fully prepared to give a student No Credit if we believed he or she was not doing their best.

The gas crisis of 1973 and projections of oil shortages, overpopulation, depletion of natural resources and degradation of the quality of food awakened in me the concern that our curriculum—basically college preparatory—was obsolete, preparing our students for a world that did not exist. I believed more had to be done to prepare young people for a more likely future—one of scarcity and severe environmental issues.

As my concerns grew, I developed an idea for a post-high-school experience on a farm where students could develop self-sufficiency skills. After eight years with Miquon, I resigned my position in 1978 and through a series of fortunate occurrences, met the people from The School of Living. They had a thirty-six acre farm near York, Pennsylvania, and after several discussions, I was given a lease on the property and created The Deep Run School of Homesteading and Community. I made a brochure and sent posters and material to high schools all over the country, doing all I could to recruit students. Several from Miquon Upper School loved the idea and four or five of the graduates came to Deep Run. I received many other applications, but on March 29, 1979, the accident at Three Mile Island happened. The farm was eight miles away. *Disaster!* Many potential students withdrew their applications.

Still, I managed to have fifteen students. The farm manager and teacher—who had become uncertain about committing after Three Mile Island—decided to become part of our school. We had a construction teacher and studied and built a passive solar cabin. Most of the students lived in three tipis we erected. We learned livestock management with our cow, several goats and sheep, chickens and geese, and pigs and rabbits. Each student spent a month caring for and learning about a particular animal. An experienced homesteader and one of the founders of The School of Living, Mildred Loomis, who was then in her late seventies, taught everything from food processing to edible weeds. We worked hard, grew nine acres of gardens, ate good food, and had many guests teach and lead discussions. It was a rigorous and successful year; however, the continuous problems and proximity to Three Mile Island became a major obstacle. Enrollment dropped and it became impossible to sustain the school. I tried for a third year, but was forced to close the school and move on.

After Deep Run, I discovered the Shoreham-Wading River Middle School was looking for a farm teacher. They had an after-school farm that grew out of a science project. Students and teachers had built a barn and tended chickens and goats. I was hired to develop a curriculum that could integrate the farm into the school day as a course that students could take. Keeping in mind that the school was in a middle- to upper-middle-class community, and it was unlikely any of these students would become farmers, I developed a curriculum called "Backyard Self-sufficiency." It was a project- and problem-based course in which the students had to turn their homes and property into a small self-sufficient homestead. Students had to make a scaled drawing of their property, and figure out where the gardens would go, how many eggs and loaves of bread their families ate in a year, and all the things they would need to learn about livestock.

Unfortunately and ironically, I again found myself living a quarter of a mile from a nuclear power plant. Shoreham Nuclear Plant was not completed, but was paying 90% of the town's taxes as an incentive for its presence, as well as subsidizing the new schools and an excellent new library in their community. But it was insidious and I knew that I had no future in this town—even with a good job and living less than a hundred yards from the beach of Long Island Sound.

In my quest to be as self-sufficient as possible I had developed a passion for baking bagels and breads. Unraveling from my teaching position, my family and I moved to Frenchtown, New Jersey, and with great effort opened The Left Bank Café in an abandoned train station on the Delaware River. We transformed this 500-square-foot dilapidated building into a very successful bakery-café, with long lines out the door on weekends. We were leasing the building and when the owner saw how successful we were, he raised the selling price to way out of reach. We lost our lease and after three years, packed up and moved to Blue Hill, Maine, to start over.

The Left Bank Café in Blue Hill became an amazing little place—in addition to serving a wide variety of European style breads, bagels, pastries, delicious breakfasts, lunches and dinners, it became a concert venue where nationally known folk, jazz, blues, and bluegrass performers entertained. No one could figure out why people like Odetta and Arlo Guthrie would come to this little café, in a tiny town in the middle of nowhere, to perform in an eighty-seat café. But they did and for ten years that is what I did—baked, booked, and worked sixteen hours a day.

For me, a café where people met to discuss topics personal and political, where folk artists shared their stories and music, was no different than a school. Revolutions were started in cafes. Out of cafes of Europe many schools of art and literature evolved; many major businesses and institutions emerged. The London Stock Exchange began in the coffee house where farmers met, and over coffee, sold or exchanged livestock.

The Left Bank employed a lot of high school students as dishwashers, bus boys and girls, and eventually as prep cooks and assistant bakers. I often asked about their schools, and practically all of them, even the most successful honor roll students, were bored, thinking of school as something just to be tolerated. Clearly, if it wasn't for the extra-curricular activities such as sports, theater and music—the only things students could actually choose to do—school would have been unbearable, the drop rate have been even higher. When I shared the experiences of my previous schools, they couldn't believe anything like that was possible and kept saying I should open up a school in Blue Hill. So, after ten years of café life, I went through the long process of selling The Left Bank Cafe and starting my third school.

Maine has an unusual law that permits the state to pay tuition for students who live in a town without a high school. There were ten schools in Maine eligible to receive tuition—old, traditional academies—one of which was in Blue Hill. When it was announced that a new, untraditional school was being organized, it became quite a controversy. My son Joe and I began working to create the school in the fall of 1996, and though we hoped to be open in September of 1997, we had an arduous road ahead of us. We had to be approved by the Maine Department of Education, find a building that met all the requirements—something that did not exist—raise money and recruit students and teachers. We formed a group of people interested in helping to start the school and met regularly, meanwhile creating a brochure, giving informational meetings in all of the towns in the area that didn't have high schools, setting up a non-profit, tax-exempt corporation, working with the state, and finding land on which to build a school building. Fortunately, we acquired land through the generosity of a wealthy and interested man who bought a four acre property, gave us an option, and allowed us to have our school meetings in the house. We had an agreement that, if the school actually got off the ground, we could purchase the property for what he paid for it. What good luck! At the same time, we faced tremendous adversaries. Many people who had long associations with the existing school did everything they could to stop us. As students enrolled in our school, we had meetings every two weeks with the five, then ten, then fifteen of them as they came aboard. We didn't wait for the fall to start; we were already a school, meeting in different places, discussing issues, making democratic decisions, and working on the design of the new building with architects.

Though our efforts were surrounded by nasty politics, we were determined to be respectful. We met every obstacle from the state, planning board, town council, and other groups that couldn't understand why the town needed a new school (especially one that would have an open campus, call teachers by first names, and let students choose what they would learn and help run the school). Our school could take tuition-paying students away from the existing school, and they feared the competition as well our philosophy. In spite of the ugliness, we opened on September 19th, 1997, with thirty-eight students. Liberty School—A Democratic Learning Community—was based on two Essential Questions: What does it mean to be an educated person in the 21st century? and What does it mean to be human in a technological, computerized society?

We eventually grew to over seventy students, with students and teachers governing the school democratically. Like Miquon Upper School, we were obligated to meet the state requirements for graduation in order to receive the tuition. Though we were basically a public school, the state accepted our untraditional philosophy, and our written evaluations with credit or no credit, in lieu of grades. Students wanted rigorous courses, as well as the freedom to make up their own independent courses, and created an interesting approach to ensuring we had a serious, stimulating student body, rather than a place where students sat around and didn't do much. The students formed an Admissions Committee, whose criteria and policy was voted on by the entire school. The committee interviewed all applicants, and a new student would be admitted for a two month trial before being accepted.

We referred to Liberty School as a college for high school students because we were structured more like a college than traditional schools. Students were responsible for their time—if they wanted to graduate, the state requirements were laid out and it was their job to meet them in any substantial way they could. Additionally, in order to graduate, students had to complete a major, multi-disciplined Graduation Project in which they explored, in depth, an Essential Question of their choosing. This project was the student's chance to demonstrate their mastery of skills necessary for becoming a life-long learner.

I retired from Liberty School several years ago and for a variety of reasons, the school closed a year later. I am now doing what I've always loved doing—writing stories, poetry, and novels. I get up every morning around four to face the blank page and see what comes. Right now, I am content to not be involved in a school, but I am still deeply concerned about the state of education in our country, and disturbed at how little has changed since I started attending school over sixty years ago. I have ideas of what a 21st century school could look like—a place that emphasizes creative problem solving, that does not waste students' time, that promotes active, democratic participation—and wonder if I will ever get back in the saddle again, with my dented and tarnished armor, and look for another battle.

Notes

1.   My book, *Adventures on Arnold's Island*, describes more fully how the year went—a wild educational adventure where academics and real life learning merged.

Journey to Democracy
David Gribble

U
ntil the age of eight I was educated at home by a governess who was employed to teach my older sister. My parents were divorced, so I was the only male in the household. During that time I absorbed many feminine values. Then, just before I was nine, I was sent to a boarding school where the only women were the headmaster's wife, the teacher for the eight-year-olds, and the matrons.

By the standards of the time the school was civilized, but the education was entirely traditional, and in the 1940s it was normal for schoolteachers in Britain to make children who misbehaved bend over chairs, bed-ends or tables and then beat their bottoms with bamboo canes. I was eager to please and seldom misbehaved, but nevertheless I was beaten several times.

I enjoyed much of the work in class, but I was tall and thin and awkward, so I had the experience, in sport and PE lessons, of being one of the least able in the whole school.

When I was thirteen I went to Eton College, where the uniform was (and still is) a black tail-coat with pin-stripe trousers and a white shirt with a peculiar sort of half-bow-tie. In spite of the archaic uniform, Eton offered a certain amount of freedom. An hour and a half before the mid-day meal was free time, and there were frequent whole holidays, sometimes even two in a week. We had a lot of work to do in those periods, but it was up to us to decide how and when to do it. We spent about half our time learning Latin and Greek, nearly all of which I have since forgotten.

I left school at the age of eighteen with no idea what I wanted to do, so my father invented a job for me in the office of a retail tobacco business that he owned. It was not long before I realised that I was not interested in commerce and would prefer to work with children, but I still believed that the traditional model of education was the only sensible one. When I was fourteen or so my mother had invited me to read *That Dreadful School* by A. S. Neill, but I had thought it was stupid.

I applied to study languages at Cambridge University in order to get a qualification, and three years later, duly qualified, I was appointed as an assistant master at a conventional boys' public school. In England the so-called "public schools" are a group of selective private schools.

This was a boarding school with none of the freedom I had known at Eton. Almost the whole week was programmed with lessons, compulsory sport and study times. As at the other schools I had known, caning was a normal punishment. Teachers had to dominate their classes if there was to be any work done. Sport was taken immensely seriously: during the time I was there a seventeen-year-old was beaten for working in a laboratory instead of watching a school football match, and a boy was actually killed playing cricket—an event that seemed to be officially forgotten within a few days. All the boys were enrolled in the military cadet force, and when, in conversation with a senior member of staff, I said that patriotism was a form of self-interest, he said furiously, "For me, patriotism is the basis of all morality, and I am *not going to argue about that.*"

I was the master responsible for the school magazine, the play-reading society and the jazz band, but even there, genuine friendship was impossible. This was particularly clear to me because one of the pupils, all of six years younger than me, was a friend of the family. We seldom met at the school, but when we did meet the otherwise impenetrable barrier between masters and boys simply did not exist.

When a boy was beaten because he had tossed a sweet to a friend during one of my classes I handed in my notice.

Purely by chance I happened on a book about Dartington Hall, the social and agricultural experiment in the southwest of England, which included a sixty-page section by W. B. Curry, who was head of the progressive school there. He seemed to have the answer to all my problems. He wrote, for instance:

> At Dartington we have had no patriotic assemblies, exercises or celebrations, and the usual methods of promoting nationalist feeling have been entirely avoided. The atmosphere of the School has been one which would encourage children to think of themselves firstly as members of the human race, and only secondly as members of a particular country.

and

> . . . if there is anything at all in modern psychological theory one must surely believe that if an education based upon respect and love and understanding became universal there would be an immense release of instinctive friendliness, a diminution of the hate which results from unwise repression and inhibition, and a great increase in human kindliness. I am the more inclined to believe this because theory and insight seem to be confirmed by experience.

and

> Adults who like to exercise authority will give orders whenever the case for freedom is not overwhelming. Adults who do not like giving orders will allow freedom whenever the case for authority is not overwhelming. We have wished our teachers to have the latter bias.

I applied for a job at Dartington and was appointed for the following term.

Curry had meanwhile retired, and I only met him once, but his writing and, above all, the school he had made possible were an inspiration for the rest of my life.

I was twenty-seven when I arrived there, but the older children were more socially mature than I was, particularly in terms of the relationship between the sexes, which had none of the slightly embarrassed tension that I had been used to. There was a natural acceptance of human values that was more rational than my own ideas, which were still being influenced by my conventional background. There was an assumption of equality between teachers and students, even though it was recognised that they had different responsibilities. During my first year the whole book of rules at the Senior School (thirteen- to eighteen-year-olds) was discarded, and the school meeting devised a new set of rules that fitted on one side of a sheet of paper. There was a largely conventional timetable, but children only took the subjects that mattered to them, and one boy, who had suffered badly at a previous school, had only two lessons a week.

All this seemed wonderful to me, but my greatest relief was that I found I no longer had to act a part, to pretend to mind about children eating sweets during my lessons, to try to assert myself to command attention. The children listened to me because they wanted to hear what I had to say. I began to unlearn many of my conservative attitudes and to discover a new independence for myself. Dartington Hall School not only helped its pupils to develop, it helped the staff as well.

I stayed there, on and off, for over a quarter of a century. I met my first wife, Jenny, when she was still a pupil at the school, and she taught me to understand it from a pupil's point of view. She died when she was only twenty-four years old, and I felt that I had lost one third of my life. The other two thirds, that made my life still worth living, were our children and the school itself. That I comforted myself with the thought of the school during that time shows how important it was for me. My second wife, Lynette, who re-established my life, was a teacher at the school. Between us we had four children who were all different personalities, and who were all educated there. I saw the school from many different points of view, at first hand as a teacher and a parent and at second hand as a pupil, and I loved it.

Then, in 1987, the school was closed without consultation by its own Trustees, against the wishes of the children, the parents, and the staff. The year before, when the junior section of the school had been closed, my wife, Lynette, and four other women had started Park School, because they felt that the Dartington tradition must not be allowed to die. Myself and two other teachers—Sybilla Higgs and Sean Bellamy—followed their example, and with a group of children who wanted to continue with the same style of education, as well as half-a-dozen newcomers, we started Sands School.

Sands was to take the principles of Dartington and develop them further. Above all it was to be made impossible for anyone to close the school as Dartington had been closed, without the agreement of the pupils and staff. All important decisions were to be made by the school meeting. Committees or individuals could be appointed to deal with particular issues, but any decisions they made could be overruled by the whole school meeting.

When the school started the meeting appointed me as head, but when it became clear that I did not and should not make any decisions the title was changed to administrator. At Sands the administrator's duty is to make sure that all necessary decisions are made through the school meeting, and, when they have been made, that they are put into practice.

I learnt new lessons at Sands. At first I had thought that there were some matters that were either too emotionally demanding or too complex for young people to have to decide about, and that as older people the staff should relieve them of responsibility for these decisions. I learnt better after a particular occasion when I was completely at a loss and the school meeting sorted it all out within about an hour. I realised that though experience may be useful, it is no more so than the sensitivity and imagination of a twelve-year-old. It is important to listen to everybody's contributions, and to make the final decisions together.

Just as Dartington had done, Sands runs most of the time without any system of punishment. It is better to rely on common sense. Someone who only does the washing-up in order to avoid punishment does not learn as much as someone who grows to understand that washing-up has to be done, and it is only fair to share the work. At Sands staff and students do the chores together.

David Wills, another educator for whom I have great admiration, gives the following reasons for avoiding punishment:

1. It provides a base motive for conduct;

2. It has been tried, and has failed; or alternatively, it has been so misused in the past as to destroy its usefulness now;
3. It militates against the establishment of the relationship which we consider necessary between staff and children—a relationship in which the child must feel himself to be loved;
4. Many delinquent children (and adults) are seeking punishment as a means of assuaging their guilt feelings;
5. When the offender has "paid for" his crime, he can "buy" another with an easy conscience.

(*The Barns Experiment*, p 22)

And in a different context:

Punishment shifts the responsibility for behavior onto the adult, instead of leaving it with the child.
(Wills' report to the Scottish Council for Research in Education, 1942)

I retired from Sands when I was sixty, because I felt too remote from the culture that the students took for granted. I could no longer share easily in their conversations, which naturally usually dealt with shared experiences.

It was about then that the first International Democratic Education Conference (IDEC) was held at the Democratic School of Hadera in Israel, in 1993. For the first few years, the conferences, in whatever country they were held, were called the Hadera Conferences, and two of the earliest were at Sands, in 1994 and 1997. The second ran for a fortnight, and was organized by two sixteen-year-old girls, who were the first to describe the conference as an IDEC.

Before the first conference I had only known of three democratic schools—Summerhill, Sands, and the Freie Gesamtschule in Vienna. Then I heard about Sudbury Valley and Hadera, and thereafter more and more places all round the world. I was astonished that there were so many, and that so few of them—even if they had heard of Summerhill—had no idea that there were any other similar schools. I began to visit them and to tell them about each other. I went to many different countries, including the USA, Ecuador, New Zealand, Japan and India. In most schools I spent at least a full working week, and then I described them, largely in the words of their own students, in my books *Real Education* and *Lifelines*.

Curry and Dartington had been my inspiration, but there was one aspect of education that had received little attention. These are the words of Curry himself:

> As to what has actually been taught, and how it has been taught, I do not think that we can claim to have departed in important or significant ways from what is done elsewhere. So that while I believe most of our teaching to have been good, and much of it outstanding, I cannot claim that in this field we have done much pioneering.

In my journeys I came across this kind of pioneering in many different forms, all of them based on the idea that children know what they need to learn and will pursue their objectives more energetically and with greater success if they are not interrupted by adults telling them to stop what they are doing and do something else.

At Sudbury Valley there is no timetable at all. At the Democratic School of Hadera there is a rich and varied timetable, but you do not have to take part in any courses if you do not want to. At the Pesta in Ecuador the staff prepared an environment full of stimulating materials, but the children did not have to make use of them. At Countesthorpe College in the UK, in the 1960s, students could choose to follow as many conventional courses as they wanted, but were also helped to find topics that were of particular interest to them personally; most used about half of their school time to follow them up. At Tokyo Shure there is a timetable of lessons requested by the students, which changes as interests change. (Tokyo Shure is the only school I have visited that does not require its students to come into school at all.)

All these systems work. Jenifer Smith, who taught at Countesthorpe during its most interesting period, has described what happened when tutor and student met.

> As you talk with me
> you unfold what is

you alone
you refuse my impositions
you expose my pretensions
you reveal your originality, your vulnerability, your vigour.
and
In the silence; amidst the talk; in the space that is yours, is the way ahead.
and
I come to know your commitment which is that of scholar, artist, poet, scientist, historian.

This trust in the ability of the young to educate themselves is important, but trust is not the only important characteristic of the good teacher.

Wills, in the quotation above about punishment, says that the child must feel himself to be loved. In my writing I have generally shied away from any such declaration, hiding my true feeling behind words and phrases like "equality," "tolerance" and "mutual respect."

Of course "love" is the right word. A. S. Neill put it characteristically bluntly.

The only possible way of education is the way of love.
(*The Modern Schools Handbook*, 1938, p. 119)

And here is David Wills again:

First and foremost and all the time the children must feel themselves to be loved.
(*The Barns Experiment*, p 60)

People often protest that the kind of educational methods I have been describing work only with children from privileged backgrounds, whose parents favor a liberal approach. They seem to think that children can understand love only if they have been loved. This is simply not true. The reality is that children who have never been loved need love more than anything else. I have seen many individuals whose lives have been transformed by coming to schools like Sands, for instance, but there are many institutions that have been set up specifically to care for whole groups of the unloved:

- Wills tells of the boys at the Barns Hostel who came from deprived backgrounds and had significant social problems, and how his approach helped them.
- In my travels I visited the Märtplatz in Switzerland, set up to help apparently unemployable young people to find out how to fit into society, and met Jürg Jegge, who for some years had run the Kleingruppe Lufingen, for children rejected even by special schools.
- Lynette and I visited Moo Baan Dek, a children's village in Thailand for orphans, abandoned children and victims of abuse, run on a Buddhist interpretation of Neillian ideas.
- We also spent a week with Butterflies, an organization for street children in Delhi, where children regarded by the general public as pickpockets and nuisances came in order to learn to read, write, and calculate, and formed themselves into responsible groups to campaign for their rights.

Ishani Sen worked with Butterflies, and she completed an idea for me that I was feeling for in a talk at the Tokyo IDEC in 2000. "For the children of the wealthy, liberal, middle classes," I concluded, "this kind of education is appropriate, but for the children of the disadvantaged it is . . ." I hesitated, and saw Ishani mouth the word "essential," and I saw that she was right.

That was something that I had always wanted to believe, but it was not until I saw it in practice in many different cultures that I became sure that it was true.

Many of the most important figures in democratic education around the world are women. Among them are Rita Panicker, who founded Butterflies, Pat Edwards, of Tamariki in New Zealand, Mary Leue of Albany Free School in the U.S.A., Ute Siess of Kapriole in Germany, Keiko Okuchi of Tokyo Shure, Helen Hughes of Windsor House in Canada, Rajani Dhongchai of Moo Baan Dek in Thailand, Rebeca Wild of the Pesta in Ecuador and Zoë Readhead of Summerhill. Perhaps this observation links back to my early childhood.

So what do I do now to promote the ideas that mean so much to me?

For some years I have been a Trustee of the Phoenix Education Trust, which was originally set up to raise the ideals from the ashes of Dartington Hall School. Under the direction of Anna Leatherdale this has now grown into an important contributor to the development of democratic education, not only in Britain but also, through EUDEC, in the whole of Europe. Among many other things Phoenix has established ESSA, the English Secondary Students' Association. This organization is run by the students themselves, is supported by two of the major teachers' unions, and was invited by the General Teaching Council to send two representatives to participate in a round table discussion of a new code of conduct and practice for teachers in England.

I also collect and edit the articles that appear three times a year on the Lib Ed website (www.libed.org.uk). The articles are written by university professors, school students, teachers and researchers, and have covered events and educators in many different countries— Switzerland, Russia, and India for instance.

In addition, I maintain the IDEN database of democratic schools around the world, and send out occasional newsletters, mostly about forthcoming or recent IDECs. They are now translated by native speakers into seven different languages. IDEN is another enterprise supported by Phoenix.

I am still occasionally asked to write articles, and once or twice a year I give talks, usually abroad, but I find that nowadays I tend to repeat myself, so I don't enjoy it as much as I used to. I haven't written a book for a couple of years, but there are two unpublished books on my website that you can read or download. *Escape from Convention* is about my own life and the development of my ideas, and *Children Don't Start Wars* argues that the worst crimes are committed by adults, and we ought to listen to children more seriously.

References

Bonham-Carter, V. and Curry, W. B. 1970. *Dartington Hall: The formative years, 1925-1957.* Dulverton: The Exmoor Press.

Smith, J. 1989. An exploration of teaching in action. Mphil thesis, Univ. of Southampton.

Wills, D. 1935. *The Barns experiment.* London: Allen and Unwin

Democratic Education:
A Beginning of a Story
Yaacov Hecht

At the age of five, in the dark shed of kindergarten, I thought for the first time about education. The teacher would often lock me in the shed, as punishment for my behavior. I remember clearly that I was not angry at her; on the contrary, I felt mostly pity. I decided that she, too, must have come from "there," from the Holocaust, like my parents, and so I mustn't be angry at her. I would sit in the familiar darkness, listening to the children's voices and think. I felt that there surely must be a better way to educate children. A way without dark sheds, without arbitrary punishment, and with respect. I didn't know then that I would devote most of my adult life to the search for this way.

When I began first grade, it became evident to me that I could not learn to read and write. I had two options: to join what the children called "the retards' class," or to conceal my condition. I chose the second option and summoned up all my natural talents and energy to carry it off. I learned all the right answers by heart, I pretended to be chronically absent-minded and forgetful, and I copied on exams.

By sixth grade I had managed, through tremendous efforts, to acquire basic reading (to this day I still can't write without mistakes). At school no one knew—I was an average student, a bit distracted, with a tendency to forget, and prone to illness around exam time; yet good at math and sports, and reasonably good overall.

Deep inside, though, I felt horrible. The huge gap between what I knew about myself and what others knew about me was almost intolerable. I lied systematically, copied, and constantly watched my back, trying to keep all the stories I had told to different teachers straight. I remember asking myself what was wrong with me. I could beat adults at chess, I was a national champion in broad jumping, I had fine achievements in sculpture, and yet, at the end of eighth grade, I still read like a kid who had barely learned to read. The letters refused to join together into acceptable words. How could it be, I asked myself, that in some areas I was strong and successful, while in others—the ones most important to my parents and my school—I was a total failure?

My parents saw my difficulties as the result of laziness. I had innumerable private teachers, and was required to sit for hours every day practicing my handwriting.

Fortunately, I didn't believe my parents. I knew that I was neither lazy nor stupid. I rebelled against them, disobeyed, and fought tirelessly for all the things that were important to me, the things that helped me survive (the Scouts, my friends, the Chess Club, the Model Planes Club and more).

When I reached high school, a huge institution of some two thousand students, I realized that no one really cared about me or my private world. The only thing that was important was the grades I got. After my ninth grade homeroom teacher claimed to my parents that I was smoking drugs (to this day I have never smoked anything, including cigarettes) because I used to fall asleep in class, I realized that I had to play the game in order to get through the next years. I quickly joined a group that would steal all the exams. Together we broke into the teachers' room, prepared copies of perfect exam papers, and passed them in at the end of the test. Later we broke into the health clinic and stole doctor's permission slips for our absences. I convinced myself that these thefts were moral and that there was no other way to beat the predatory system. In physics and math—the subjects I was good in—I tried to take exams without stolen test papers, but I discovered that crime has its own side effects. I could not answer even the questions I understood. I had gotten used to not thinking during exams, and so the next time I stole those papers as well. My school grades were high and even the principal knew me and treated me kindly. At the same time I was giving lessons on morality in my homeroom class and was active in the Scout movement, but behind my successful façade, I was in fact a criminal. Only I was aware of this harsh truth, and I was very much alone with it.

At times I wonder: Is this how regular children turn into criminals? Children that no one sees, whose human qualities no one recognizes, as they are required to do educational tasks that are cold and valueless to them, ones they can't cope with? How many of the "bad kids" in the education system are actually the miserable products of its requirements?

At age fifteen I did not ask these questions, but I felt unclean. I became entangled in the web I had woven around me, and even now it isn't clear how I would have ended up, if it were not for the war.

When the Day of Atonement War broke out, almost all the men around were called up for many months. We, the youth, began to run the city. I worked nights at the Hadera bakery, in charge of distributing the bread as well. In the mornings I worked with my friends, the Scout leaders, in elementary schools, where we ran activities for kids who were left without teachers. In the afternoons I delivered mail. After a few weeks the Hadera municipality set up a strong, active Youth Headquarters, which ran the entire city with the full backing of the leaders of the community.

This activity went on for a half year, and during that time I felt needed, successful, and enterprising, and was surrounded by people who appreciated me. When I returned to school, a teacher saw me in the schoolyard and scolded me for my absence. For me, it was like a kick in the head—all that time they had all been studying and taking tests! A blood-filled war had been going on in the State of Israel and at school—nothing. Business as usual.

From my shock, an understanding began to flower. I suddenly

realized that true learning comes from doing. In the Scouts, we were learning; in our volunteer activity we were learning. School, on the other hand, was a tool to measure grades and a workplace for thousands of teachers.

The first choice I made as an adult was to be the Troop Leader of the Hadera Scout troop, in parallel to the last part of my army service. Within a short time the number of scouts grew from two hundred to close to a thousand. We were considered a particularly active and special troop. We had many activities outside in nature, and also in the city in its various neighborhoods. My fantasy was to create a community with a close relationship among its people, not based on judgment or criticism, but rather on caring and common interests. And indeed it was not long before a very special atmosphere of cooperation and friendship was created. A large part of the troop's activities were devoted to the group leaders themselves, as the group became an increasingly central part of their lives. This was a place where we struggled to fulfill even the wildest of our dreams. As I had imagined some years before, the activities of the Scouts replaced school as a significant educational activity.

For a certain period of time I was happy, but after a while there began to be cracks in my satisfaction. I would say to the leaders: "The Scouts are you." But in time I understood that this was not accurate. As time went on I began to feel that I was lying—they were merely realizing *my* plans and initiatives. The Scouts were me. The important lesson I learned from this touched upon the connection between charisma and cooperative activity. A cooperative act requires more compromise and the ability to step aside in time. I began to seek a way in which the desires and skills of every one of the participants would be expressed.

When the first year of my studies in the University was over, I went to England—to find Summerhill.

At the University I had been told that Summerhill was long gone. That Neill was dead. That the place had burned down. No one had any address for me. But I took the trip anyway, and in England I discovered that Summerhill was very much alive, and that Neill's wife continued to run the place in the same spirit.

For the first time in my life, I met children who loved to learn. I saw children for whom all options were open—to go to the swimming pool, to study math, to play tennis, to learn history, to climb a tree, etc.

And they could choose. To my astonishment, the swimming pool and the tennis court were not always preferred over the math or history lesson. But it was obvious that every choice was made out of free will and with enthusiasm. When I was a student at school, as I have already told, I loved to play ball and I hated to learn in my classroom. Even the good students in my class saw learning as a chore, or at best "something important to do." Not one of my friends had experienced learning as something he loved. We saved our feelings of love for games or boy-girl relationships in class.

At Summerhill, I saw kids who *loved* to learn. I sat in on a "meeting"—the weekly general assembly at Summerhill—and I saw kids speaking their minds, without fear, and without trying to humor the adults around them.

Although I had some reservations (mainly concerning the place's management as a boarding school, without any involvement of parents), my visit to Summerhill had a considerable impact on my thinking. The structure of the school I was aiming for became clearer to me: a democratic structure, as in Summerhill, which would include the influence of the nuclear family in the school processes, with the understanding that in the center of that entire process was the free choice of the child.

The vision of a democratic school was only in its very early stages, but the main components of what I wanted were already clear to me:

- a choice of areas of learning: the students choose what they want to learn and how
- democratic self management
- evaluation focusing on the individual—without comparison with others and without tests and grades
- a school where children grow from age four till adulthood (eighteen and up)

In Israel, I discovered, there was no school that included all of these principles that I was looking for.

During my first year at the University I met Sheerly. Years before our first son was born, our main topic of conversation as a couple was about raising and educating children. Our relationship helped me to consolidate the way I would go after graduation. It was clear that I was going to make a change, but for some time I had deliberated between focusing on the education system or the university itself.

Eventually, through ongoing dialogue with Sheerly, I realized that in order to raise our children in the way we believed, and in Israel, I would have to found a school that suited our concept. I put notices up at universities and colleges, inviting people who were interested in thinking about establishing a different kind of school, which would operate according to the four principles that I previously described, to come to the first meeting in my home. About twenty young people came to that first meeting, most of them students. We began a process of learning, which continued on a weekly basis for an entire year.

At the end of two years of exhausting labor, we stood at the gates of the school feeling that we had "done it." Actually, we were only at the beginning of a long, hard, and wondrous way. The way of the Democratic School of Hadera.

We opened the first year of school with a curriculum that was divided into two; half a day of compulsory studies and half a day of electives.

Gradually, the students, teachers, and parents developed strong opposition to the compulsory lessons. They had a slogan: "Coercion does not encourage creativity." But some of the parents and staff persevered with the idea that without the framework of compulsory lessons, the system would "fall apart" and the children "wouldn't learn anything." The arguments were many and the atmosphere was tense. I needed some proportions.

In the middle of our second year, Sheerly and I took a trip to visit a friend in Boston. I took with me a list of alternative schools in the area, hoping to discover that we were not alone in the world, and to get support from the experience of older schools.

The year was 1989. The Internet was a distant dream, and all the information that I had gathered came from friends and rumors. In Boston we went from school to school, but we found no schools that offered freedom. We certainly didn't find anything that resembled what we had. It was only on our last day of vacation that we were told about "some strange school that might be worth your while to see," about ten minutes from our friends' home.

It was Sudbury Valley. The moment we arrived in the parking area, we realized that we had arrived at the place we were looking for. (Years later I tried to solve the riddle: how could we have felt what we felt from a hundred yards away? The answer was related to the way the children were moving in their surroundings—like free people, at home). This was our first meeting with Daniel and Hanna Greenberg, who established the school and work there to this day. When I returned to Israel, equipped with books and articles and strong impressions of my visit to Boston, I knew that now everything was going to change. The following year I sent a delegation of students and staff members from our school to Boston, and at the same time we hosted a group from there. This was in addition to long discussion in the staff about the significance of the experiences of the Sudbury Valley people.

The following summer, on the third anniversary of the school, the Parliament passed a decision to cancel all *compulsory studies*.

Already during the first year of founding the school in Hadera, a year considered difficult and intensive by all, I found myself involved in supporting the founding of two additional schools: one in Jaffa (Tel Aviv) and the second in the Tefen Industrial Park (in the Western Galilee).

People around me found this strange. We had just established the school in Hadera—was it worth our while, under the pressures of the first year schedule, to support additional schools' establishments? I saw it as a necessary process. In 1987, after a long dying period, the Open School of Rishon LeTzion closed. Its closing was a sign to me of the difficulty of sustaining an unusual school within the regular system. In fact, all the experimental/open schools that were established during the 70s in Israel were unable to go on for long; some were actually physically closed, while others changed ideologically. This disturbed me and I tried to understand what had happened. I saw that every school that tried to be different was under heavy pressure from two main directions. One was external pressure from the direction of the educational establishment, which was expert at taking the "different" and changing it to "similar"; the other was internal pressure within the schools themselves—adults, parents, teachers and students, who were afraid to remain in an isolated position, radically different from the accepted one, and were leading processes of change towards the "middle," towards being "like everyone else." Erich Fromm describes in detail this process of a pendulum swinging between uniqueness and conformism in his book *The Escape of Freedom*. When we founded the school in Hadera, it was clear that as an isolated school we would not be able to withstand the pressure we'd be subject to. We assumed that we would have to establish a wide-ranging educational movement in Israel, in order to compel the educational establishment to confront an entire movement rather than a solitary school. We also assumed that this kind of move would give parents and teachers an inner feeling that they were not alone in their positions, but rather, that they were backed by a comprehensive movement.

Today, over twenty years since we began our journey, the Democratic Education Movement of Israel has some twenty-five schools in which about seven thousand students study, representing a wide range of publics from all of Israel's population. We have founded the "Greenhouse for Educational and Social Initiative," an academic course in the HaKibbutzim College, Israel's largest teachers' training college. In this course, over two hundred students study Democratic Education in a four-year program. We have developed a new educational framework, "A Democratic Education City," for cities and towns that wish to create an all-inclusive municipal framework that implements the ideas of democratic education. We initiated the founding of IDEC—the International Democratic Education Conference—to unite all those working for democratic education around the world, and today more than thirty countries throughout the world participate. At the heart of all these initiatives is the Institute for Democratic Education.

I would like to end with a story that I think has the heart of my vision in its folds.

Getting Lost

When I was about seventeen years old, I went on one of my many hikes over the sand dunes north of Hadera. I took along a pair of binoculars and planned to do some bird-watching in the area. It was a hot, exhausting day. Grains of sand stuck to my sweaty skin and perspiration poured down my face. I was thirsty, and found none of the usual pleasure I took in bird-watching. Disappointed and upset, I resolved to go home and turned to the west, plotting my path in the direction of the highway. I knew the way well, but irritated by the combination of perspiration, impatience, and scorching sun, I got lost.

I searched for what seemed a long time, but all the sand dunes suddenly looked exactly alike. For a moment, I imagined that I would be stuck there forever, when I suddenly noticed a hill that I had never climbed before. A spark of curiosity led me to it. I knew the dunes well, but I couldn't remember seeing that one before. I climbed it, cursing myself for my foolish curiosity. And then I reached the top. I will never forget how it felt: right there, in the middle of the dunes, surrounded by greenery, a lake the size of a football field sparkled with blue, clear, inviting water. Whooping with joy, I scampered down the sand dune, tearing off my clothes as I ran, and dived into the cool water. Amazed by my discovery of this unknown lake, I swam for quite a while, splashing about and roaring with rapture. Then I got dressed and easily found my way back to the highway.

A week later, I invited a few friends to share my discovery. "You won't believe it," I told them. "Wait until you see how amazing this lake is." This time we drove there, approaching the lake by the nearest access road. Then, walking quickly, we climbed the hill. As we stood there, looking over the clear water, I could feel my excitement mounting, but to my surprise and disappointment, my friends were not impressed. "What, that's it? You're so excited by this little lake," they said. "Don't you know that just a kilometer away from here, there's a huge water reservoir right in the middle of the dunes? What's so special about this tiny lake?" I tried to explain to them how special the place was to me, but to no avail. Since then, I have brought other people to the lake, but discover each time that I am unable to recreate that same sense of excitement among others, and the interest in the lake stops with me.

This story epitomizes what happens during the learning process. Learning is a story of searching, discovery, of a great excitement and intimacy—all of which are difficult to convey to others.

I believe that all learning is the discovery of something new. The experience of discovery, the moment when something new is discovered—to find a plant that I have been seeking for a long time, to come across a book I have never seen before, or any other discovery, whether about the world or about myself—is one of the most powerful and moving experiences there is.

The History of a Homeschooling Magazine
Helen Hegener

I've been writing about homeschooling since 1983. That is, professionally; my writings about families and children and learning—everything that comprises what we've come to know as homeschooling—go much, much farther back. I did a quick search of my name the other day and came up with almost 5,000 results, including many articles and essays I'd totally forgotten about. My perspective has changed over the course of close to thirty years, and the homeschooling movement has undergone many significant changes. But I can go back to our earliest issues, my first writings about families learning together, and most of what I wrote back then is still relevant today, and still worth reading. I like to think that's a sign of a good writer, but maybe it's just a sign that some things never change.

I was pretty little the first time I remember skipping school. I think it was the second grade, in the small town of Healdsburg, California, about seventy-five miles north of San Francisco. Every morning I walked about a mile to the Fitch Street Elementary School with my cousin Barbara—we'd skip along and sing songs and pick flowers along the way. The highlight of the trip was when we'd stop to pet the beautiful collie who would always be asleep on the front porch of Barbara's aunt's house. The big friendly dog looked just like Lassie and we loved her. She would always follow us a little ways toward the school, then turn around and go home. But one morning she didn't turn around, she kept following us, closer and closer to the school. Barbara and I tried to shoo her toward home, but she'd just wag her tail at us and give us a toothy, endearing doggie-grin.

Then we remembered that Barbara's aunt was gone for a few days—her brother had been coming over to feed the dog. The big collie was lonely! Well, we could take care of that problem. We turned off the sidewalk out into an orchard and headed for the creek we knew ran along the far side. We spent the whole day romping with the big collie, picking wild onions and grapes and making mudpies and catching tadpoles and just lying in the tall grass, happy to be free from schoolish concerns. It was a grand day!

I'm sure school had been out for hours when we finally headed home—we lived right next door to each other. The collie turned off toward her house and Barbara and I wandered in, tired and dirty from our adventures, ready for a good hot dinner. Barbara's mother met her with a quick spanking, and a stern lecture about responsibility, and sent her to bed without dinner. My mother sent me to get scrubbed up, then set dinner in front of me, and wanted to know all about our adventures, in great detail. She tucked me into bed saying maybe it was about time we thought about getting a dog of our own—she'd talk to Dad about that soon. Comparing notes with my cousin the next day, it struck me how differently our respective parents had reacted to our truancy, but I shrugged it off as just the way things were.

The overriding message to my young impressionable mind was that school just wasn't anything to get upset about, unless you had fiercely strict parents like poor Barbara. My mother used to tell us wonderful tales of when she and her sister and brothers would skip school and go riding or swimming or treasure-hunting in the hills of northern California. She always made those adventures sound far more interesting and compelling than going to school. One favorite family story was about how her brothers once dynamited their small one-room schoolhouse right off its rock foundation, and school was out for several weeks after that, much to the delight of kids for miles around.

I missed a lot of school when I was growing up, and the last grade I actually completed was the seventh—barely. My attendance record was shot full of holes, and things went downhill from there. By high school I'd given up on the idea completely and dropped out, preferring to spend my time reading, writing, riding my horses, or just hanging out. Our home was always full of books, encyclopedias, and magazines on a wide-ranging series of subjects, and like the rest of my family, I was an absolutely voracious reader. We traveled extensively, both here in the U.S. and abroad, and my ever-curious parents made sure we always checked out historical sites, museums, zoos and other local places of interest. Even without school my young life was full and fascinating and more adventurous than most kids my age could even dream about.

Long before I had children of my own I was telling people that mine weren't ever going to school. People would smile condescendingly and let me explain why, and then they'd explain in return why not sending my someday-kids to school would be a very bad idea. Most experienced homeschoolers are familiar with the so-called reasons, such as stunted socialization skills, poor testing abilities, and a general inability to get along like other kids would be taught to get along. Somewhat naively, I was okay with that. I figured the benefits of not being tied to schoolish expectations would somehow outweigh the negatives. Of course, at that time I also fully expected to raise my kids in the Alaskan bush country, where being able to load and fire a rifle, handle a riverboat or a dogteam, or build a log cabin with a chainsaw and an adze were quite necessary and valuable skills to have. Diagramming a sentence? Not so much.

As often happens, life had other plans for me—and for my children. When my two oldest sons, John and Jim, reached school age we found ourselves living a few miles from an Alaskan town called Palmer, which, while not exactly out in the bush, wasn't exactly middle-American suburbia, either. Moose and bears frequented the neighborhood, and I decided my young sons didn't need to run into them on the mile-long walk to the school bus stop. Sub-zero temperatures were the norm in winter, and I didn't want my children exposed to that either. So I asked around and discovered that the State of Alaska ran a correspondence program that was open to any Alaskan child who lived more than two miles from a school, and since we were about three miles away, we signed up for kindergarten and first grade, respectively.

The entire family, which by then included a baby girl, Jody, thoroughly enjoyed the programs, administered through the local

Palmer Elementary School. We were assigned a teacher who oversaw the process through monthly in-person meetings at the school, but otherwise we were on our own. We received big boxes of books, pens, papers, crayons, story tapes, arts and crafts materials—it was almost like Christmas! The story and song tapes became great family favorites, and our kids still remember the words to many of them. As a special project we built a paper mâché globe by pasting strips of newspaper around an inflated balloon and painting it to look like the planet Earth. The teacher overseer was so impressed she asked to hang it in her office—and the boys just beamed about their "globe" being selected for such an honor!

Both boys passed their respective grades with glowing reports, and we figured the next year we'd repeat the process, moving each up a grade. But again, life had other plans for our family. In late August of that year my dad suffered a debilitating heart attack and we suddenly found our young family moving to Washington State to help with my parent's ranch. We spent the rest of that summer learning about horses and chickens and hauling hay and firewood—and when fall rolled around again I blithely headed down to the local school office and asked how I could enroll my boys in their state correspondence course. They just gave me a blank look and said they didn't know what I was talking about.

By the time school opened John and Jim had made friends with the neighbor children, several of whom were about their own age. The boys decided that since everyone else from our little valley was going off to school in town, they'd like to try it too. So one brisk fall morning they walked down the creek, met up with their friends, and waited by the last gate in the valley for the local school bus to come rolling up the dusty mountain road.

It only took about a month for the novelty to wear off. We started hearing reports of lunches being stolen by other kids, jackets torn in playground bullying, one boy ridiculed because he was coloring things the wrong color, another made to miss lunch because he went to the restroom without asking first. When a teacher rapped John's knuckles with a ruler because he was talking to a friend in class we decided the school experiment was a failure and the boys never went back.

About that same time a friend of my mother's had given her two copies of John Holt's newsletter, *Growing Without Schooling*, issues number eleven and twelve. Mom had already taken my youngest brother and sister, ages twelve and fourteen, out of school permanently, and she passed Holt's newsletters along to me when the boys started running into minor problems at school. It was the first I'd heard about an organized movement to take or keep kids out of school, and reading those thin typewritten newsletters was like a breath of fresh air!

Our determination redoubled, we ignored the increasingly threatening letters from the local school superintendent. The last letter they sent advised us they'd arranged a meeting we were to attend, and that we were being charged $25 per day, per child, for every day the boys were absent from school. At $50 per day the bill was undoubtedly adding up pretty quickly, so we took evasive maneuvers and told them we were planning on returning to Alaska. That seemed to end their interest in our family, although in that very small rural community we were pretty certain they knew we were still living in the area. We figure that telling them we were leaving let them check off some box on a form somewhere, and we never heard from the school officials again.

Sometime in the summer of 1983, on a trip to Seattle to discuss raising calves with a friend who was already successful in that business, I decided that we needed a computer. I'd grown up with computers; my dad was a programmer and a systems analyst for the big room-sized IBMs of the late 50s and early 60s. I'd played with punch cards and programming boards as a child and I knew these were powerful tools, capable of wondrous things. So when I found out I could buy one—a lovely little blue and gray machine called a Kaypro II—for only $1,500, I didn't even hesitate. I plunked down my money and grinned all the way home.

Mark was a bit puzzled about what we needed a computer for, but he was game to learn about it. For the first few weeks we mostly played games; it came with a few built-in standards like Ladder, Aliens, and a version of Pac-Man, and the whole family enjoyed these newfangled electronic diversions. I did some bookkeeping and letter writing on it, and the boys explored the drawing program. Then in the fall of 1983 I saw a short newspaper item about a homeschool conference in Spokane, Washington, two hundred miles from where we lived. It advertised homeschool advocates and authors Dr. Raymond and Dorothy Moore as the featured speakers, and conference attendees would receive a free copy of their book, *Home Grown Kids*. I tore out the newspaper article and pinned it above the bed, trying to decide whether or not I should make the trip.

The conference was being sponsored by the newly-formed Family Learning Association, a service organization created by local homeschooling pioneer Kathleen McCurdy. Not having any idea what I was getting into, but excited about the prospect of meeting other people interested in the then-new concept of homeschooling, I finally drove the two hundred miles and took my seat on a hard metal folding chair in the large and impressive Spokane Convention Center.

I don't recall much about the conference other than liking what the Moores had to say and how they said it. They seemed very knowledgeable about the potential of parents teaching their own children, but they were also warm, friendly, sincere and encouraging. They spent a long time answering individual questions after the seminar, and they were kind and patient with everyone. Little did I know that a few short years later these remarkable pioneering leaders would become good friends—and trusted allies in the fight for homeschooling freedoms.

What I primarily remember from the conference was meeting and joining a small group of people who were drafting a bill to make homeschooling legal in Washington State. I drove back to Spokane two or three times a month for the next few weeks, attending meetings and drafting sessions and coffee klatches for local legislators, often with Mark in tow. We organized the first statewide gathering of homeschool leaders in Washington and presented our bill draft, then we gained a good sponsor and set about garnering more support. Kathleen McCurdy, who had organized the conference, became the bill's lobbyist, and when she headed for the state capitol in Olympia to begin work in earnest, I went along, as much out of curiosity as anything else.

That winter I started a little one-page newsletter to keep local homeschoolers and alternative schoolers informed about our progress with the bill. At some point that December, seeing how well the newsletter was being received, I decided that what the greater homeschooling movement really needed was not just another newsletter, but a full-fledged magazine with articles, columns, photos, artwork and all the rest. John Holt was publishing GWS and the Moores were publishing The Family Report, but they were both just newsletters. I wanted to produce a real magazine, and in true unschooled fashion, I didn't let my lack of knowledge about the publishing industry deter me even a little.

We have a big red spiral-bound notebook, one of those two hundred page, college ruled notebooks divided into five subject areas. Written across the cover in black marker are the words: *"Home Education Magazine,* Issue 1, Volume 1 (putting it together)." This notebook was literally the handwritten blueprint for the first issue of the magazine.

Inside are notes such as this listing from the first page: bulk mail rates, licenses? permits? Advertising—where and how—costs? printing—available options, need a title—cover? advertisers—how to obtain, what to charge, subscriptions—twelve issues, $20/year or $2/issue, welcome contributions—no pay yet. The date was December twenty sixth, 1983.

The next page is a listing of potential content: Editorial, Articles, Interviews, Resources and Reviews, Kids Korner, Homeschooling Hints, Directory, Legislative News, Letters, Questions and Answers, Local Support Group News. Interestingly, most of those features and departments can still be found in today's *Home Education Magazine.*

On page after page the first content of the magazine is written out in longhand, in blue ink—in some places items are scribbled over and corrections or additions made, either in my sloppy scribble or in Mark's distinctive hand. Editing was done later, in red ink—but there's little of that. At the top of each page the word Finis is circled in red. At that point the entry was typed into that old Kaypro II computer and undoubtedly fine-tuned for printing.

The first issue of *Home Education Magazine* was twenty pages; ten double-sided sheets of paper stapled along the left-hand side. It featured an editorial, a couple of articles, an interview with a homeschooling family, reviews of several educational items, a book review, a report from the Washington Legislative Action Committee, a few good quotes and a short listing of helpful homeschooling resources.

That first issue sported a sharp graphic header designed by my artistic brother, Bill, and our young son John provided a bit of childish artwork for flavor. I sketched a couple of small images to run with the quotes that related to learning, but that was it as far as graphical content.

We weren't aware of clip art or copyright-free images yet, and we didn't think photos would reproduce well on a print shop's printers.

There was a meeting scheduled in Spokane the first week of January, 1984, to go over the homeschooling bill, and I thought that would be a good place to introduce our new publication. I drove over to Spokane and a couple of hours before the meeting began, I took our laid-out pages to a quick print shop and had them run off one hundred copies of each page. I stopped at a McDonald's restaurant and collated up about fifty copies over a burger and fries, and when I got to the meeting I passed them around the room. To be honest, I don't remember much about the response. Our little publication just seemed like another way to promote the legislative effort, and while I'm sure it was well received within the group, I don't remember any specifics from that debut evening.

When I got home with the remaining copies we collated and stapled them, then sent that first issue to everyone we thought would be even remotely interested. We sent copies to John Holt and Dr. and Mrs. Moore, to friends we'd made around the state while working on the homeschooling bill, to legislators who had shown support, and to anyone with any connection to homeschooling whom we could find a mailing address for. Imagine our surprise and delight when we started receiving letters of appreciation from around the country, and checks from people looking forward to our next issue!

By the time our second issue went out we'd learned what a saddle stapler was, and how to make artwork and illustrations and photos work, and we were developing connections with homeschool support groups in several states. We added a section of Homeschool News from many states, and on the inside front cover we proudly published letters from John Holt and Dr. Raymond Moore, both wishing us well with our fledgling publication.

Home Education Magazine grew and changed over the years as we added columnists, changed editors, went from black and white to color and became one of the first magazines to venture into digital content. *Home Education Magazine* was one of the first publications to have a website and domain-related email addresses, and the HEM forums on America Online were the first electronic access to homeschool networking for many, many families. I can't begin to count the friendships we still have today that began on those early America Online forums and the OneList email discussion groups.

Today, *Home Education Magazine* is still a well-recognized leader in homeschooling, and our online presence is evident in several popular blogs such as the HEM News and Commentary, HEM's Closer Look, and the HEM Guide to Homeschool Resources, as well as morphing into popular social media such as Facebook, Twitter, MySpace, Stumbleupon, Digg, and the ever-expanding range of applications available now. We have twelve years of the magazine online in our digital archives, and content from each issue is added to the collection, making the HEM Archives one of the largest online libraries of homeschooling content available anywhere.

But beyond all the social networking and technical advancements, our focus was never on publishing a magazine as much as it was on supporting an important movement for educational freedom, for the right of every parent to take an active part in determining what their children's education, and thereby their children's future, would be. We were instrumental in the founding and development of the National Homeschool Association, the National Home Education Network, and the American Homeschool Association, and our commitment to homeschooling is evident in every issue we publish: *Home Education Magazine* is a publication by our homeschooling family, and for homeschooling families everywhere.

Looking For Trouble
Matt Hern

I spend lots of time wandering around mouthing off, saying obnoxious things about contemporary schooling, so I get asked about my own school experiences pretty often. If I had had either traumatic or phenomenal school experiences, it would make it easy to explain what has become a twenty-year exploration of radical schools and alternatives to school. It would be easy to explain my antagonism to compulsory state schools if somewhere along the line there had been a deeply formative childhood juncture, or a tipping point, or something. It would be a good narrative but it's not the case. There has been no epiphanic moment when radical deschooling ideas just dropped on me. They emerged bit by bit out of exigency and genuine need.

*****

My schooling was, frankly, rather unexceptional. I grew up about ten miles outside a small town on Vancouver Island, on the far west coast of Canada, and with no neighbors around, I spent a ton of time by myself, poking around the beach, shooting hoops, willing myself (futilely) to become Mike Bossy redux. I got sent to a private school when I was a young teenager (I still can't imagine what my folks were thinking) and in short order, got kicked out. I caused as much trouble as I could possibly engineer through high school, eventually got through it, did well enough to get offered a little money by a fancy university, and did a few degrees. That's not much of an interesting story.

In terms of formative factors of my childhood, I would point to a couple of pieces, which in some combination have driven lots of my thinking. First, I have terrific parents and a lovely extended family who have always had my back. Second, spending all that time on my own, unprogrammed, without friends around, letting my mind roam, not only remains really important for me personally, but also for my ideas about kids. I really think people need to get good at spending big chunks of time by themselves, thinking ideas through and imagining their lives outside the bounds of supervision and monitoring.

Third, I would say that I have been engaged in radical politics for pretty much forever. Part of it, especially as a teenager, was just wanting to piss people off. I come from a good liberal/lefty family, so saying I was an anarchist got people hot, but nothing like the shit it caused at school. Which, of course, is exactly what I was after. But in time, after a ton of reading and meeting good people in the punk rawk and activist worlds, I really did embrace social anarchy, or left socialism, for real. More on that later.

The story goes like this: In 1991 I was young and in love, with both Selena and New York City, where we were living. But when she got pregnant, it dawned on us that we were very young (twenty-two and twenty-three), had no legal status in the U.S of A, no money at all, and no freaking clue what we were getting ourselves into. So we beat a quick path to Vancouver, BC, closer to my family. When our daughter Sadie was born in early 1992, we tried hard to find part-time jobs that would let us share in childcare and putative bread-winning, but it was difficult to find passable employment, let alone jobs that matched our imagined schedules.

So (absurdly, in what has become a very profligate habit of

absurd decision-making) I decided to do an M.A. at the Institute for Social Ecology, in Vermont. The degree program had an internship component, so Selena and I decided to start a school, which would kill two birds: we could make ourselves jobs and I could fulfill my program requirements. Plus we'd be able to quit our dumb-ass daycare jobs, we'd have a fun project to do together, we could work part-time, and I'd have something to write about.

And more or less it worked. We found an organization in town that helped us get the Eastside Learning Centre off the ground, and through them we were able to secure a little funding. Amazingly, it all came together and some kids showed up. But what a fucking mess! We were really young, Selena had her teaching degree and I had a little experience, but we were woefully under-prepared. The parents were a motley crew, the kids were wild, and it was in a broke-ass neighborhood, so we charged minuscule tuition on a sliding scale that very often slid to zero. Plus we had a little baby and we were starting from scratch. But we had no fear and it often went well.

And it was great for my writing. I had no formal training or schooling in education and no idea what I was doing, but I relied on radical notions of equality and horizontality and was eager to figure out what that might mean with children. Every day I was confronted with an endless and liquid series of ideas and circumstances and relationships that I had some sense of how to approach, but nothing solid to work from. So every day I would charge home at lunch, take the baby from Selena, and as soon as I had a moment, frantically start reading John Holt, Ivan Illich, John Gatto, Grace Llewellyn, Leo Tolstoy—anything that anyone could feed me. I was so eager for perspective that I tore into the books, half-desperate for help in understanding what the hell had just happened to me. When Selena got home we would talk and try to make sense of our days. Then I'd write about it.

The Learning Centre was a great little place. We had between twelve and twenty kids, all under the age of twelve, and we did anything and everything we could think of: we took constant field trips, built and tore things apart, dug gardens, traveled, went to the library a lot, sat around and made all the decisions together. It was mostly like having a really big family meeting right in the middle of our great East Van neighborhood, where all the families came from.

There were two basic premises that we worked from. First, self-determination: when people, even very little kids, are pursuing activities of their own volition, with their own motivation, they tend to do them much better and more honestly than if they are being forced. Marionetting people, even—and especially—if you think it is "for their own good" is ethically suspect and deeply ineffective, and it lays the groundwork for a culture of domination. Schools, even the nice ones, are built around the premise that they know best how kids should be spending their time. I don't buy it. As Ivan Illich once put it, it is the fantasy that "Man can do what God cannot, namely manipulate people for their own salvation." It is the bedrock of schooling and inhered deeply in liberal/progressive notions of education that adults can and should dominate children; coerce, bribe, threaten, cajole and/or maneuver them into a tightly prescribed set of behaviors and studies. It is the wellspring justification for the entire constellation of tests, grades, behavior, and classroom management, monitoring, supervision and assorted manipulative techniques and governmentality of schools. It's well past time to cut all that off at the root.

The second core premise we built from was taking democracy seriously. In the early years we toyed with renditions of voting and then various consensus models and they all worked to certain degrees, mostly depending on the kinds of kids we had. The goal was to put everything on the table for common control. To my mind the actual configuration is less important than the constant commitment to flatten decision-making structures right down so that all people and kids can all have a genuine voice in core decisions. The goals of actual collaboration, respect and equality are good in themselves, but they build a foundation of shared responsibility. When kids know that the place, the building and the project are really theirs, they invest themselves and genuinely care about its welfare, which makes for not just a more ethical and engaged milieu, but a space that's easier to clean because people are taking care of it.

I've really hung on to these two core ideals and they've continued to inform and challenge my work ever since. Too many schools (and institutions in general) pay lip-service to ideals of respect and freedom and democracy, but I think it's worth peeling back the marketing, the platitudes and the double-speak and really looking hard at what is going on. All too often it's the same old domination, sometimes dressed up in nice language and liberal ideals, sometimes just stark naked and unapologetic. All schools and institutions—the ones we are closely involved with most certainly—need to be examined rigorously and evaluated honestly, not just for their everyday functioning, but for their political and ethical foundations as well.

Improbably, we kept that little school alive for four full years until the City and their building inspectors finally drove us out of the big old warehouse we were occupying. Then, even more amazingly, right as we were out of options, we were able to take all our kids and stuff and families and merge our Centre with Windsor House, a publicly-funded democratic free school in a suburb about a half-hour from our neighborhood. It was a quasi-miracle that Selena and I were able to get jobs immediately, that WH was willing to have us, that our philosophical approaches were so closely compatible. Selena has been working there ever since and both our kids attended.

Windsor House has been around for more than thirty-five years now, continues to fight hard within an antagonistic system to maintain a non-coercive pedagogy, and is still a pretty compelling place (see Helen Hughes' chapter in this book). It was sweet relief for Selena and I to have a large and engaged staff to share the load with (in all ways); we got a break from running an independent school in a poor neighborhood, and we had the ongoing pleasure of having Helen as a mentor. Being part of Windsor House really was, and continues to be, a pretty much seamless (if colossally messy) investigation into what a laboratory place for self-reliant and collaborative learning might look like.

So by 2000, I was happily working away at Windsor House, doing fun projects, taking kids on long camping trips, and completing a doctorate in Urban Studies, when I noticed that many of the teenagers at the school were drifting away—emotionally, intellectually, and/or physically. It didn't seem coincidental that many were poorer kids from our neighborhood. So I gathered seven of them around our kitchen table and started asking them: if we were to start something new, something that would be perfect for you and your crew, what would it look like? It took us a lot of months of weekly meetings to come up with something, and we went through lots of ideas, but eventually it became clear that they described themselves as at their happiest—as flourishing—when they were being creative: painting, taking photos, making zines, sculpting, carving, writing, building bikes, shooting video, animating shorts, drawing. So I said, "Let's start a place to do that."

We did, and it has gone almost exactly as we might have imagined and hoped. We ran into a little grant money and in 2001 we opened the Purple Thistle Centre on Commercial Drive in a four room office-like space above a video store.[1] We had just enough money to pay the rent and utilities for a year, so once we moved in, tore out the carpet and tidied the place up we had nothing, no money to buy supplies and not a ton of ideas about what we would buy if we did.

But no fears. I asked my neighbor, who is an artist with a long history of working with the community, if he'd be willing to run a painting group. For free. With a pile of rowdy kids. And you gotta find all the supplies too. Dan being Dan he was happy to do it and soon we had a well-attended weekly art class going. Then one of the kids found a local professional photographer who was equally generous, and they soon built a darkroom out of a closet, dug up all kinds of donated supplies and cameras, and that was our second piece.

We just kept going. Everyone who was involved met on Monday nights and we talked about the place—what we wanted, ideas, plans, hopes, fears. We learned how to run the place collectively with just one (highly suspect) adult as part of the organizing crew, and very little money. But kids kept coming up with ideas for classes, workshops, projects and trips, and we kept finding ways to do them. I spent lots of time looking for money and applying for grants, we kept dragging in new kids, the Centre kept filling up with crazy art and books and computers and zines and photos and supplies and junk dragged out of alleys. We also did enough creative remodeling that the place looked rather unlike what its owners were hoping for. That, combined with the fact that kids were spilling out of the place at all hours of night and day, and there were always packs of people playing hockey in the alley, smoking out front, playing music too loud or just being the youth of today, eventually, after three great years, got us evicted.

Which was really a great blessing. The place had gotten way too small, the landlords were dickheads, and it was time to move. Again, we were incredibly lucky and found the perfect spot—a big ol' cavernous ex-sweat shop in a great building full of artists, just a short walk away, and equidistant between three poor and working-class neighborhoods. The place was a mess—no power outlets, no walls, insulation hanging everywhere, floor all torn up, no lighting, nothing really. Except a lovely and supportive landlord. It was ideal.

And now, five years down the road the Centre looks awesome. It is 2500 square feet that we have steadily and relentless built and retrofitted to fit our needs. It has an office and library, huge zine collection, major animation room, computer lab stocked with ten smoking machines, a huge darkroom, bike fixing and tool area, silk-screening room, art area and lots else. We're loaded with supplies of all kinds, run a ton of events and classes and groups, the place is open at least six days a week and everything is always free.

There are a couple hundred kids who use the space on a regular basis—some just to check their email or read a zine for fifteen minutes, others who are there constantly. It's a lively and fun place that we say is open to all ages, which mostly means thirteen to twenty-five, but we don't check ID. To me, though, the coolest part is that it is run on a genuinely collective, horizontalist basis.

There are approximately fifteen kids (sometimes more, sometimes less) who sit on the collective. They each have a set of keys, and in return agree to take one four-hour shift per week to keep the place open, and maintain the place drug, alcohol and assholism-free.[2] They are also asked to develop or nurture one public project—a group, a class, an event, some particular set of supplies. In this way we have the place open from afternoon until late in the evenings at least six days a week for drop-ins, plus we have an ongoing and emerging curriculum that is participant-driven and run. The collective still meets every Monday night and using a liquid consensus process makes all the decisions that govern the place, from who to hire and what classes to run, to holding events, to budget decisions, to any conflicts that arise.

I come to the meetings only occasionally, when asked or if there is something I want to present, and have every confidence the collective can run the day-to-day operations smoothly. I do all the fundraising (almost exclusively grant-writing), take care of all the meta-stuff like permits and leases and bills, mentor the collective in various ways, and help out whenever asked.

I also have a couple of projects that I have taken on, among them two full-time training programs that are run during the day at the Thistle for kids who need extra support. These programs hire between eight and twelve kids full-time and run for six-month stretches, and we try to have one running at all times. I also have developed a native/non-native exchange program with an isolated community in the Northwest Territories called Fort Good Hope that we run whenever I can come up with the cash.

But that's enough about the Thistle: I am bragging a little more than I meant. In large respect, though, that's where most of my ideas about deschooling and community and radical social change are getting incubated.

Those ideas have always been very closely connected, maybe indistinguishable from, my larger politics, and those politics have been germinated and nurtured by my neighborhood. I have lived for my whole adult life in East Vancouver, and really all within a few blocks just off Commercial Drive. It's always been a fabulous neighborhood and I think we have a shot at fighting off the creeping virus (bacteria?) of gentrification and doing our radical working-class, immigrant, and activist history proud.

And that's kind of always been the heart of it for me. I'm all good with thinking about deschooling, unschooling, home learning, alternative schools and alternatives to school—but if that isn't explicitly connected to a larger politics, if this isn't about remaking the world, then fuck it.

In looking to radical alternatives-to-school and deschooling, we need to be looking explicitly to horizontal participation, commonality, community, individual and local self-reliance: radical democracy taken seriously. And for me our Eastside Learning Centre, Windsor House, and the Thistle have all been all bound up with that politics.

*****

Now, almost twenty years down the road (!) and hordes of great (and sometimes truly brilliant) kids coming through our lives, I feel like maybe I have a tiny bit more clarity about what we have been doing (an increasing clarity which actually is neatly dovetailing in reverse mirror speed with my very evident intellectual decline). The Thistle is still surely a big part of my heart and brain, but to a large extent it runs itself. Now I spend as much time with my own kids as they are willing: Selena and I had another daughter in 1997, plus we have taken in many kids over the years, several of whom are now very firmly family and I care about/for dearly. I teach at a couple of universities here in Vancouver to pay the bills. I founded and still work with a sprawling Car-Free Vancouver Day project, try to drink less and work out more, write plenty, try to produce quality books, still find myself traveling and lecturing pretty constantly, and like many other middle-aged dudes am very happy to spend huge blocks of time in my garden growing food.

All that distills down to two essential lessons I'm taking from these two decades of work: first, don't wait for an epiphany. Epiphany suggests to me a moment of clarity, of the Truth descending down and everything becoming clear. I can't imagine that happening and even if it did it would be false. It is a fundamental arrogance, Illich's "educational hubris," to think that any body of theory, any grand narrative can describe how kids should be spending their time. Don't start with master theory, start with some kids and a place you love. Start with the people and families around you, then figure things out from there.

Schools have always started with their reified pedagogy and then forced students to adapt around it. I'd say turn that equation on its ass. Sit down with the kids around you and some friends you want to work with and ask: what do we need to thrive? Then go straight at it with an open heart, figure it out as you go, let 'er rip, and don't worry about money. As Colin Ward once said, "We need a mass of solutions, not a mass solution"—and that's exactly right. We need as many people as possible creating as many places as possible; we need a radical pluralism, not just of people and values but of institutions too. And we need everyday people to lead it.

The second lesson is that our work has to stay rooted in transformative projects. All this alt-school and deschooling stuff really has to be about remaking the world, about making the world a better place. If a really cool school or project is just providing nice experiences for already privileged, sheltered kids, then that's a regressive force, not a progressive one. We have to be looking explicitly to collaborate with the least privileged folks in our communities. Our goal has to be making the world a freer, more respectful, egalitarian, democratic and ecological place, and given the monumental role compulsory state schooling has had in constructing the world as we know it, we should be shooting for nothing less.

Notes

1.   I needed a name on short notice for a grant application, so I dug this up and it just stuck. Purple thistles are tough as hell and they grow everywhere—beside the road, in abandoned lots, in fields, they thrive pretty much anywhere. They are lovely to look at but will fuck you up if you try to hurt them. They are also incredibly resilient, self-seeding, and hardy. You get the metaphor.

2.   The Thistle has only ever had three rules/agreements: 1) No drugs or alcohol + no coming messed up, 2) No sleeping over. People are welcome to stay working/hanging out, it's a 24/7 facility, but we can't turn into a shelter, and 3) No assholism. This is a blanket rule that covers sexism, racism, homophobia, not cleaning up after yourself, being a jerk, being sketchy, etc. It's commonly understood, doesn't require much explanation, and has worked extremely effectively.

The Evolution of a Child Listener
Helen Hughes

My schooling was very unremarkable. I lived in a middle class neighborhood and went to a big brick building with a girls' entrance, a boys' entrance, and separated playing fields. We were separated into age groups as well; I was terrified of the older kids and disdainful of the younger ones. I could read and was able to do math in my head before going to school, so the early years were very boring.

In school I learned to do as I was told without question, move my lips but not sing, and daydream without being noticed. I lived for recess and noon hour, where we got to go outside and play skip, O'Leary, hop scotch, and marbles. I was a great little skipper and hopscotcher, but my O'Leary ball was not the right kind because we couldn't afford the one that bounced well, and I couldn't get the hang of marbles. Nonetheless, it was enough to keep me almost sane.

Every so often I would pretend I was sick so I could stay home. My mother would indulge me a certain amount, but if I tried it too often she would say, "Walk to the church steps and if you still feel sick then come home." She knew that when I saw my friends on the field I would be drawn in.

It was in elementary school that I developed the talent for replaying the last few words of a teacher's question if it happened to be directed at me. I had a repertoire of vague responses that usually got me off the hook, so I wasn't punished for daydreaming. I noticed that some others weren't so lucky, and were constantly in trouble.

When I was going into grade six we moved, and I found myself in a much rougher school. I had never heard dirty jokes before, and I went scarlet when I heard them. I was fair game. Teased mercilessly, I was miserable for two years until I went into junior high. All I remember of that time is humiliation and boredom.

In junior high school, I encountered a teacher who was the essence of evil. She ran the home economics class like a prison. We were all terrified all of the time. She wore a white, slightly translucent nylon uniform that showed shadowy outlines of underwear, stays, and girdles. Her shoes were crepe soled, and she could sneak up on you and bark an order in your ear. When you regained your senses, you were left wondering how much of what you had been saying, she had heard. You knew that eventually you would pay.

I learned nothing in junior high school. Every ounce of intelligence I possessed was used to keep me from being bullied and shamed. My mother made my clothes, which immediately marked me as a target. I frantically baby-sat, even though I didn't really like kids, to earn enough to buy the store-bought clothes that everyone else wore.

At noon, the girls all walked clockwise in little bunches around the perimeter of the building; the boys horsed around, moving more slowly in a counter-clockwise direction. There was much giggling and pointing from the girls, and much shoving and wrestling from the boys. It was no wonder that at the school dances the girls all hugged one wall and the boys hugged the other. I suppose someone must have danced, but it certainly wasn't anyone from my group!

In high school things changed. I made some good friends and got involved in the politics of School Council. We didn't, of course, vote on anything of importance, but we did get to raise money for sports equipment and organize the school dance. Curiously enough, we didn't notice that we organized the school dances the same way they had always been organized. We didn't realize that we could have invented something new. We were curtailed by the invisible forces of "it has always been this way and will always be this way." I did, however, enjoy my friendships, especially that of my dearest friend, who never excluded anyone. Halcyon days they were, halcyon and clueless.

I have a few indelible memories, however. The fire drills were always executed in our lunch hour, and if we didn't get out of the ancient death trap fast enough, we were marched back in and made to do it over and over until we hit the magic number. One balmy spring day, after our fourth attempt, one of the senior students went up to the principal, who was looking at his watch and frowning, and said, "I'm going home for lunch." He left. The principal, a wily old man who was purported to have a steel plate in his skull from a WWII injury, conferred with the Fire Marshall and dismissed us. It was my first conscious brush with the dynamics of power.

Intrigued, I began playing with it lightly. My father was a teacher, and although my parents didn't maintain a heavy supervision of me, I didn't want to incur his wrath. I began with chewing a matchstick. When a teacher told me to take it out of my mouth, I mildly demurred that I wasn't aware of a rule against it. She said it wasn't lady-like, and I responded that I wasn't aware of a rule against that either. The next move was a kindly talking-to by one of the younger female teachers: "Do you realize what it looks like to others?" Indeed, I did! This was followed the next day by the principal telling me that it was against the rules to have matches in school. I didn't fight it, I just switched to a toothpick. By then it was turning into a campaign that interested the other students. How lovely! In those days, we could cause a kerfuffle by chewing a toothpick. We didn't have to do drugs or shoplift, we just had to wear our skirts too short, the boys wear their hair too long, and the adults were aghast.

They then had the good sense to leave me alone, and I tired of the game and stopped.

I took home economics because my parents wouldn't let me take a study period, so even though I had developed a severe dislike of the subject, it was better than the other option which was shorthand. Clueless as I was, even I picked up the impression that once you learned typing and shorthand, you were doomed to be somebody's servant for evermore.

Home ec it was. Every day the teacher would start the lesson with the same question: "At what temperature do you cook eggs?" And we would chorus: "A low temperature!" The first question on every exam was the same.

Curiously enough, I did well in home ec, and replaced a yard-long zipper four times so that I could get it perfect. It earned me a scholarship!

The rub was that I hated cooking and when I married at nineteen (What was I thinking?), I would sit on a stool and read recipe books instead of slinging the veggies and potatoes into a pot and broiling a piece of meat. The carrots in my fridge were usually in need of Viagra, as I never seemed to be organized enough to get them peeled and on the stove with the potatoes, so they became limper and limper as time went on.

You would think that at least I would know how to cook eggs, but the truth is that I didn't relate my classroom lessons to real life. It was several years later that I pulled myself together enough to notice that my eggs were always rubbery. Finally the penny dropped. I should cook eggs at a low temperature!

Needless to say, I endured a fair amount of ribbing about my home ec scholarship.

I fully intended to play hooky at some point in my schooling, but wasn't quite sure how to do it. The only people I knew of who played hooky were the girls of questionable morals, who were so contemptuous of a goody-two-shoes like me that I didn't dream of approaching them to find out. The boys who played hooky were, according to an unspoken but very clear opinion, young thugs in training. I was terrified of them. So on a spring day in my last year of school, having missed the bus and panting my way down and up the ravine short-cut, I suddenly bethought myself, "Why am I doing this? Today would be the perfect day to play hooky." By then I was ambling along the sidewalk trying to figure out where to go, when a teacher in a car stopped and offered me a ride! Several things rushed chaotically around in my head. "Should I take a ride with a *teacher*? Can I make an excuse? Is this a sign? What will my friends think if I drive up with a *teacher*?" I took the ride and never did play hooky, and now it's too late. That is one of my few regrets about high school.

When I graduated, I went to a one-year teacher training course at the University of British Columbia. They were desperate for teachers, and I wanted the shortest possible amount of further schooling that would allow me to start earning a decent salary. I really wanted to be an air stewardess, as their jobs seemed very glamorous. I had never been in a plane, however, and had a terrible fear of heights. I was guided into teaching by my fiancé. In those days young women were not expected to think for themselves.

As it turned out, I loved teaching. It was very ego-building to have a class full of children sitting in rows of seats, listening to my every word. My moment of truth came when I was in my fourth year of teaching and was writing grade six social studies notes on the blackboard. For some quirky reason I decided to write notes on the other board that contradicted the notes on the first board. The students dutifully wrote down the notes and I quizzed them on the following day. The usual ones parroted back the information pretty accurately and the usual others didn't.

When all was said and done, I turned to the class and said, "Didn't any of you notice that this sentence here (gesture to the right) contradicted this one here (gesture to the left)?" There was a stunned silence, and then one brave young lady raised her hand and said, "I didn't know you wanted us to think."

Amazingly, *I* started to think. I read *Summerhill* and was, in the parlance of the day, blown away. I started to experiment by putting obvious errors on the board, and being delighted when they were spotted. I had my students prepare lessons and teach their peers. I began being absent from the room to see how they would manage. I began my career as a child listener.

In spite of all that, it didn't really kick in until my own daughter began to wilt in grade two. She had stomach aches except on the weekends, she couldn't sleep, her prodigious art output dwindled to a trickle and I became seriously worried. My bonnie child became pale and listless. It wasn't that she couldn't do the work, she did very well academically. She had friends and liked the teacher. It was the system that was doing her in.

At that point I was teaching in a parent participation preschool, and I loved having parents as part of the team. A group of us got together and decided to open up a school of our own.

We started a little co-operative school in my house on Windsor Road. When we tried to find a name for our fifteen-student group, we had fifteen different ideas, and when we voted, each one got one vote! After a while everyone agreed that we could call it Windsor House until we thought of a better name. Here we are, thirty-seven years later, still looking.

The school dissolved at the end of the first year because we had all known what we didn't want, but none of us had much of a grip on what we did want. We had a big house on a very large lot, so the children spent most of their time playing Crocodiles in the basement or outside climbing trees, running madly around and working out intricate games.

One summer we put a large piece of plastic on the steep slope of the lawn with the hose dribbling at the top. The children slid and careened down, soon realizing that skin slid faster than shorts. They disrobed, discarding bits here and there, without a thought of impropriety. Soon they were all stark naked, having a lovely time. We had very easy-going neighbors, luckily, and although I did hear a few amused remarks years later, nothing was said at the time.

The adults, however, were very busy offering candle-making, spinning, weaving, story time, field trips, reading groups, woodwork, and vinegar and baking soda volcanoes. The children availed themselves of these opportunities sporadically, but their eyes really lit up when they produced one of their interminable plays, and we were all held hostage because we didn't want to damage their little psyches.

The activity the adults liked best was the problem-solving sessions that we imposed as our method of discipline. They were brutal. We made a point of hearing from everybody about every aspect of a problem. We were not satisfied until everyone agreed on a solution. It was perfect for my articulate daughter, but misery for my active little son. It was in these early years, when we weren't trying to do much else, that the thinking and reading and experimenting was at its height. Problem-solving evolved by creating rules to keep people from going "on power." It became a bit of a monster. Every once and a while it was jettisoned, and we staggered along with a Queen or King, or Judges. Then, when that delegation of power had been thoroughly abused, we would revert to problem-solving again.

Eventually, the adults made their way to the nook in the kitchen to drink herbal drinks and talk about the Windsor House philosophy. By the end of the first year we had gelled into three groups. The ones who wanted more structure (read coercion) went down the block to another parent's house and had lessons in the morning. They didn't last the year.

The second group wanted less structure (read effort), so they took their families down to live in a cave in Mexico, and gave the children a set amount of money each day to buy food, which they would be expected to prepare for themselves. They stayed several years.

The last group, consisting of my family and a family that had moved from California and bought a house nearby specifically so their children could go to Windsor House, carried on as before. The group grew to fifteen fairly rapidly, and our philosophy evolved to being very non-coercive and relationship based.

These days I am the front person (known as President to satisfy the hierarchical groups we interface with) of the Society for the Advancement of Non-coercive Education (SANE). We have just pulled off a major triumph in our school district. SANE proposed a Neighborhood of Learning partnership with Windsor House, which is a publicly-funded school. In a heart-stopping meeting, the Trustees voted unanimously to support it, and so we will be able to provide for members of our community who are sort of "whole-earth, attachment parenting" in our very own building with community driven initiatives. It is so exciting I can hardly stay in my skin.

SANE will be starting an in-house after-school day care for Windsor House students this coming September. In the following years we will set up a pre-school, a seniors drop-in, a well-baby clinic, a theater group, a bike repair shop, and so on.

I am hoping it will morph into an ever-changing, community-determined, learning, playing, and resting center for all ages. I would like to see 24/7 daycare provided so children would always have a safe place to go. I would like to see a Learnary, where people meet with others to share their passions and skills. I am determined to see a Community Council, where anyone who wants to may participate.

Lastly, I would love to be involved in a mentoring institute, where we share our experiences and thoughts, read books and discuss them, visit other centers and cross-pollinate. I would be on one end of the age continuum, and my yet-to-be-born new grandchild will be on the other, teaching me in ways I have yet to experience.

Here are descriptions of the Riverplace Learnary and the Windsor House Institute of Mentoring:

The Riverplace Learnary

It is our belief that young people should be raised in collaborative communities. Since churches are no longer serving that purpose for many of us, we are setting up a space for this to happen in. Our objective is to raise our own consciousness about real respect, especially respect for young people.

The Riverplace Learnary will eventually be a building where people will flow in and out, using the space as they see fit, changing the contours as they pass through. The space will have a form and basic organization that, flexible though it may be, will boundary the activities for emotional and physical safety.

Through the Open Space component, people will organize into interest groups through email or by using the Open Space Wall, and gather to engage in activities and classes of their choosing. Anyone who wishes to take advantage of the WHIM (Windsor House Institute of Mentoring) component will meet after the activity and discuss the interpersonal dynamics that they observed or were involved in. They will share their thoughts and experiences to improve their ability to work respectfully in community with others, especially young people.

The facility itself will have four components:
- a community kitchen/lounge/decision-making space;
- a childminding space;
- an Open Space wall for postings, with rooms available for booking;
- a mentoring institute room.

The main ingredients of a good learning environment are:
- Learner: with self-knowledge about personal learning styles and an enthusiasm for learning
- Mentors: anyone with knowledge about any given subject, a love of that subject, and the ability and desire to share with others
- Spaces to meet: can be anywhere: at the Riverplace Learnary, in

the park, on the internet, in a living room, on a boat, in a coffee shop, up a tree...
- Time: any time that suits the co-learners
- Payment: whatever people work out amongst themselves

The unchangeables (corner stones, foundation, core principles that define who we are) are:
- Collaborative: using the idea of brainstorming—putting out all kinds of ideas, refraining from negation, picking up of useful ideas, and crafting solutions that have the backing of the whole group, while understanding that all solutions are temporary
- Flexible: no canon of pedagogy
- Non-coercive participation—guilt free
- Agreement to do conflict resolution and not practice hurtful behaviors
- All ages: baby to seniors

Structures:
- Fluid concept of time
- Fluid concept of places to meet
- Fluid concept of attendance
- Fluid concept of payment

We do not want to have survival dependent on one funding source, so we want to develop a broad base. We may hire a fundraiser. We want to use innovative approaches that build a secure base over time.

We already have many of the key ingredients: the Open Space at Windsor House; the mentoring institute at Westmoreland House; the community space at Windsor House; and the daycare that opened in September 2009.

Westmoreland House Institute of Mentoring (WHIM)
People gather to share their thoughts and experiences to improve their ability to work respectfully in community.

WHIM consists of an email list of people who choose to be involved. There is no leader, and no single person taking responsibility.

People will involve themselves as much or as little as they like. Lurkers are welcome.

The only thing we would ask people to pay attention to is the subject line in all emails. Be sure the subject line is pertinent to what you are posting, so that all of the recipients can delete the postings that are not of interest at the time.

You may post any activity or event that interests you and might interest the others on the list. The idea is to attend various events, and then meet later to discuss the dynamics of the group you were in. Our objective is to raise our own consciousness about real respect, especially respect for young people.

We ask that groups work collaboratively, but we do not wish to monitor this. Reports from various groups are welcome, but there is no obligation.

Every once and a while, one of us might be moved to call a gathering of all involved in this adventure, to discuss how it is going, but this would have no attendance requirement.

People who would wish to be off the list can simply remove themselves.

We have done all of the things I am talking about at various times and in various ways, but now they will be brought together to create a vibrant self-directed learning community.

Recalling the Indigenous
Don "Four Arrows" Jacobs

I went through a status-quo school system in the mid-west for K-16, graduating from high school in 1964 and from a university in 1968. No problems. Played the game. Was a model student on my way to law school.

Then came Viet Nam. Rather than be drafted, I joined the Marine Corps officer program. Flight school, gung ho the whole way. And then, at last, I woke up.

Perhaps it was the ultimate realization that "my" war was bogus, and that I had been sucked into it as a result of all the brain-washing I had received throughout my schooling. Maybe I just started seeing what was happening in the world and how it related to education. At any rate, I returned to civilian life with a chip on my shoulder. I also had a more critical view of the "white-washed" realities in the world. I say white-washed because my early life had resulted in me rejecting my own Cherokee heritage. My mother discouraged my associations with this part of our ancestry, perhaps to protect me. Her father had committed suicide. By the end of first grade I figured it was not a good thing to be "Indian." I remember the first grade. I remember that I had forgotten my Roy Rogers lunch box (and at the time never would have guessed that Roy Rogers was also part Indian). Mom drove it to school for me but had not taken time to powder her face or paint her lips and her Indian features were obvious. When she left the classroom, all the children began chanting, "Donnie's Mom's a squaw, Donnie's Mom's a squaw." I looked at the teacher for help but she merely smiled a smug smile I never forgot.

After the Marines, however, I questioned everything, including the negative assumptions I had about the Indigenous Peoples and what they had to offer the world. In 1974, I returned to college to get a teaching degree so I could turn schooling upside down, or so I thought. I'm sure I was a pain in the neck to the program. For example, during my first student-teaching assignment, I had the students in my eleventh grade American History class literally teach themselves. Each day one person would lead the entire class on a self-selected topic that he or she had researched for the presentation. The students were so effective in this process, I sometimes left the classes alone to go for bike rides or attend to personal business. I almost got kicked out of the program as well as the school, until the students and their parents rallied in my support for "the best class and the most learning they ever experienced."

The experience turned me against a career in public school teaching and I got a job as a professional firefighter/EMT. To get a raise, I went back to school and took classes in fire science. For one class, I was asked to do a slide show about a change I wanted to see in the fire service. I did one entitled "Physical Fitness and the Fire Service." I was a marathon runner and handball player at the time and worked with a number of obese, cigarette smoking colleagues. I had also seen statistics that showed that my profession led the nation in mortality rates, and not because of the danger of the job. Instead, we led all occupations in heart attacks, most of which occurred on the way to or from the scene.

The slide show was a hit and my teacher recommended that I send it to the National Fire Protection Association to see if they would like me to write the first book on this topic. I did and the NFPA published a series of my books over the next eight years that led to national fitness standards for firefighters. Unfortunately, my own department fought all my efforts to initiate fitness programs and I decided to go back to school so I could practice in the new field of health psychology. To do this would require a doctoral degree, however, so I applied to an accredited but highly alternative "self-directed" doctoral program and obtained my degree in Health Psychology while interning at the Wholistic Health and Nutrition Institute. My dissertation, "Organizing Health and Fitness Programs in Business and Industry," was published by World

Publications, publishers of *Runner's World Magazine* and *Getting Your Executive Fit*, and was the first book to describe the economic benefits of fitness. At the same time I published *Happy Exercise: An Adventure into the World of Fitness for Children*, also published by World. This was a story about a fictional rabbit rescued from a forest fire who helped children become active and fit. He taught children the hazards of sugar and challenged television commercials that touted cereals as healthy when they contained 80 percent sugar. He taught the young people to look at television commercials critically because they did not always tell the truth. One month after publication, Bob Anderson, the owner and publisher of the book, told me he had a number of advertisers for his magazine complain about a children's book that accused businesses of not telling the truth on TV. He said he would have to remainder (kill) the book as well as the other one.

With these first publications, I learned that messing with the system was not going to be an easy task. These would be the first of a number of books that would be "banned" and the story of these books reveals, I think, a story, like others in this book, that can help the reader understand what motivated me to be an alternative educator.

After graduating, I remained working as a medic for a while but also taught as an adjunct professor at U.C. Berkeley. As a result of some of my coursework, I had become interested in hypnosis and I taught hypnosis certification to Marriage, Family, and Child Counselors. One day I was reading through the seventh edition of a first aid book, *Emergency Care and Transportation of the Sick and Injured*, by the American Academy of Orthopedic Surgeons. A sentence in the introduction stood out: "Be careful what you say at the scene of an emergency because words, even words uttered in jest, can become fixed in a patient's mind and cause untold harm." It struck me that this was an example of fear-induced, spontaneous hypnosis. I thought of how young children whose teachers told them, "You will never amount to anything!" were affected in the same way as someone at an emergency scene hearing, "You will never walk again." I then wondered why, if negative words could be hurtful, positive ones could not be helpful. I began in-the-field research for a book about this possibility. I spent years talking to my patients until I was branded "the voodoo doctor." Norman Cousins, a well-known author of a book entitled *Anatomy of an Illness*, endorsed my manuscript and this led to Prentice-Hall publishing *Patient Communication: The First Hour of Trauma*. The book was a big hit, like *Happy Exercise*, for a month or so, until I was informed by the legal department that they would have to remainder the book. It seems some attorney said, "This stuff should only be used by medical doctors." When I challenged them to show me anything in the book that was not valid, they said it was valid, and that firefighters and medics might be able to help stop bleeding or reduce blood pressure, but that the risk was too high that they would be seen as practicing medicine. It seemed to be okay if they said negative things because they did not learn about this phenomenon, but not to say positive things that could help people survive, even if I said, "This should be used only as an adjunct to standard medical care." The book was remaindered anyway.

At this point, it seemed that every educational innovation I employed or wrote about was challenged by the system, so I decided to go to work as director for a large residential treatment program and school for adjudicated youth. My first day of work, an alarm went off. I looked outside and saw a number of counselors jumping into the school vans and driving off. I asked my secretary what was going on and she told me some children had run away. She said they would hide in the sugar cane fields until it got cold and then the cars that surrounded the area would spot them when they walked out of their hiding spots. They would then be placed in concrete rooms for observation for twenty-four hours, placed in yellow jump suits, be restricted from recreation opportunities and P.E. while in school, and would have all visitation rights suspended for several months.

While my secretary was speaking to me I looked outside and saw the two children's heads bobbing up and down in the field. My horse, Brio, was in a nearby corral and I grabbed a radio, went outside my office, jumped on the horse, and rode into the field after the boys. In short time I came upon them. I told them I was the new director and they could turn around and come back with me. I canceled the patrols.

On the way back to the ranch I asked the boys what they thought they could do to make the situation right. They replied that they knew about the punishments waiting for them. They had experienced them before. I told them as new director I had different ideas and repeated my question to them. By the time we arrived, they had agreed to wash all the vans that had gotten dirty; get jobs to pay the overtime salaries of two of my counselors who responded; write letters of apologies to their house mates and a few other things I now forget. No jump suits, no concrete room, no suspensions of recreation or family visits. When I shared this with my employees, I knew they did not like my plan.

The next morning thirty-five people, including one janitor, were lined up outside my office. Each warned me that I was making a mistake. These were tough boys and girls and such leniency would put all the staff in danger now. I took notes and fired everyone who strongly stood against my arguments. Within a month, I hired replacements and placed all seventy children on "Obecalp" instead of the high doses of Ritalin they taking. "Obecalp" is "Placebo" spelled backwards. We took them off their real meds and put them on sugar pills. Everyone started an exercise program of race walking. Farm animals were assigned to students based on their personalities. Some were put in charge of horses, others pigs and cows. All the soft drink and candy machines were removed and the institutional food increased in nutrition.

I also brought in Larry Brendtro, the well-known author of *Positive Peer Culture* and *Reclaiming Youth at Risk*. Together we set up a positive peer culture program based on his original research. We had a number of American Indian youth and we incorporated a variety of Indigenous stories, including rites of initiation opportunities for the children that were based on the Navajo twin hero story, "Where the Two Come to the Fire." There is so much I would like to say about this program, but suffice it to say that within fifteen months of my arrival, the physical take-down report required for state auditors showed a reduction from one hundred twenty-two per quarter to only fifteen, with *no* runaway attempts.

The improved program, however, had enemies. The Mormon Church felt the program was not sufficiently punitive and wrote letters to the state so stating. They had sufficient power, and ultimately, I was fired. For years after I kept a bumper sticker that read, "There is one person in every organization that really knows what is going on. That person must be fired."

I decided, however, that it was time to get back into public education to implement the effective programs *before* children engage in drive by shootings or robberies. I applied to Boise State University's Curriculum and Instruction Doctoral program, was accepted, and earned my second doctorate. During this time, Newt Gingrich and Rush Limbaugh came on the scene as did the well planned anti-environmental movement that Limbaugh sold for the far right on his radio program. I wrote the first book deconstructing Limbaugh's assertions, *The Bum's Rush: The Selling of Environmental Backlash,* but could find no one who would publish it. One large publisher, who loved the book, told me "We don't want to take on Limbaugh."

So I self-published the book, got endorsements from most of the big environmental groups, and marketed the book myself, only to find that no one wanted to take him on at the time. Several universities canceled my speaking engagements when ranking or influential people learned what I would be talking about.

By now, I had become convinced that the traditional ways of knowing that American Indians understood had a significant role in modern education for everyone. Fate intervened and I became Dean of Education at Oglala Lakota College on the Pine Ridge Indian Reservation. There I learned more than I taught, but managed with an incredible team to bring culturally relevant programming and full accreditation back to the teacher education program that had been canceled by the State of South Dakota for failing an accreditation audit.

In my University of Texas publication, *Unlearning the Language of Conquest: Scholars Expose Anti-Indianism in America,* my contributing authors, including the late, great Vine Deloria, Jr., reveal why our Western world does not want to acknowledge the truth about the Indigenous worldview and Indigenous approaches to teaching and learning. It is because, like most of the alternative education programs in our world, it offers authentic respect for the ability of students to learn naturally, through many paths that each recognize and respect the numerous ways that everything is connected. Perhaps someday the Indigenous models for teaching and learning and the common themes that run through the different First Nations will be studied by all educators so that the "alternative" will become mainstream; I hope this will happen before it is too late.

Inside-Out Learning
Mark Jacobs

"O uch! You hit me!"

I was stunned. There I sat in ninth grade global studies in public school. It was not just any public school; it was Pelham Memorial High School, in Westchester County, one of the wealthiest counties outside of New York City.

So what had I done? I was a quiet fourteen-year-old. My two biggest fears were adults, and of course, girls. I hadn't spoken out of turn or said anything disrespectful—I hadn't even passed a note. What was my big sin that Thursday morning? I'd yawned. I'd yawned and my hulking fifty-something teacher, less than affectionately nicknamed "Froggy" by some of the other students, had walked down the aisle and slapped me—one of the good kids!—in the face.

That slap was my wake-up call in more ways than one. First, I never slept in Froggy's class again. Second, I stopped assuming that the supposed expert educators, into whose hands I had been given, actually knew what they were doing.

As I recount some of the lowlights of my traditional public school education, it is important to understand that by my educators' own standards, I was a success. I don't think I ever received a grade lower than A or "very good" in all of elementary and junior high school, and I'm not even sure I ever got as low as a B in high school. I graduated seventh in my class of almost 200. I even participated in extra-curricular activities. For me the system worked. Or did it?

I still remember many elementary school nights lying in bed in tears with my well-intentioned mother trying to console me. Over and over again I would ask, "Why?" I wanted to know why I was being forced to spend my time learning certain material in which I was just not interested. I would ask: "Why do I have to learn about the histories of the kings of England and their wars?" "Why do I have to answer the hundredth spelling or part of speech question?" And most often, "Why is this important? How will it help me in my life to spend my time doing this assignment?" Sometimes, I would try to make a deal with my mother. I'd say, "Tell me how this assignment has value and I'll do it." She could hardly come through on her end. Still, I would cry and shake my fists at the powers that be, and then I would get out of bed to do the work and get another A. All that my teachers saw were my excellent assignments. All that the guidance counselors saw were my high grades. They were proud. I was unhappy. I hated school.

At least I had the social aspects of school. I had the opportunity to be with kids of different experiences, intelligence, and backgrounds. So what was our educators' grand plan for teaching us how to get along with each other? How were we, the socially inexperienced, supposed to know how to talk to each other, to work out conflicts, to balance our own wants and needs with those of others? I think the plan went something like this: Follow the rules. Go to the teacher when others don't follow the rules, but don't go too often. You'll be fine.

But I didn't feel fine. This approach led to might making right. I was afraid. Mostly, I was afraid of not being liked, of being judged by my peers—and boy, did they judge. The way to be cool was to make fun of other kids and of course it was the strong kids making fun of the weak ones. I don't mean to suggest I was a weakling—I was actually a closet jock—but I was *socially* weak, ill-equipped with the fast comeback when being teased. So it wasn't long before I was clearly not one of the cool kids.

I still cringe at the memory of Kim's second grade birthday party. This was the age when pretty much everyone in the class got invited— so I was there. We were at the Ground Round, at a big table playing telephone. You remember that game: somebody whispers a line into the next person's ear going around the table until the hardly recognizable final sentence is repeated. I was near the end, anxiously waiting for my turn to hear the whispered words. I listened, and what I heard makes my stomach tighten to this day, "Mark's scared of the great white shark."

One year earlier I had attended another birthday party. Some parents had allowed their kid to bring fifteen first graders to the Pelham Picture House to see *Jaws*. I remember sitting in the dark room watching that first scene: The young woman goes swimming in the ocean at dusk. The music starts, building to a crescendo at the same moment her eyes roll up into her head and she is pulled into the ocean's depths. Okay, I admit it. I couldn't take it. I was six. I got up and went to the lobby to call my mother to take me home. I wasn't cool enough or socially aware enough to realize the consequences of walking out of a scary movie in front of my classmates. I was just scared and wanted to go home. So I did.

One year later, I had still not lived it down. There I sat in front of my half-eaten hamburger with everyone laughing at me for my cowardice from a year before. I was ashamed and embarrassed. I still haven't watched *Jaws*.

Now, I realize that this event didn't happen in school. Kids are mean to each other outside of school, no matter where they are being educated. The point is that no one was teaching us how to behave together. The "Sit quietly in class and follow the rules" imperative hardly provided the tools to equip us for the wide-ranging social experiences we would have to face throughout our lives.

In high school, it was even worse. There, everyone but the coolest kids learned to keep their heads down. Don't look at them, don't interact, and usually you won't get picked on or hurt. This didn't always work—I still remember being bullied in the locker room and in the hallways, but I learned tricks of non-engagement to get by. But, is getting by really the goal? Is a school community based upon the rule of the strong really what we want our children to participate in? I don't think so.

One of the best decisions of my life was to leave high school early. The Clarkson School, housed at Clarkson University in the upper reaches of New York State, is a program in which forty to sixty students combine their senior year of high school with the first year of college.

Most public schools would allow the college credits thus earned to apply to completing high school requirements. This enabled me to flee my unhappy, unrewarding experience of high school for a college environment.

Thinking back upon my year at Clarkson has often helped me to identify some of the components of a good education that are missing from traditional K-12 schools. First and foremost, we had the ability to choose our classes. Sure, there were requirements, but these made sense because of how they fit with our intended majors. Second, social integration was not ignored. We had regular house meetings run by caring and thoughtful counselors in addition to having Outward Bound-type trips with all the participants in the program. Finally, we were given real responsibility for most components of our lives. There was laundry and balancing my checkbook. It was up to us to go to class or sleep the day away. We had people to go to for help, but the ultimate responsibility was ours.

Clarkson is an engineering school, and as such, doesn't have liberal arts programs. All of the non-math/science courses, regardless of the field, are given by the Liberal Studies Department. One of the courses I took through this department was called *Great Ideas in Western Culture*. This introductory literature and writing course, taught by a man who looked like he was still dwelling in the 1960s, taught me something that all my previous education seemed to ignore: it taught me how to think.

We read books from Plato to Marx, from Descartes to Pirsig. Our opinions were valued and the professor would engage us in meaningful analysis of these works and how they applied to our lives. In addition, he taught us how to write. I find it interesting that I had taken honors English classes all through high school and as part of these, had written numerous papers in a variety of styles, yet I think back on this college course as the first time I learned how to write. In part, it may have been the extensive comments and corrections I received on everything I submitted. But more than that, I believe this was the first time I was writing on subjects that mattered to me. We were given the flexibility in the topics of our papers so that each week we could write about what we cared about. I wrote and I wrote, and yes, I learned.

My major at Clarkson was mathematics, which I chose because

1) I have always excelled at math, and 2) I enjoyed doing math. These are two solid reasons for making this sort of decision, but, as I had to learn on my own, there should have been many more factors that I considered. My *Great Ideas* class taught me more than how to write: it taught me that I had questions—big questions—about life, the world, love, religion, and justice. I came to believe that I could answer these questions; Plato and Descartes had come up with their own answers, so why couldn't I?

I transferred from Clarkson to Clark University so that I could study philosophy. I was inspired, yet saddened at the same time, because I felt like my real education was just beginning. How had I wasted so much time? How had so much of what was truly important been ignored in my education up until now?

I loved college and graduate school. I continued to excel, but more importantly, I continued to be inspired. I'll leave out the details of my higher education because I want to focus on what came later. Skip ahead to my senior year of college. Decision time: what would I do next? I was graduating Summa Cum Laude, a member of Phi Beta Kappa, and the recipient of the Philosophy Department's highest award, but what would I do with this? There wasn't a huge demand for itinerant philosophers. Some of my friends were off to graduate school in philosophy, which was tempting, but that path pretty much led to one and only one job choice: college philosophy professor.

I loved philosophy, but when I considered what most philosophy professors do, I was uninspired. Teaching philosophy generally involves the repeating the ideas of the "great thinkers" in an attempt to help class after class understand what these writers had believed. Most philosophy undergrads simply battled to understand what the "great thinkers" had said. I was different. I had decided to study philosophy because I had questions that I had tenaciously worked to answer during my undergrad years. Indeed, I had spent three years developing my own philosophy, blending metaphysics, epistemology, and ethics. But I knew I was the exception. I was a philosopher, not a teacher of other philosophers' ideas. I wanted to teach kids how to live, how to figure out their lives for themselves, how to confront the biggest and most difficult questions in their own way. Philosophy professor didn't seem to be a good fit.

Skip ahead more years. There I am, married, running a peace and social justice center, with my son about to turn school age. Here comes the big question: where should he go to school? Public school? Not after my experience. Private school? I hadn't heard of ones in my area that inspired me—they seemed to be just high-powered versions of public school. Homeschooling? Just me and my kid, without the daily involvement of a group of other kids? Maybe.

Then it came to me: if I wanted my child to have the best possible education, then I would have to start a school. There was no way around it. I turned to my mother, the same woman who had watched me suffer through public school. She had been a special education teacher and I asked her if she was up for starting a school together. Happily, she agreed, and thus was born the idea for Longview School.

I wanted to avoid the mistakes made in my education. The primary problem with schools that we saw, and felt after many of our own experiences, was that the kids weren't interested in what they were learning. We swore not to fall into the same trap, and as a result, spent lots of time creating the most exciting lessons possible, covering the whole range of the curriculum. We prepped, we listened to kids, we watched what they seemed to like, and we nudged. Nudging is a form of soft coercion: "You'll have fun if you do this science experiment," "You can build with Legos after you come to math class," etc.

For about six months, we tried our model of "exciting" lessons mixed with ample free time. Then it was time for some honest self-assessment. We found that the lessons we thought were so exciting were only a little interesting to a few kids. We found that there was a great deal of anger from kids about being nudged into activities that they were not interested in doing. This sounded all too familiar. We had set out to create a school that avoided the frustrations I had gone through in school, and found that our school led kids to feel the same way.

As a result, we went back to the literature. We read about Montessori schools, Waldorf schools, open classrooms. We reread *Summerhill* and Sudbury Valley School's *Free at Last*. We looked into the Sudbury Valley School, which has been improving its model of education for forty years now. We read and we talked. We read some more and we debated. Finally, we decided to try the Sudbury model for a week or two in order to see what would happen. Here we are now, over seven years later, and our two-week experiment has turned into a philosophy I believe in with all my heart and soul.

So what is Longview School like? I can tell you that it will be difficult for you to imagine if your education was traditional. Still, open your mind a little and give it a try.

In a Sudbury school like Longview, kids decide how to spend their time all day, every day, almost entirely without exception. There are no required classes. None. Not ever.

At this point, nearly everyone asks, "So how do kids learn?" and to answer this, we have to look into one of the primary assumptions of modern and traditional education; namely, that learning means acquiring knowledge.

I believe traditional education took a wrong turn when it began to focus almost exclusively on the acquisition of knowledge. Acquiring knowledge is certainly important throughout a person's life. In fact, it's so important that it's unavoidable, and most of what we need to know we learn simply by living our lives. As a result, I feel it is a lofty but misguided approach to base a curriculum on gathering knowledge, and a waste of precious educational time. We remember such a small percentage of what we learned in school anyway, unless we were interested in it.

Of what then should a curriculum consist? The Longview curriculum has seven components: play, conversation, democracy, justice, clerkships, classes, and internships.

Play

Since children decide how they spend their time at school, it is not surprising that they choose to spend a lot of time playing. In the literature on child development, play is considered a primary modality of learning for children from birth to age five. Unfortunately, many educators believe that learning for those older than five must be serious business, a bitter pill that must be swallowed. At Sudbury schools, we believe that play is one of the best ways to learn, not just for very young children, but throughout one's schooling, and even in one's adult life. Because it is so engaging, people tend to retain what they learn during play, whether it is social skills (such as conflict resolution) or academic skills (such as reading, writing, mathematics, etc.).

Conversation

Conversation is surprisingly absent from traditional schools. Kids are expected to spend most of their days being quiet, listening to teachers or engaged in seat-time busywork. Sometimes they can speak, such as to answer a teacher's questions or to chat in the hallways, at lunch, or in gym, but these are the exceptions and are mostly seen as recreational, not educational.

Take a moment to reflect upon your own life. How have you learned what you know? For most people, honest reflection shows that conversation has been a primary mode of learning. As adults we learn through conversations with friends, relatives, co-workers, teachers, experts, and even with our children. Kids deserve the opportunity to learn in the same way.

In Sudbury schools, students spend most of their time talking to others. This includes conversing with peers and with adults. These conversations cover an incredible range of topics, from the seemingly mundane to the highly technical and philosophical. These interactions are an essential part of their education.

Democracy

Longview is run by our School Meeting, a democratic body composed of students and staff, each with one vote. This is not a mock democracy with the semblance of power, but rather a fully empowered school government. Every significant decision affecting the school is made by this body including making and reviewing the rules, planning field trips, planning new classes and activities, allocating school funds, etc. The School Meeting could decide to spend the entire bank account on candy, or to paint the school neon pink. It could theoretically make all sorts of bizarre decisions, but as a matter of practice, it doesn't. When kids are given real power, they take it seriously and make good decisions a high percentage of the time (I would venture to say much more often than most of our elected city, state, and federal governmental bodies). Plus, there is no better way to understand that a bad decision has been made than for it to take effect and to have to endure the negative consequences (within the limits of safety, of course). Then, when School Meeting revisits the issue, it reliably improves its decision based upon its actual experience. The democratic basis of their school provides students with the necessary practice to participate in a democratic society upon graduation.

Justice

At traditional schools, each conflict is resolved by a teacher, who is usually eager to squelch the disruption of the lesson, or by an administrator, who tries to reconstruct an incident based upon scant information. This approach teaches kids that conflict resolution is supposed to be done by adults in positions of authority and that the kids bear little responsibility in the process beyond complying with their punishments. Sadly, justice is often not served. In contrast, at Sudbury schools students learn what justice and fairness are through their participation in a judicial system modeled upon the US courts. We have a Judicial Committee (JC) which is chaired by a student, who acts as the judge, plus two other students and one staff person, who act as the jury. The Judicial Committee hears cases and metes out justice. Over time, every student at Longview is in the position of trying out each of the different roles in the judicial process, including judge (JC Chairperson), juror (JC Committee member), defendant, complainant, victim and witness. This enables students to formulate their own conceptions of justice through first-hand experience. At the same time, it makes them value the school rules, which they have created and supported, rather than scoffing at what seem like senseless restraints.

Clerkships

Learning responsibility is quite challenging. This is especially true for children when they are given few opportunities to practice being responsible. In so many schools, students spend their time doing busywork that has been created solely for them and that will be thrown in the garbage once they complete it.

At Longview, students share in the work of running the school. Much of the work students do is necessary for the smooth operation of the school. The kids know this, and as a result, they take their jobs, which we call clerkships, quite seriously. The following is a list of clerk jobs at Longview: Admissions Clerk, Attendance Clerk, Birthday Clerk, Calendar Clerk, Chores Clerk, Computer Clerk, Fire Safety

Clerk, Law Book Clerk, Library Clerk, Mail Clerk, Office Clerk, Physical Plant Clerk, Supplies Clerk, Town Crier, Treasurer, Judicial Committee Chairperson, Judicial Committee Chairperson, School Meeting Chairperson, and School Meeting Secretary.

Students hold positions for two-month periods. There is not enough space to describe each clerkship in detail, but the work includes paying the bills, balancing the bank statements, running both democratic and judicial meetings, maintaining the lawbook, running fire drills, keeping judicial records, overseeing the completion of daily chores, etc.

Classes

Students at Longview learn in both traditional and non-traditional ways. Our classes, other than being small and personal, look similar to classes in any school. The greatest difference is that we offer a class only when it is requested by one or more students. There is no core curriculum through which students are forced into cursory exposure to the range of academic areas regardless of their interests. Instead, students learn to become experts in the areas in which they are most interested. Then, throughout their lives, they are able to apply this experience in gaining expertise in each new endeavor. In this way we teach excellence and resourcefulness as opposed to competence and compliance.

Longview classes are quite diverse. They typically include traditional subjects such as reading, writing, math, science, art, and language, as well as unconventional subjects such as biking, canoeing, salsa, and Dungeons and Dragons. Many students never choose to take a class, while others try a class here or there, while yet others take multiple classes each day. All of these approaches are honored at Longview.

Internships

Another questionable turn in education happened with the shift from the apprenticeship to the classroom model. For older students, Longview offers the opportunity to explore the real world of work. Students do unpaid internships for local businesses in return for getting first-hand experience in jobs in which they are interested. This helps students make career choices based upon first-hand experience. Internships are valuable even when a student hates the placement;

learning from experience that you don't like being a lawyer, a veterinarian, or an acupuncturist could save years of wasted study.

In conclusion, kids at Longview are successful. They are not successful in the way I was successful at school, namely, by being able to conform to an imposed system wholly unlike the real world. Longview kids are successful at using a school modeled upon the real world in order to help them develop themselves into independent, responsible adults with real-world skills who know themselves, their talents and their abilities well enough to design happy, productive lives. What more could we want for our kids?

Walking Off the Beaten Path
Shilpa Jain

For the last ten years, I have been part of Shikshantar, a people's movement to radically rethink education and development. Up until a year ago, I was based in Udaipur, India, a lovely city in the northwest part of the country, complete with huge lakes, lush gardens, fantastic palaces, and diverse cultural communities. Shikshantar comes out of the spirit of fierce resistance and history of Udaipur (one of the few cities in India never taken by foreign rule), and also out of a nearly four-thousand-year-old conversation around truth and the dignity of the human spirit. We are trying to expand the depth and breadth of learning opportunities available to those locally, regionally, and around the world. We do this by challenging the monopoly of factory-schooling and its complementary modernizing institutions, while simultaneously supporting people to regenerate ways of learning and living that are more consonant with the values they seek for their societies and their lives.

If I tell you my background, I have a feeling that my story and its trajectory might seem a little ridiculous. Let's take school: I grew up in the suburbs of Chicago and was a straight-A student for twelve years. I was sent to gifted classes from first to eighth grade, and then to honors and advanced placement classes throughout high school. I won awards in a wide range of subjects and activities, from science to good citizenship to public speaking to tennis. I graduated third in my class, was accepted to Harvard University, and voted "Most Likely to Be a Millionaire" by my classmates (which goes to show you how little they knew). By society's standards, I was a success.

But, here's the catch: all that scholastic achievement didn't really mean anything to me. Although many people equate A-grades with intelligence, I certainly didn't; scoring well on tests just came easy to me. While many of my classmates would work long hours, struggle and suffer to get high grades, I would breeze through my homework and be in bed by 9:00 p.m. So why should I feel I'd accomplished anything? The whole arrangement was just a game.

And, it seemed to me to be an inherently unfair set-up. First, it was highly selective. Because I scored well on some random tests in the first grade, I was given chances to do interesting things for the next twelve years, while the vast majority of my classmates, who didn't score as high, were condemned to dull monotony. In my gifted classes, I was able to research current affairs and come up with creative solutions to global problems; I read powerful literature and challenged myself with neat puzzles. My classmates, however, were stuck doing repetitive math problems in workbooks and reading boring textbooks. Why weren't they given chances to be stimulated or grow in new directions?

I knew my classmates weren't average or stupid. All of them were gifted in different ways—at making friends, resolving conflicts, playing sports, making people laugh, drawing—but that didn't seem to matter at all in school. Their talents were classified as extra-curricular or deemed disruptive and distracting to effective classroom management. If it couldn't be measured by a test, it didn't count. Most of my friends and classmates were taught to think less of themselves, made to believe they weren't smart, and, as a result, often became withdrawn or aggressive over time. But I knew that their qualities and gifts were important—essential for developing functioning friendships and healthy lives—and without them, school would have been completely unbearable for all of us.

Another part of the game was competition, which I completely hated. Competition pervaded schooling and then spilled over into all other aspects of living. Children and adults were compared and ranked in everything, from intelligence and beauty, to height and weight, to money and possessions. In fact, it seemed my peers and I were constantly placed in a race towards the top (or away from the bottom). But the endless fixation with superiority and inferiority was cruel and unforgiving, and I hated the ways it would make everyone feel. The myth that competition brings out the best in you is total nonsense! Most often, it seems to bring out the worst of the ego: conceit in the winners, self-loathing in the losers. I am sure my sensitivity and aversion comes, at least in part, from my upbringing as a brown-skinned minority in the racism of America. Whatever the root of my repugnance, though, the extraordinary emphasis on competition gave me yet another reason to doubt the purpose and process of schooling.

School wasn't something I enjoyed or took pride in, but something I *had* to do, something that even at its best was an irritation. But I was lucky. Because school came easy to me, I didn't have to waste too much time on it, and in my childhood and adolescence I got to do things I really liked: reading fairy-tales, creating art, writing poems, making up new games, dancing. Best of all, I could interact with people of all ages and backgrounds. My neighborhood was like a World's Fair— there were Filipino, Pakistani, Taiwanese, Latino, Arab, Haitian, and Caucasian neighbors—and I learned so much with them, and from them, about religions, cultures, knowledge, and friendship.

With the support of my parents, and especially my older brother, I also had the chance to travel and work in different places. When I was eleven, I began to help my father with the computerized billing for his water cooler business; by the time I was fourteen, I did it on my own. When I was fifteen, I won a partial scholarship from my school to participate in the American Field Service program and spent the summer in Italy with a host family. My first time traveling alone, it was an incredible experience. I found myself speaking Italian without a teacher or any formal instruction. I navigated in new places, from the big city of Rome to the small villages in the countryside, and made many new friends. I realized my ability to do things by myself, and the independence was intoxicating.

When I returned home, though, that new sense of a powerful self led to several clashes with my parents and teachers. I wanted the freedom to learn and do as I saw fit, and felt confined by the schooling system and social expectations. School didn't become more difficult, it became more time-consuming and stifling. As I got older, there were more exams, more homework, leaving me with less time to pursue my other interests. One of the great losses I felt was in my art; I couldn't draw or paint or create as much as before because I was expected to concentrate more on "practical" courses, such as science and English and math. I searched for other avenues through which to express my interests and creativity and, in the latter years of high school, became busy with extra-curricular activities: tennis, human rights issues, public speaking, school newspaper, inter-cultural club, social service work, environmental concerns club.

Through these activities I was able to give expression to my urges for justice and a better world. I remember that my concerns with women's issues, violence, poverty, environmental damage, racism and human rights seemed unusual to my peers or teachers (they called me a rebel and a feminist). I believe that my unlearning around education grew out my activism because, over the years, I began to realize that the outlets for expressing my concerns were incomplete and, ultimately, futile. I tried to work within the system—using its tools, strategies, programs, and institutions—and went through several stages of hope and disillusionment.

I began doing charity work when I was thirteen, serving the elderly and poor, collecting food and clothes, raising money for other resources and services. After a year or two, I realized that these activities didn't do anything to change the system that neglected poor and elderly people. Instead of supporting people's skills and talents, or questioning economic systems, charity tried to alleviate suffering by doling out material objects. It missed the big picture. Social service workers tended to see problems as isolated phenomena and concentrated on individual shortcomings or difficulties. They failed to make a connection to larger political-economic institutions and forces.

After coming to this understanding, I tried a different approach. The problem was not with individuals. No, the institutions were just malfunctioning; they weren't working for all people. We needed to reform the system, to fix its failures, so that it could benefit everyone and not just a few. After all, the civil rights and women's rights struggles in the United States were about changing the government's laws and policies, in order to give everyone a fair chance to succeed. I began to focus more energy on environmental and human rights issues. I thought that by writing letters to government officials in the U.S. and other countries, and by supporting legal cases, I could voice my concerns and help to initiate changes.

I wrote to President George H. W. Bush in 1992, when I was fifteen, and urged him to attend the Earth Summit in Rio de Janeiro. I listed all the reasons why it was important for the U.S. to participate, given its tremendous use of the earth's resources and the ill-effects of its industries. I also described how the U.S. could be a world leader of a different kind, by seriously curbing CFC and CO2 emissions, thereby protecting the ozone layer, as well as preventing the greenhouse effect. What did I receive in return for my impassioned plea? An autographed picture of George Bush standing at the Grand Canyon, squinting at the camera, and a canned reply letter from one of his secretaries, stating that his advisors were considering if U.S. interests would fit with the goals of Earth Summit. Later, under Bush's orders, the U.S. delegation undermined the summit's proceedings and I was cured of my illusion that the "democratic strategy" of letter-writing, petitioning, and campaigning could fundamentally alter government policies. Clearly, there were bigger power games at play, and I began to see that "U.S. interests" were something separate from the interests of Mother Nature, the world's majorities, and even most U.S. citizens.

I then thought that we could address the failures of the political-economic system, if we started earlier, before the problems began. We could use the world's best institution—education—to make a difference. If children and young people got a good education, maybe a better and fairer system would emerge for everyone. This theory was tested in college, where I was involved in a program called CityStep. Each year, my classmates and I worked with five different groups of children, ages eleven to thirteen, from various schools in the area, and used dance to build their self-esteem, creativity, and teamwork. Each year would be amazing: kids who were shy and withdrawn would come out and be expressive in performance; new friendships were made;

confidence restored. But, our program took place for only a year or two, and only for one hour, three days a week. What about the rest of the time? What about the constant onslaught these children faced through the cruelty of schooling, an idiotic media fixated on rampant consumerism, and the abuse, divorce, or alcoholism in their families? CityStep might temporarily boost children's immunity against this onslaught, and even heal some wounds, but it couldn't challenge or resolve what was causing loss, hurt, pain, turmoil, and conflict in the first place. That suffering would not only remain, but would grow more powerful over time.

Slowly, I began to understand that all the well-meaning activities allowed by the larger system—charity, letter-writing and petitions, extracurricular programs—were only "reforms." They could temporarily fill the cracks in the system (or disguise them), but never remove its rotten core. In the last several years, I have to come to realize that what I saw as failures were actually evidence of the dominant system's success. Its tools, institutions, strategies, and personnel are structured in such a way that they *must* produce these individual, social, and ecological crises.

Exposing the myths of reform was almost as powerful as becoming cognizant of the hypocrisy and elitism of Harvard. Here, I have to admit, I was late in realizing the absurd self-indulgence of academia. Although I saw early on that Harvard was filled with incompetent professors and anti-intellectual students, I still hoped it could be a place of deep learning, radicalism, and activism. But, by the time I graduated, I began to see it for what it was. For one, Harvard subscribes to the same narrow notions of intelligence and talent as mainstream schooling does. Indeed, it defines itself by these notions and capitalizes on competition, selecting only one of every fifteen people who apply for admission, three-quarters of whom are already among the top 5% of their classes. Most of those accepted believe that they deserve their admission—it's just due to their hard work—but few ever think to question the validity of the schooling system, especially since their entire lives, they've been told they are successes in it.

At Harvard, we learned to fine tune our elitism. Our position on top is constantly affirmed; in speech after speech, we are told how we are the best, the brightest, the cream of the crop. It's seductive and often leaves one feeling giddy with power. In fact, even as we were further classified and cut down throughout our college experience, most of us still believed that the world was ours. We could do anything and be anything we wanted, and we would be in control. A Harvard degree was a one-way ticket to the elite bastions of politics, business, professional services, and academia. We would be the experts, presidents, and CEOs. Who were we to question the system? We would run it and rule it.

Of course, this is rarely articulated so openly. Instead, Harvard claims it has a noble goal: to continuously make significant contributions to the body of human knowledge. As students, we were made to believe in this goal. It justified our hours, days, and years in deep study of some obscure piece of info-knowledge. We were preoccupied with writing papers, reading old texts, completing problems, absorbing, constructing and deconstructing knowledge. All of it seemed very good and important. But in this time-consuming process, most of us became distanced from the world and more fixated on our own selves and our own (economic) futures. Rarely, if ever, did this info-knowledge challenge current injustice and exploitation. In fact, we weren't even exposed to it. It was only after I left Harvard that I discovered how many brilliant critical social thinkers never made it to my professors' syllabuses.

I realize that in putting forward such an outspoken critique of Harvard, I risk alienating a number of people, including many of my friends and former classmates, who still believe that Harvard is a good place for real learning. I should qualify what I wrote above: I did learn a lot there, but not in the way that many of you might expect. I can recall less than 5% of what I studied, but I did meet some amazing people who feel passionately about their work and who continue to struggle to live in accordance with their beliefs. (Of course, I have met such people everywhere; they reaffirm my faith in the ubiquity of the human spirit.) At Harvard, I had a chance to truly see the system, not for what it was theoretically supposed to be, *but for what it was*, and for that I am grateful. The rest—the elitism, the selfishness, the rigid belief in info-knowledge and rationality, the arrogance—I have had to unlearn, and I am still unlearning. It isn't easy, but it must be done.

After graduating, and spending a year trying to unmask the Development industry in Washington, DC (which is another *great* story), I came to be a part of Shikshantar full time. My first year there was laughter and art and intellectual rigor and sweat and persistence and new friendships and hand, back, leg work; travel, surprise, energy, love. My work itself was a mix of research—on conflict, creativity, the work and life of Rabindranath Tagore—and action—supporting workshops, facilitating discussions, working with children and youth on art, theater, new games. I had the chance to understand real-world crises and conflicts, from struggles against big dams to the death of the small farmer. I was also blessed to meet extraordinary people who, maybe by others' standards, might be called just ordinary. But, in them, I saw wisdom, dedication, and firm belief in truth. As I am, they are positive that the world can be a better place—more just, harmonious, beautiful, meaningful. And they made their actions consistent with their beliefs.

Unlike my activities in high school and college, my work with Shikshantar is all connected to larger critiques of the system and to regenerating new possibilities for living and learning. Here, we are not trying to fix the system's "failures," because we understand that the system is succeeding with what its architects and followers intended it to do: control, loot, and, in the process, destroy the majority of the world's people. If we remember this "success," then each action we undertake, both personally as well as socially, can dent the system and make space for something different. In this way, these actions are not putting a band-aid on something that is dreadfully sick; rather, they name this sickness openly and search out ways of healing our minds, hearts, bodies, and spirits, and also ways of keeping them healthy.

To believe that I have the capacity to learn things in life with "regular" people, to know that I don't need to be sheltered in ivory towers and elite circles, to have faith in myself and my potential—isn't this the foundation of human life? I know I don't need credentials to prove I have learned something, just as I know that many people who label themselves experts and professionals are doing the worst kinds of damage to individuals, communities, and nature. Instead of succumbing to the diploma disease and hiding behind degrees, I (and many "walkouts" I know) set up and follow through with my own learning interests, especially around self-sufficiency, community building and healing.

For instance, in August 2001, I spent two weeks working on an organic farm, Angelic Organics, in Illinois. My hands were in the dirt, in the earth, planting, weeding, and harvesting. And from the earth came sweet and beautiful gifts: peppers, corn, melons, onions, tomatoes, greens, herbs. I saw a rainbow almost every day. I slept outside, in a tent beneath the stars, with the crickets lulling me to sleep. I milked goats, brushed horses, fed ducks and chickens. I laughed with new friends, listened and spoke of struggles in everything from globalization to love. It was magical, this farm and its simple spell. It reaffirmed my faith that there are amazing people in the world, who stand by the strength of their convictions to live honestly, with integrity, and whose concern for life and living come through in every step and breath.

A few weeks later, two planes crashed into the World Trade Center in New York City. A month later, the United States launched a war on innocent people, mainly because their country's despotic government (once favored by the US) insisted on blocking multinational corporations' access to oil and natural gas reserves. I asked myself: *Is this the same world?*

As many times as my faith is shaken, it is renewed. Sometimes, I feel like despairing. When I acknowledge World Bank's and multinationals' power, when I listen to biased media, when I see the devastation wrought by the schooling system, or when it seems thousands more are going to die for America to salvage its ego and continue its greed, all seems dark and horrible. Then, as if they are sent by a higher force, I meet people who are struggling with the system, challenging and standing up to it. I meet someone who is unfolding their life in a new way, demonstrating that we can be different. My faith returns; it is transformed and rejuvenated. There is hope, and I am part of it.

Some Thoughts On My Education and My Work
Herbert Kohl

I attended PS 82, PS 104, Macombs Junior High School, and the Bronx High School of Science, all in the Bronx. My kindergarten teacher was wonderful. She was a member of our working class Jewish, Italian, and Irish community and knew all of our parents. She also cared about us and her classroom was comfortable, and I assume that we learned what was expected in kindergarten in 1942. I had a few problems in the first grade, as I didn't understand why I should have to learn to read. My teachers called my father in one morning—meaning he had to miss some work—and she asked me to read for him. I said "Jane" for "Dick" and "Dick" for "Spot." I didn't even look at the page when I read. My father was embarrassed and said that when I returned to school the next day there was no question that I would be attentive to learning to read.

At home, my father told me that I had to cut out the occurrences of the word "the" on the front page of the *New York Times* and I would do it every day until my teacher told him I was caught up. He wasn't kidding, I got the message, and from then on academics was never a problem no more. Until high school, it was simply a matter of what was expected of me within the family and it wasn't hard at all. Until junior high I had very nice teachers, a number of whom were trained in progressive education methods. Though I hated competing with other students and often suffered from asthma, school seemed pleasant enough. In the third through the fifth grade I especially loved walking almost a mile to school with my cousin Marilyn and my friends Ronny and Bobby, wandering aimlessly to school by myself, looking in store windows, or stopping at the candy store and perusing the comic books. During my elementary school days I rather enjoyed school and liked my classmates, though I was a bit of a loner. Public school was, and still is, a very comfortable place for me. The sixth grade was sometimes unsettling because there were gang troubles around the school and walking home could be perilous.

Junior high school was another thing altogether. Many of the teachers were old school Irish disciplinarians who didn't particularly like Jewish kids. One of them, the school disciplinarian and social studies teacher, was a chronic drunk. I was in a Special Progress class and we did the seventh, eighth, and ninth grades in two years. So far as I'm concerned, except for print shop and English, I could have skipped all three years. My homeroom teacher was one of the few Jewish teachers at the school, but she left in the middle of my first year, replaced by a young teacher who, for some reason, didn't treat us with respect. We drove her out with the help of our parents, whom she also didn't care for. In retrospect I think it was a matter of social class. She simply didn't understand or respect working class life.

In junior high I grew about five inches and became more sociable, liked to play basketball and softball, and had my first girlfriends. I don't remember learning much, but did encounter a book in the school library that transformed my life (see my essay *The Tattooed Man*). I also pretended to be part of a gang until I had a few unpleasant encounters with actual gang members and decided it wasn't for me. I still don't like to fight even though, growing up, I learned how to defend myself.

Bronx Science was a new, exciting, and very important experience for me. I entered Science in 1951, during the time of Joseph McCarthy and the House Un-American Activities red hunt. My family and many of the families of my friends had members who were socialists or communists, and we all knew card-carrying members of the Communist Party. The teachers at Science were, in my experience, wonderful. They knew and loved their subjects on the highest professional level, and many did work in mathematics and the sciences independent of their teaching. Others, like Eleanor Burstein, my English teacher, helped students like me encounter poetry and literature for the first time. There were no books in my home. It was from her teaching that poetry, fiction, philosophy, and almost anything that came in book form became a necessary part of my life. To this day I love and collect books.

At home, there wasn't any exposure to painting, sculpture, classical music or jazz. My parents did take me to the Metropolitan Museum of Art once or twice, rushing me by all of the nude paintings and those that represented Jesus. This, presumably, was to prevent me being corrupted by sex and Christianity.

At Science, music and the arts also contributed profoundly to my growth. I remember my friend Ralph Lehman and I encountering a poster announcing that Paul Badura Skoda was playing the *Mozart Piano Concerto* at Carnegie Hall. We were just wandering around 57th Street on a Saturday and ended up buying standing room only tickets. I remember thinking that we were really lucky that Mozart was being played in New York that year. I had just encountered his music in class at Science and had no idea that there was a thriving classical music culture in the City.

Through my friends I discovered Birdland and the Village Vanguard, and became a jazz aficionado. It seemed to me that through what I was given at high school, I had moved from planet Grand Avenue in the Bronx to planet Earth. It was very exciting, and in all of my educational work I have wanted all of my students to have similar gifts of discovery and to find challenging and exciting worlds they would not have encountered but for good teachers and schools.

I also discovered and became a participant in political and social activism at Science. Many of our teachers were called before the McCarthy Committee and HUAC, and as students, we were active in defending them. One of the most beloved teachers at the school, Julius Hlavaty, the Chairman of the Mathematics Department, took the Fifth Amendment and refused to rat on anybody. As a consequence, he was fired. We were all enraged and devastated. This taste of demagogy and fascism, added to our sense of the impending Holocaust and Hitler's repression of us Jews, colored my entire youth. We were embattled, and struggles for justice were a matter of life and death. I became a socialist through my grandfather and an activist though my experiences at the Bronx High School of Science.

In addition to national politics, I was directly involved in student government politics in New York City. At Science I became active in the student organization, being secretary, vice-president, and eventually president of the student body. I was also the school's representative to the New York City Inter-city Student Council, which represented all eighty-six high schools in the city. In my senior year I became president of the council and along with the vice–president, Robert Maynard (who became the only African American owner of a major daily newspaper in the US, the *Oakland Tribune*), became involved in issues of racism, police brutality, and student power. We even held a school strike over the *New York Daily News* running a series of articles demonizing high schools in New York. Along with the articles, the paper printed pictures of kids with knives (these were the days before guns in schools), of students making out in school stairwells, and of other students menacing teachers. We discovered that all of the pictures were posed by professional models and exposed this and ended up in conversations with the Mayor's office, the Police Department, the Superintendent of schools, and members of the media. This was unfortunately a short-lived action as the leaders (myself included) all graduated and our successors showed no taste for struggle.

My experience as an undergraduate at Harvard was different from my high school experience. First of all, I was away from the Bronx and I loved it. I wanted independence and got it. Much to the chagrin of my parents I chose to major in philosophy and minor in mathematics. And much to the chagrin of my philosophy professors, who encouraged me to pursue a career in academic philosophy, I took classes in modern theater, fourteenth century Italian painting, seventeenth century English poetry, the twentieth century novel, advanced mathematics, and the social sciences. I went where the great teachers were, and have never regretted it. Douglass Bush teaching John Donne and Ben Jonson was inspiring. Lynn Loomis's classes on modern algebra and functional analysis introduced to me pedagogical strategies that have been part of my teaching repertoire throughout my educational career. And there was so much more. My life-long interest in theater and my work creating plays with children was profoundly influenced by

Chapman's modern theater course. My tutor, Marshall Cohen, guided me on a personal basis in reading philosophy and integrating the arts into my thinking about the world. I am an expert in excellent teachers and have been privileged to know many throughout my life. One thing I learned at Science and Harvard was that first-rate teaching comes in many forms, shapes, and colors, and knowing this has helped me build coherent educational programs with very diverse groups of people.

However, all was not smooth at Harvard. It was a social nightmare for me, one that, during times of stress, was punctuated by attacks of asthma. I was literally out of my class and felt awkward. There were times when I wasn't sure I belonged; others when I tried to belong too much and took on airs and attitudes, in imitation, I thought, of what a "good Harvard man" is like. Of course people knew I was a sham.

The hardest thing at Harvard was my encounter with anti-Semitism. It didn't change my complex feeling of being a Jew from a somewhat mixed, secular and anti-Zionist family, but it did enrage me. There were a few times when I exploded, but for the most part my rage was tempered. I had too much to gain from what I was learning to blow it on the kind of prejudice I knew I would spend my life encountering and fighting.

My dream after Harvard was to return to the streets, to go home to the kind of rough and tumble neighborhood I grew up in, and to teach in a public elementary school. Then, as now, I thought that the two things I wanted to do and had to do with my life were write and teach.

After a year at Oxford and Paris, and another at Columbia in the graduate school of philosophy I finally followed my inner voices, my daemon, and became an elementary school teacher and a writer. Of course I learned from my students, but I've written a lot about that and won't go into it here. I also learned from the parents of my students and from the community activists, like David X Spencer and Jose Gonzales, who put their lives and careers on the line for justice, and who became lifelong friends.

There is one other extended learning experience I had that deepened my understanding of pedagogy, and showed me, in a more profound way than I could have imagined, the centrality of education to the struggle for social and economic justice. That was my and my family's twelve-year friendship with Myles Horton, the founder of the

Highlander Center. It lasted from 1977 until his death. Myles' presence infused me with energy and love, and his storytelling and actions had an immense impact on my life. We traveled together to Belfast in the midst of the troubles, and to the coal mines in the Rhonda Valley of Wales during the coal miners strike in 1984. My wife, Judy, and I spent time with Myles at Highlander and at our home in Point Arena, and our daughter Erica worked with him and Highlander while she was in college. The result of this was Myles' autobiography, *The Long Haul*. It would take me a book to talk about what I learned from Myles, but I think it would be best for people to read the book and learn from Myles themselves.

I have been blessed by being given the gift of learning from superb educators both within and without formal settings. I love schools and love learning on the fly. I love learning from reading, from conversation, and from confrontation; from looking and listening; and from living within a racially diverse and cross-cultural family and community. Hopefully, I am able to transfer this affection to my students through my teaching and to others through my writing.

I don't consider the education I advocate and practice as alternative to anything. I think of it as good education. My development as an educator emerged from my practice in the classroom, informed by a vision of a decent world where resources were shared, creativity encouraged, and individual growth was accompanied by social responsibility and a commitment to social justice.

My earliest teaching experience was in a fifth grade class of students who had rejected schooling. I began trying to lecture to the class, use copying from the chalkboard, textbooks, and threats to try to compel learning. It simply didn't work, and since I refused to blame the students for my failures as a teacher, I struggled to develop other ways to get them to value what they were learning and to enjoy being together as a community of learners. I quickly learned a few things. Giving students choices instead of trying to force them to do only one thing calmed them down, got them thinking, and taught me what they cared to learn and how they liked to go about learning. Mixing group, individual, and full class learning during the course of the day allowed for flexibility and comfort. Providing the students with rich materials that had compelling content seduced students into engagement with complex ideas. Crossing disciplinary boundaries and introducing theater, the visual arts, technology, storytelling, reading and research as part of a whole led to personal and group enrichment. Drawing on the students' own experience, getting to know parents, and becoming familiar with the community created trust. It made it possible, not just for the students, but the community as a whole, to feel that I provided a valuable service. In sum, over the first few years of teaching I learned to become connected, as a teacher and a learner myself, to my students, and to begin to understand their skills, talents, dreams, and ideas.

From the very first day I began teaching I was driven by a refusal to accept any limitation on what my students could learn. I therefore rejected any prior stigmatization that had been imposed upon them in their school histories. I worked very hard at becoming a good teacher and I loved it. Being with children and contributing to their growth has always been a joy and blessing to me. However, as I began to observe my students open up, I began to see how unhappy and badly treated other students at the school were. I saw overt racism and brutality, as well as more subtle, though equally damaging, institutionalized or rationalized racism and I often got in trouble for confronting it directly.

I had learned from my grandfather, as well as other socialists and labor activists, that the only way to change something was to confront it—intelligently and strategically, but nevertheless without fear of losing a job or being criticized or ostracized. Over the course of my teaching I have been involuntarily transferred out of a school where I was successful; I have been engaged on the side of the community in battles over the control of schools; I have confronted administrators, other teachers, and the union over issues of racism; and at the same time advocated for excellence in public education. It is in the public domain—not home schooling, private schooling, or alternative schooling—where I have located my work. And I have achieved successes beyond my dreams, seen sad and discouraged children emerge as powerful, caring, thoughtful, and skilled adults. I also experienced communities coming together over educational issues, and through attempting to help children, learn to organize and advocate to help themselves as well. I have also been honored to play a modest role in the civil rights movement and a number of anti-war movements, to have been a fellow traveler of movements for social and economic justice wherever they emerge. And perhaps my writing over the past forty years has contributed to developing richer, more effective, and socially responsible education. I hope I have done my grandfather proud.

Finally, I have always advocated that all students should have every opportunity to acquire the basic skills of reading with intelligence and sensitivity; calculating and understanding the role of numbers in their life; engaging in the arts and tutoring the social and personal imagination; learning their own history and developing a critical and analytic knowledge of history and economics; learning the scientific method and understanding the role of experimentation and verification in life as well as in the lab; and becoming part of social action for community development. The consequence of good education, for me, has been the development of the habit of lifelong learning and, on the part of my students, the feeling that they can continue to learn and have something to teach their own and other people's children as well.

I am now seventy-one and living in Point Arena, California. I am teaching a seminar on essay writing. The half dozen members of the class have made personal commitments to writing, and the experience has allowed me to focus, once again, on improving my own work while helping others develop. I'm also working on a number of other projects. One, in conjunction with the Stella Adler Studio of Acting, consists of developing, along with actors and educators, a book that advocates funding for the arts in public schools, and proposes ways to consider the arts as basic skills. Hopefully the book will appear in the context of a campaign to promote public proponents for arts in the schools. This is a way of reminding people of the importance of nurturing the personal and social imagination during a time when schooling is becoming increasingly sterile.

Another project I'm working on is developing a toolbox for progressive educators. It would gather together specific resources for teaching social, economic, and human rights; civic participation and community development; ecological thinking; geopolitical understanding; change, innovation and invention; communication and media (including propaganda analysis); planning and design; and finally, conflict resolution. This is a very ambitious task, involving bringing together specific published resources, games, original documents, teacher created and locally published curriculum material, and visual and computer based materials that deal with subjects not usually included in the curriculum. These subjects have been chosen to help teachers create progressive and critical understanding in their classrooms or small schools. They specifically and unambiguously are meant to help teachers introduce sensitive issues into their work no matter how restricted their latitudes of freedom are becoming with the current obsession with high stakes tests and "teacher-proof" materials. They will also involve soliciting and creating new materials. If I ever get this done they will be what might be called chicken soup for subversive teachers.

I have also been thinking about developing a project that engages teachers, educators, community organizers, academics, and parent advocates in developing the skills of writing for the public. The goal is to create a public voice that advocates for children and teachers who have a democratic vision of teaching and learning. For me, it means advocating for progressive educational ideas (a definition of what this means in the context of twenty-first century education would entail a book, which at times I have thought of writing); Mike Rose and others have been thinking along the same lines. This is still in the talking stage.

There are a few books I have been working on or planning. I'm working on a book, along with Kevin Truitt, former principal of Mission High School in San Francisco, on what we call edutherapy, that is, support for school leaders that is more like dramaturgy than training or evaluation. I have also been thinking about doing a book about basketball, my life, and, more generally about the role sports plays in the psychological and social development of youngsters in our society. In addition, I've been working with my daughter, who is planning to write a biography of me. And I have thought of working locally with junior college students, helping them develop writing skills and think about a viable, economically sustainable, imaginative future.

The most complex and difficult project I imagine undertaking is a philosophic and pedagogical work on learning which would bring together my experience, thoughts, and understanding of how people learn and how teaching fits into all of the different ways of learning that human beings utilize.

All of this is keeping me busy, though I continue to be troubled about how much work needs to be done to create greater justice and equity throughout the world. Fortunately, at this point in my life I have time and ideas. My commitment to social and economic justice is stronger than ever and I hope to continue to be of use over the coming years.

Create the World That Ought To Be

Arnie Langberg

Until the middle of my sophomore year at MIT, when I was notified that I was being placed on academic probation, school had always "worked" for me. Which, of course, was the problem; I had never had to work for school.

Lynbrook High School, on Long Island, was a generally pleasant place and I graduated fourth in my class primarily because of my good memory. If I could stay awake in my social studies class, I could answer all of the test questions at the end of the week because they had been fed to us during the teacher's daily lectures. Actually, it was a bit more complicated than that: the teacher would ask our class questions based on our reading assignments, and as long as I wasn't asked on Monday, another student had to answer them, and I was then ready with the answers later in the week.

Math and science were a bit more challenging, but I was always good at puzzles and enjoyed finding my own way to solve a problem, rather than just feeding back the teacher's answer—which was required in the social studies and English classes. I was generally cooperative, perhaps even compliant, because being good at the school game made the school, and my parents, happy.

In my senior year, the principal called me into his office to discuss plans for my future. Guidance counselors had not yet been invented, or hadn't yet made it out to Lynbrook, so Mike Brennan, the principal, counseled the boys, and Marge Swarthout, the geometry teacher, counseled the girls.

Mike looked at my transcript, saw that my math and science grades were very good, and asked if I had considered a career in engineering. My father was an engineer and we had a family business; it seemed like a good choice. Mike then recommended MIT. I had never of the school, so he showed me a catalog with a beautiful picture of the Charles River on the cover and I agreed to apply.

What I didn't realize at the time was that my grades in all subjects were very good, but Mike had much more respect for the sciences than for the humanities, and overlooked the rest of my transcript. I did enjoy the technical subjects more, but that might have been a reflection of the quality of the teachers Mike had hired in each of the subjects.

Either way, I attended MIT, and tried to adjust to living on my own for the first time, while also keeping up with a required course load that included chemistry, physics, calculus, engineering drawing, humanities, physical education, and ROTC. It was overwhelming, and I felt that I couldn't keep up with everything all of the time. Somehow I scraped by academically the first semester, even managing to find time for intramural sports, but the biggest problem was the food that, as freshman, we were required to pay for. Eventually, I poured a dish of ravioli directly into the toilet, thereby cutting out me, the middle man. The food problem led to one of my first decisions. A student whom I did not know invited me to dinner at his fraternity house. Though I had no interest in the fraternity, the magic word "dinner" attracted me. On my third visit I beat the house champ at ping-pong, and they asked me to become a pledge; because of the food, I accepted.

They asked me to join for the "wrong" reason, I accepted for the "wrong" reason, yet I found something I hadn't known that I was searching for—a sense of community! A group of guys in the class ahead of me truly became my "brothers," and still are to this day. Ken had attended John Dewey's lab school at the University of Chicago,

Tom had gone to a prestigious eastern prep school, and Mark was a Polish-born Holocaust survivor. Their diverse educational and life experiences resonated with tendencies within me of which I had hardly been aware. I was a student at MIT, but my real education happened in the fraternity!

As these new aspects of my life grew in importance, I became even less engaged in the classes. I found one or two professors that inspired me, but began to question my career path. When I actually failed my first class, thermodynamics, and was put on academic probation, I was forced to do some serious soul-searching.

My parents were devastated, but helped me consider my alternatives. I could drop out and work for a while, transfer to a different university, or try to find a way to survive within MIT. I had already made an investment in this third option, both in terms of my parents' financial contributions and my connection to the fraternity, so I met with the head of my department to investigate just what I would have to do to stay.

I had become interested in the humanities, but we discovered that I would only be allowed a maximum of ten such courses to count toward graduation, since MIT did not grant the BA degree. Combined with the minimum number of engineering courses that I needed, it looked like I was going to come up a bit short. My professor and his secretary helped me to identify psychology as an acceptable bridge, with the Institute considering it a technical elective, and my considering it a branch of the humanities. I ended up graduating on time in four years with essentially a triple major!

During my senior year another key moment occurred when I was back in Lynbrook for the Christmas holidays. My old high school science teacher, E. Evans Carr, who was the best teacher I ever had at any level, called. His brother, the head of the science department at a nearby high school, was looking for a chemistry teacher, and Mr. Carr wondered whether I might be interested. I was flattered to know that Mr. Carr even remembered me, let alone considered me a good teaching candidate, but I didn't pursue the position, mostly because I didn't want the responsibility of the chemistry laboratory. His proposition stirred something in me, however, and I began to seriously consider a teaching career.

I stayed at MIT after graduating and worked as a research assistant in the psychology department, on a study of vocational choice. No surprise there! I went back home at Thanksgiving to see if my old high school might have any job possibilities. I discovered that my former geometry teacher was going to become a full-time guidance counselor at the end of the year, and expressed interest in replacing her. Mike Brennan told me he would have to discuss it with the board of education because I didn't have a teaching credential, but I was offered the job to begin in September 1956, with the proviso that I obtain my teaching license within three years. This "alternative" practice had begun as a way of attracting teachers to subject areas with a scarcity of qualified applicants. It also provided me with an exemption from the draft, because mathematics teaching was considered an essential occupation. Lynbrook had changed significantly in the five years I had been away. What had been a small village was now a suburb with a large influx of New York City families who had high aspirations for their children. The school buildings were inadequate to handle the increase in numbers, so our high school had to go on double session; my hours ran from 8:00 am to 12:15 pm and the junior high school took over the building from 12:45 until 5:00.

This combination of high aspirations and limited time was frustrating to the students, their parents, me, and at least one of my colleagues. Dick Powell was a science teacher who had also graduated from Lynbrook and attended MIT, and he, too, had received a call from Mr. Carr. His first year teaching general science was the year before I joined the faculty.

For most of my first teaching year, I was busy keeping up with the curriculum, and fortunately had the assistance of Marge Swarthout's one hundred years of notes. One evening in early April, I decided to call on Dick to express my frustration with our teaching situation. We took a walk and hashed out what might be done. Five hours later we had developed the idea for a "club" that would engage in serious academics after our regular school day.

We discussed particular students whom we believed were equally frustrated by the limitations of our school situation, and decided to invite twenty-one of them from the classes of '58, '59, and '60 to help us flesh out our ideas. We met a few times before the end of the school year to decide what we wanted to do, how we would do it, where and when we could meet, and how to open it up to other students. We told Mike Brennan of our plans, and I believe he thought that it was going to be a sort of science club for gifted kids, so of course he was supportive.

In September 1957, three months before Sputnik, one of the students got on the school's public address system and announced the creation of a new after-school activity that would be academically demanding; applications would be available at an orientation meeting on Friday at the end of the day. We ran off fifty applications, assuming that serious academics and Friday afternoon would limit the number of students, from a school of five hundred, who might be interested. One hundred and twenty showed up—which was quite a statement about the situation—but there was no way that Dick and I could work effectively with that many students. We interviewed each applicant to try to determine who among them was most likely to commit to the concept, and ended up selecting fifty, including the original twenty-one who had helped us put it all together.

From September 1957 until June 1967, Dick and I and groups of students created a stimulating intellectual environment as an extracurricular activity! Participants in Iota Society (a name that Dick and I arrived at on the same day at about the same time, though two hundred miles apart) studied literature and philosophy, sponsored field trips to museums and concerts in New York City, and brought concert artists to perform in the school and our community. This continued even after 1961, when the school was able to get off double session.

There is one other aspect of my Lynbrook years that was very important to my development as an educator. When I originally asked Mike Brennan about teaching, I told him that I would like to teach both math and English, but his response had been, "English teachers are a dime a dozen." A few years later, Mike became superintendent of schools and my old gym coach, Wally Hawthorne, became the new principal. I was in the school office between semesters, when a young female English teacher broke down and screamed at Wally that she couldn't turn her back on "those hoodlums," and that she wouldn't teach that senior English class even one more day!

When she left I told Wally that I would be willing to take on her class as an extra assignment. I knew he cared about those guys (a class of sixteen senior boys, most of whom had never read a book) and wanted to see them graduate. I told him I would guarantee that they would graduate, but wanted no interference in what or how I taught. I was pretty radical for Lynbrook, and a leader of the teachers' union, so I was not Wally's favorite teacher, but I think he respected my ability, and so accepted my offer.

Those sixteen students had even more reason to be upset about my becoming their English teacher. First of all, I was a math teacher, and second, I was part of the Iota group, the smart-ass kids. Third, I had almost come to blows with one of them when I had been serving time as the "warden" of the school lunchroom! (An assignment Wally thankfully relieved me of as compensation for teaching a sixth class.)

From day one I treated them with respect. Of course, I try to treat everyone that way, but that had not been their previous experience. I told them that I would not give them any grades until I had earned their trust, but once that occurred, we could go as far together as they were willing to go, with high school graduation the goal.

Their first assignment was to write a paper telling me as much about themselves as they wanted to share. This was to help me to create a course that responded to their interests, and inevitably, I discovered a whole range of interests and abilities. I responded personally to each, without giving a grade. I did, however, correct their spelling errors, and with their permission, shared their comments with the rest of the group. I told them a lot about myself, too, and together we created a "curriculum."

They already had a sense of group identity—the "dumb" class. I was one of the first teachers who had shared personal details with them, and from then on we had no problem filling the time with discussions based upon their interests or mine. At the end of the week I gave them a spelling test made up only of words they had used incorrectly in their papers. Initially they were angry, but I told them I wouldn't grade the tests, though I did want them to learn how to spell the words they chose to use, and I would continue to test until they got them all right. By the end of the semester they would ask me to give them a test and demand to be given a grade!

After the writing and spelling were resolved, the next challenge was getting them to read. I myself had not been inspired by any of the books

Lynbrook High had imposed upon me, and chose instead a book that a prep school friend had lent me during my freshman year at college, Salinger's *Catcher in the Rye*. A couple of them stayed up all night reading it and their enthusiasm infected the rest of the class. We read four novels that first semester, and over the course of the next years, the number increased and included *King Lear*, Kafka's *Metamorphosis*, Herman Hesse's *Siddhartha* and Camus' *The Stranger*.

With the exception of the spelling test, all of the other exams I gave them were essay-type. Again they reacted angrily, saying that they preferred multiple-choice or true/false testing, despite the fact that they seldom passed any of these. They said that at least these tests were fair, while essays were a matter of opinion and if they differed from the teacher, they would fail. I told them that as long as they could defend their opinion I would never fail them, and my job was to teach them how to write such a defense. It took a quite a few non-graded papers before they developed enough confidence in their abilities, and trust in me, to request a grade on their essays.

As I write this I realize how much more exciting I found the Iota Society and that particular English class than my regular math classes, with their state-imposed curriculum. I thought the difference was the passion of the students, whether they loved the material or hated it, as compared to the math classes, where the work was merely a chore to be done. But apparently it was also my own passion, which surged when I had the power to tailor the curriculum to the interests of the students.

After eleven years, I left Lynbrook because the school system had regressed into mediocrity. The community voted down a bond issue to replace our high school, the oldest operating in the county. As a leader of the Teachers' Association, I met with the school board to suggest that to compensate for the inadequate building, they should offer the best salary schedule in our area. They said that they would be happy to pay me more, but considered most of my colleagues unworthy of such a proposal. Rather than feeling flattered, I was insulted by their condescending attitude, and one particular colleague—my wife Dagnija, whom I met in 1961 when she joined our staff as the French teacher—encouraged me to look elsewhere.

Great Neck offered me a job teaching math because of my reputation as a coach of the Mathletes, an interscholastic competition.

The head of the department wanted to take a sabbatical, but no one in his department wanted to teach calculus, because they were afraid of the high-powered kids and their parents. I moved from lower-middle-class Lynbrook to upper-middle-class Great Neck and into the highest level courses in my field.

I had become comfortable as a fixture at Lynbrook, with students and parents tolerating my eccentricities because they knew my reputation for high quality work. I was worried that I would have to "behave" in my new job, at least until I had established myself. I discovered, though, that most of my students were Iota-caliber academically, and very engaged politically. As I taught calculus, they introduced me to radical approaches to social and political issues, and helped me to rethink my views of the education system. I was challenged to move out of my comfort zone.

The late sixties were an exciting time as a teacher, although most of my colleagues were less enthusiastic about student activism than I. I negotiated a class schedule with my students wherein we would do math at the beginning of the class, and as soon as we had accomplished that, we could devote the rest of the time for discussion of the events of the day, both in school and the larger world. For the most part, the students became more efficient in their use of the "math" time, knowing that we would only move on to the other subjects when they could demonstrate that they really understood the required material.

During these days I became aware of the culture of the school, and it was probably the first time I'd considered school culture to be an important topic. My students told me that my style of teaching created a moral dilemma for them. In a high-pressure environment, where getting into the "right" college was essential, the demands of their other teachers were often overwhelming. Although they enjoyed my classes, they felt that the work for other teachers was getting more of their attention. This was the beginning of a conversation that eventually led to the creation of the Great Neck Village School.

Some important events took place during the three-year incubation period leading up to the opening of the Village School in September 1970. A student Board of Education had been created to give students a voice at the district level, and those students helped to hire a new Director of Secondary Instruction. Tom Sobol, who later became

Commissioner of Education for the State of New York, brought energy, enthusiasm, and sensitivity to the ideals of the students, while being able to operate within the political realities of the system. There was a "Peace Day," when more than half of the students in two high schools created a "curriculum," with speakers and films about the war in Vietnam, which loomed particularly near for those students of draft age. In one of the schools, there was a confrontation about allowing military recruiters without providing draft counseling about alternatives.

In response to a sit-in, one of the schools allowed the students to operate an alternative curriculum called the Free School. Using spare classrooms, the public address system, and the copy machines, classes taught by students, people from the community, and a few teachers were offered. The only requirement was to have a faculty advisor, and the students asked me; acknowledging that I was to be a mere figurehead, I, of course, accepted.

The first semester of the Free School worked very well, but by the second semester the old school culture began to win out. Students couldn't find time to participate in the new curriculum, which they might have preferred, because they had so much work to do to keep up with the demands of the conventional school. Four of the student leaders, realizing the schizophrenic nature of trying to live in both curricula, decided that they would prefer to have their own school. They invited Tom and me to a meeting to tell us that they were going to start a K-12 private school.

We agreed that Great Neck could afford such a school, but neither of us was interested in a private one; we wanted to make these changes in the conventional public schools. The students didn't believe it was possible to work within the system, but Tom convinced them that, from his position within the district, he might be able to help them accomplish it. From February until May of 1970, four students, Tom, Dagnija, and I met three times a week at the school district administration building to develop the plan for what became known as the Great Neck Village School. (As of this writing, the school still exists, thirty-nine years later!)

When the School Board approved the proposal, they provided funding for three teachers and only allowed grades eleven and twelve for the first year—but we were on our way! We decided on a sixteen to one student/teacher ratio, giving us a total of forty-eight slots to fill by lottery, from among the students who would apply from two high schools (two hundred and twenty students actually applied). The founding students sent out letters to all potential candidates and arranged an evening meeting for parents and students to hear a presentation and have their questions answered. I'm probably exaggerating, but I remember seven hundred people showing up!

Tom opened the meeting and then turned it over to the students, who did a great job of describing what would be a totally personalized learning community. They fielded all of the questions expertly until one parent stood up, pointed at me, and asked what I was doing there and what my role was going to be. The students and I had never really discussed this, so I said that I was there was because I had survived adolescence, and was someone whom the students trusted. I was the resident adult! Everyone laughed, but no one disagreed.

There are many stories about my five years at the Village School, including how we found the other two teachers, how we existed without grades, credits, or even a curriculum (in the sense of one-size-fits-all), and how we created an alternative elementary program (short-lived, unfortunately). But there are two stories that are particularly relevant to how I became a visionary educator.

The first occurred halfway through our first year, when the students called a general meeting about me. They accused me of not being the person they thought they had hired, because I was just sitting back and waiting for them, rather than offering any of my own ideas. I replied that I had not wanted my enthusiasm at finally being in a place where I was free from the constraints of a conventional curriculum to run roughshod over their own enthusiasm and interests. They politely told me that they wanted my ideas, as long as I realized that they might accept some and reject others. This was the first of a couple of balances I had to restore for myself.

The second didn't arise until the second year, when two of my advisees came to me to tell me that they were going to transfer back to the regular school because our school was not meeting their needs. A third student presented the same issue in a slightly different way when she told me that she didn't get enough of my time, but saw me giving priority to those students who had previously not been successful in school. She said she understood why I would do that, but that if that was how the school operated, we would eventually lose students like her. Thus, those three students and I spent a couple of weeks trying to redesign the school so that it could better serve, equally, the needs of the highly motivated as well as the academically fragile.

With the help of the rest of the staff and students we created an "honors" program. Each term, at least one course would be offered that would demand dedication to significant amounts of work, at home and in school. If a student was not yet willing to take this on, there would be other options, but the level of expectations would remain high for those who chose to participate. One student, an eleventh grader whose reading comprehension score was at the sixth grade level, took an honors class on revolutions in science because his advisor co-taught it with me. In most other schools, he would have been denied this option, but he worked hard, sought help when he needed it, and the project he chose was to explain to the rest of the class Plato's Allegory of the Cave. His presentation was the most lucid explanation of this work that I have ever heard!

During my fifth year at the Village School, I received a letter from a group of parents and students in Evergreen, Colorado, who were writing a proposal to start an alternative high school as an extension of an existing K-9 alternative school. One of my advisees responded to the group's questions about our school, but my interest was piqued; my wife's family lived in Denver and we spent every other summer out there. Additionally, during that year the Great Neck school system experienced serious political turmoil, and when we received notice that the Colorado folks' proposal had been approved, and they were looking for a principal, my wife and children encouraged me to apply.

I had never aspired to become a principal, and had turned down the offer of head-teacher at the Village School, figuring that a staff of three and a student body of forty-eight did not warrant any hierarchy. Once Tom Sobol left, however, and we no longer had "our man" in district administration, it became clear that there were aspects of operating a school that we were ill-prepared to deal with. I identified three such aspects, which became my rationale for applying for the Evergreen job. The first was the need for a buffer—someone to insulate the staff and students from pressures generated by the district administration and other external political entities. Without such a person, the whole school had to respond each time a new question arose, which interfered with the students' pursuit of their own educational plans.

The second need was for someone inside the program who could resolve a situation in which the community could not reach a consensus. If there were no person within, the decision was made by someone outside, which was especially problematic because the alternative school culture was so different from the rest of the system.

The third was the need for perspective, for keeping in mind the good of the entire community, and for reconnecting to the principles and passion that led to the creation of the program in the first place. Ideally anyone in the school could serve this role, but the principal must do so if no one else steps forward.

My first of two interviews for the position in Colorado was with a large group of students, parents, and a few teachers from the K-9 school. I enjoyed engaging with the students, in particular, and was chosen as one of three finalists. The second interview was with two parents, two students, and two school district administrators, one of whom would become my immediate supervisor.

There are two moments in this interview that are worth sharing. After they finished with their questions, they asked me if I had any questions for them. I had three: I did have a family to support, so what was the salary? Will my children be allowed to attend? And, following the original meaning of the word "principal" as principal teacher, would I be allowed to teach?

I was satisfied with the answers, and they then asked me if I had any other concerns about taking the job. I told them of a friend who had a similar job in New York, and often found herself the radical at the administration building and the conservative in her own building. My soon-to-be "boss" asked me how I intended to deal with this dilemma, and I immediately responded that I hoped to be the radical in both places! They hired me, and I think I was.

There are many stories about what was originally called Mountain Open High School—now part of Jefferson County Open School in Lakewood, Colorado—but I will limit myself to a few.[1]

Once the staff was hired—a process worthy of a chapter all to itself—and they, along with the students, created an initial schedule for the school, I was asked again what my role was going to be. I told them that I thought all decisions could be put into one of two boxes, labeled major and minor. My job as principal was to make all of the minor decisions and only one major, for which I must be held accountable to the entire school community. That major decision, of course, was "in which box should a particular decision be placed?" If I kept a major decision to myself, I would be in violation of the collaborative culture we were trying to create. If I burdened them with minor matters, I would be infringing on their time for their educational pursuits. Even in areas like the budget, where I had legal responsibility, I encouraged students and staff to join me according to this of my leadership style.

I received a memo from the district administration that had three non-negotiable items. Mountain Open had to cost no more per pupil than any other district high school, had to hire according to the same contract, and had to satisfy the same graduation requirements. With over three hundred applicants for the original six staff positions, the contract was not a problem, but it was in response to the other two "demands" that we began to establish just what sort of school we were going to be.

As I read through the budget book for the district, I discovered we were only receiving money based upon the academic portion of our curriculum, while other high schools had funding for athletics and a significant number of extracurricular activities. We had chosen not to offer these, but had many of our own alternatives, with extended trips being an essential part of our program. We were able to convince the district to add $10,000 to our budget, bringing us up to the level of the other schools, and with that bought two vans that enabled us to travel all over North America.

When I read the graduation requirements for what was considered an exemplary school system, I was actually embarrassed. To graduate from a three-year high school in 1975, a student needed three years of English, one year of American history, one year of world history, one year of mathematics *or* science, one year of physical education *or* music, and eight electives. In December of our first year, we held school on a Saturday so that parents and community members could join us in brainstorming our own, more demanding, graduation requirements. A committee of students and staff worked with me for the next couple of months to reduce the nineteen pages of notes from that session to our first set of alternative graduation requirements.

We had three kinds of requirements. For those areas such as reading, writing, and mathematics, we expected demonstrated *competence*. Seat time in the classroom was not the measure, nor was a standardized test; instead, we required performance in authentic situations that would demand these skills.

For physical health and hygiene, and for civics and service, we established the category of *experience*. Here we were interested in developing life-long behaviors leading to physical, mental, emotional, and civic health. As in everything we did, the student's self-evaluation was the central assessment, which had to be supported by teachers, parents, and fellow students. In many cases, members of the larger community also joined in providing support for the students.

The third category we called *exposure*. This included all of the arts, foreign languages and cultures, psychology, economics, and other areas that are important to becoming a well-rounded member of society. We took responsibility for the breadth of their education, opening up subjects that they might otherwise have avoided. Each student had a personal advisor to help her choose how much depth to pursue in each area, based upon her interests, talents, and dreams.

Although Open High has evolved to a different set of graduation requirements, based upon the Walkabout model originally suggested by Maurice Gibbons, I included the details about our original set for two reasons. First, we expected more of our students than the conventional requirements (which was apparently not the case in many other alternative programs), and this helped to convince the school board that our program was worthy of their support.

Second, the conventional grading system was clearly inadequate for evaluating this complex personalized approach to schooling. Packaging the results into credit based upon seat time would have changed our emphasis from the quality of a student's work to an arbitrary measure of quantity. Student portfolios, bolstered by the strong advisory structure, provided richer and more relevant information to both students and parents than a mere collection of A's and B's, or even averages calculated to the third decimal place.

I want to conclude this section with what I regard as my two legacies to the school. The first is a definition of curriculum based upon my own experience and my dissatisfaction with all of the other definitions I encountered in my research:

> Curriculum is that process whereby the school facilitates the integration of a student's experiences, in-school and out, planned and unplanned, into a coherent framework having personal meaning for that student.

Imagine, if you will, building a school that was based upon this definition. In fact, this definition grew out of the school we created! The other legacy is a set of alternative goals I created when I realized how most conventional goals are words on plaques with little connection to the daily lives of students and teachers. I am as proud as I can be when I attend an Open School graduation and hear that the language of the student presentations is still that of the five goals I proposed thirty years ago. Jefferson County Open High School will help every student to be able to:

> Rediscover the joy of learning
> Engage in the search for meaning
> Adapt to the world that is
> Prepare for the world that might be
> Create the world that ought to be

I left Open after eleven years for three reasons. I was concerned that I wasn't being challenged and that things were coming too easily for me. I was also aware that the district saw *me* as the school, rather than really learning about the wonderful things our teachers and students were accomplishing. Most important, though, I was afraid that our school community had become too dependent upon me. I encouraged other long-time staff members to also consider moving on, partly to allow new blood into the school, and partly to export what we had learned to other schools.

During my final year, I was invited by the President of the Denver Classroom Teachers Association to make a presentation about our program. In response to a number of questions about how what we were doing in a small suburban school could apply to large urban schools, I said that I would be willing to work with them immediately if they were serious about wanting to change. A member of the audience, whom I later found out was Jim Scamman, the Denver Superintendent of Schools, stood up and pretended to write me a check. He followed this up with a phone call to determine if *I* were serious, then asked me to make an offer.

Dagnija and I spent the weekend walking through the woods in Evergreen discussing how to respond to such a unique opportunity. The Denver Public School system was just recovering from more than a decade of battles over desegregation, during which time the Federal Court had exercised supervision over the entire operation. Many families who could afford to had abandoned the city schools and escaped to the suburbs. My "offer" to Jim was to spend half of my time creating a laboratory school that would attract people to Denver and reverse the exodus, and the rest of my time helping the principal of a large high school with a predominantly Latino population transform his program into a number of smaller units, each with the chance to create its own subculture.

Shortly before hiring me, the district had undergone an outside evaluation of their existing alternative schools. The findings were summarized in three statements: These are not alternative schools, they are dumping grounds. The teachers are victims as much as the kids. They lack leadership.

At my official job interview, Jim said that although he liked my proposal, he first needed me to fix the problems identified in Gary Phillips' report. He offered me a position created specifically for me, Administrator of Alternative Education, and because I had the support of both labor and management, I accepted.

I was very careful during my tenure in Denver to try to maintain that balance. When I had been hired in Evergreen, in the mountain area of Jefferson County, one of the central administrators said to me, "Do what you want up there, but don't infect the rest of us." The Denver Superintendent asked me to do just the opposite! Within my first months he twice offered me principalship of a conventional high school, but each time I turned him down because I felt I could have more influence from my administrative position. During my six years in DPS, I responded to requests for assistance from principals and teachers in twenty-six different schools.[2]

My second year in Denver I was asked to apply for a grant from the U. S. Department of Labor in order to create a replica of High School Redirection, a school in the black ghetto of Brooklyn. I resisted initially, because dependence on outside funding usually guaranteed the short life span of such programs once the new money dried up. However, in spite of this pattern (which did, unfortunately, hold true), I applied because the program would be required to provide child care for students' children right within the school, and because it would be the first alternative to grant its own diplomas. Although we received an award of $800,000 for three years, the district had to match the money and the board only accepted the grant by a vote of four to three. Forces within the district were concerned about "the integrity of the Denver diploma," and some were convinced that we were encouraging teen pregnancy by providing child care within our building.[3]

During the first year of Redirection, Bill Randall, Colorado Commissioner of Education, stopped by on his way to work to see if he could be of any help. As we chatted, he suggested that perhaps the State Department of Education could adopt our school. I was interested, but told him it might be a bit premature, since we hadn't even completed one semester. But I mentioned the idea to the students and staff, and one year later we invited Bill, and forty of his colleagues, to the school for a lunch prepared by our students—an event that was written up in the Denver newspapers. This developed into a partnership that benefited our students and teachers, as well as the State Department folks, but unfortunately, angered our district administrators who, I believe, regard the Department of Education the way most of us think of the IRS.

Early in our fourth year, I put in a budgetary request for funds to stock our school library, but got no response, even though such funds had been previously approved. This was my first semi-official hint that the district had decided not to commit to our program beyond that year. We did, however, have fifty seniors who were working on their graduation expectations, and it didn't seem fair that they couldn't find the resources they needed within their own school building. Because of our relationship with the State Education Department, I had become friends with Rick Ashton, head of the Denver Public Library, and called him to ask if he would create a branch within my school. I personally guaranteed any losses the library might incur, and it was the best $100 I ever spent!

In 1992, when DPS refused to continue Redirection, I quit but did not go quietly. They tried to close our school in the middle of the senior year of the first graduating class, and blamed it on Children's Hospital across the street. I knew that the hospital coveted our building, but had recently attended one of their board meetings to help create a unique partnership. The hospital had identified thirty teenagers in the area who had serious health problems that prevented them from attending conventional school, but were not serious enough to warrant continual hospitalization. Our students and staff unanimously agreed to invite them to use our cafeteria as their "classroom," and for many members of both student groups it was a life-changing experience.

The President of the Hospital Board telephoned the superintendent to assure her the hospital didn't want our building until the first group of students had completed their senior year. We contacted friends of our school throughout the country and abroad, and asked them to write letters to the Denver School Board in support of our continuation. There was an article in the *New York Times* about us and we appeared on Tom Brokaw's news show. The most ironic part might be that one of our graduates, a black male in a district where the percentage of black male high school graduates was minuscule, read his poetry at his graduation ceremony, which was covered on national television!

Back when the newspapers had covered the adoption of Redirection by the State Education Department, Commissioner Randall received a long letter from a recent immigrant, who wrote that he had finally found something to restore his hope in America. Bret Dofek and I became friends, and we created a program called Education for Moral Courage, based upon his experiences in his native Czechoslovakia. From the age of nineteen, he had spent fifteen years in prison for resisting occupiers, first the Nazis and then the Russians.

We made presentations to educators, met weekly with a fifth grade class in the suburbs, then developed a three-year long project with Harrington Elementary School in inner-city Denver, based upon five virtues that we felt were non-controversial and comprehensive.

These were Caring, Determination, Flexibility, Idealism (which the third-graders renamed "Hope") and Reliability (which they renamed "Trust.") We worked with the teachers and students to integrate these virtues into all of the conventional subjects. Concurrently, two college professors and I offered the principal and teachers a graduate course in school culture so that the precepts addressed in the classroom would be reinforced throughout the school environment. This work was funded by a grant from the Governor's Youth Crime Prevention Initiative, the legislation for which he actually signed at Harrington.

Another project I helped to initiate after my official departure from DPS is the Colorado Harmony Project. The Denver Musicians Association, along with the Langberg Foundation (which my family and I began in 1992), work together to provide professional artists as partners for classroom teachers in under-served schools. In high income neighborhoods, most children are exposed to the arts within their homes, but this is seldom the case for families of lower socio-economic status.

The emphasis on high-stakes standardized testing has reduced the presence of the arts in most schools to almost nothing. Too many schools have become joyless places offering fragmented curricula. The experience of the arts is innately joyful and integrates all aspects of the human being—social, emotional, and intellectual. Harmony helps to restore a balance among these areas, which have been eroded by the pressures of the current political/educational climate.

People still contact me for help with schooling, some wanting advice on how to survive within the system, others seeking assistance in starting new alternatives. In all of these instances I think I provide what my friend Herb Kohl has labeled "Hope Mongering." We have plenty of fear mongers around, but while their alerts are code orange, my glasses continue to be rose-colored!

Notes

1. If you wish to know more about this wonderful school, please get a copy of *Lives of Passion, School of Hope*, written by my friend and colleague Rick Posner. Rick has maintained contact with more than eight hundred alumni, and his book is largely their story.

2. If you are interested in the details of my attempts to deal with this new challenge, especially the challenge of working for the first time with a staff none of

whom I had hired, AERO has a DVD of my keynote speech from 2007 in which I describe it in great detail.

3. You can find the details of Redirection's four years of existence in *Public Schools That Work*, edited by Greg Smith.

The Shoestring School
Mary Leue

The Shoestring School was the title once given to The Albany Free School by a Reichian journal, after publishing an article I wrote about it. I guess it was an appropriate term. How did this odd hybrid come into being? I would have to think back pretty far to be sure. Perhaps that's where it starts.

As I think back, it wasn't my actual schooling that provided the seed from which the school was to grow, but my reading of Louisa May Alcott's stories about her family and the school she dreamed someday to create, but in the end, only wrote about. Still, my own experience in school was favorable enough to have been an incentive.

My schooling was pretty standard for middle-class suburban families, and I enjoyed it very much. I did well, and being a quick learner, went off to a small Ivy League women's college at the age of sixteen. This was much too young for serious learning, but it most surely did not deter me from enjoying the fleshpots of a posh undergraduate lifestyle, even during the depression years of the thirties! After graduation, I enrolled in a graduate nursing program at the Children's Hospital in

Boston, where I lived during the program's three year span, growing up a bit and learning some universally applicable life skills.

Toward the end of my last year in training, I met a fascinating grad student from Harvard who had contracted scarlet fever, and was quarantined at the Children's Hospital. We married, and began having children, first in Brunswick, Maine, where he began as an instructor at Bowdoin College, then in Denton, Texas, where he was an assistant professor at Texas Woman's University. Sending the older three kids to school in Texas taught me how bright, curious children could be transformed into rebels or robots by being forced to attend mediocre schooling. So when I found a job teaching history and Latin at a new private school nearby, I persuaded my husband to allow them to transfer. Watching them develop new skills, enthusiasms, and talents was a reminder of how much difference there was between average and excellent schooling!

After nine years in Denton, a new opportunity for a position at the State University of New York at Albany opened up, so my husband applied and was accepted. Moving back to the crowded Northeast was, in some ways, a shock after the easy-going lifestyle and open spaces of our Texas years. By then, we had five children, and the two youngest were of the age to attend Albany's public schools—which turned out to be both draconian and disastrously routinized by elderly teachers who had long since lost their inspiration! Both children were very unhappy, but at least my daughter Ellen soon moved up to a "laboratory" high school taught by university students who were supervised by master teachers. My son Mark, though, was trapped in the school system from first grade onward.

Both kids then accompanied my husband and me on a year-long Sabbatical at Oxford University in England, where their village schooling was relatively uninspired but reasonably tolerable. Upon our return to Albany in 1970, Mark attended a school whose children came from mostly lower middle-class families. That year turned into a daily nightmare for him, the combination of an overcrowded classroom, an overworked and elderly teacher, and persecution from many of the boys in his class, whose hostility and derision were aroused by Mark's long hair and his friendship with the single black kid in the class.

It was early in the summer that I visited a Unitarian church in nearby Schenectady, whose minister was allegedly a closet hippie—or so I had been told. I guess there was some truth to the allegation, because his sermon was on the subject of a book he had just finished reading: *Summerhill*, by A. S. Neill. The sermon was eloquent and I returned home fired up with inspiration for solving Mark's ongoing issue about his schooling!

The first thing I did was to buy a copy of *Summerhill* and read it from cover to cover. Then, that fall, when it came time for Mark to return to school, he balked, having heard me describing Neill's ways of "doing school" to my husband. Sometime around November he began importuning me to teach him at home, knowing that I had taught school when we were in Texas. I finally persuaded my husband to let him drop out, but when the school learned I had done this, they called the man from the "Bureau of Attendance and Guidance" (i.e., the truant officer) who began an impassioned harangue, warning me of the terrible things that would occur to me should I refuse to bring Mark back at once. I had prepared for this by speaking with a man from the curriculum office of the State Education Department, who had offered to give him "State Guidelines," and I was in luck, because the political "line" there favored "innovation."

The officer called back and apologized for his previous manner, assuring me that what I was doing was fine, and said he would be happy to give me any help he could if I should run into any problems; in fact, he became not only respectful of our operation, but really sympathetic with our purpose when we finally started our little school in the ghetto, since his chief clientele came from the same "population" as ours did, and he knew the problems that could arise.

About two weeks after Mark and I got started on our tutorial venture, I ran into a friend with six children in another of Albany's "finest" public schools. When she heard what I had done, she begged me to take on her three youngest, who, she said, acted as though their lives were on the line every morning when going-to-school time came around, and whom she usually ended up having to accompany there. One of my chief worries had been that Mark would feel isolated from his friends, and this sounded great, so I agreed at once, and we were in the school business!

The year we spent at my home went swimmingly. We all loved

the experience, and since it was the year of the student strikes and the Cambodia crisis, as well as the initiation of Earth Day, it was a very exciting time to be "free" of school. It was exciting for me, too, to be actually conducting my own little "unschool," planning and carrying out my own design of curriculum, which included a lot of projects like picking up twelve trash bags worth of cans, bottles, and other garbage thrown down an embankment by the side of a public road near the house (on Earth Day), helping at a day care center set up for the children of university strikers and others, putting on home-written plays, learning to develop film, making our own movies, cooking and baking, and generally enjoying ourselves a great deal while learning the three R's.

Toward the end of the year, we took a vote and decided to keep on with the school the following year, even though the other three were moving during the summer and we would be back to a population of one. At this point, I decided to ask for advice and arranged for a brainstorming session with Alan Leitman, an educational filmmaker in Newton, Massachusetts, whose films dealt with the development of successful alternative education programs in various places: notably the experiments in Philadelphia associated with the Parkway Program, but on an elementary level.

We met in a resource center for early childhood education, and Alan gave me several suggestions. The first was that I ask a local newspaper to do a feature on our little school, then that I rent a few films depicting the kind of school I was interested in creating and show them in community places, to attract families who would want our kind of school for their kids. He also suggested that I visit a few "free schools" in the New York State and New England regions, to see how they actually look in action. He warned me to start small, to learn my "trade" at each stage of the process, before moving to a larger operation, and in general, to ensure that the enterprise was sound every step of the way; we needed to make sure we really knew our business and were accomplishing what we set out to do, not just playing "kid games." That advice still governs everything we do.

I began that very day, visiting Jonathan Kozol's Roxbury Community School on the way home, and three others over the following few days: one in Buffalo, one in Syracuse, and a third, the Fifteenth Street School, in New York City. A week later, an article appeared in the newspaper that included large pictures of the five of us gathered (untypically) around our round dining room table surrounded by books and papers. It also mentioned that I would be showing three films on "free school" education at the Unitarian Church and at the university, which I did the following week to crowded rooms of fascinated adults whose appetite for information about this new "thing" seemed boundless. Out of these three exposures to the public, I found a group of four families interested in sending us their children and in working as a group to help us find a suitable building and at least one other teacher for the seven kids who would be involved.

Suddenly, providentially and wholly unexpectedly, a young high school teacher named Bruce, who was also a friend of my older sons, gave me a call and asked if he could drop over to chat. Puzzled, I agreed, and lo, what he wanted to talk about was his wish to quit high school teaching (where his best friend had been recently fired for refusing to shave off his beard) and come to teach with me at our fledgling school, now christened "The Free School" by my four students. I agreed enthusiastically, and introduced him to our little group of parents at the next strategy meeting. They were equally delighted.

By this time, June was over and our school was out for the summer. One other mother and I set out in earnest to find a building where we could hold forth, and right away, the first snags began to appear. There were no buildings to be had that we could afford that would give us what I knew to be an absolute necessity in a school site—one large room for gatherings, roughhouse, and general togetherness; plus enough additional space for activity rooms, eating, and a lab; at least one good bathroom; an office; a good-sized kitchen; and play space outside. We literally searched for weeks, surveying the entire region. We began desperately asking churches for space in their Sunday School quarters, were refused by at least three church boards, and suddenly, just as the end of summer was nearing, were offered the rental of an entire church building for $100 a month by a black minister whose congregation had bought a fine stone church across town and were moving out. This was a frame building in a state of great neglect but essential soundness, and we grabbed for it frantically and with great relief. We had yet to even begin to prepare the space for the school, and after a hasty consultation with our parent group, and with the reality of our financial straits before our faces, we all agreed on this building in the inner city. The price was right, the size was ideal, and our appetite for renovation was boundless, none of us having done any!

Immediately, we all set out to put it into usable shape. Working virtually around the clock, sharing coffee and sandwiches far into the night, we worked to cover up the grime with new paint, even going so far as to paint floor-to-ceiling blackboards in several rooms, scrubbing whatever we could not paint, attaching as a fire escape an iron staircase we found at a wrecking company to an upstairs door which had opened onto thin air, for a reason none of us ever fathomed. By the time school started, we had already grown to love this place, funky as it was, but indisputably ours!

One event that had charmed and excited me, but which proved a harbinger of trouble to come, was the fact that, no sooner had we opened our doors (to let in fresh air as well as to bring in ladders and so on) than hordes of curious black children began coming inside, asking us a zillion questions and begging to be allowed to stay and color or play school. These ranged from the ages of three and four up to twelve at least, all from southern black refugee families who had come seeking work in this northern city, and all wanted to know, "What dis place?" When they learned that we were a school ("A school? You a school? Yo' kids goin' play heah?), asked us, "Kin ah come?"

We began having dreams of attracting a whole schoolful of neighborhood kids as students. Our universal answer to their questions was, "Go ask your momma, and if she says you can, you tell her to come and talk with us and then you can come here, OK?" The older ones would ask, "Do it cost money?" and my instinct was always to say, "No, it's free." My hunger for the children was always greater than my financial sense, and I guess I haven't yet changed that. Fortunately for me, Bruce felt the same way about the children as I did, so at least at this point, there was no trouble. But it was coming.

Our first serious conflict was between Dorothea, the wife of a university professor who happened to be black, and two boys whose father had been the black caretaker of the church, and now of the school. This middle-class black woman had strong feelings about the violence of black children from the ghetto—and her son was timid!

Within the space of fifteen minutes after she had tossed both boys downstairs for intimidating her son, we had a virtual lynching mob of angry relatives of these two boys at the door of the school, brandishing iron pipes and other weapons, and bent on redress! We managed to downplay the conflict, but it was a foretaste of what was to come out of our naive and explosive effort to conduct a free school for middle-class people (among others) in the midst of a totally neglected and furiously angry welfare proletariat (I cannot think of any other term that so aptly fits the characteristics of this group).

The school year got underway in early September, initially with eleven kids, all middle-class. Bruce and I found we could work together very well indeed, and our parents seemed happy with the new experiment. We met weekly to discuss funding and other considerations, and seemed to get on very well together. One day late in the month a charming young woman, Kathy, appeared at our door and asked if she could teach with us, having just graduated from an Ohio school of education. Of course, we agreed enthusiastically, and the children all fell in love with her.

Our only problem was finding enough money to pay salaries, rent, phone and utilities. We came up with all sorts of strategies for raising this money, and participated enthusiastically in doing so. We had bake sales, rummage sales, garage sales, and candy sales, all good middle-class strategies our parents could throw themselves into enthusiastically. None of them raised much money, but they were a lot of fun. Soon three other families joined us, and we really felt we had a nice little school going. Gordon, the younger of the black boys whom Dorothea had pushed downstairs, asked to become a member of the school, and we all agreed amicably—even Dorothea and her husband. Things seemed to be going amazingly well.

Then two things happened, sometime in December or early January. Two new families brought us their children. These new families proved a problem far greater than their children. One father, Lamont, an assistant professor of psychology from the university, newly married to a young widow with three children, the oldest of which was our student, was determined to assert his parental authority—with this boy in particular. It was clear that he believed that Denny had been spoiled by his mother. He had considerable skepticism about the nature of our school to begin with, and as his PhD thesis was on the subject of non-violence and we were located in the ghetto, Lamont was prone to seeing violence everywhere.

We had developed a school policy of encouraging children to work out their own solutions to interpersonal problems via a council meeting system of self-governance, as well as by other problem-solving devices, which did not necessarily prevent violence, but taught them how to handle problems that, left unsolved, would have led to violence. Lamont's interventions, or efforts to intervene, in the governance of our school struck us as authoritarian in impact, as our policies struck him, evidently, as anarchical.

Parent meetings began to acquire the characteristics of a battleground, with factions lining up pro and con school personnel and policies, but mostly con. It was an uncomfortable time, and its effect on the school was to cause those of us who were actually at school from day to day to decide to adopt a policy of permitting only those who were actually involved in being there to make rules as to how we could or should do things. Any parent who chose to be there would automatically be a part of that decision-making process, but other parents could only request, advise or suggest, but not demand or direct. It was our first real move toward absolute internal autonomy, and is still in effect. I still believe it is the only possible way we could have managed things in such a way as to make them work, but the cost in loss of families was great at the time. All but four of them withdrew their kids at the end of the school year.

But this division was only the beginning of our troubles! The other new family was a divorced wife and her son Bobby. Susannah was living with a black militant, still a big no-no in our society, at least for middle-class families—and even now, I believe, grounds for loss of custody of a woman's child with some family court judges. We got caught in the midst of the custody battle for control of where Bobby would live and go to school. His father, a pathologist at the local medical school, had as his lawyer a former city court judge who elected to focus on our school as the second grounds for his client's custody of Bobby; the first, of course, was his client's ex-wife's current partner.

The first thing we knew about this was when we were visited, in rapid succession, by an attorney from the office of corporation counsel for the city, the chief of the fire department, an official from the building department, and a man from the county health department. One after another, these officials told us that we would be summarily shut down, some saying unless we complied with their requirements, others saying just shut down, period. I must admit, we felt pretty alarmed, so we called an emergency meeting of parents, and began frantically trying to find out what, if anything, we could do to meet the situation.

Then the children got into the act. I guess that was my fault. I had felt badly crowded by the threat and had decided to bring out our big guns. I told the kids what was going on, in pretty colorful terms—and they decided to set up a picket line outside the school protesting the unfairness of the city. Then I called in the media. The signs made by the kids were most eloquent, and the photographers had a "human interest" field day—for which, read "fair game for taking pot-shots at the city government"—especially at our perennial mayor! Reporters and picture-takers from both newspapers and all three TV channels swarmed, and we were a short-term sensation for the silly season.

But ... we weren't closed down. We made some changes, did some housekeeping, and let a lot of people know that we took their comments seriously. Gradually, the heat subsided. I made an appointment to talk with the mayor. He was very understanding, but made it very clear how much he deplored my having used the weapon of publicity. I was very apologetic and contrite. It was a real father-daughter scene. I think he was quite relieved to have us off his back.

So ended our first exciting year of the "official" school. Toward the end of the school year we had finally received our tax-exempt status from Internal Revenue, and since this had been reputed to be an extremely difficult feat to accomplish—and I had done it without legal representation or even setting up a corporation—I felt elated. Our funding problem was still an acute one, and I believed that having tax-exempt status would encourage people to donate money to us. Along with the same mother who had helped me to find our building, I now took on the task of seeking out a grant or grants to help us solve this problem. She and her husband wrote out a series of eloquent grant proposals and sent them to several corporations reputed to have given money to other schools like ours. We got back a sheaf of polite and encouraging "no's."

It was also very clear to all of us by now that our present building would not be suitable for occupancy the following year, so we set out to find a replacement. Quite early in the summer we located an ideal one—a large row house in the old Italian section of the south end, owned by Italian Catholic war vets, which had been first a German church, and later an Italian language parochial school. My first attempt to raise enough money for a mortgage was to write a small grant proposal to three local millionaires who had expressed an interest in families living in the inner city.

I was inspired to do this because I had met two of them personally, and had heard from our teacher Kathy that the third had a reputation for benevolence; he was a friend of her father's and owned an electrical contracting firm that occasionally hired ghetto black adolescents. Alas, we had only begun to learn that, like poor black parents themselves, most prosperous middle-class people are exacting in judging the potential usefulness of a school in money and status terms, and so, shunned ours.

Having been refused by all three of them, we had to look elsewhere for the money we needed. Actually, the neighborhood provided us the solution to our financial problem. What was going on was a violent and destructive process among two groups, one a long-term, stable, and largely elderly Italian population, some first generation, most second generation, who had lived and raised their families in row houses they owned and kept up—and the other, an ever-increasing number of black welfare recipient tenants living in the row house apartments that had been sold to absentee landlords when their Italian owners grew prosperous and moved to the suburbs, leaving behind only the poor and the elderly.

These black families, mostly single-parent, had many children who were growing up largely unsocialized and unsupervised amid squalid neglect and despair as their mothers struggled to survive. In many cases, these mothers moved from decaying building to decaying building, attempting to raise children with no parent support whatsoever; often, they struggled with hostile and contemptuous welfare and clinic personnel, and justified the existence of their children by defending their behavior against all comers, no matter how dysfunctional that behavior might be. In other words, this was an armed camp, and battle lines were clearly drawn.

The advantage to us in this unfortunate, even tragic, situation was that the Catholic War Veterans as a group were determined to sell their building, even at considerable sacrifice, just so long as they could turn their backs on this neighborhood. We got a very good bargain. I also managed to find a sympathetic mortgage officer willing to take a risk with us, and the school was able to move out of the storefront we had been using for three months into our new building before the end of November. Almost immediately, we began attracting new families, a process which was enhanced by the fact that we asked the newspapers to run a feature on us, which they did.

Life in our new neighborhood proved to be at least as exciting as it had been in the old one. The black children living within a block of us began begging to come inside, even beating on the door to be let in (we still have the cracks in our door panels to show for it!). Middle-class white mothers shrank back from the assaults of these black children in terror, and a couple even took their darling little blonde girls out of the school, claiming that it was too chaotic for them, that their children needed more "structure." When we sent the neighborhood children home for permission to attend our school, most were refused. The word seemed to have gotten around the neighborhood that we were not a "real school."

So we decided to start a pre-school that they would recognize as "real," because it would be relevant to their need to find a cheap, reliable, and friendly place to leave their small children while they went to work. This we could do. Soon, we had a group of around eight three- and four-year-olds, mostly black neighborhood, with two mothers in charge. This took place on the second floor of our building, which really was ideally suited for the purpose.

But we still had our financial problem. It was quite clear that we could not expect to survive indefinitely paying teachers nothing, yet we were equally determined not to become a high tuition school. At this point, I thought of Jonathan Kozol's suggestion for solving this problem in his book *Free Schools*: run a business. There was a three-story house for sale on the next street over, owned by an Italian family disgusted with the deterioration of the neighborhood and well enough off to buy elsewhere. I bargained, and we got it. Now I had to get a tax exemption from the city for this building. I went about gathering information on the hows and whos of setting up a non-profit corporation, and finally managed to get it accepted by the state. Non-profit status by the city was more difficult, but I finally managed that, too, thanks to a sympathetic attorney from the city's Office of Corporation Counsel. We also began attracting families who wanted an apartment to live in, and who decided to let their children attend our school, usually because they found us friendly people to deal with in a very unfriendly world.

Over time we acquired several old buildings on the two parallel streets, most of them abandoned by their slum landlords, and so available from the county by public auction for ridiculously low prices. In the process of rehabilitating these buildings for occupancy, we acquired a lot of skills—plumbing, wiring, sheet-rocking, carpentry, glazing, floor sanding, plastering, masonry, roofing, and so on. We found our rehabilitation skills very popular indeed among these new families, and began gathering to help one another in weekend "work parties," at which as many as twenty of us would pool our efforts on one place, accomplishing rapid and low-cost miracles of building rescue and refurbishment. School families from farther away became attracted to this village atmosphere and began moving closer, either by finding a nearby rental apartment or by actually buying up an old or abandoned building.

More and more, our streets became after-school and summertime "play streets," with the few remaining Italian people serving gladly as built-in stoop supervisors of their activities. Since most of our buildings were located on parallel streets, their back yards touched. When we had acquired them, these yards were filled with rubble, so we began clearing them out, planting gardens, and using them for socializing. Our properties had begun taking on more and more of the characteristics of a village, as we enjoyed our barbecues, birthday and holiday celebrations, and generally spending more time together.

Our challenge was always to become fully relevant to the families of the neighborhood who had only the public schools of the ghetto as an alternative to us, not just or primarily to the families of the children we had begun busing in from other parts of the city. The goals of these parents all too often clashed head-on with those of their children! The parents wanted evidence of academic success. The kids wanted justice and fair dealing among themselves. We found ourselves spending far more time teaching kids to deal justly with personal conflicts of all sorts than with the three R's, although our arts and crafts program was always excellent. We understood how educationally relevant this effort at the learning of self-government was, but on the other hand, we did not want to lose kids, and parents had begun letting us know how dissatisfied they were with this emphasis.

Since we actually agreed, it was a struggle, because the kids' natural priorities were perfectly valid in their own terms, and had to be respected—and yet, we needed to teach skills as well, especially with such a potentially explosive mix of children from suburban and ghetto families! Our council meetings at this time sometimes took several hours out of the day. My approach to this issue included a strong belief that teachers themselves need to be very clear and straight in their thinking and stable in their emotions in order to deal with the demands made upon them by kids with great needs, and yet we could not afford to hire therapeutically trained teachers, nor did we wish to, believing that both children and teachers should be free to make the choice to be in the school!

It wasn't easy for any of us. One teacher, pressed too hard by a very provocative black boy of around eight years old, suddenly "broke," picked him up and slammed him onto the floor in great fury! Fortunately, the child was not hurt. Yes, there had been provocation, but such a reaction was intolerable—to the teacher as well as to everyone else. We set up a personal growth group that met every week for three to four hours, at which time teachers and others who wished to join could work through their hang-ups. Teachers who had come to teach with us as a novelty began seriously settling down and investing themselves in a more permanent and more monogamous pattern of living. The new group became a kind of center for this new village that was coming into being, serving both to create a common ground of interest and to offer interpersonal support for dealing with the strains of getting through the hang-ups that divide people.

By 1978, so many young couples who were connected with us in one way or another were getting pregnant and coming up against the up-tightness and cost of obstetrical care that we decided to organize a pregnancy and childbirth support group. From this beginning, we moved on to the setting up of a center in the basement of one of our buildings, which offered medical and legal self-help education at no or very low cost to anyone who wanted to use us. We named it The Family Life Center. One of our reasons for doing this was certainly a need to solve the problem of the high cost of medical insurance for our school people, but the interesting thing was the fact that the more we worked with families to help them get what they wanted, the more we realized how revolutionary our concept was, and how much of a logical extension of the concept of a school that belongs to the families who use it.

Other agencies we thought up were what we called the Money Game, a mutual investment group that enabled people with low incomes to invest in bank savings plans usually available only to people with surplus capital; Matrix, a birthing center for which we found medical backup among doctors who favored midwife-managed birth; and Rainbow Camp, an old lodge on a small lake in the mountains near Albany where city-bound children could learn self-sufficiency and familiarity with nature.

I officially retired from any real connection with the school in 1998, and gave myself a treat by taking on an offer from a German airline to fly around the world, stopping off several times to spend as much time as I chose in between flights with families in several countries! Leaving the school community was a huge change for me, and it took me more than a year to shift gears!

At the age of ninety, I live in an old farmhouse in the hills of western Massachusetts on land I inherited from my mother and her best friend, which they had acquired in 1908, before my mother married, and where they ran a summer camp for working girls from the mills of Boston until 1917, when the U.S. entered the First World War. The land extends some distance along the road, as well as deep into the woods, and also includes a parcel of timbered land across the road that extends up the mountain. Two of my five families live on the land in houses they have built, and we have developed a Family Land Trust for sharing the land. We farm extensively, raising a lot of vegetables and fruit, keeping chickens, and sugaring in the spring.

I also manage a small desktop publishing business and maintain three websites. I miss being at the school, but they really didn't need me any more, as the school carries on successfully with its present staff! This fact is a source of real pride for me, especially since so many free schools didn't survive beyond the 70s.

T.G.I.F.
Dennis Littky

Are you playing the game or really learning?

In seventh grade, I realized school was a game that I could play successfully. I also realized that there were students in my class who weren't into playing the game, but were interested in learning. In social studies, we got credit for doing extra reports. My dad worked next to an AAA office and brought home books on each state for me. I would copy a few paragraphs, draw a beautiful cover, and turn it in. An A, every time. In science, the teacher asked us to do a big yearly project, a poster describing how something works. Once again, my artistic and copying abilities came in handy. I got A's in science for the prettiest posters—all copied out of books. I still knew I was playing school, and somehow I also knew that I wasn't really learning, but I was too busy with the game to figure out what to do about it.

High school and college felt the same. I had to work too hard to keep up with the game to even think about learning. I saw people caring about learning around me, but their care and intellectual exploration didn't always seem to translate into good grades. I spent my time acquiring my A's and B's, and got into the University of Michigan. I thought things would be different there, but I continued to feel that I needed to study hard just to get by (as well as join a fraternity, play intramural sports, and meet new co-eds). All through the year, I didn't really think or comprehend. I just read and took notes. I was doing what I believed a college student was supposed to do. If you watched me, you would say I was a good student. On Friday afternoons, my fraternity would invite a sorority over for a frat house TGIF party. After a few hours, I would actually take my books (all of them) and go to the library. I went through the motions, but didn't learn a thing on those grim Friday nights.

I remember an English class where I read *Heart of Darkness* six times to try to understand it well enough to pass the test. I passed with an A. A friend, fascinated with Joseph Conrad, read other books to follow his passion rather than studying for the test. He got a D on the test, but I knew he was the real learner. While studying for finals, I'd get glimpses of my own real learning from time to time—my mind would finally start to sort out and reassemble the bits and pieces of learning I was throwing at it. But mostly, I just moved on to the next exam, the next paper, the next task at hand—and the results weren't always the A's of high school. I was still playing the game, but no longer getting the prize.

Do you think you can do a better job? What happens when you try?

As a junior, I took a psychology course where we spent a day at a state mental hospital. I was truly engaged. I was fascinated. I was good at working with the patients. I found that I loved to read about schizophrenia and the mentally ill. You couldn't stop me. As my mind turned on, my grades improved, and I became a real learner, finally.

I entered graduate school at the University of Michigan, studying psychology, and started teaching an undergraduate psychology course. Those who signed up for my class received a room number, the time and days of the week the class would meet, but no instructor's name. I arrived to the first class wearing chinos, boots, and a crewneck sweater and sat in the back of the room chatting nervously with the students, many of whom were experiencing their first college class. I was clean-shaven, with neatly trimmed hair, and a consummately boyish appearance; I looked as much a freshman as the real ones sitting around me. In walked a handsome, stern-faced man with a close-cropped beard, wearing a dark blue three-piece suit and carrying a briefcase and an armload of books. The class quieted down. Without smiling, the man turned to the board and wrote his name, Mr. Wolfe.

"Class," Mr. Wolfe barked, "There will be surprise quizzes in this course—a lot of them. The only one you'll know about will be tomorrow."

I raised my hand. "Mr. Wolfe, now that we are in college, do we still need surprise quizzes?" Mr. Wolfe set his jaw. "I work on a bell-shaped curve. The same number will get A's as fail in this course and most of you will earn grades somewhere in between. That's the law in this class."

I raised my hand.

"Is this important, young man?"

"Don't you think it's kind of discouraging to know that a set number of us will fail regardless of how hard we try?"

"That's life."

"What if we all work hard, do well, and deserve A's?"

"A bell-shaped curve doesn't work that way."

"I know, that's exactly my complaint."

By now, students turned in their seats, stunned by the aggressive fellow in the back of the room. Mr. Wolfe continued his labored description of the course. My hand shot up.

"What is it this time?" Mr. Wolfe snapped.

"I thought this course was supposed to get us out into the world and actually work with mental patients."

Mr. Wolfe slammed his books on the desk, packed his briefcase, and turned on his heel. "Young man, if you think you can do a better job, then get up here." He stormed out of the room.

"I'm gettin' out of this class," one student said, and got up to leave. Others followed his lead.

"Hang on one second," I said. "Wasn't I speaking for all of you?"

"Yeah, I guess you were," a thin, bespectacled freshman said.

"That teacher seems real unfair," another student said.

The discussion continued. Finally, I stood up, walked to the front of the room, smiling this time.

"Hi, I'm Dennis Littky, your teacher."

The students applauded.

The first unit of the class was aimed at looking at the way people learn. My antics confronted those issues head-on, engaging the students, getting them involved in the class, and giving them a flash of real learning.

What have you learned from the leaders you've worked with?

I hurried through graduate school studies in education and psychology, excited about my work as a teacher and therapist with autistic students, as well as my work in the back wards of mental hospitals. I took the non-traditional route and became a community organizer and project director in Ocean Hill Brownsville, an experimental decentralized school district in Brooklyn with about 9,000 students. Thrown into a project in which students were learning to read through programmed instruction, I realized that the students could do the reading workbooks, but didn't know how to read. They were playing the game.

Ocean Hill Brownsville made me politically aware. The chief administrator, Rhody McCoy, was a real inspiration. Rhody worked every minute. To see him, I would come in at 5:00 a.m. He was not afraid to die for his cause. Just think of how that frees you. Getting fired is nothing. There is nothing to be afraid of, nothing to control your decisions, except what you think is right. The horrible, protracted 1968 New York teacher strike happened because Rhody transferred six teachers out of his district. The union closed the schools, and the national media described the strike that resulted as the "Black vs. Jew Confrontation of Ocean Hill Brownsville."

Rhody felt that standardized tests did not show what young African American children could really do. He had his staff fill in every correct bubble on the students' answer sheets and sent them to the New York City Board of Education. Every student scored 100 percent on this "disrespected test." Rhody then asked me and a colleague to create reading and math tests that were diagnostic and that the school's paraprofessionals could give to the students one at a time. We created the tests, trained the paraprofessionals, administered the tests one by one, and had baseline scores for each student. We gave these same tests at the end of the year, providing teachers, students, and parents real evidence of whether and how each student had improved.

I finished my thesis while working in New York. In addition to my research on work in the classroom, I wrote about the politics in getting things done in an urban school district, using my work as a case study. New York City closed down the district as a way to get Rhody McCoy out, and my work there ended.

What does a school created for real learning look like?

Long Island's Stony Brook University hired me to run an experimental teacher training program for the Dean of Education. Because you can't train teachers who spend most of their time sitting in a university classroom, I started placing juniors in the schools for a year before student teaching. But many of the classroom teachers were not very good—thus their classrooms were not great places to train teachers to be innovative. So, I started to train the school's teachers at the same time, giving them university credit for their training.

We prepared to start a paperback reading program. Everyone was excited. Then an announcement came over the P.A. system: "Starting Monday at 10:10 a.m., everyone will start a new basal reading series." At that point, I knew I needed to be in the position to decide on curriculum, programs, and structures. Change had to happen from the inside. In 1972, the job opened up for the principal at the Shoreham-Wading River Middle School, a new school in one of the districts where I worked, so I applied. Although I had a Ph.D. in Psychology and Education, I didn't have principal certification. Somehow I got hired. Three years after earning my doctorates, I went back to school to get my principal certification and a master's degree.

I had the chance to put all my thoughts, ideas, and readings into practice—this was exciting. I hired twenty-two teachers, searching the country for passionate, smart people who wanted to be school-starting pioneers. Everything I learned came together in practice during the first two weeks of workshops as we prepared for the start of school. It felt like I was using my potential to the fullest. I recently found an old journal, one among many that teachers wrote and shared with me weekly. Summing up what I then believed would work and now absolutely know works, the teacher wrote:

...the week-long workshop began on Monday morning the 26th at

7:00 a.m. with twenty-two people grouped around a large table in the cluster. The nervousness expressed in smiles and chatter was predictable. Dennis quieted us down and started telling/sharing his vision of a school for kids. He touched upon several points: "A school for kids—they should take a more important role in making decisions—kids should work with us—kids ought to know more about the education process—the arts—usually seen as specials—should be integrated—kids as consumers vs. producers—we want producers—kids traditionally consume; give them real roles and let them produce—flexibility." He spoke of advisory groups that each of us will have, with fifteen kids in a group. It will be like a homeroom but the function will be counseling, advising, keeping tabs on those kids (and their parents), creating at least one stable and permanent non-choice fixture as a constant throughout the year. Dennis also spoke of the importance of involving the community as part of the school.

The politics started in the community. We were all young. I was twenty-seven, the youngest principal in the state of New York. A conservative faction in the community tried to fire me. They put pressure on the school board, which decided to have a community hearing. I was not willing to die for the cause, like Rhody, but I was willing to fight. Because I hadn't finished my certification, this community group said I was unqualified. I told the board to change my title if they wished, but I wasn't going to be forced out. I remember saying I would work as the custodian, but I was not leaving. I then became the "instructional leader," instead of principal. We kept strong, and the opposition folded. Six years later, after we had developed an incredible school (written about in Joan Lipsitz's *Successful Schools for Young Adolescents*), the original opponents were the most positive supporters.

We developed one of the first advisory systems in the country at Shoreham-Wading River Middle School. We broke the six hundred students into three small schools. We had internships and interdisciplinary curriculum. We helped the students start real businesses. We had intense parent and family involvement through neighborhood teams. This work set the stage for the next four decades, both for the school and for the work I would go on to do.

I had spent ten years as an educator, somehow working eighty-hour weeks that didn't feel like work. This was what I enjoyed doing the most. I didn't feel burnt out. My long hours felt very successful. Most evenings, including Fridays, the staff ordered pizza and stayed late, working together. Even so, working like that made me realize that I needed to develop other parts of myself. I realized I had only two speeds: hard working or not working. So I left when the school was strong, the teachers tenured, and my assistant principal ready to take over.

How fiercely are you willing to fight for what you believe in?

I headed to a cabin I had bought in the woods of New Hampshire—no water, no electricity, on the side of a mountain looking out into Vermont, New Hampshire, and Massachusetts. I spent three years there, using up my savings. I cut wood for heat, learned to rebuild a cabin, became a state legislator, started a town newspaper, and traveled. Because most of my time was needed to winterize the cabin and keep wood cut, to keep warm, things were done on my schedule with a much slower rhythm.

As my bank account ran down, it was time to return to work. During that time, I was still always trying to make change by organizing a community and passing laws. I had developed a commitment to the small, poor town of Winchester, New Hampshire, where the junior/senior high school had become the laughing stock of the state. The principal was leaving, so I decided to give it a shot...and got it. I would be the principal of Thayer Junior/Senior High School.

The staff members were already in place, many set in their ways. When they looked at me, they thought and said, "He'll be gone soon." This battle to gain trust and turn around an unsuccessful school culture was exciting, and different from my previous experiences. Over the years, we decreased the dropout rate from 50 to 2 percent, and increased college attendance from 10 to 55 percent. We had developed a national reputation as an outstanding small school. In 1984, Thayer was selected as the first school in Ted Sizer's Coalition of Essential Schools, a movement based on Ted's book *Horace's Compromise* to make schools places where real learning happened. We were already doing so much of what Ted argued for—we had strong advisories, a powerful internship program, an integrated hands-on curriculum, and a set of nineteen skills in which the students needed to demonstrate proficiency to graduate. It didn't matter if they learned these skills in classes, internships, or out of school. Thayer had so many visitors that we decided to start a monthly TV show that trained teachers around the country on our work.

Then, six years in, the school board changed and the new one decided to fire me. We won the two year battle. There was a town vote, and after a tie and a new election with special New Hampshire state guards, our candidate won—and the board reversed the firing decision. Simultaneously, the state Supreme Court also supported my rehiring. The story made national news: we were in *Newsweek* in 1984, Susan Kammeraad-Campbell wrote the book *Doc: The Story of Dennis Littky and His Fight for a Better School*, and NBC made the movie *A Town Torn Apart*.

What are the actions you can take to create new ways of making real learning happen for young people? What are you doing to prepare to make that happen?

After winning the battle, I stayed on for another six years, using the Winchester vote of confidence to heal the community. In the meantime, I kept talking with Ted Sizer, who wanted me to come to Brown University's Annenberg Institute for School Reform to spread the word about the Coalition of Essential Schools' work. I was looking forward to a year off to travel, explore, and have a different life before jumping back in. Ted wanted me immediately, so we compromised. I traveled to Fiji, New Zealand, Australia, Bali, Vietnam, and Thailand, spending a month in each place. My only hotel reservation was for the first night in Fiji, and that was paid for with a couple of bottles of Jack Daniels I'd bought from the airport duty-free store.

In January 1995, I started at Brown, and it soon became clear that the university was not for me. I felt that the best way to influence the system was to work in schools, and have students, teachers, and the community speak for themselves about the results. The Rhode Island state Commissioner of Education, Peter McWalters, talked to Elliot Washor and me about designing a new career and technical state high school. Elliot and I had worked together at Thayer. We went way back—he had been my student at Stony Brook.

We said yes, and boldly asked if we could create the school in a completely new way. We'd dreamt of and prepared for this day for a long time—we were ready. Peter agreed, fortunately, and the ride began. We set up a non-profit organization, The Big Picture Company, to do the work. We quickly raised a million dollars, hired a staff, and began designing the Metropolitan Career and Technical Center, better known as the Met.

At fifty years old I didn't think I would be running another school. Yet here I was, so I might as well use it as an opportunity to put together all my thoughts and try not to compromise. How often do you get a chance to start a new school from scratch, with money to build a brand new facility? Elliot and I closed our eyes and dreamt about what education would look like if we didn't know there was such a thing as school. We truly started from scratch and asked ourselves, "What's best for kids?" We wanted our low-income students to get strong enough to be able to stand on their own. We wanted them to love learning and want to keep learning. We told Commissioner McWalters that we would develop a school that depended on students using their hands and minds, while working with experts in the community, and with strong and sustained family involvement. We would help students do real work around their passions. We wanted engagement. We wanted students to get into a "flow" with their work. There was no reason or justification for classes where twenty-five students are being taught the same thing in the same way. We wanted exhibitions—showings of students' work with detailed written evaluations, not grades.

People tried to stop us. The state legislation tried to take away the $400,000 we had to start the school. The first vote nearly came down to a fistfight between the leader of the Black caucus and a legislator. With plenty of support, including from our "angel," local heavy-hitter Stanley Goldstein, founder of CVS Pharmacy, who provided financial help and political cover, we won. The Met started with fifty students, and we have not turned back.

Everyone laughed. No grades, no tests, no classes? But at our first graduation in 2000, all of our students were accepted to college. The Met had a 97 percent attendance rate (compared to 77 percent citywide in Providence) and a 2 percent drop-out rate (compared to the city's 41 percent). People began to take note. Tom Vander Ark, director of Education for the Bill & Melinda Gates Foundation, came to visit. He sat with Elliot and me and said he wanted to talk with the students. Into the luncheon he went, and Elliot and I sat wondering what he would think. An hour later, Tom came out smiling. Elliot and I shortly had five million dollars to scale the model to twelve schools. Then three years later, Gates gave us another fifteen million dollars.

In 2009, we have sixty-six schools in the U.S., nineteen in the Netherlands, and five in Australia, and we're still growing. I am proudest of the fact that we did this in a tough time educationally. We never wavered. We stayed strong to our philosophy even if it was often in conflict with state standards and No Child Left Behind.

We had a great reputation as school-starters, but Elliot and I wanted more. We wanted to influence and innovate. We were never just about schools. We always wanted as many students as possible in our country to have a great education. The state of Rhode Island built its state high school guidelines around The Met. Now every high school in Rhode Island needs to have advisories, internships, and alternative methods of assessment. The University of California's college system changed its admission policies because of our work. We changed Big Picture Company to Big Picture Learning to broaden our work to schools, innovation, and influence.

What does real learning after high school look like—and why do we need it?

During the past five years, I became more and more concerned about the abilities of colleges to work with first-generation students and students of color, few of whom went on to college and even fewer of whom were graduating. Graduates from the Met and other Big Picture schools were doing pretty well compared to others with the same demographics, but still, too many were coming home. Colleges keep telling the world that the high schools must do a better job. Lots of experts even claim that if high schools gave students just one more math class, the problem would be solved.

But that's not going to solve the problem. Colleges are teaching the same way, with the same content. Lectures and big classes are still the main way to teach. But our college population, and the world, have changed. So, although I was still, with Elliot, Co-Director of The Met and Co-Director of Big Picture, I began to research what it would take to start a college. I felt that our Big Picture philosophy would work even better with college age students than high school students.

Along with the new initiative's Co-Director, Jamie Scurry, after three hard years of running into lots of walls, we found a college partner, Roger Williams University in Bristol, Rhode Island, and named our new program College Unbound. We selected our first eight students, hired staff, and put together an advisory board. On August 5, 2009, we started. The students kicked off their college careers with a road trip, traveling by bus to visit each of their cities and families from coast to coast. Travel is powerful—it changes you, knocks you out of your groove, and makes you figure out how to learn what you don't know.

College Unbound will change the lives of its students, their families, and their communities, and we're planning on changing the system and practice of higher education to make it accessible and meaningful to far more students. We hope to put pilots inside thirty universities as we influence policy and funding changes to increase graduation rates of first-generation college students, to give them a great liberal arts education, and to make real-world learning happen for them not only in college but throughout their lives.

The years have been about following my passion, keeping honest and consistent about my philosophy, and never taking no for an answer. I believe in and depend on being proactive—I never go into anything without thinking it through and being prepared. I make time to think, to look back, and to see what's ahead. Every Thursday night of my work life, I write a "TGIF." It's a memo, thoughts about the past week, ideas about next week, notes on what I read, and observations about what's happening in our world. It goes out to everyone at every school I've ever worked at, and they write for it too. In thirty-seven years, I've never missed one. TGIFs remind us what we've really learned, and what we believe in.

Making progress is up to all of us—knowing what we believe in, and fighting for it. Good luck.

I Feel So Lucky to Be Right in the Middle of It
Grace Llewellyn

I'm savoring the first sweet sips of a promising romance. Last Thursday night while we were talking, my new man got a little quiet. I don't know him very well yet, and wasn't sure what the quietness signified. I said, softly, "Hey . . . how you doing? You okay?" After a pause, he ventured that something I'd just said had hurt his feelings. "Tell me more," I said, and over the next few days we dipped into eddies of that same conversation, both of us coming to understand each other, and perhaps even ourselves, a little better. Such a simple, essential relationship skill: to notice another's withdrawal and invite them back into the light. To question with equal parts gentleness and attentive persistence. Such a basic human exchange. And yet—

As I sit down to describe my own schooling, the usual lackluster adjectives come to mind. Boring, deadening, dull, dry, monotonous, repetitive, rote, uninspiring, irrelevant. At this moment, however, that's not striking me as the only tragedy. There's also this: that, apparently, nobody in my life—no parent, Sunday school teacher, grandmother, big brother, piano teacher, neighbor, teacher whose pet I was—thought there was a problem with that lack of luster in my first career, with my decades-long withdrawal into an ordinary and awful silence. Nobody probed beyond the routine conversation:

Q. "How do you like school?"
A. "It's okay I guess." (Or "Fine," or "Well, it's pretty boring.")

As I see things now, if a kid speaks apathetically about the biggest time commitment in her life, that's nothing to let lie. Full-time boredom begs further questions. It invites a conversation, one which might lead to helping that kid change her situation (negotiate new reading assignments and projects? switch classrooms? switch schools? quit school?). But even more importantly, this conversation would draw the child out. Through it, she would begin to articulate the nuances of her own feelings, her perspectives, her analyses, and the muted rainbow of choices available to her even in the situation exactly as it is.

People who are more interested than I am in the story of language publicly ponder the distinctions between two Latin tributaries that feed the word "education:" *educare*, having to do with molding and rearing, and *educere*—to "draw out" or "lead forth" (like elicit, and deduce). Well, I would say that even a little bit of educeric mentoring—an occasional long and attentive Socratic conversation *about* my schooling—would have itself created a dramatic shift in my experience of that schooling. I think about these things as I consider the ways that my book, subtitled *How to Quit School and Get a Real Life and Education*, has affected teenagers who *don't* leave school, and as I consider the choices I will face as a parent—because now, at the ripening age of forty-five, through the miracle and the heartbreak of adoption, I'm about to become one. But when I was a child, nobody drew me out and helped give me back to myself through these kinds of conversations. If they had, I might have a very different story to tell.

I grew up in the public schools of Boise, Idaho, in the seventies and eighties. I impressed my teachers and peers with my ability to spell, remember times tables and algebraic formulae, read music, solve logic problems, write poems and essays. Everybody thought I was smart and talented, and at least in a shallow way, they admired and liked me for this. I hungrily ate up their respect, but my heart and mind were rarely committed to the schoolwork that earned it. As I got older, I also became acutely aware of parties I was not invited to, social skills I desperately lacked, school dances where I stood diffidently watching embracing couples rock side to side with their eyes closed.

And there was the great divide. Although I didn't have the language to describe my perspective at the time (and now see that deficiency as a compelling issue in its own right), in retrospect, there was a huge disconnect between school and what I perceived as my life. Life-outside-of-school had its dark shadows, dysfunctions, and deep wounds, but I was unquestionably right there in the middle of it. I made choices and digested the consequences. I devoured books, fantasized about my future and about fairyland (at seven) or boys (at thirteen); I talked and fought and walked and played with my siblings, and then my friends, and then my boyfriends. I played the piano unhurriedly, quietly scrutinized fascinating older family members, and practiced my balance beam routine on a slice of masking tape on my bedroom floor. I pondered theology, God, hell, and eternity; I danced and dreamed of dancing; I secretly wrote short stories and sent them off to *Seventeen* magazine; I experimented with my mother's makeup and tried on clothes and smiles and disco moves in the mirror. When I think about my brothers' and sister's childhoods—they were often out catching frogs, riding horses, wandering the hills—it's easy for me to criticize my own choices. I was more of an indoor person, spent a lot of time in a fantasy realm, and I was secretive, all of which I can judge as unadventurous and unglamorous. But without a doubt, I was living my own life.

Funny thing is, *lots* of the time, even outside of school, I had to do things I didn't really want to do—listen to my dad go on and on about how to take care of camping equipment, help my mother in the kitchen, get out of bed on Sunday morning to go to church, endure long cramped drives through Wyoming wedged between two squabbling brothers. But even the compulsory aspects of my life outside of school were fundamentally and qualitatively different from the compulsory nature of my life in school, because outside of school I *belonged*. I lived in relationship—often painful, of course, but also alive and dynamic. In contrast, at school I checked out emotionally. I had friends but we weren't allowed to talk much, and our friendships grew mainly after school. There were teachers I respected, whose attention and respect I in turn enjoyed, but the territory of our interactions—an ugly room with cold light, crowded with fashionably dressed near-strangers, terminated by a loud buzz we called the "bell"—wasn't conducive to that quality or depth of engagement that nourished me outside the school walls. That quality, and that depth, as far as I could tell, belonged to life and not to school.

The main exception to my story that "life was alive and school was dead" was high school choir with Jerry Vevig. Thank God there was one human being who showed up for his work in such a way that for two or three hours every day, school wasn't school; school was life. Mr. V brought important work that he expected us to do. He had a competitive streak and when our jazz choir went to festivals, he wanted us to win, which more often than not we did. He could be angry and critical and harsh and demanding, but at least for me, that didn't create a problem. He loved music so much, and he loved to bring music to life *in us*, and by extension, I believe that we perceived his rather unsentimental love *for* us. There was never a feeling with him that we were just messing around biding time and creeping dully toward the emancipation of graduation. Everything we did in that room made sense. And thanks to Mr. V, I began imagining that I would become a high school music teacher. I, too, could bring water to a desert.

There was another moment, too. In my senior year, I wrote an essay that caused a stir—mainly within me, in the process of writing it, but also in the teacher's other classes when he read it aloud to them. It was a concoction braided from my real life, a tale my grandmother had charmingly told me, and wishful thinking—an almost love-drunk report of an impromptu Shakespeare performance at a multi-generational house party, interrupted by mischief-causing raccoons and a prowling billy-goat. Looking back, the feeling I had writing it (*this is life: celebratory, vivid, disastrous, communal, creative, expressive! and I can bring at least the telling of it into this un-celebratory place we call school*), the enthusiastic response of other students, and my teacher's own praise, further suggested that I might eventually come back to school, reincarnated as a teacher, and bring my certain vision that life and learning could and should be a banquet, rather than the overstewed mush we swallowed daily. Somewhere between Mr. V's choir room and my pseudo-autobiographical essay, I knew I would teach school, and eventually I knew I would teach not music, but literature and writing. I could hardly wait to become the personal savior of hundreds of bored teenagers.

I soon rode off to a fancy college on the Greyhound bus, and while I had much lateral energy devoted to friends and lovers and vegetarian cooking and Bulgarian folkdances and a tall stack of books I'd discovered through the *Next Whole Earth Catalog*, my forward energy was all about my certain future as a high school English teacher. If I had been in a different frame of mind—eager to take my time exploring the world and human culture, the way I had been as a younger teenager—I might have thrived in that small liberal arts college environment. In fact, although socially I wouldn't have been ready for it, if I'd entered the scholarly world of Carleton at the age of sixteen, I bet it would have thrilled and captivated me. As it was, I had a few intellectual epiphanies, but mostly I hurried through to get to the other side: my brilliant teaching career.

I began teaching and from the start—right from my student teaching days—it didn't go according to plan. For a few of my students I did get to play the muse, helping to reconnect them to the life pulsing inside their own skin. But for the most part, I found myself disappointed and occasionally shocked. How on earth had I assumed things were so simple? First, that all teenagers everywhere semi-consciously wanted (and *should* want) nothing more than to discuss and read and write about life, art, and literature; and all they were waiting for was a lively young woman to pirouette out from behind her steel desk and whisper, "Hey, guess what? While we're in this room together we don't have to pretend we're already lying in our cemetery plots! And today we get to read Whitman—how cool is that?!" Furthermore, how had I sustained my fantasy that public schools gave—that public schools *could* give— teachers the power to enter their classrooms as passionate artists, as Dionysian revelers? If my schooling had been characterized by dullness, my teaching was now characterized by heaviness. All the curricular requirements and rules and standardized tests, the already-entrenched distrust of teachers and aversion to books weighed heavily on me (even as I write it I can barely breathe), and as far as I could see, these things blocked the real work I wanted to do with my students. You would think I would have known before I committed to teaching that the Red Sea wasn't going to just part before me, that school teachers were not actually hired in order that they might pour their souls into the work of inspiring their students. But somehow I had refused to pay attention to this damning information, even though it was all around me.

It wasn't long before I began suspecting that I was going to have a hard time cultivating my vision in an institution so rigid and disrespectful to young people as the public school system. Little things happened all the time that fed this suspicion. One day early on, for example, I was substitute teaching high school band in Oakland, California. The furnace in the music wing of the building wasn't working, and I was cold, so I wore my wool cap. This, my first students of the day informed me, was Against the Rules. I didn't ask them why, didn't care. I explained—a bit condescendingly, if I remember right—that while it was an excellent idea to follow most rules under most circumstances, common sense and good judgment should trump rules, especially petty ones, in unusual circumstances. I was certain that no one would fault me for warming my skull under these particular circumstances. As they played, I stood front and center on the podium until I realized that my energy was more needed down in the rhythm section behind me, where the drummers were goofing just a bit. I left my post and simply stood among this cluster of good-naturedly cheeky boys, and the band played on. That's when one of the vice principals stepped in to check on how the little lady sub was doing. It was always painful to see how an administrator would react in such situations—as if their internal rule book was more prominent in their consciousness than their ability to simply sense whether everything was okay. Everything was definitely okay. The group of sixty-plus kids was playing a song, and playing it pretty well, and there were no spitwads flying, nobody throwing chairs, nobody even dancing in their own chair. But the poor guy's face panicked immediately, as he looked at the vacant spot where he expected to see the Teacher. Unsupervised children, big problem—I could see that in his eyes. Then those eyes landed on me. "Take off that hat!" he yelled. I would say "screamed," because it was loud and high pitched and vociferous and full of panic, but that seems a little dramatic. In an instant panic myself, I snatched the hat off my head. At this, the song fell apart and the kids dissolved into laughter. "We *told* her," they said. He was still confused, scanning the room low and high for a possibly maimed authority figure, and he backed out toward the door in a zigzag. The rest of us, in various states of amusement, shock, and newly acquired sobriety, eventually reassembled our ensemble.

Later, the man figured out what had happened, and came back to apologize profusely—"I just thought you were a *student*," he said beseechingly, several times. Even though the real students and I had the pleasure of our private joke about the incident, it really did bother me. Stuck with me. I mean, the guy *screamed* at me ("yelled," really, doesn't convey). For wearing a hat in a cold room. And that part is okay. I know people have stupid moments; I've had at least several thousand myself. But when he apologized, it wasn't for what he did, it was just because he had accidentally treated an *adult* the way he saw fit to treat *teenagers*.

Lots of things like that happened, though most of them don't make such good stories, and in some of them it's me, or a student, who plays the bad guy. I began investigating how I might enact my fundamental vision—to create an oasis of life and joy in what I perceived as the dry and scaly world of school. At first, I fantasized about opening a very inexpensive ten-or-so-student private school,[1] and my investigation to learn how a person might do such a thing lead me rapidly through stacks of newsletters and books about alternative education and odd experiments. Suddenly, I was reading John Holt, whose words would transform my thinking about school, teaching, learning, life. "Of course," he said in *Teach Your Own*, "A child may not know what he may need to know in ten years (who does?), but he knows, and much better than anyone else, what he wants and needs to know right now, what his mind is ready and hungry for. If we help him, or just allow him, to learn that, he will remember it, use it, build on it. If we try to make him learn something else, that we think is more important, the chances are that he won't learn it, or will learn very little of it, that he will soon forget most of what he learned, and what is worst of all, will before long lose most of his appetite for learning anything."

I thought again about that quality of vitality, of connection to life, that I had hungered for as a student and then longed to bring into schools as a teacher. I had arrogantly (and inaccurately) assumed that what sparked me would—and should—spark any random cross-section of American teens. Now I understood that much of what kids needed was to be given their own lives back, to be able to follow their own inklings in their own ways in their own time, without an adult telling them what to do and then telling them how well they had done it. John Holt argued that this happened best outside of school, and I was a quick convert to his philosophy of unschooling.

For a while I drifted about, like a November leaf. Then, out of a lingering desire to make sure I wasn't giving up too easily, and also because I didn't really know what *else* to do at the moment, I took a job. It was a dream job, in many ways, teaching a delightful and clever batch of seventh and eighth graders, surrounded by a brilliant, definitely not dull and lackluster community of teachers, in a highly regarded private school in Colorado. I experimented, to the best of my ability and under the generous blessing of the headmaster, with giving my students great gobs of freedom within the broad definition of our territory, Language Arts. And I kept my eyes and ears and heart open, hoping to understand each of their lives such that I could teach in as connected a way as possible. But despite my best efforts and, apparently, the best efforts of other passionate teachers more skilled and experienced than I, the missing ingredients still seemed to be missing. These kids were usually bored. Stressed, too—boredom isn't always a result of things being too easy. Bored, stressed, disengaged, eyes aglaze. Less so than at most public schools—probably a lot less—but public schools were not my yardstick. I was still trying hard to bring vitality and freedom to my boxy little room, though it gradually sank in that *I* couldn't deliver the necessary life and freedom; its source had to be, could only be, the very lives and hearts of my students themselves. By the autumn of my second year, the back of my camel had accumulated many straws, and all it took to finally crack the poor beast's spine was an incident in which—during an extended field trip—two teachers scolded a couple of my favorite students in a way that I perceived as harsh, uninformed, and unfair. I finished out the school year with the most sincere devotion I could muster, but what I most wanted now was for these particular kids, the actual human beings sitting with me day after day, to know about the option of unschooling. I didn't consider it my business to tell them about it directly, but I decided that the *Teenage Liberation Handbook* needed to exist. Soon thereafter, I realized that since John Holt had died some years back, and I therefore wouldn't be able to beg him to write it, I'd better get started myself.

I began my formal (though undercover) research by asking my students about their perspectives on their schooling, and their perception of its role in their future success. And I pondered the conundrum of the magic Mr. V had been able to create, versus my own—and many others'—inability to do this. I chalked it up partly to the fact that music classes were elective, whereas my language arts classes were required for all my students; but I knew this was not the whole picture. Mr. V's temperament and skills were simply different from mine, and while his work was terrifically important, my own work—which ironically rose out of my failure to teach powerfully within the schools—has also been important. I imagine the world has room and need for both of us.

So I wrote the *Teenage Liberation Handbook: How to Quit School and Get a Real Life and Education*. I often say that it came through me rather than from me, because it did. Some force bigger than me definitely took over. Of course, I think the same thing about children—that they come through, not from, their mothers—and that in no way lessens the work of pregnancy, or the pain of labor. Birthing that book was the hardest thing I've ever done, at least aside from getting along with another human being. But eventually I finished. I remember a conversation with my brothers Ned and Richard, who had read the manuscript. It wouldn't be fair to paint them as true believers in my Cause, but they were certainly supportive of me and contributed helpful feedback, as well as insightful perspectives on science and technology education. One evening I said, wistfully, "It would be so cool if, like, one person actually read this thing and it made a real difference in their life. Maybe even to the point where they decided to quit school." "Yeah," said Richard thoughtfully, tentatively. "And that might happen. It probably won't happen on a large scale, but it would be nice." Fifty thousand copies and eighteen years and boxes and boxes of impassioned letters later, it has, miraculously, happened. The book has its own life now. It has grown up and left the nest to make its own friends in the world, and we don't usually even stay in close touch anymore.

After the *TLH*, I compiled and edited a couple more books—*Real Lives: eleven teenagers who don't go to school tell their own stories*, and *Freedom Challenge: African American Homeschoolers*. (Eventually—I'm violating chronological order with this sentence—my friend Amy Silver, a shining beacon of a homeschooling mom, invited me to co-write with her, so together we conjured *Guerrilla Learning: how to give your kids a real education with or without school*. It's her book more than mine, and I'm finding it useful as I contemplate the luminous and monumental task of motherhood.) I opened a resource center for homeschoolers, which quickly drained my patience and my funds. I published a newsletter called *Unschooling Ourselves* for a couple years. I accepted invitations to speak at homeschooling conferences and learned that I wasn't very good at public speaking. I compiled a mail order book catalog for homeschoolers. I answered a lot of mail and failed to answer more. In my other life, I performed and taught bellydance and had many great adventures. But during that post-*TLH* flurry of activity, I mostly thrashed about, scanning tea leaves for my next marching orders.

And then, finally, came camp. In 1996 I launched Not Back to School Camp, wherein (that first year) ninety unschooled teenagers from all over the US and Canada converged for a week outside a tiny Oregon town to share their skills, passions, and hearts. Before we went live, I worried. Would it take? Would it catch fire? How would we—me and my staff of ten beloved friends and family members—make sure there was magic, that there was *life*? The worry was needless, of course, because most of these kids already had a strong connection to the centers of their own lives, and they brought this connection along with them and threw it in the pot. Fourteen years and thirty-five sessions later, the fire and the magic burn a little brighter every time we meet.

These days, I continue to direct Not Back to School Camp, finding new questions and goals each year that keep my work fresh. I'll soon write a new introduction for the *Teenage Liberation Handbook*, and will then publish a twenty-year anniversary edition; I look forward to articulating some of the spirals my thoughts have traveled over the last couple decades. I've gradually cleared more space in my life for dancing, and I'm beginning a non-school teaching adventure as the facilitator of a practice called Soul Motion, which combines meditation, encouragement to dance freely and ecstatically, and an invitation to connect with others. I bellydance weekly in a Moroccan restaurant. I do my best to be a good friend, sister, and aunt, and I have at least a dozen big aspirations regarding this odyssey of mothering I'm—finally!—about to begin.

I might say that my own attention has returned, full circle, to the desire to foster—particularly through my roles as director of NBTSC, fledgling Soul Motion teacher, bellydancer, and soon-to-be-mother—a vivid and felt connection to life, to a sense of celebration and gratitude, to knowing myself, and others knowing themselves, as conduits for creative energy. My take on this, these days, is a little more forgiving than it was when I wrote that Zorba-esque high school essay twenty-eight years ago. It has room, now, for ordinariness, for crescendo and decrescendo, for dark nights of the soul, even for that unattractive, mysterious, and fertile landscape named "boredom." (Unschoolers, too, it turns out, can suffer from dull days and dry spells—though a probing, compassionate conversation with an interested adult often works wonders to help this move and transform.) But my spirit soars in moments like this one: at the edge of a clearing in the forest, I'm talking with a couple campers who have broken each other's hearts. A flicker of movement seduces my eye and I lift my gaze. Over in the field, a little past the group of people adjusting the tilt of a solar oven, a young woman dances across the grass in a series of exultant leaps. From somewhere behind me in the trees a distant, warbling flute seems to echo her. And I think to myself: *this is life—celebratory, vivid, disastrous, communal, creative, expressive!* I feel so, so lucky to be right here in the middle of it.

Notes

1.   In fact, my fantasy looked and felt a lot like something that my friends Blake Boles and Abbi Miller are doing in real life at this very moment: they call their organization Unschool Adventures, and for the duration of this month, November 2009, they've rented a house in Oregon a few hundred yards from the ocean, and they're sharing it with seventeen teenagers who don't go to school. The teenagers, plus Blake, plus Abbi, are all writing 50,000-word novels, as participants in National Novel Writing Month, or NaNoWriMo. I visited last week

and was impressed and touched by the group's dedication, camaraderie, and shared sense of mission. I feel a little thrill, in fact, that although my own work did not go in this particular direction, somebody else's did.

It's In My Blood
Basir Mchawi

My first memories of education and learning have to do with my maternal grandmother. Ethel Sousoi was an entrepreneur and store owner in Manhattan, but by the time I was born, acute rheumatoid arthritis had ravaged her body. Grandma was confined to a wheelchair, but her health challenges did not slow her down. She loved teaching, learning, and writing, and from her wheelchair, conducted literacy classes in our project apartment in the Bronx for a group of older women. Though I couldn't have been much more than four or five years old, I remember sitting there, watching and listening.

In a closet in our apartment, my grandmother kept a mimeograph machine that she used to publish a newsletter/magazine called Pathway of Roses. Fairly regularly, Grandma and my mother would type articles and draw pictures on stencils and put them on the mimeograph machine. Pathway of Roses was printed, collated, bound, and mailed all over the world.

When I was nine, Grandma gave me a Webster's Unabridged Dictionary, which I still have in my home office today. The dictionary had over two thousand pages of dictionary entries, as well as an atlas and almanac-like sections. By the time I first held it, my engagement in education had been well established—via genetics and direct experience, I was ready.

I was born in the South Bronx, and lived in a tenement for

my first years. Due to a serious housing shortage and some rough tenement conditions, my mother looked for other alternatives, and we ended up in Throg's Neck projects, a public housing development, in the Northeast Bronx. Although there was a lack of money in my neighborhood, the word poverty, with all its negative connotations, did not apply. Everyone had some money issues but it didn't matter that much. Families did what they had to do to survive with dignity. In those days, most of the projects in New York were integrated; Blacks, Latinos, and Whites played together, hung out together, and went to school together. It was that way up until the puberty period, when things changed rather drastically.

I have to thank my mother for my intense sense of cultural identity. I always knew that being of African ancestry, I was different. My mother added some definition to that reality by making sure I had knowledge of the culture being created by African people around the globe. When I was no more than eleven, she took me to a concert featuring Count Basie and Ahmad Jamal. The music of Charlie Parker, Dizzy Gillespie, Billie Holiday, and Louis Jordan wafted through our apartment as it all spun off the phonograph. We traveled to Harlem and hung out at the Apollo Theater; friends and relatives from the old neighborhood came up to spend time with us in Throg's Neck; there was no cultural deprivation in my life.

Having that rich home life made school a breeze. I recognized the importance of learning by what I saw at home and applied those lessons at school. I always did well on tests and had a rather prodigious vocabulary. I was bused out of the projects and sent to a school in the then all-white Pelham Bay area. It was difficult for the white teachers and students to adjust to a Black kid who knew all the answers and did the best on all the tests. I suppose it was similar to what Malcolm X describes in his autobiography, when he talks about going to school in Lansing, Michigan. Although no teacher tried to totally dash my dreams (as was Brother Malcolm's experience), several of them were more subtle; they made sure that I did not get all the recognition I deserved, but knew I couldn't be stopped. At the same time, there were a few teachers who actually encouraged me and treated me like the other students. A few.

For junior high school, the Board of Education built a school on the border between the projects and the white working class neighborhood that surrounded us. While the school itself was integrated, the classes were not. The top classes in each grade had one or two Blacks and/ or Latinos, but that was it. Part of my competitive streak comes out of that; we were always under the microscope. It was as if there were an experiment going on and the Black and Latino students were the experimental subjects. You had to learn to handle your business on all levels. The Irish and Italian folks from the neighborhood were no joke either. Some were certainly in training for positions in the mob and other "organizations," and had even already settled into gangs and social clubs. Those of us from the projects all banded together if some problem developed. It was a pretty long run, with a shortcut across the highway, if we had to get home quick.

In keeping with my doing well on tests, I passed the test for Bronx High School of Science and spent my high school years there. Bronx Science was an alienating experience. Though the academics probably helped out later, my social circle was limited. There are a couple of folks from classes that graduated after me that I still communicate with every once in a while, but no real lasting friendships developed. Once again there was only a smattering of Blacks and Latinos throughout the school, and since the entire school was "special," there were only one or two students of color in each class. In order to keep my sense of who I was, I continued to hang out in Harlem. Whether playing hooky to go to the Apollo or spending time at Elder Michaux's bookstore on 7th Avenue and 125th Street, I did what I had to to keep my identity.

Despite a lily-white curriculum in school, I was motivated to read books by African people. I read James Baldwin, Chester Himes, Dr. John Henrik Clarke, Kwame Nkrumah and a host of others. The world was changing in front of our eyes, and I wanted to be a part of that change. The Civil Rights Movement was important but it wasn't for me. The Nation of Islam and Brother Malcolm were more relevant for urban youth. When Malcolm spoke, his words resonated deep inside many of us. We began to recognize that the Honorable Elijah Muhammad was the architect, but Malcolm X was the organizer and popularizer. There were many brothers out on the streets of the Bronx and Harlem selling Muhammad Speaks, the Nation of Islam newspaper. The message of self-reliance, self-determination, self-respect, and self-defense just made sense. By my senior year in high school I was going to jazz clubs and immersing myself fully in the emerging Black Arts Movement. I ventured into Harlem to connect with the sense of activism and Black pride that was developing; even then I was clear about the relationship of culture and politics.

If it had been an issue of money, I would have had to go to a public college or university, probably one of the CUNY schools. But I was still testing well and was able to put together enough scholarship money to attend New York University. What a time to be in the Greenwich Village area. Everything was converging: Black Arts, Black Power, the Black Student Movement, the radicalization of college campuses around the world, the Anti-war Movement, and the creation of a "counterculture" all came together at once. There was enough activity to make your head swim. I had started to write in high school and was able to use my writing as a means of connecting several of the emerging political and cultural struggles. I was able to perform and publish some pieces in anthologies and magazines. The major contradiction was how to attach all of this motion to the communities and neighborhoods that many of us students had come from. The answer was education and building our own institutions.

As students, several of us identified with the struggles that were taking place in the neighborhoods we were from. The struggle for community control of the schools in New York was one of the most important battles of the time. The Ford Foundation provided funding for the establishment of a series of community controlled, experimental "demonstration" school districts. This was to see if communities of color could improve on the failure of the gargantuan centralized bureaucracy that was strangling schools, parents, students and teachers. The impact of centralization was especially bad in Black and Latino neighborhoods. Schools that were comprised of mostly Black and Latino students experienced troubling levels of failure and dysfunction. There were few Black and Latino teachers—and even fewer administrators—in the New York City school system.

Three demonstration districts were established; Ocean Hill-Brownsville in Brooklyn, IS 201 in East Harlem, and Twin (Two) Bridges on the Lower East Side of Manhattan. As students, we felt that these experiments needed our direct support, and we came from all over the city to volunteer our time and energy. I focused most directly on IS 201, which was a train ride away from the housing project in which I still lived. A series of divisive teacher strikes took place and all manner of ethnic, racial, and religious accusations were made when the administrators in Ocean Hill-Brownsville reassigned several white teachers. Should the community have that kind of power? The resulting "compromise" created a series of "decentralized" school districts that provided the appearance that some change had taken place. The irony was that the "community" school districts that were created had no real power and were centrally controlled. Not only that, but the educational unions, the UFT and CSA, regularly supported corrupt candidates for election to "community" school boards. The compromised system remained in place until Mayor Michael Bloomberg was given authority to recentralize the schools, and place most important decisions in the hands of the Mayor and his advisors, in 2002. Unfortunately, under Bloomberg, it has only gotten worse.

My first full-time job after college was in the IS 201 demonstration district. I became a teacher at the Community Education Center (CEC) on East 126th Street. I thought that it would be important to cultivate an audience for all of the actions that were taking place across the country. Education was the key. At the CEC, we held classes during the day and supported the efforts of schools in the district. In the afternoon and early evening, we ran a variety of classes and after-school programs, and offered tutorial services and homework help. The work I did there had an indelible impact on me. I saw what happened when parents and community members were directly involved in the education process. That type of engagement is always superior to what the bureaucrats and "experts" have to offer. It leads to possibilities of tremendous personal and institutional growth and development.

As a senior in college, I had gotten married and moved to Brooklyn. My experiences at NYU and IS 201 led me to get involved with a new community organization in Brooklyn called the EAST. I was also building a family and sought the company of some like-minded individuals. The EAST was a reaction to the Ocean Hill-Brownsville debacle—if we could not control municipal institutions, we needed to build our own. The founders of the EAST included teachers and students who had been in the thick of the battle of Ocean Hill. Jitu

Weusi (then Les Campbell) was the pivotal figure in building the EAST. Students from the African American Students Association (ASA), an organization of high school and junior high school youth, also played a great role. Then there were the disgruntled teachers and parents who were tired of all the BS they faced daily in the public school system, along with community activists and college students. The EAST was an idea whose time had come. All the right forces came together to make it happen.

The EAST was described as a "cultural and educational center for people of African descent." It started out as a cultural center, bringing popular musicians from downtown into Bedford Stuyvesant in Brooklyn. The weekend sets became nationally known as musicians like Pharoah Sanders, McCoy Tyner, Max Roach, Sonny Rollins, Betty Carter, Lee Morgan, Reggie Workman and a host of others came to play at the cultural center located at 10 Claver Place. But the development of the institution did not stop there. The EAST became an umbrella and an incubator; a number of enterprises were started, and the creative energy that was generated lead to the creation of still more ventures.

Probably the most important creation of the EAST was the Uhuru Sasa Shule. Uhuru Sasa means "Freedom Now" in the Swahili language. Influenced by the work of John Churchville—who founded the Freedom Library Day School in Philadelphia and the Nairobi Day School in East Palo Alto, California—Uhuru Sasa became the anchor of a national movement to build and develop Independent Black Institutions (IBIs). It became the largest of the independent Black schools, attracting over three hundred K–12 students at the height of its development. 2010 marks the fortieth anniversary of the founding of Uhuru Sasa, and graduates are planning a series of events to mark this important milestone. The events will culminate at the thirty-ninth annual International African Arts Festival to be held in Brooklyn in July 2010.

It was not enough for the EAST to have a weekend music series and a school. There was also Black News, a monthly newspaper/magazine; Akiba Mkuu, a bookstore; Kununana, a health food store and food co-op; Mavazi, a clothing and variety store; EAST Caterers and the EAST Kitchen; The Sweet EAST, a snack shop and restaurant; and A View From the EAST, a radio program heard on a commercial radio station

(WLIB). All of these endeavors were developed out of the principle of Ujamaa—cooperative economics. Ujamaa is the concept of African socialism as promulgated by the President of Tanzania, Dr. Julius Nyerere, and one of the Seven Principles developed by Dr. Maulana Karenga, and associated with the holiday of Kwanzaa. More than a matter of economics, however, the EAST sought to create community-based ventures that addressed the specific community needs for food, clothing, and information.

During my tenure at the EAST I took on many responsibilities. When I first arrived, I juggled my EAST work with teaching English at JHS 275 in Brownsville, but after a few years the contradictions began to get to me. At Uhuru Sasa we made everything work to the benefit of children. Parents were highly important, committed and involved; the curriculum was relevant and new; teachers were firm and caring. I had to compare this with what I saw every day in public schools. JHS 275, at the time, was one of the roughest junior high schools in the City. On one occasion, local gangs broke in the school while classes were in session, and I had to fight to save the UFT chapter chair from a serious beating. I handled myself well in the classroom, and used some of the Uhuru Sasa model with my students. I brought in relevant materials, engaged parents and had them take some responsibility for their children's work. We went on field trips and I always invited parents to accompany the class. We went to see the National Dance Company of Senegal, to a variety of movies that reflected the times, to museums, and when the weather got warm, to Prospect Park just to cool out. The problem was that there were only a few teachers who were both serious and skilled at 275. Most of the time, I felt terribly out of place and alone. It wasn't long before I decided to work at the EAST on a full time basis.

An organization like the EAST made you reach maturity rather quickly. You were given responsibilities that were often daunting and required considerable skills. It was usually sink or swim; you had to solve the problem and develop the proper strategy. Jitu Weusi was great at making those kinds of assignments, and no matter how painful, you would stretch until the job got done. On several occasions I had to undertake international diplomatic missions, often meeting with heads of state and high-level officials. On the domestic front, I took on the task of providing information. For several years I was the editor of Black News, as well as the producer and host of our radio show, A View From the EAST. On the political side of the equation, we recognized that we were in a position to influence electoral outcomes in Central Brooklyn. Influenced by the struggle—spearheaded by Amiri Baraka and the Committee for a Unified Newark (CFUN)—to elect Kenneth Gibson in Newark, New Jersey, we held a Black Political Convention and made local politicians and candidates come to the community to articulate their viewpoints. We entered into an organizational relationship with CFUN by joining the Congress of African People (CAP), a national alliance of revolutionary nationalist/Pan-Africanist organizations. Central Brooklyn became a hotbed of political activity and several electoral victories followed, as Brooklyn became a model of Black empowerment.

We were not afraid of taking direct action when conditions called for it. We staged demonstrations and boycotts when incidents of police brutality or racist violence occurred. Uhuru Sasa students would participate in these activities, giving practical application to many of the ideas introduced in the curriculum. The EAST also took up a leadership role in the African Liberation Support Committee (ALSC), an organization dedicated to the support of liberation struggles being waged across the African continent. These were heady and important times.

But the EAST was not immune to internal contradiction, and in hindsight, many of us recognize that errors were made. Instead of having others run for political office, we should have done it ourselves. The current confusion in the New York City political scene would be no more chaotic if we had decided to get EAST members elected to political office. We also did not realize how vicious the government would be in attempting to destroy the EAST. The organization was monitored and infiltrated. Internal differences were exploited using COINTELPRO (US government counterintelligence program) type operations, and other organizations masquerading as "progressive" would be used to compromise the security of the EAST. The IRS, the NYPD, and NSA all took their shots, and as the government onslaught continued, by the early 1980s the EAST organization was practically defunct.

Despite the demise of the EAST, the importance of the

independent Black schools movement must be emphasized. At the height of the movement, independent Black schools flourished throughout the United States and the Caribbean. In Brooklyn, several offshoots of Uhuru Sasa became schools themselves. By the late 1970s, there were so many independent Black schools in Central Brooklyn that an organization, the Brooklyn Family Schools, was developed to foster inter-organizational cooperation. Several institutions born out of the EAST still exist today, including the International African Arts Festival, Black Veterans for Social Justice, and the Council of Independent Black Institutions (CIBI), a national organization of independent Black schools.

After the EAST, I became part of a smaller organization with some of the same goals and objectives—Shule ya Mapinduzi (School for Change) and the corresponding Mapinduzi organization—while going to graduate school. I took on the position of headmaster of Shule ya Mapinduzi and used some of the lessons learned at the EAST to guide our development. I was intent on using professional development to improve our instructional outcomes, and used books like Pedagogy of the Oppressed to provide theoretical frameworks for teaching practices. We brought in several educational experts to provide staff with ideas about better engaging students in math, science, and language arts, and hired excellent part-time instructors to work with our students in music, art, physical education, and martial arts. Our full time instructors, although sometimes not as credentialed as their public school counterparts, were excellent. The dedication, commitment, and positive attitude more than made up for the lack of training in Eurocentric institutions of higher learning. We remained in constant conversation about the teaching/learning continuum.

One day I looked up from my office desk at Mapinduzi and saw three of my own children. In a small school environment, suddenly it got a bit too personal. As Shule ya Mapinduzi continued to evolve, I decided to move on but remain involved. I started teaching at the college level, always using the lessons learned in the independent Black school movement.

Race remains a central issue in education at all levels. Discriminatory practices infect pedagogy, curricula, hiring, discipline, student achievement, funding—you name it. Africans, Latinos, and other peoples of color are often excluded from discussions about educational reform. The current charter schools explosion is designed to foist flawed Eurocentric educational models on unsuspecting Black and Latino communities. Not only that, but charter schools attempt to put public dollars in private hands. This effort at privatizing public schools is taking place in the United States, Central America, South America, Africa, and Asia. Corporations have realized that there are billions of global dollars that can be diverted into the coffers of large multinational conglomerates. Rarely are the victims of these scams included in the conversation. Think about it: some person from the suburbs wants to come to a large city and tell the Black and Latino residents how to best educate their children. No discussion, no conversation, no Freirian investigation, no look at history or prior educational successes, just take some shit that works in Duluth, Minnesota and bring it to Harlem or South Central, Los Angeles. As bad or worse, experiment on us or build educational research projects studying Black or Latino children. I don't think so! White people are often comfortable having educational discussions about children of color without African and Latino experts present. What is wrong with that picture? Maybe we have to redefine "expert." As principal of the middle school in Roosevelt, Long Island, I was confronted with the New York State Education Department "expert" on middle schools. Had he ever been an administrator in a middle school? No. Had he ever taught in a middle school? No. He just read some books and did some research. Got a PhD. Some expert! It's this simple: Someone reads some books about bicycles and bicycle riding, but never rides a bike. Someone else knows how to ride. Who's the "expert"?

I interject my discussion about race here because of some of my experiences over the last twenty or so years. I left academia when my career stalled due to racial discrimination. I sued a college for discrimination and retaliation and won, but had decided to go back to K–12 public education to support my family while that battle went forward. I taught at Boys and Girls High School in Brooklyn for a few years before I was identified to join the staff of Chancellor Richard Green, New York City's first Black chancellor. While at central headquarters, I used the skills I developed at the EAST, Uhuru Sasa, and Mapinduzi to move a positive educational agenda forward.

After a short time, Chancellor Green died suddenly of complications associated with asthma. I have to believe that race had something to do with that whether it was the poor health care we receive or the extra stress related to being New York's first Black chancellor.

My next major struggle was the creation of Ujamaa Institute, New York's first African-centered public high school. Ujamaa means "familyhood" in Swahili. In the early 1990s, reform efforts in New York focused on the creation of theme oriented high schools and there were very few people of color involved in the reform discussions. I developed a model for a small African-centered high school that would look at the educational and social strivings of African and Latino young men. I took much of what I had learned at Uhuru Sasa and Mapinduzi and put it to use once again. The model included many progressive elements, such as flexible use of instructional time, values based education, cooperative learning, heterogeneous grouping, and a multicultural curriculum. Ujamaa Institute was described as "African-centered," which meant that the African experience forms the center of analysis. That African experience is defined broadly to include much of the population of North, South, and Central America, the Caribbean, and of course, the African continent itself. Now why did I say that? A firestorm arose around the concept. I was accused of fostering "segregation" in NYC public schools, but no one looked at the fact that New York had one of the most segregated school systems in the country. I was accused of racism and sexism. What was actually racist was the high dropout rate, the low levels of academic achievement, and the historical obliviousness to the plight of Black and Latino families. Regarding sexism, all along I had talked about a coeducational environment, but was anticipating the clamor that arose a few years later about the status of Black and Latino young men.

I enlisted the help of then NYS Assemblyman Roger Green to deflect some of the political flak. The Aaron Diamond Foundation signed on by providing a planning grant. It took almost four years to get the school open and it opened with twenty students in a room adjoining my office at the central administration headquarters. It was a short-lived victory. My support base began to erode as new chancellors, new school board members, and new superintendents came into play. There were also several betrayals as key players sold the concept out.

The name was finally changed and all of the elements that made Ujamaa unique were removed. I, too, was removed. The irony is that in later years, as white women advocated for an all-girls public school, there was no outcry. There are currently several schools that are all-male in New York City, but no evidence of African-centered curricula. There is a great deal of resistance to such ideas. That is a struggle that must continue. Ujamaa Institute was first.

One of the items that Ujamaa Institute projected was recognition of the "devaluation of African/Latino intellect." There are numbers of people of all races who believe that people of African ancestry (and Latinos) are intellectually inferior. Even in our post-Barack-Obama-election, post-racial America, such notions still exist and are grounded in the mythology of white supremacy. The idea of the "achievement gap" is also rooted in this notion. To me, the achievement gap is socially constructed. Give African people inferior schools, inadequate health care, fewer economic opportunities, and then wonder what is wrong when children impacted by these practices don't do well on "standardized" exams. Further, don't allow culturally focused teaching and learning methodologies, which have been shown to be successful, to take root in so-called "inner city" schools. Many of the solutions are right in front of us.

After Ujamaa, I went on to work with incarcerated youth and in adult education. I then spent a few years as a high school and middle school principal in Roosevelt, Long Island. Roosevelt is a small community in Nassau County that is surrounded by suburban wealth, and another example of social construction of the achievement gap. Roosevelt's population is largely African American with an increasing Latino presence. The commercial base, while I was there, consisted of a gas station, a supermarket, and a McDonald's. The surrounding communities had lucrative businesses and superior real estate tax rolls. Roosevelt's schools were needy and the higher in school you went, the greater the disparity. In the years I was in Roosevelt, significant academic progress was made. Students did so well that the New York State Education Department had to reverse a decision to take over the school district based on academic need. Instead, State Ed used the Roosevelt financial situation to remove a newly elected school board and totally disenfranchise the residents of Roosevelt. Homeowners had to pay school taxes without having any say about what would take place. Whatever happened to "no taxation without representation?" Several years of mismanagement followed as the New York State Education Department ran roughshod over the aspirations of the Roosevelt community. It was once again having a conversation and making decisions about education without the involvement of the people whose lives would be most directly affected. If we can advocate self-determination for peoples and nations around the world, we must call for self-determination for Black, Brown, Yellow and Red people throughout the United States.

Beginning during the Ujamaa Institute period, I was asked by radio visionary Samori Marksman to design and host a program that would tackle educational issues, and I started Education At the Crossroads, which continues to be broadcast on New York City Pacifica station WBAI every Thursday evening. I attempt to engage the WBAI audience in an ongoing dialogue about education and education issues. I do so rather broadly, understanding that all education is culturally based, and that as former President of Guinea Ahmed Sekou Toure once said, "Revolution is first an act of culture."

I am currently the chairman of the International African Arts Festival (IAAF), an organization that continues to spread the legacy of the EAST by conducting a multi-day cultural arts festival in Brooklyn every summer. Aside from its primary cultural thrust, the International African Arts Festival is at its center an educational organization. I also teach within the City University of New York (CUNY), but am about to directly enter into the public school wars for one last shot at this critical moment. I still have more work to do and there are more victories to be won. Whether it is genetics, experience or a combination thereof, the struggle around education is in my blood.

What I've Learned
Deborah Meier

It was the early, heady 1960s. I was immersed in raising three very young children and trying, simultaneously, to change the world. I was deeply immersed in civil rights work, peace activism, and helping to keep alive a small, democratic socialist group led by Mike Harrington. But I was also short of cash. So, based on what a neighbor on Chicago's Southside told me, I decided it would be easy to pick up $35 a day being a public K–8 substitute teacher. It would work with my schedule—I could offer maybe two days a week while my kids were in nursery school and kindergarten, and I needed only to take a few courses (which were, in themselves, interesting as an insight into "ordinary" schooling)—so off I went.

I was dead wrong. Being a substitute teacher was the hardest thing I had ever done, and I was clearly a failure at it. But both of these factors intrigued me, and I relished the chance to get a sneak-peak into Chicago's mostly black public schools. After my second year as a substitute, though, it was getting tiring, and I accepted an offer to teach morning kindergarten at the school that my own children attended (which was also mostly black). Me, a kindergarten teacher? Well, again, it seemed like an easy way to pick up a little money and stay close to home. Besides, it was a small school—maybe three hundred kids in grades K–6—and its teaching staff included a large number of local women who were full-time teachers and neighborhood activists. Surely, I thought, this was bound to be easier than subbing all over the city!

Despite the fact that I avoided being a babysitter in my youth and that I refused to take a single course in education (against the wise advice of others), I fell in love with kindergarten teaching and became fascinated with my fellow teachers. I had led a privileged life, attending progressive independent schools in New York City, Antioch, and the University of Chicago. Taking courses at the local teachers college was my first exposure to more traditional public schooling and public school students; getting my teaching certificate at the Board of Education was my first experience of being treated with contempt and condescension. Although my own children had already embarked on long "careers" in public, urban schools, it was utterly new to me. My twice-a-week exposure as a sub offered me a new insight into the nature of America's inequities, the difficulties in creating a truly democratic ethos, and building a movement for change. The public schools were a force, wittingly or not, for preserving the status quo.

I meant to see how, exactly, this might be changed. What are the small and telling ways in which we reinforce the prevailing class structure in our schools, and how do we perpetuate various ways of imagining possibilities? How is it that so many hard working and devoted women tolerate being treated so shabbily in their schools and yet stick with teaching, year after year? Why are mothers so fearful, and often angry, when they come to the school door and hand over their loved ones to the mostly well-meaning staff within? I wanted to find answers.

On a much smaller scale, the life within the classroom itself grabbed me. It was a place of endless fascination and constant intellectual, social, and moral struggle and delight. My first post-subbing classroom had thirty-five four- and five-year-olds and no assistant. Yet my energy was inexhaustible. Even though I only taught for half a day, it was, quite frankly, always a full-time job. In my personal time, I scoured my home and my neighborhood for interesting objects, read books that might be useful for my classes, and met with families in the school and neighborhood to make better sense of what I was seeing and hearing with the children. I had my students dictate stories to me and created little books for them to read, which I then read aloud back to them. The kids' stories were full of wonderfully rich language, a fact counter to what I had been told about these "language-deprived" children.

My experience in those first few years of teaching was central to my forty-two-year career in urban public schools—as well as to teaching Head Start in Philadelphia and kindergarten in Central Harlem, then founding a series of public elementary and secondary schools in East Harlem, and finally, founding the Mission Hill school in Boston's Roxbury neighborhood.

Yes, poverty and racism have a powerful out-of-school impact on the lives of our children, which school alone cannot "undo." But undoing these factors is not the task of schools; the task of schools is to redo schooling so that it meets the strengths that all children bring with them, and joins with their families to make sure that schools are the richest and most inspiring places they can be. All children come to school with their imaginations intact, even where trauma or sensory deprivation has wounded them severely (which can occur to privileged children as well). What traumatized children require is a space to reflect upon life, not boot camps to further alienate them from their human aspirations.

I discovered early on that standardized tests were the most deceptive instruments, hiding rather than exposing the intelligence and capacities of children with societal disadvantages. Through careful and well-documented efforts, I learned that the kids I taught often gave smarter and well-thought out responses to short-answer and multiple-choice questions than their middle-class white peers, yet those answers were often marked wrong. Whether we were talking about a second grade reading test or a fourth grade math test, what was being picked up from the children were abilities that had less to do with reading and math than educators assumed. Forty years later we can still see this, even on SAT questions!

I also discovered early on that young boys were doubly wounded in schools for reasons both obvious and subtle. The earlier schools sought to inculcate so-called "academic" skills, the deeper the damage and the more permanent the "achievement" gap.

I found, too, that the remarkable early independence that poverty requires of the young is rarely rewarded in schools and, indeed, is often turned into a disadvantage, along with all the other early skills that come from having to cope with a less accommodating (coddling) environment.

And on and on.

Along with some of the most exciting progressive educators in the 1960s and 1970s, I had an opportunity to explore these questions and imagine how schools could be redesigned to better unleash the intellectual capacities of all children—starting with their natural talent for play and imagination, invention and exploration, and building and creating both material and abstract ideas. I came to see that the harsh discipline we criticized underprivileged, poor families for was often a tough-love response meant to prepare their children for a punitive and discriminatory world and to protect their children from authorities over which these families had little control. It may, in today's terms, be a maladaptive response—but who am I to say? Maybe the institutions of society need to be changed before such adaptive strategies can be dropped.

I reasoned that, if I could create an alliance with these families, I could create a school that would, at least to some degree, allow us all to utilize our intelligence better in the raising of our children. Rather than focus schooling on behavioral discipline we could focus on the intellectual disciplines—from art, science, history, and literature. Was it possible to find the kind of collegiality that was necessary to sustain me personally, and could it collectively produce something more than any one of us could produce in our own isolated classrooms? Collegial critique—a setting in which people were both supportive and critical of each other—was far harder than I envisioned, and more time consuming. Also, the trade-offs in seeking such collegiality were more open to question than I expected. In spending our time in critique, we reduced the time available for other forms of professional growth and for paying attention to our own immediate classroom/student tasks. Finally, there were trade-offs that I hadn't anticipated between a staff-governed school, in which decisions were largely made collectively, and a family-style school, in which parents felt their voices were critically important. The cohesiveness and empowerment of one often encroached on the other, particularly with respect to those parents who had more choices and a greater sense of entitlement.

It would be untrue to say that I succeeded in all my dreams for the classrooms or schools I was most responsible for creating. But I'm not sure I expected to. I probably thought that I'd at least find the right answers to more of my questions, even if they didn't become norms. None of the above issues have ever been resolved for me, and they are all ones that I wish I could tackle once again with the energy of my youth. Sometimes I regret that I didn't stay put at CPE/CPESS schools, instead of reaching for more grandiose schemes.

None of the schools I founded were protected from the drive toward standardization that has surrounded them in the last twenty years. Above all, I never figured out how, in the world of here and now, schools could survive without very particular conditions—strong godfathers, politically strong leadership, and a few politically savvy parents, for example. Sustainability, short of revolutionizing the entire system to one's way of thinking or breaking altogether free of the public system, has eluded me.

In fact, it's the first school—CPE I—and the last—Mission Hill— that have remained more or less intact, in terms of their practices. Begun in 1974, CPE I is still alive today, thirty-five years later. And although some of its fundamental practices are now in question, and may or may not survive its sixth principal (its third in the last five years), for nearly thirty years it took on the fundamental challenges of providing an equitable education without dropping its continuity and tradition. Graduates returned as teachers and parents, and we were able to all keep in touch over the last three decades or more. The next three schools have had a harder time, although CPE II is still a popular and successful school, and River East could still be if it hadn't run into a deep political crisis that led to the removal of the principal and, essentially, the closing of the school itself. CPESS, the secondary school—in some ways the most radical and deviant of all the schools I helped found—survived, alas. I say alas because, after the first twelve or thirteen years, it dropped most of the characteristics it was famous for and became a fairly traditional secondary school of last resort. But the impact on its first ten graduating classes has been immense; this July they are holding a reunion to celebrate the skills and values they believe CPESS embodied.

Many of the many other schools modeled on CPE and CPESS still survive. Some have reverted to quite traditional practices while others still resemble the founding dreams and practices. And many teachers and parents are out there trying to reinvent our stories.

Here are some of my assumptions about schools that have proven only partially accurate. I presumed that a strong community of parents and teachers working together would be nearly impossible to rend asunder and could protect their school in times of trouble. The assumption might be true, but working together under adverse circumstances—especially if the formal leadership (the principal) has other intentions—is far easier said than done. The inequality of power between the school's constituency and the central system is often too huge. Parents and staff sometimes can work together to remove a hostile or inadequate principal, but even a friendly administration can eventually throw up its hands and say, "enough." Meanwhile, teachers and parents who have other responsibilities can soon retire from the fight. Even if schools can select their own leaders—which is not built in to the leadership process in New York City—sustainability is not guaranteed.

I read, with envy, the literature from my old independent New York City school, and I visit and talk to current students. I often marvel at how they have kept intact the dreams of their founders for nearly half a century—even some with quite radical beliefs. But I note also how many have made drastic compromises over time, even given their greater freedom.

Relationships to what I'll roughly call "downtown" required me to rethink assumptions too. I had hoped, even in New York City, that I could focus 97 percent of my energy on the world within the school—kids, families, and staff. Given that the schools I was involved with were not closely defined by their physical borders, I didn't even need to play as much community politics as many other principals might have. And given various favorable factors, I assumed I could play the political game only when I chose and take risks that other principals didn't dare take. However, in New York City, I also really wanted to change the world around me. I was aware that these favorable factors often inhibited my effectiveness. "Oh well," others might say, "*she* can get away with, *she* has other resources, *she*. . . ." Often these assumptions were untrue. I had, for example, no additional resources at CPE I or CPE II, but there was an "aura" around me that suggested I had privileges and contacts, that I "knew" powerful people. In fact, part of this aura was a sleight of hand on my part, and far more people can and do play it just as I did. You use whatever you can! But you pay a price for it too. It makes your work seem more insuperable to others, if not unfair.

The offer to move to Boston came at a time when we lost the fight over designing a mini-system for both more autonomy and accountability in our New York City schools. This mini-system would have created a free learning zone containing 10 percent of the public school system. While the original proposal, funded by the Annenberg Institute to the tune of nearly fifty million dollars, had been approved by the schools chancellor, school board, state commissioner, and union, it didn't survive due to two critical changes: New York City got a new city schools chancellor and New York State a new state commissioner.

This interlude of "out of the school" work, including a year traveling around as a Senior Urban Fellow at the Annenberg Institute at Brown University, was interesting, but I missed the daily life of school—its three-ring circus of dilemmas and, above all, the sustained human contact with kids and adults. I was running out of good stories to tell, those anecdotes that particularly suit this or that Big Idea.

I had already "retired" from my New York City work, so I accepted a challenge offered in Boston. In 1996, Boston offered a few schools the chance to explore the same idea we had proposed for New York City with the freed learning zone, albeit on a smaller scale. A move to Boston seemed fine, and this time I could do it from inside the schoolhouse. I could start a school which would be exempt from most downtown rules and union rules as part of a network of pilot schools. The offer also came from a superintendent I knew from other national projects and assumed I could trust. At sixty-five, I was sufficiently old enough to want to work not quite so hard, and I figured that with more freedom from downtown the job would be less anxiety-producing. I still had so many unanswered questions going back to my first years of teaching, and now I could focus my attention on those again. Creating waves was another matter; Boston already had an organization that was set up to do the latter and didn't need much from me. This organization was modeled after one we had created a decade earlier in New York City—a network called the Center for Collaborative Education. So I took full advantage of the opportunity to keep my eyes on the daily life of school while others handled the system. It was an extraordinary success, both Mission Hill and the Pilot School network. But they all are now struggling with how to sustain themselves under changed district leadership and retiring founding principals.

In short, one pays a price for how one succeeds—everything from legitimate and understandable envy and fear ("what's she out for?") to less attractive but natural jealousies that cover up a failure to exert some courage and independence on one's own. And such responses complicate life when one needs a favor, which is probably inevitable even for completely private schools. We are all embedded in the larger world and every act sets off reactions. Life is full of compromises. It's a tautology. It's even part of what we need to teach kids about—how to compromise. It's not an accident that at Mission Hill, the "office" was my office, the staff office, the parent office, and the place where calls came and went and notes were written on the board. When kids were sent to the office, I wanted it to be a learning experience where they could hear me talking to downtown—cajoling, arguing, conspiring. I wanted them to read the notes on our faculty blackboard about our comings and goings. (The kids at some point asked for their own board.) We added extra computers to the office to insure that kids would have additional reasons to hang out there.

But of course, in my case, I chose a public and political stance because it was that combination of fascination with the actual life of the classroom and school—each child and staff member within it— alongside my lifelong love affair with political democracy that drove me. I thought, occasionally, about keeping a lower profile. I had a friend who did just that and ran a remarkably different kind of public middle school for over thirty years that was known only to those in the know. It just wasn't in me to do that. From day one I used the pen to express my educational ideas. I wrote friendly, accessible (I hoped) letters to parents starting the year I taught Kindergarten half-time in Chicago. I wrote weekly letters to students' homes in every role I subsequently played. From the start, I wrote articles about schooling for various non-teacher magazines—primarily *Dissent* (a socialist magazine with a long history), *The Nation*, and so on. When I began to get concerned with the role of standardized testing in education, I joined with others to form the North Dakota Study Group and examine and resist such forms of evaluation. I began to speak on the subject around the country, and I wrote a few pamphlets and booklets aimed at teachers and parents in an effort to demystify testing. Until I became a "real" principal, I was active in the UFT-AFL-CIO and wrote for the union press. I joined the initial founding board for the National Board of Professional Teaching Standards (which is where I met two future superintendents I served under). I was elected to my own local school Board and had a chance to see the world from that stance. And so on.

Of course, I was lucky to be the recipient of a prestigious MacArthur award just after starting CPESS. Being marked as a "genius," rather than just a dedicated school person, was immensely useful in elevating the status of my opinions about the world of schooling. And I was fortunate to be part of several movements after the end of the civil rights and peace movements of the 1960s and 1970s. Lilian Weber and Hugh Dyasi of the City College Workshop Center provided a kind of stimulation and excitement around my ideas that many of today's teachers do not run into in the course of pursuing their professional development. Vito Perrone's response to Head Start testing initiated the North Dakota Study group, a mini-movement that gave us precious opportunities to argue and discuss ideas that were not fashionable. Finally, a decade later, Ted Sizer's book *Horace's Compromise* led to the formation of the Coalition of Essential Schools, a network of hundreds of schools throughout the nation where I felt at home. And each of these led to other offshoots. From Weber, I got to know Eleanor Duckworth and Pat Carini's work, and our schools had the chance to see themselves not as lonely mavericks but part of an important stream of thought with historic roots and well-established ideas. Later the free school and home schooling movements offered new ideas and ideals to my work.

So it was not entirely surprising that I was constantly frustrated by the claim that whatever I did had no political significance because it was the impact of my "unique" public circumstances, etc. It was as if "they" were purposely undermining my expertise and example by putting my work on a pedestal and sending the message that it couldn't be generalized. In fact what I did might have required fewer compromises had I not had such a public life.

But we are all unique; and I was neither the best student in any of the schools I attended nor a remarkably good writer or stylist, and my political connections were as much pretend as real. Besides, as my best friends will attest, I have plenty of natural faults that made my work harder. It's *choosing* to see oneself as a "player" and having the luxury of being able to fail that I excelled in—if one wants to put it that way. Far more of us can do that, in our own way. We need to help one another do it.

What we do can be done to scale, but we need to start from the premise that "doing it our own way" includes making one's work accessible and reviewable by the public. If all good to great schools are unique, expressing the character of their place and particular people, then a good to great system has to start there: encouraging such uniqueness, not undermining it. I was just plain lucky to be in the game when two such systems (District 4 in East Harlem and the New York Alternative School system) existed under Tony Alvarado and Steve Phillips. It took less subterfuge to build one's unique school with these people around as protectors, although even then it needed a few other guardians! And, alas, in the end, they were undermined too.

What it comes down to is each of us taking advantage of our own particular circumstances. That, after all, is what we're educating for. Happily, the purpose of education is consistent with the struggle to create good schools. If we share that struggle with our staff, families, and above all, kids, it needn't be as lonely as we sometimes make it.

Can these coalitions and paradigms from the past sustain a new generation of like-minded maverick reformers? Will they refashion it in ways that might, at first, seem disturbing to me but will, in the end, emerge the stronger for it? Will these difficult trade-offs be met in ways I did not know how to do, or will the trade-offs themselves be new ones I never encountered? A new language will be needed as so much of our language has been co-opted (e.g. school autonomy and empowerment now excludes the ability to make decisions about the essentials of schooling) and the paradigm of accountability to one's public is built on the model of profit-making businesses with their shoddy record of public responsibility!

Of course, in the end, each of us comes to this with a unique history and enters it at a unique time and place. We step into the stream of progressive education, which has roots that are centuries old, at a particular curve. Our own particular stance will depend on whether the current is faster or slower, the bottom mushier or harsher. I wish I could come back a century from now and see what others have made of the work we did, much as we took the work of the late nineteenth- and early twentieth-century reformers and tried to refashion it.

School:
A Manageable Interruption
Chris Mercogliano

I attended my neighborhood public schools in Washington, DC, until the ninth grade, at which point I was sent to a Jesuit prep school about ten miles north of the city. My elementary education was pretty standard. Kindergarten was half-day and left me with two enduring memories. During afternoon nap, I made sure to place my mat next to that of a little girl who lived a couple of blocks from me because she was very pretty and all I could think about was kissing her. One day the teacher finally caught me in the act. I was firmly reprimanded and from then on had to lie down on the opposite side of the room. My second memory is lying in wait on the way home from school in order to beat up another boy in the class who was attracted to the same girl.

All I recall from first grade is being totally smitten with the teacher, who was young and nice, and had the most wonderful milk chocolate skin. There was plenty of competition from the other boys, but I don't remember any fights to win her favor.

Mrs. Weiss was my second grade teacher. She was older and matronly and didn't like me because I would finish my work faster than everyone else and then begin teasing the girls who sat near me and doing other disruptive things. I distinctly remember her saying to me once, while she hauled me off to the principal's office for the umpteenth time, that I was going to be one helluva good lawyer some day because of the way I so fervently argued my innocence.

My third grade teacher was also older and matronly, but very cool, too. Mrs. Leckie understood that the best way to handle rambunctious boys was to assign them responsibilities. So she put me in charge of accounting for the school savings bond money and sent me to the bookroom when there was a need for more books, or to find the janitor if there was a maintenance issue in the classroom. Then one day a substitute teacher appeared and we were told Mrs. Leckie was sick and wouldn't be back for a while. In fact, she never returned at all, and I learned the following year she had died of cancer.

It was in fourth grade that I fell in love for the first time. Stephanie had moved to the neighborhood from another city and I thought she was the most beautiful girl I had ever seen. Lucky for me, she lived near my best friend, Greg Sprehn, and so every day after school I would hang out on their street until it was time to go home for dinner. But before long Stephanie began showing affection toward some of the other boys in the class, and I grew so jealous that I began saying mean things that reduced her to tears. I vividly remember the day the teacher told me to stay put while the other kids went off to the lunchroom. Mrs. Koch, a stern, middle-aged woman whom I was not terribly fond of, told me in no uncertain terms that the way I was treating Stephanie was unacceptable. This time I didn't argue because I knew she was right and was already feeling pretty bad about the whole situation. Mrs. Koch then called Stephanie in so that I could apologize to her, and that was the end of it. One of my only "educational memories" dates from Mrs. Koch's class. She was a bird lover and had brought in a lot of books about birds, as well as several pairs of binoculars and a small telescope that she allowed us to use to watch birds in the wooded lot next to the school. She even took us on a birding expedition and taught us to identify a large number of different varieties. Those experiences awakened a lifelong love of birds in me.

My fifth grade teacher was older, matronly, and stern, and nothing about that year stands out, except perhaps for joining the school safety patrol. My post was on a busy Wisconsin Avenue corner, and I can recall taking very seriously the responsibility of helping other kids cross the street safely.

When I was in sixth grade my stepfather told me he would pay me ten bucks if I got straight A's. In those days we were graded on nearly twenty items, and I don't think he thought I could pull it off. Handwriting was my downfall. Each quarterly report card would come back with seventeen A's and a D in that dreaded subject. At the end of the year, however, Mrs. Fields, who was older and matronly, but kind, informed us that if we took home and cleaned a safety patrol raincoat she would raise one of our grades a notch. I pleaded for three coats and she would only agree to two, but when my stepfather saw my final tally of seventeen A's and a B he declared it close enough and gave me the reward anyway.

My most vivid memory of junior high school is how huge and intimidating it felt. I will never forget that first morning in the auditorium, sitting there surrounded by my elementary school pals and waiting for my homeroom assignment. There was no effort to disguise the tracking system in those days and my good grades turned out to be my undoing. By the time my name was called, I was sitting all by myself because every one of my friends had been placed in lower tracks. When I settled into my homeroom desk I looked around and did see quite a few girls from my sixth grade class, and because of that I was elected class president, which was nothing more than a popularity contest. I suddenly felt important nonetheless, but then I quickly learned how pointless and boring the student council meetings were, and I withdrew my name from consideration in the second semester election.

I have no academic recollections from seventh or eighth grade, other than that school continued to be easy because my mind worked quickly and I was a good test taker. What I do remember was the tremendous social pressure I felt when I found myself thrown in with an entirely different social group. My elementary school friends had all been working class kids like me and I found it a struggle to fit in with a bunch of stylish and self-assured kids from the middle and upper middle classes. Plus I wanted to maintain my relationships with all of my friends from the past too. It was all very confusing, and it was then that I think I felt lonely for the first time.

My mother and step-father, neither of whom had college degrees, held upwardly mobile aspirations for me and thought it would be a good idea if I switched to a prestigious prep school in the suburbs because it would improve my chances of getting into a good college. Also, my stepfather harbored extremely racist views and the public schools were on the verge of instituting forced busing in order to achieve court-ordered desegregation. He did not want me going to school with black kids, and that was that.

My feeling of being out of place multiplied exponentially in high school. Now I was in the midst of spoiled, upper middle class suburban boys and strict and sometimes physically abusive Irish priests. To make matters worse, we had to remain on campus until 5:30 p.m., which separated me even further from my childhood world. Thankfully, school continued to be a breeze, due to the aforementioned reasons as well as to the fact that I think the school was coasting a bit on its puffed-up reputation.

Very little stands out educationally from those four depressing years. I can't say that I ever remember feeling inspired. Mr. Homayouni, at least, managed to make trigonometry and calculus entertaining. A thick cloud of pipe smoke would form around his head as he furiously filled the blackboard with equations. Then he would step back beaming at us and say, "Now boys, isn't that *beooootiful!*" Other days he would regale us with stories like the one about the time he used the laws of probability to win big in Vegas. While I didn't find his passion for math particularly contagious, at least his class didn't drag on like most of the others. There was one other class worth mentioning. As a senior I was able to take an elective in European literature taught by the German professor. Reading novels and short stories by writers like Kafka, Mann, and Conrad opened me up to a much deeper way of looking at myself and the world around me, and I enjoyed writing the interpretive essays that Herr Farrell required us to do. Also as a senior I was allowed to put together a month-long independent study project in the spring. Heeding Mrs. Weiss's prediction and my parents' wishes, I decided to check out the legal profession. This entailed shadowing three judges in different branches of the court system, as well as spending a week in the Public Defender's office. For once I felt like I was learning something important.

The most formative moment of my adolescence, however, had already occurred two summers earlier, when I was a volunteer counselor at a camp for autistic and retarded children. It was there that I discovered how much I enjoyed working with kids and that I met Betsy, my future wife of thirty-five years with whom I would travel to Albany, NY, three years later so that we could volunteer our services at the Free School.

But first I spent a year at Washington and Lee University in Virginia, which had offered me a generous scholarship. It was an excellent school. The classes were very small; the professors were creative, supportive teachers; and at the time there were none of the ridiculous core requirements that exist today. Browsing through the course catalog, I felt like a kid in a candy store with a pocketful of cash. The hard part was choosing only four. And I'm not sure it fully struck me then, but each one was *entirely my choice.* I thoroughly enjoyed all of my classes and my understanding of the world began expanding at an exhilarating pace.

Ironically, although Washington and Lee was known as a very conservative place, it was there that I became quite radicalized. Some of this was the result of the courses I had chosen: in sociology I learned about the vast inequities that are built into the American economic system and my readings in political science exposed the sordid roots of the war in Viet Nam. Outside of class, too, my experience as a volunteer in the Big Brother program and a tutor in the local elementary school taught me firsthand about the stark realities of poverty and the failure of the public schools to address the needs of poor children. By the end of the first semester I had become so troubled by the state of our society that the thought of spending three more years in such a privileged environment studying about the situation was intolerable. I had no idea what, but I had to do something right away to make the world a better place.

Much to my poor mother's dismay I requested a leave of absence from the university effective at the end of the school year. In the meantime I obtained permission to undertake an off-campus independent study project in education. The whole thing was a shot in the dark, really; I knew nothing about educational theory or philosophy and the university had no education department. My entirely self-concocted program would consist of spending my days observing in a rural elementary school and doing as much independent reading as I could accomplish during that time.

Before leaving town to live in a shack on a small dairy farm, I stopped by the student bookstore to grab whatever was on the education shelf, which wasn't much. Serendipitously, however, because it was the early 1970s what I found were the writings of a number of critics of the very same educational model that had brought me to my currently confused and unsettled state. A book with the strange title *Summerhill* caught my eye first, and being short on funds I sat right down beside the bookshelf to crack it open. I couldn't believe what I was reading–a school in England where young children were already directing themselves and learning because *they* wanted to. It seemed totally insane, but also brilliant. I couldn't put the book down, and when I was I finished I gratefully returned it to its place. Here was total confirmation of my decision to strike out on my own.

I left the store with about a dozen books by authors like Dewey, Kozol, Silberman, and Kohl, none of whom I had ever heard of, and drove out to the farm, eager to dive into my project. After a few weeks of observing and reading I began to wonder if I might want to become a teacher. The only trouble was that I had just quit college and teaching required a college degree. Fortunately, I found the solution to my predicament in the back of Jonathan Kozol's book, *Free Schools,* where he listed the names and addresses of a dozen or so of the urban, grassroots schools he had just described. It occurred to me that one of them might be happy to have the volunteer services of a nineteen-year-old with minimal experience and no college credentials. I should add here that Betsy, who was in college in Connecticut, was going through an inner crisis similar to mine, and when I mentioned the idea to her she said she was interested too.

I handwrote individual letters to each of the schools, but one by one the postman began bringing them back because the schools had already folded. Finally I got a single response. It was a brief note from Mary

Leue, the founder of the Free School in Albany, saying that I sounded nice and why didn't Betsy and I stop in for a visit sometime?

Betsy and I spent the summer working to bankroll cash, and in September we set out in an old bakery van that I bought for $300, on the side of which friends had painted a giant rainbow. We slowly wandered north to live in a rustic cabin Betsy's sister had built on the shore of a remote Adirondack lake. By the week before Thanksgiving winter was already baring its teeth, and so we wisely decided to head south, which the geese had already done a month ago.

Looking at the map and seeing that Albany was right on the way back to Washington, we decided to take Mary up on her invitation to visit the Free School. It was a little like landing on Mars. Nothing in my previous experience prepared me for such a high octane free for all. But when Betsy and I compared notes at the end of the day, we both felt drawn to come back after spending Thanksgiving with our families.

When we returned we moved into a two-floor collective in an old building behind the school that Mary had purchased, where four or five other young teachers and volunteers were already living rent-free. No one was getting paid at that time, and so together we made a game of trying to keep our overhead as low as possible.

I found the school daunting to say the least. But what at first seemed to me like total chaos gradually began to make sense. The kids were all so alive and passionate, and the adults clearly loved each and every one of them. Big and little people from different races and social classes had formed a true community free of prejudice, one that by some strange magic became quite orderly when there was a serious issue that needed to be resolved. I began to realize the reason so many of the kids were so fair-minded and responsible was because the adults trusted them to be that way and there wasn't a slew of rules and policies to cover every contingency. I saw kids learning basic academic skills, though it often didn't happen in set ways or on a set schedule. I saw how eager children are to learn when given the chance to do so for their own reasons. And likewise, I saw how important it is to give new students whose attitudes toward themselves and toward learning have been damaged by punitive, standardized schooling time to just play, and hang out, and experiment with their new-found freedom. And most importantly, perhaps, I saw unhappy, antisocial kids slowly shed their defensive armor, and, if we could keep them with us long enough, take charge of their lives and discover how to form intimate relationships with others.

Clearly the fact that I saw miracles happening nearly on a daily basis had to do with the school's wholly unconventional approach to education, and so Betsy and I stayed on and both became permanent members of the staff. Betsy left after nearly twenty years to become a midwife, and I stepped down as director two years ago in order to write fulltime about issues affecting the lives of children, something I had begun doing in the wee hours of the morning and weekends and summers back in the late-80s.

Looking back, I think my primary role was to help sustain the school through its first two generations, to act as a bridge between Mary's founding vision and the dedication of a new group of young teachers and families who have rooted themselves in the community. Looking ahead I feel that my mission is to support the work of this third generation and beyond that, to carry the wisdom I have gained from my thirty-five years at the Free School out to the world at large, and, wherever possible, into the heart of the mainstream.

The Call of the *Zeitgeist*
Ron Miller

There were very few indications, during my early life, that my entire adult career would be devoted to unconventional ideas about education and cultural change. I grew up in comfortable and ordinary circumstances, in a quiet residential neighborhood in a suburb of Chicago. I enjoyed a warm and stable family life. My father and uncle ran a successful family business and always promoted the conservative attitudes that are typical in such cases. I took their worldview as simple common sense, and held onto it for most of my youth even when most of my peers were drawn to antiwar activism and the counterculture of the late 1960s and early 70s. To this day I sometimes shock friends and colleagues (and amuse myself) by recounting that while many teens of that era were wanting to take down the Establishment, I put up a poster of Richard Nixon.

I attended very conventional, well funded public schools all the way through high school, and I thrived in them. I was a bright student and was always interested in learning. I played in school bands, was editor of my high school newspaper, and got involved in various other clubs and activities. On the surface, at least, I had no reason to complain about schooling. It worked for me, and was even rather fun. Still, there were a few wrinkles along the way. In eighth grade I must have tired of my "good boy" image and I became the class clown; by the end of the year my classmates gave me an award for "snappiest answers under pressure." I frequently made fun of one teacher I didn't like, talked back to another, and shrugged off the inevitable slide in my grades. It was a very mild rebellion, and by the next year, I got serious again, but as I look back I realize that it was, indeed, an existential revolt against the authority of school. Some buried part of my identity was allowed to show up, in a meekly comedic way, before going back into hiding.

When I went off to college, I wasn't focused on any career in particular, and deliberately sought out a program where I could roam across the liberal arts without declaring a traditional major. I found the opportunity at a 60s-era experimental program at Michigan State called Justin Morrill College. I took courses in philosophy, psychology, literature, and intellectual history, and seminars on broad interdisciplinary topics. Still politically and morally conservative, I nevertheless took ownership of my learning and resisted the constraints of academic disciplines. I had my own questions about human nature and history, and followed my inquiring mind wherever it led. Eventually, it led me to radical ideas that burst the protective bubble of my suburb-topian identity, and I discovered the still relatively new literature in humanistic psychology—launched by the ideas of Carl Rogers and Abraham Maslow—which proposed that human potential is far, far greater than our present culture allows or even recognizes. This was the great turning point for me. From my junior year of college on, I no longer took modern industrial/consumer society as the pinnacle of human achievement, and began to explore alternatives.

I pursued my inquiry into humanistic psychology through a masters program at Duquesne University, where the focus was on a radical, existentialist approach called phenomenology. The primary teaching of this philosophy is that the realities of society and the larger world are not fixed and objective, because human beings actively create meaning from experience. The authority of society can be challenged—indeed, needs to be challenged—when new conditions or new understandings change our experience. (This insight was at the heart of Thomas Jefferson's vision of democracy, by the way.) I realized that formal education is the process by which a culture exercises its authority over experience and meaning, and I further realized that we were entering a post-industrial world where this authority was becoming obsolete. I was drawn to radical educational ideas and I first discovered the work of

Maria Montessori. I spent three years taking the training for Montessori teachers and working with young children. As a young man having big ideas but little prior experience with children, I was not a very good teacher. But that experience, especially my interactions with suburban parents who demanded conventional signs of educational success, fueled my deeper inquiry into the cultural and political meanings of schooling.

Montessori schools are popular in many places because they provide such tidy and orderly environments for children, and they showcase young children's intellectual powers. But I realized from the start that Maria Montessori hadn't just invented a clever method for turning out well behaved child prodigies. Rather, her writings about education and society were laced with the same critical analysis that I had come to through my studies and reflection: human nature, she insisted, is capable of so much more goodness and spiritual fulfillment than modern civilization allows to be expressed, and if we would provide children with nourishing, rather than coercive, learning environments, we would see a cultural transformation, a nonviolent revolution, that might create a better world.

This vision appealed to me. I had not rebelled angrily against my own upbringing or society's flaws and injustices; I had come to a radical understanding by gentle means, through quiet study and exploring the comfortably middle class "human potential movement" that followed from the suggestions of Maslow and Rogers. How did a sheltered, bookish introvert from the suburbs leave the worldview of his family and friends behind and turn into a passionate advocate for cultural revolution? The best I can figure it, I think there must be some truth in the concept of *zeitgeist*—an actual "spirit of the times" that lurks in the depths of our collective unconscious. From the beginnings of the harsh industrial age, a romantic counterculture arose to challenge it, and in the 1960s it gathered strength as a viable postmodern, post-industrial worldview. This counterculture is not simply an intellectual or political movement, but seems to be a new stage in the evolution of humanity's consciousness, the spirit of a new cultural phase.

Although I stubbornly resisted the youth movement, with its hippies and hallucinogens and subversive music, I became much more sensitive to this emerging *zeitgeist* as I matured and expanded my understanding. It helped me make sense of the world. I could sense that the culture I had inherited was entering an age of decline and eventual transformation. I've always thought it was a bit ironic that in my doctoral dissertation I revisited the 60s but with a reversed sense of loyalties; now I saw the rebellious youths and their radical mentors as the heroes, and the true villains were the defenders of the Establishment. It wasn't the Dionysian excesses of the 60s that attracted me (I never would have fit into the Haight-Ashbury scene), but the opening of new possibilities for radical democracy, spirituality, and reconnection to nature. Out of the toxic smog of the industrial age, a more *holistic* worldview started to become visible, and I was caught by its spirit.

Montessori's vision spoke directly to this awareness, and very soon I saw that a whole range of dissident educators spoke to it as well. The prophetic educators who have resisted industrial schooling since its inception—from Johann Pestalozzi and Bronson Alcott, to Rudolf Steiner, to Franciso Ferrer, to A.S. Neill and Ivan Illich and John Holt— were, like me, moved by a romantic/holistic understanding of life, and thus their pedagogies, as diverse as they were, could be described collectively as *holistic education*. My career path was ordained when I came across an article in *New Age* magazine by Jack Canfield (before he became famous for his "chicken soup for the soul" books) that named this philosophy for me. It was one of those moments when the soul recognizes its purpose, when an individual finds his or her calling. Holistic education.

I returned to graduate school—at Boston University—to pursue a multidisciplinary inquiry into the historical and cultural roots of American education. Although I loved the intellectual atmosphere of academia, there was some friction between my personal scholarly mission and the expectations of my professors. "Holism" was considered a fuzzy, new agey topic, not a legitimate subject for academic study, and my wide ranging interest in diverse educational philosophies was seen as too broad. My advisors would not accept my dissertation and suggested revisions. Nevertheless, I rediscovered the gentle but inspired rebel in me, and refused to confine my studies to fit these constraints. I left the program and self-published what I had written because I had a story to tell the world, even if it would not satisfy my professors. This book, *What Are Schools For? Holistic Education in American Culture*, established my niche in the educational literature and went through several printings. I thought it appropriate that a study of educational rebellion would itself be published as an act of rebellion. Twelve years later, wanting to prove that I deserved the academic credentials after all, I returned to B.U. to write a more acceptable dissertation (this was my study of the sixties), which was then accepted by a respected academic press and published as *Free Schools, Free People: Education and Democracy After the 1960s.*

When I first left the doctoral program, I had no interest in teaching at the college level. My role was to be an advocate or popularizer of this new worldview, and so I launched the journal *Holistic Education Review* in 1988. I sought out whoever was writing about whole-brain learning, multiple intelligences, ecological literacy, planetary citizenship, peace education, and spirituality in education, and invited them to contribute their ideas. I also contacted advocates of Waldorf and Montessori education, homeschooling, progressive education, and other alternative methods, and asked them to join a conversation that would, for the first time, bring their perspectives together. In 1989, I collaborated with seven people who stood out as leading voices in these movements to plan a conference on holistic education, which took place near Chicago the following year. Out of that meeting arose a network we called GATE—the Global Alliance for Transforming Education. We held additional conferences over the next few years, and issued a manifesto, "Education 2000: A Holistic Perspective," that was fairly widely circulated and still shows up sometimes today. (One of the highlights of my career was attending a conference in Guadalajara, Mexico, and watching 300 people huddling in working groups to discuss our document in Spanish.)

In the 1980s and 1990s, those of us drawn to holism, human potential, and "new age" ideas earnestly believed that we were part of a revolutionary wave that would soon transform modern civilization. The rising interest in spiritual practices, alternative medicine, organic food, feminism, deep ecology, green capitalism, homeschooling, and other emerging paths seemed very promising. The Berlin Wall came down, and we thought this was a signal of the new world in the making. If we could introduce holistic education into the mainstream, there would be a revolution in educational thinking and practice. If we could distribute enough magazines and books, and hold inspiring conferences, we would change the world. Obviously, we were a bit too optimistic. The modernist/industrial worldview is tenaciously and violently clinging to power. The reactionary and authoritarian agenda of educational standardization has completely marginalized holistic approaches. Today, twenty years after the founding of *Holistic Education Review* and GATE, there is no holistic education movement, only a widely scattered group of individuals and small, isolated alternative schools even using the term.

For several years I taught in the education program at Goddard College, historically a leader in progressive, innovative higher education. Instead of teaching courses, I worked as a mentor to adult learners who followed their own self-designed study plans. (If I had been more hip in the seventies I would have gone to college there myself.) I advised many idealistic people who wanted to bring radical pedagogy to their schools or communities. On one hand it was very gratifying to see these visionaries go out into the world to plant seeds of educational revolution. On the other hand, I heard too many discouraging reports about the obstacles and opposition they often had to face. Their passion for nourishing young people's learning and growth was so often thwarted by this culture's obsession with "standards." We were sending these brave, lone crusaders to do battle with an empire, and unless they could establish their own countercultural islands, they were coming back in frustration. A few years ago I left Goddard (temporarily, at least) for a change of pace, and I am currently teaching conventional undergraduate courses in American history and contemporary world issues. Given the constraints of vocation-oriented higher education, my pedagogy isn't as radical or holistic as I might like, but I have to admit that I enjoy being the "sage on the stage" for once, and it's worthwhile challenging these young people to stretch themselves intellectually farther than they would have gone on their own.

I continue to write about holistic education. Like everyone else in the known universe, I've put up a website to promote my ideas. But I've come to accept that the transition to a holistic worldview, if it succeeds at all, will be a long, difficult process, not a magical "paradigm shift." I don't spend my time and energy touring the country to give workshops or speak to audiences, nor am I trying to build a national or international organization. I've come to accept that an educational revolution will follow, not lead, a much larger cultural evolution, and that this will take a while. To the extent that parents and educators feel the pull of the emerging *zeitgeist*, or simply abandon the sinking ship of industrialized schooling when they see how badly it damages their children and students, a self-organizing revolution may take shape. "Self-organization" is a property of organic systems, as described by some holistic scientists; in response to changing conditions, systems can make a qualitative leap to a new level of complexity. Social and cultural institutions, too, may respond to a changing world by spontaneously self-organizing in new ways. People and institutions respond to the call of a new spirit of the times. They don't need prophets or teachers or leaders to do so, although some of us, who for some reason are especially receptive to the *geist,* are able to give voice to the emerging new consciousness. So I continue to write and edit and publish. That is what I feel called to do.

What Do You Mean, You've Decided? We're Supposed To Decide!
Jerry Mintz

I was born in Worcester, Massachusetts, a small industrial city. My father was a scrap metal dealer and my mother was a piano teacher. I went to public school and never liked it much. When I was very young, our family would visit my mother's parents in Boston every week or two. My grandfather, William Blatt, was a lawyer and occasional judge. He had been president of the Massachusetts Law Society, but his real passion was writing and philosophy. He knew so much about Shakespeare that he wrote a play called *After the Curtain Falls*, which consisted of additional acts of Shakespearean plays, written in iambic pentameter. It was performed all over Europe.

At some point during these visits, my grandfather would sit down with me and ask me what I wanted to learn. That simple act was the most powerful influence on my idea of how learning should take place. People probably thought he was crazy, talking to a seven-year-old about atheism and agnosticism, about what makes things humorous, about the ego, the id and the superego, the causes of the world wars, Einstein's theory and great discoveries in science, about anything I wanted to know. But I remember these things to this day.

My grandfather also wrote epigrams, little sayings that sometimes appeared over the headlines of the *Boston Globe*. I remember clearly sitting around the dining room table as he, my family and I would go over them to decide which would go into his series of published booklets. In fact, to honor him we recently published a book of his epigrams with cartoons made by Albert Lamb.

In looking at one of the epigram books, I noticed a folded piece of paper fall out. On the paper was a note to my father, written after some sort of argument. It said, "Dear Dad: Read *Blattitudes* #5, 8, 29, 53, 62, 77, 96, 122, 183, and 202 before talking to me. Jerry."

These are some of them:
5. Everyone is entitled to a few hundred faults.
8. Forgiving is a great luxury. Only the rich in spirit can afford it.
29. Tolerance is the willingness to admit that you may be wrong. As for me, I am never wrong.
53. Conscious ignorance is helpful, unconscious ignorance is dangerous.
77. The kind of people who can't say "no" to themselves can say it very easily to others.
183. Don't assume that because your children love you that they approve of you.

It must have been some argument!

Strangely, as close as I was to my grandfather, I hardly felt any loss when he died. Perhaps it was because he had suffered with cancer, or because we had moved further away to New York. But I have always felt that the real reason was because he is still inside of me, keeping me company with his ideas and wit.

Perhaps as a result of my early experience in that learner-centered approach, I was always skeptical of school. Our family moved to Long

Island when I was twelve years old so my mother could be near her beloved sister Josey, who was a poet and artist. My mother continued teaching piano and my father got a job with Josey's husband selling filters and sewage systems for his company.

Fortunately my family never put any pressure on me to do homework or get good grades, and I never cared about them. When I was about fifteen I got so fed up with school I wrote this poem:

I hate this darn unthinking school
Which professes to teach you the Golden Rule–
"You fool me and I'll make you a fool"
Against this I will rebel

Many's the time when I've hated to stay
When the bored, boring teacher had nothing to say.
But "No!" says the teacher, "You can't go away!"
And this I will also retell

So I learned what the bored, boring teacher had taught
And, thusly, I learned to be bored on the spot.
And ever since, I've been bored at the thought
Of the trash that the school has to sell

Oh, I'm sure education in school's not all bad
And I'll know things of interest when I am a grad.
But the camouflage job on the interest is sad
And the learning won't set very well

And so every morning at just 8 O'Clock
I rush in the school and behind me they lock
The door to my prison, and I start to walk
Through the prison, from cell to cell.

Not long after that I organized some of my friends into a group we called "The Thinker's Club." Except for me, we were all the elite students from the school. The other members went on to Harvard, Yale, and Princeton; became doctors, lawyers, and business leaders.

We got together about twice a week and our agenda was to brainstorm any questions we wanted to discuss, without censorship. There were no adults involved. Actually, a lot of the questions we discussed came from me. If we didn't know the answers we went out and found guest speakers, or went to see rabbis, ministers, and philosophy students, etc. I realize now that this was the first school I ever started.

Recently, I came across a woman who was a member of our club. She's now a grandmother and a law professor. She said the club had a great influence on her. I know of another member who became a professor at U. Mass. at Amherst, and another who founded a computer company in California. For me, this club had a far more important influence on my life than the high school we all went to. Although that public high school is often listed in the nation's top one hundred, I call it the best high school of a failed system. For example, when I was a junior I was one of ten students out of seven hundred applicants who were accepted into a cancer research summer program, where we learned about and did real cancer research at a Long Island lab. But the following year, taking high school biology, I found it so irrelevant that I barely squeaked by with a D, and I didn't care.

As a teen, I discovered that there were alternative colleges, but my parents wouldn't let me go to Antioch College in Ohio. Instead, I wound up going to an "experimental" program at Hofstra University, New College. It was supposed to be innovative in that we took each subject one at a time for six weeks. But that meant there was a midterm every three weeks, so it was really like glorified high school. While I was there I came across a Goddard College catalog. It was beautiful, actually written by a poet, Will Hamlin. My parents said I could go if I got a scholarship, not expecting that I would.

One of the most important courses I took at Goddard was Community Laboratory, taught by Alan Walker. In that course we went into the community and started things. Since I had been a licensed ham radio operator since I was fourteen, one of the projects I started was an amateur radio club. Another was a science 4-H club, in which I taught local children some of the techniques I had learned while I was in the program at the Long Island laboratory. We were testing a theory I had developed upon discovering that 17,000 German beekeepers had an extremely low rate of cancer (neoplastic disease). Of course, I had a budget of only fifty dollars. When I had to leave the college for its two-month winter work term, it seemed natural to me to turn the research over to the club, the oldest member of which was thirteen! Goddard put out a story on that, which got national attention, and in the end, an apiary found my work very interesting and took over the research.[1]

That experience turned out to be a turning point for me as I found myself evolving from science, which I thought would be my field, to education. I did it more or less this way: from science to medicine to psychiatry to psychology to sociology to education. This route to education has led me to view education itself in a very therapeutic and holistic way.

My next major project while at Goddard was to start organizing a democratic recreation center in the town of Plainfield. I proposed this as part of a major independent study, but the study was not approved. It seemed to me that the college liked to talk about community involvement but was afraid of what would happen if someone actually did it. So I decided to do it anyway and signed up for three regular courses. We got the use of an old former warehouse and renovated it ourselves with the kids. The recreation center eventually opened, dedicated by Philip Hoff, who was governor of the state at that time.

But the college was not amused that I had gone ahead and done the project after they rejected it. Even though I got good evaluations for the courses I took, they used the progressive philosophy against me, saying that I could not have properly done the best I could because I had spent so much time on the project they had not approved, and took away credit for the whole semester!

At that point, I nearly quit the college, but because I had a glimmer of hope of getting the credit back, I returned. One of my next independent studies was to research the causes of juvenile delinquency. I hitch-hiked around the country looking at various facilities, interviewing students, and eventually wrote a paper called *The Philosophy of Juvenile Delinquency*. Essentially, I described much delinquency as a form of unconscious civil disobedience, expressing the anger that children had about being discriminated against. I also used sources such as Albert Camus' *The Rebel*. One day I received a note from the professor who had approved the study, giving me a deadline for submission. She had been on the committee that had taken away my previous semester's credit, as if that were the reason I was doing it, and now I needed some artificial prod. This angered me so much that I told her that the paper was done, but that she would never see it. Actually it was good enough that a congressman and James Farmer, the great civil rights leader, eventually used it. After the professor's daughter and son-in-law read it, they convinced me to let her see it. Upon reading it, she immediately began to fight to get my credit back from the previous semester. I never got it but I felt it was a moral victory.

When I organized the recreation center I had never heard of Summerhill or of democratic schools. I did eventually read *Summerhill* and then one day, while I was hitch-hiking in Amsterdam, NY, I saw another hitcher who was wearing a peace symbol. He told me he got it in Trafalgar Square in London. I asked him if he had heard of Summerhill and he said he had gone there, and that Herb Snitzer, a photographer, and Zoe, A.S. Neill's daughter, had started a school based on Summerhill in upstate NY. I contacted them, visited, and did my work term there instead of at my uncle's chemical laboratory on Long Island. I loved working there, but wanted to see if I could do something that Neill said he couldn't do—start a democratic school for children who were disadvantaged and from low income families.

My Goddard thesis was called *On the Starting of a School,* and it outlined the process I used to start a democratic school in Plainfield. The idea was to have a school for local children and foster children, who would be boarding. That project eventually split into two schools while I was away getting a Master's degree (so I wouldn't have to go to Vietnam). The day school ran for thirty years and was mostly for Goddard faculty children. The school for foster children is still going almost forty-five years later. In its early years, as a pioneering group home, it was so successful that many other similar group home/schools were created, which led to the closing of the state's only reform school.

Meanwhile, I was in Yellow Springs, Ohio, at what has now become Antioch New England Graduate School. I began to organize a democratic recreation center there. We were only supposed to spend one semester in Ohio, before interning in Baltimore. When I found out that the Baltimore school district required a loyalty oath, I refused to go and informed the director that I had decided to stay in Yellow Springs and work on the development of the recreation center. *"You've* decided!" Roy Fairfield barked at me. "We're supposed to decide! What will you do if we say you can't stay? You'll stay anyway, right?" I told him that I would. "Well, then, just write and tell us what you are doing!" We've stayed friends for four decades.

In organizing the center I had been meeting with an interracial and cross-cultural group of kids, and had found funding from the community council, as per Arthur Morgan's suggestion. Morgan was the creator of Antioch's pioneering co-op learning program, in which students spend half their time in actual jobs. It was the first such program in the country, and Morgan was in his mid-nineties at the time.

When we couldn't find a building to meet in, and the Presbyterian Church, which had an empty wing, had turned down our request, Morgan gave me one of my most important lessons: As I was telling him the situation he turned away from me and slowly started reaching for the phone. He started to dial. I thought he might really be senile— he wasn't even listening to me—but it turned out he was calling one of his former students, who was one of the two millionaires in town. His name was Morris Bean.

The conversation went something like this: "Hello, Morris. This is Arthur Morgan. I'm fine. You remember several years ago when the Presbyterian Church was expanding and they said that they were going to serve not just their own congregation, but the whole community? They did some fundraising. Well, there are some young people here who are trying to start a recreation center and they're looking for a place to have that recreation center. They have funding and support, but the church turned them down. Now, you put money into that, didn't you? Yes, I thought so. Well, if you'll just get me the list of some of the others."

As Morris Bean was getting the list of other people who had contributed to that fund, Morgan looked up at me and said, and I'll never forget this; "I think that this is ethical!" That was an important lesson for me from the old Quaker about how to get things done.

A week later, I got a phone call from the Presbyterian Church at 1a.m.—they'd been rethinking my request and wanted to know if we were still interested in using the wing of the church for the recreation center and if I could come to a meeting the next morning. A week after that, we opened, the first interracial center in the town. It evolved into a community center that continues to this day. I wonder if the people in Yellow Springs know that this is something else they owe to Arthur Morgan.

After finishing my MAT and helping the school in Plainfield get off the ground, I decided to see if it would be possible to apply these ideas to public school. I got a job working with underachievers and students with reading problems at a public high school. The program was voluntary and soon we had a sort of little free school in the middle of that public school. But I eventually realized that the system would change me before I changed it. I wrote a slightly fictionalized account of the experience called *I Was a Spy in the Public Schools*.

After a similar experience as a teaching principal in a rural K-8 school, I happened across a small publication put out by the state commissioner at that time, Harvey Scribner. It was called the Vermont Design for Education. It was very radical and I got angry because I had just been a victim of trying to apply those same ideas. I contacted Scribner and met with him. I asked him where these ideas could be applied. He said "Nowhere! It's just a design!" So I asked him if I should just start my own storefront school. His answer? "Yes."

When I discovered that the law had been changed to give the commissioner final say on school approval, I started Shaker Mountain, named for a hill behind the little rural house my father had helped me buy, which later became the boarding part of our school.

Most of our first students were street kids. We had no minimum tuition and fundraising was always a key to our survival. For the first few days of our school we met in any space we could find. Somehow the local school officials got word that we had started this school with a handful of their chronic truants, and went around trying to find us. They would come in to one of the sites we had used and yell, "Where's Mintz's school?" The people would say they didn't know where we went.

Eventually we rented a small former grocery store. My office was in the walk-in cooler. The kids played basketball in the back storage area using a peach basket. One day the posse of assistant superintendents found us, bursting in the front door yelling at the kids, "Don't you know you are all truant?!!" I then showed them a letter from the state attorney general, indicating that our legal status had not been determined and would be decided by the commissioner's office. They left in a huff, red-faced!

I learned most of what I know about democratic education through Shaker Mountain. In our first year we heard about a Mohawk tribe in upstate New York that was being charged taxes for going across a bridge from one part of their reservation to another. They happened to be in New York and Canada. They blockaded the bridge in protest. We took a school trip to the area and had the great luck to meet the founders of what became the Native American Traditionalist movement. One of the most important things we learned was the decision making process that the Iroquois Confederation had developed. We discovered that Jefferson and Franklin learned many of their governmental concepts from the Iroquois. We adapted our democratic process to use processes we learned from the Iroquois to honor the minority and ultimately make better decisions.

A few years later, in 1971, I got a call from my Mohawk friends, again at 1a.m. They told me that seventy Mohawk students had been kicked out of their public school for speaking their own language and wanting to know their own traditions. They asked if we could come over to the reservation to tell them how to start a school. The next day we made a slide presentation in Ann Jock's small house on the reservation, crammed to the gills with interested families.

"Don't we have to get the government to pay for it?" some asked.

"No," we said. "You have the resources to do it yourself."

The next week, the first Indian Way School started. The next year the second one started at a reserve near Montreal, and more later. The Mohawk language was saved. Other Native American survival schools started all around North America.

Another short fast forward: It had been more than twenty years since I had visited the Akwesasne Reservation and a friend of mine asked me if I could take her to visit the Mohawks. After driving many hours we arrived and somehow found Ann Jock's old house. She had died a few years earlier. I didn't know what to say when I walked in the open door. There on the other side of the room was a Mohawk man about thirty-five years old. He looked up at me and said, "I knew you were coming. When I think about someone three times in a week I know they are on their way!" I had last seen him when he was fourteen and now he had his own fourteen-year-old and was helping the new incarnation of the school we had helped them found in his back yard, which now has about a hundred and fifty students.

The school I founded in Vermont became one of the most traveled schools at the time. If we had had a small travel budget, we might not have gone many places. Luckily, we had no budget at all. Every group had to figure out the finances of any trip they took, so that meant we could go anywhere, and we did. We'd sometimes work our way along, speaking at colleges, passing the hat, cleaning restaurant parking lots for meals. There is such a wealth of stories about these trips that telling a few would not suffice. Eventually we went to every state on the continent, Mexico, and most of the Canadian provinces. Any student who was part of those experiences developed the confidence to do just about anything in his or her life.

At the school itself, there was no set curriculum. Instead, our curriculum was created retroactively. At the end of the year we made a list of some three hundred classes and activities. They were then arbitrarily divided into subject areas and the student checked off which things they did.

We gave no tests or grades in the school, but we used some standardized tests to gauge the school's success and to give us feedback for our own purposes. The average student improved at almost three times the national rate in all subject areas. Sometimes I could hardly understand why. But I think the key is that children are natural learners, and if they retain or regain their confidence as learners they can learn anything they need or want to at lightning speed.

In 1986, I was asked by the National Coalition of Alternative Community Schools (NCACS) to help their organization. I took a leave of absence from Shaker Mountain and went to Pennsylvania to help them develop their network, increasing their numbers from fifty to five hundred. I didn't know it then, but I was on a new path. A few years later, in 1989, I founded the Alternative Education Resource Organization (AERO). The venerable School of Living invited me to do my work through their organization and it remains that way to this day. I liked working with the School of Living because they had pioneered in the fields of land trust, environmental protection, consumer protection, organic farming and organic foods. In fact, the School of Living was the name founder Ralph Borsodi had used for his family homeschool when they moved to the wilds of Westchester County, NY in 1920!

AERO is a direct outgrowth of my experiences with Shaker Mountain and the NCACS. It always bothered me that there were millions of students suffering out there while our small numbers of kids were thriving in our schools. Through AERO I've been able to help students, parents, and teachers find or found alternatives in their communities.

It was also especially important to me to help people start new alternatives. So we have special listserves for school starters, workshops at our conference, and on-line courses to help people who are starting new alternatives. We've helped people start more than thirty-five new alternatives in the last few years, something I am particularly happy about. The only way I know of to bring about the education revolution we need is in this way, brick by brick.

I now do a lot of traveling and consulting and the challenges have been interesting. For example, demonstrating democratic process to schools of three thousand students in India, as well as at a school in which the oldest student was five years old! In the latter case, I remember thinking that I would have to at least give them a suggested agenda. No sooner had I explained to them that a meeting could talk about problems in the school or good ideas for the school when almost every hand shot up with agenda items! You see, my own background was relatively conventional, and even though I teach it and demonstrate it, I am continually blown away by the power of democratic meetings and real learner centered empowerment.

In the mid-1990s, I edited the *Handbook of Alternative Education*, published by Macmillan, and the *Almanac of Education Choices*, published by Macmillan and Simon and Schuster, listing for the first time under one cover over six thousand learner-centered educational alternatives. That had been a goal for me for a long time. Our database has grown to over twelve thousand. In 2008, we put up a new website in which this database may be accessed free, at Educationfinder.net.

In 1993, Yaacov Hecht, founder of the Democratic School of Hadera, pulled together a dozen of us who were involved with democratic education and had attended a conference on multiculturalism in Tel Aviv. This has led to an annual gathering of schools and programs involved with democratic education. It has come to be called the International Democratic Education Conference (IDEC). It isn't an official organization, but each year a different school agrees to host it, organizing it out of the IDEC listserve that AERO manages. The IDEC has been in England, Austria, Ukraine, Japan, New Zealand, India, Germany, Australia, and Canada.

In 2002, we brought a group from AERO and the Albany Free School to the IDEC in New Zealand, and received support to host the IDEC for the first time in the USA in 2003.

It was an amazing conference. We had six hundred fifty people from twenty-five states and twenty-five countries, including one hundred from Third World countries. We raised $65,000 so they could attend. I don't think I ever worked so hard, as did Dana Bennis, an AERO staff member who was the conference director. It brought us to a new level of consciousness. Since that time regional IDECs have sprouted, including the EUDEC, a European branch that had its first gathering last year of hundreds of participants.

Isaac Graves was a fifteen-year-old who had graduated from The Free School (Albany) as an eighth grader and had traveled with us to the IDEC in New Zealand. Upon his return he said he'd been wasting his time in public school, became a homeschooler, and helped us organize the 2003 IDEC. After the conference he came up to me and said, "AERO needs to build on the success of this IDEC. We need to have an AERO conference next year and I could organize it for you." So he became our conference director at sixteen and has continued in that role for the last seven years. It has become one of the most important parts of AERO.

After the 2003 IDEC, a group of people from the New York City area were lamenting the fact that there were no democratic schools there. We started meeting regularly at a charter school in Queens, eventually breaking into two committees. One came up with an elegant proposal for the Gates Foundation funding of a public democratic school in New York City. That just sat on a bureaucrat's desk until I embarrassed them into meeting with us through one of their listserves.

They did, and were taken aback with several aspects of it, and it still went nowhere.

Our other committee worked on the creation of an independent democratic school centered on Alan Berger, who had left his job as a public school assistant principal. We had meetings every two weeks for over ten months. I demonstrated organic curriculum and democratic process, and proposed a demonstration two-day school so people could visualize it. This led to the opening of Brooklyn Free School in Park Slope, Brooklyn, now in its fifth year. It has a sliding scale tuition, is interracial and non-discriminatory, and uses the Iroquois democracy as Shaker Mountain did. It has sixty students and a waiting list of fifty.

Alan and I both hate waiting lists. We encouraged anyone in the New York City area who wanted to, to start a new alternative.

Pat Werner, a veteran New York City teacher and AERO member, had been wanting to start a democratic school for many years, but she had almost given up on the idea. Then I did a consultation with a family whose daughter had quit school to become a homeschooler. I helped her pursue her idea of setting up a homeschool resource center that could potentially evolve into a Manhattan free school. We had several meetings and a demonstration day. I invited Pat to attend. This rekindled her interest and she eventually organized a group of these and other interested parents, and Manhattan Free School opened its doors in September 2008 and has thrived in its second year.

The calendar says I am now at retirement age but I still feel far away from what I set out to do. I do remember what it was like to be old. That was fifteen years ago and I don't intend to go through that again. I had a double hernia, a ruptured disk for which they brought me to the hospital by ambulance in a stretcher, and two heart surgeries. After the second one I sat up in the middle of the night and wrote:

And then one morning you don't wake up
Everyone says how surprised they were
You would have been the most surprised
But nothing surprises you any more!

At that point I contacted a friend who was a naturopath. I realized I had to completely change my lifestyle to a healthy one. I haven't eaten any red meat since. I've learned a lot about herbs and healthy food. My friend wanted to equip me to take care of myself, as a good physician should. I didn't change because of vanity or nobility. I had to make these changes or I was going to die.

I think we need to do the same with our education system. Half measures won't do it. If we really understand the idea that children are born natural learners, everything must change if humanity is to survive.

Since making those changes I have gradually lost weight. I am still overweight but weigh less than I have since I was in my twenties. My stress tests, blood pressure, and cholesterol levels all come out well. Also, my table tennis game is the best that it's been in my life; my rating is at its highest ever, partly due to my current coach, who was a former world champion. I now realize that I will be young until I die.

Twice a week I volunteer at a local Boys and Girls Club to teach table tennis. I've done this for many years, but we now have more people on the challenge ladder, fifty-five, than ever before. Several of our players have been state champions of their age division. Of course I organized the table tennis club into a democracy. The students have passed sixty-five rules, elect their own supervisors, ages eight to fourteen, and run the club six days a week, which I believe is the reason it is so successful.

I've learned a tremendous amount through that club. The students are mostly minority and go to public school. Ordinarily the club doesn't allow the older teenagers to come into the room for kids twelve and under, where the three ping-pong tables are located. The reason is that teens often bully younger kids, but they make an exception if the teens are in the ping-pong club. Those kids never bully, only mentor. Again, I've been surprised at the power of the democracy in that little club.

When I arrive at the club I need to have a pen and notebook in my hand because as soon any anyone sees me the children run from all directions to sign up for a lesson that evening. Although I'll work with as many as fifteen in two hours, they know I'll never get through the list and I work with them in the order that they sign up.

All of this reminds me again and again that kids are natural learners. I like teaching table tennis because it is a way kids can get confidence in themselves as learners that is not academically threatening. I am reminded that all learning needs to flow this way, from the paradigm that kids want to learn. Traditional education seems to operate on the opposite paradigm, that people are naturally lazy and need to be forced to learn. Of course, it is a self-fulfilling paradigm that is not true, but becomes apparently true after many years of extinguishing children's natural ability to learn. This then is used to justify things like homework, grades, and competition.

I remember once when a consultant from another club was visiting us to work with the Boys and Girls Club staff. As he was given his tour of the club he was struck by the table tennis ladder with its many names stuck on by Velcro.

"It's not just that I've never seen such a large table tennis ladder, but if that was at my club, it would have to be protected by Plexiglas—the names would be all over the place!"

"You know what protects that?" I asked

"No, what?" he said, perplexed.

"Democracy! When we made it the kids passed a rule in their democratic meeting that if anyone but the elected student supervisors moved the names they would go to the bottom of the list. Only once did a student ever challenge that!"

A young ping-pong student who was listening to all this interrupted, "No!" he said. "Twice!"

Note

1.   As a quick side note, one of the key kids in that 4-H club, who was from an immigrant family, eventually dropped out of high school after I graduated from Goddard. He floated around, got into trouble, but took the GED at the age of twenty-five, and then decided to go to college. There, he rediscovered his love for biology, getting 130s on tests. He got a scholarship to Dartmouth Medical School. I got wind of this and caught up with him as he was finishing his surgical residency at a local hospital. He said he didn't think he would be a surgeon if he hadn't been in that 4-H club. Not long after, I went for angioplasty at the same hospital, and he left his practice as director of another hospital's intensive care unit, for the day, in order to be with me during the procedure.

Clonlara, an Irish-American Creation
Pat Montgomery

Early Education
St. Margaret's Catholic School in Greentree, a borough not far from Pittsburgh, Pennsylvania, was a four room schoolhouse with two grades in each room (first to eighth). There were about thirty-eight to forty boys and girls in each room, taught by the Sisters of Divine Providence. I came home from school on the first day and announced that I "wanted to be a nun like Sr. Mary Herman," my first grade teacher. The idea stuck fast. Our town was too small to have a high school of its own; kids had to go to bigger, nearby towns following graduation from eighth grade. Instead, I headed for the Divine Providence Motherhouse in Pittsburgh's north hills, to prepare to become a nun.

The Order was a teaching one, primarily, so I was destined to become a teacher. Parochial schools were virtually bursting at the seams in 1953 when, at the tender age of eighteen years, I became a seventh grade teacher at a suburban Pittsburgh parish, St. Norbert's. At the time, my convent class and I were just beginning to do college work. It was legal then to teach without a teaching certificate as long as a person was working toward getting one. That "work" took eight years, relegated as it was to summertime and Saturday classes.

My second "school" was the acreage around our rural home, an old house—over one hundred years old at the time—with no running water and with wires strung around the door frames bringing electricity. The truck farm that my parents maintained to feed ten mouths at the height of the Great Depression lay at the end of an unpaved street. To the east was a neighboring dairy farm, and behind it all was a rambling woods. My brothers and sisters and I had the run of the place. When the work was done we were free to go to our favorite spots. For one it was atop a haystack to read, for another it was into the kitchen to putter about baking and cooking, and for another it was to the shed to whittle or saw or weld. For me it was to the woods.

I explored briars and shrubs, found the choicest blackberry bushes, collected tree bark, twigs, and branches, built shrines and May altars and primitive coops to provide shelter from the rain and listened to the sounds around me. This time and space in nature was my classroom, and it was years later before I realized it had served a very important function for me. It wasn't until the 70s, 80s, and 90s that I observed other youngsters who were free to do similar things with little or no interference.

Recognizing a Need

The seeds of doubt about conventional educational practices were firmly planted in my mind and soul when I was called on the carpet one day by my superior, the school principal. She chastised me for allowing the five-year-olds to hold my hand on the playground. One had even taken the long, black rosary beads suspended from my waistband and circled them over her head in the air like a lasso before I tucked them into the folds of my habit. According to the principal, "Children lose all respect for a teacher when they are allowed such familiarity. The proper place for a child is to be kept no closer than the length of a teacher's arm."

I could almost accept the ruling when applied to the youngsters in my classroom, all forty-seven of them in the twelve- to fourteen-year-old range, but it didn't seem to apply at all to the little ones, the five-year-olds with their brimming enthusiasm and playfulness. That began in me an ongoing critique about the way kids were treated by the adults who taught and supervised them. My observations amassed over the next eight years that I remained in the religious community, and they continued when I taught in public schools upon leaving the convent. Schools—whether parochial, public, or private—were adult-centered institutions. The developmental needs of growing youngsters were given lip service but no real attention and no accommodation unless that happened to suit the adults' propensities to control. Kids were not trusted.

I gradually established a vision of a place where children were not compelled by law to attend, where their natural curiosity and energy was respected, a place where they were free to explore and to play without interference from teachers, however well-intentioned they might be. It was while working on a Master's degree at the University of Michigan that I met—by reading his *Summerhill; A Loving World*—A. S. Neill. His words resonated with the beliefs I had amassed over the years of working with other people's children. I visited Neill in March of 1967 at his school in Leiston, England. This helped me map the route that I would take to assure that my own two children, and many others over the years, would enjoy peaceful, child-led learning and growing.

Reality in Motion

In October 1967, my husband, Jim, and I started Clonlara School for our own (then) two- and three-year-old children. Lacking funds, I asked my father for help. He sent $4,000, the contents of his mattress stash at the time. (Many Depression survivors avoided using banks.) We used that as the down payment for the house on Jewett Street, and we chose the name of the school my father attended as a child in Ireland.

Twelve years later—in 1979—I started a second program to assist parents and students who chose not to attend any school at all in favor of using the world, or at least their communities, as their classrooms. This was called Clonlara School Home Based Education Program.

Life at Clonlara School (on campus in Ann Arbor) was never static or predictable. Teachers often say they learn from the children they teach. For me, that was always the distinction between the "free" school we created and all of the other teaching experiences I had had. Adults at Clonlara are not the central focus; kids are. So this leaves an adult free to observe and participate on an equal footing with the other adults and youngsters—the community of learners. People would ask what a typical day was like, especially journalists who were writing a story about us. All we could tell them was to come and experience it themselves, and many did.

One public school teacher who was on leave to visit non-public schools came to the younger kids' group one day. She arrived at 8:45 a.m. to be there at the very start of a day. She stood against the wall of the front portable classroom and watched this group playing in the dress-up area, that one reading a book, these few painting, that one running outdoors to play on the swings, and me busying myself to be sure that tools were available as needed and that I was, too. Around 11:00 a.m. she turned to me and asked, "When does school start?"

It wasn't unusual for six or seven kids and an adult to head for the van upon hearing the sirens of fire trucks go by, following at a safe distance to see what was causing the ruckus. Travel was an integral part of our lives. Most often it was travel in our rich community: to libraries, museums, parks, the farmer's market, theaters, gravel pits, pig farms, and the like.

On an average of four times a year, though, we traveled far. In 1971, for example, we convoyed in two vans and a parent's car to Kennedy Space Center in Florida to view the last manned space flight of the series. Youngsters and adults planned the long trips together for weeks and months in advance. Two teachers and ten kids went to Ireland for twelve days one May to visit the other Clonlara School; the one my own Dad attended as a child, and to honor him, the one for whom our school was named. Clonlara School kids and staff accepted an invitation to go to Tokyo Shure for two weeks and to return the favor by hosting staff and kids from Japan for the two following weeks.

One annual trip was fixed in our calendar, the National Coalition of Alternative Community Schools (NCACS) conference, which was hosted by one or another member schools anywhere in the U.S. Planning the trip, taking advantage of the various sights along the route, and being gone for weeks at a time was a major event in our year. Kids from Metropolitan School in Columbus, Pinewood School near Denver, Santa Fe Community School in New Mexico, Dr. Pedro Albisu Campos School in Chicago, Uppatinas School in Glenmoore,

Pennsylvania, Horizons School in Atlanta, Lamborn Valley School in Paonia, Colorado, The Farm in Summertown, Tennessee, John Boston's home school group in Escondido, California, all grew up together as it were.

Ellen was a Clonlara School student up to the high school level when she transferred to Community High, Ann Arbor's public school alternative. She graduated and was accepted at Amherst College in Massachusetts. Arriving there, a newby from far away, she felt pangs of loneliness, fearing that she'd know not a single soul. Then she heard her name being called from across the Diag; it was Josh from Upattinas whom she had met at many an annual NCACS conference, himself an incoming freshman far from home.

If we had musicians—either adults or kids—we had music classes that year; if not, we didn't. What was done and what was offered as school fare in any given year depended upon the interests and talents of the members of the community. It was a changing scene in this and in virtually every other way. It has undergone changes over the past years, too, of course. I suspect that this will always be true. See for yourself: www.clonlara.org or arrange a visit. Chris Mercogliano's book title, *Making It Up as We Go Along*, truly encapsulates what happened at Clonlara.

John Holt was an early proponent of alternative schools, but he gradually veered away from advising people to start schools in favor of having parents teach their own. One fall day he got a visitor from Japan who asked him about the free school movement. John phoned Clonlara and the National Coalition of Alternative Schools office that it then housed. That began a Clonlara-Japanese connection that prompted numerous trips between Clonlara staff and Japanese parents, students, teachers, and journalists over the years. Clonlara maintained a healthy presence in Japan, serving both home educating families and the alternative schools community there.

One day in 1978 a family visited Clonlara School asking for help in teaching their ten-year-old boy at home. That was such a novel idea then that it engendered lively discussions amongst staff. When I determined what sort of help the family wanted, I concluded that we could certainly offer that. One staff member was perplexed: "What an enigma; it's a conflict of interest, Pat. We can't do this."

My reasoning was simple: when I wanted something brand new for my own children, I did what I needed to do to bring it about. Why shouldn't these parents have the right to do the same thing? What they asked for (a few textbooks, association with an established school for legal protection, etc.) was easy enough to share. Thus began the second of Clonlara's programs. It grew to include families from each of the states and from, over time, forty-two foreign countries. In size, it was the tail wagging the dog; Clonlara's campus day school serves from forty-five to sixty-five kids each year, ranging in age from five to eighteen years. The Home Based Education Program serves thousands of youngsters and their families each year. Word spread and its clientele soon spanned the globe. Clonlara served families in Japan, Sri Lanka, Australia, Ireland, Spain, France, Sweden, and Holland early in the eighties. So far, enrollees have been residents of forty-five countries other than the U.S.

The climate for home education was not a welcoming one in the late 70s and early 80s. In Michigan, for example, the Department of Education tried to quash the hopes and plans of prospective home educators by making unreasonable demands like having a state certified teacher in the home each day for 180 days of a year. Efforts to negotiate with the state Superintendent's office were not well received. It became obvious that the educational establishment was unwilling to sit idly by while people chose to keep their children away from schools. The amount of money lost to each school district when children did not attend (especially on the annual student-count days) was the primary reason for the opposition. Having no other recourse, Clonlara filed suit in circuit court against the Michigan Board of Education (MBE) in 1985, claiming that the department was acting illegally in its attempts to regulate home education. The court agreed. The MBE appealed to the Michigan Court of Appeals. They lost again, so they appealed to the Michigan Supreme Court. Finally, in 1993, the Supreme Court handed down its opinion, again in agreement with Clonlara's claim.

And Down the Days

I stepped out of the day-to-day administrating and teaching at Clonlara School and its Home Based Education Program five years ago to complete several projects that I brought into semi-retirement with me. All are Clonlara-related in the areas of alternative education, including home based education. I consult with teachers, do workshops and other presentations at conferences in the U.S. and in Europe, and elsewhere as requested, and I serve as the Chair of the Board of Trustees of Clonlara School and as a Board member of four other public, private, and religious organizations. Near and dear to my heart is the time I get to spend minding my grandchild, Madeline, age three, and spend with my two other grandchildren, Felix, age thirteen, and Simon, age nine. Jim passed away in 2007, leaving behind our close-knit, loving family— my daughter and son and their families live within walking distance of one another here in Ann Arbor. I am writing (though not nearly enough), and going rather cautiously into old(er) age.

To be fair, I must confess that had I not had children of my own, I might never have taken any action toward fulfilling my vision. It was a combination of my own experiences and having children who would have to endure school that propelled me to act. I must explain that I used to state that I started Clonlara School for my children, but they were only two and three years old at the time and could not even have had an opinion about the matter. More accurately put: my children were my impetus for starting the school I had in my heart.

One of the blessings I count most joyfully is the large number of fellow travelers I have met along the way, like-minded individuals who have shared their lives and journeys with me in various stages, some close at hand, some farther afield. People like Lu Vorys of Lamborn Valley School, Sandy Hurst of Upattinas School, Phil Moore of Upland Hills School, Syl Flores of Kentucky and Mazamitla, Mexico, Keiko Okuchi and Asakura Kageki of Tokyo Shure, Merle Swan Williams in Bermuda, Pipob Udamittipong in Thailand, The Drysen Family (Magnus, Maria, Viktoria, Aurora, and Aron) in Sweden. Xavier Ala in Spain, Birgit and Hartwig Lohff of Germany (removed to France because of the poison climate for home education in their homeland). These friendships reinforced my resolve many times; they inspire me still today.

A Teacher's Job
Susan Ohanian

I was a good student, and so I liked school. I was even a teacher's pet. But my strongest memories of my schooldays are of my classmates who didn't flourish, especially Ricky. Our town didn't offer kindergarten and from Day One we five- and six-year-olds struggled with cursive under the direction of a very strict, stereotypical schoolmarm. About once a week, Ricky got so scared of our teacher's scorn of his mistakes that he wet his pants, leaving the evidence of his fear and shame in a puddle on the wooden floor.

These many decades later, I see that puddle in my mind's eye and I have great regret that, at age five, I didn't know how to tell Ricky that I cared about his misery and was horrified by our teacher's behavior. I regret that I remained silent and continued to bask in the glory of being a good student. All I can say now is that the images of those puddles on the floor have haunted my career as a teacher.

After picking up an MA in medieval literature, I crossed the country to New York City to get a job in publishing. A few years later, when the New York City Board of Education issued emergency credentials, I snuck into high school teaching through the back door.

This means I was never acculturated into the routine of writing lesson plans—or following state guidelines. It also meant that during my first year—teaching in a school larger than my home town, a school that really did have "up" staircases and "down" staircases—I went home and cried every night over how inept I was. I did try to follow departmental guidelines, and when one of my students refused to read the prescribed *Johnny Tremain*, I went to my department chairman, who gave me the best pedagogical advice I have ever received: "Then find a book he *will* read."

What a revelation: official word that it is the teacher's job to find material that appeals to the reluctant student. I immediately carried this principle further, figuring that what's good for the one gander should work for the rest of the flock. I began looking for material of high appeal for *all* the kids. In those pre-copy machine days, my evenings were consumed with typing up lots of short stories. You could get a ditto substance high walking into my classrooms. I went into school early to steal paper from the office and when they locked the cupboards I finally bought reams of my own.

Since I was willing to type up all this material, one of my students persuaded me to type up a story she had written. One story led to another, and pretty soon we had an ongoing soap opera filled with murder and mayhem. Students arrived from all over the building each morning as I stood in my doorway passing out the latest installment. I dearly wish I'd saved a copy of even one installment, but they were in such high demand I always got talked out of every one. Funny thing: I never let this material *into* my classroom; I just aided and abetted a whole lot of writing and reading *outside* the room.

In the years that followed, I taught everything from first grade to fourteenth, and my career was dominated by that simple principle learned the first year: find something they *will* read.

For sure, I taught seventh graders for too many years ever to write, "*The Student will. ...*" in a plan book. On a good day, the best any teacher can say is, "The student *might.*" The best thing we teachers have to take to our classrooms is not our copy of international-class standards, but *ourselves*, who we are as people. This is what is so scary about teaching. We don't teach standards; we teach our selves.

Despite all the hoopla and the data crunching, there isn't anything critical for elementary school kids to know: not igneous rocks, not Iroquois, not Washington's battle plan, not apostrophes, not algebra. The only important thing for a kid to know at the end of eighth grade is that books can offer information and pleasure. Despite this fact, we are all stumbling along with the corporate-politico pronouncements of how school is 'spozed to be, and so we insist on teaching igneous and apostrophes. And when the kids don't learn it, we become the injured parties, victimized by the crazy kids.

But occasionally, if we are lucky—and stubborn, too—we are visited by those flashes of insight that come from close classroom observation, the kind of insight you couldn't deliver to a Standardisto with a dump truck. Then we realize that it's the textbooks and the scope and sequence charts with all the skills lined up in neat little rows—all the accouterments of Standards—that are crazy, not the kids.

Let me tell you about Carol, who didn't read a book all year, not one. Oh, I could pull her along with her classmates through the Iroquois worksheets I'd prepared to help kids get through their unbelievably fatuous social studies textbook. And I knew just how fatuous that text was because during a weekend of sanctimonious, self-prescribed martyrdom, I decided that as a reading teacher I should know what my students faced during their school day. I took home all the "content area" textbooks and read them. It was the next-to-worst weekend of my life, superseded only the great ice storm of 1998 when my household went a week without electricity, heat, water, and flushing toilets.

Carol and I did not manage to find a book that made words sing for her; we never even found words to make her smile. Carol kept to herself. She was silent and uncommunicative both with me and with the other students. I remember just one exchange she had with another student all year. Ofelia was complaining about her mother being too strict. "She thinks she can still hit me, but I'm taller than her now." Carol, the loner who never participated in classroom conversations; Carol, the pasty pale girl with stringy dirty-blond hair, always wearing a heavy, dark sweatshirt, making no concessions to fashion among a group of seventh graders who were obsessed by clothes and style; Carol stirred in her chair and announced vehemently, "My mother better not come near me or the cops will lock her up again." For seven months, I had never seen Ofelia, obsessed with her rings and her nail decals and her corn rows and the lace inserts in her jeans, ever acknowledge Carol's existence, but now she was curious. "Who you live with, your grandmother?"

"No way!" declared Carol. "She's worse than my mother. I live with a foster mother. She better not touch me neither."

Eyes downcast, Carol slumped back down in her chair, and that ended the conversation. I found out later that this child had been so abused as an infant that she'd been taken out of her home at age two. According to faculty-room lore, part of the abuse involved setting her in a frying pan on the stove.

In the ways schools are judged, and even in the way I judge myself, Carol was one of my failures. She came to me not caring about books and despite all my effort, she left the same way. Nonetheless, at the end of the year Carol offered me one brief crystal moment that still sparkles more than two decades later.

Maybe I should call it an oatmeal moment. The seventh and eighth graders, who occupied the top floor of a three-story brick fortress of a building, heard that younger kids were having end-of-the-year parties; they pestered for a party, too. My colleagues insisted that the nasty rotten kids didn't deserve a party, and so I was on my own.

I don't know how many cookies I baked in the three nights before the last day of school, but it was definitely an industrial-strength effort. It seemed as though every kid and his out-of-town cousin heard that cookies were available. More than a few kids I'd never laid eyes on before showed up to wish me a good summer—and to eat a few cookies. Jimmy, whom I'd regarded as terminally lethargic, must have eaten two dozen. He raced through my room every time the bell rang to signal a change in classes, grabbing yet more cookies and calling out, "Hi there, Miz O," as he dashed by.

By the time my afternoon classes arrived all the chocolate chip cookies were gone, leaving only oatmeal with raisins. Danny, Delmore, and even the prissy and proper Roderick were indignant. "Where are the chocolate chip? It ain't fair! How come everybody else got chocolate chip and all we get is rank oatmeal?"

I held back tears of frustration and anger. *Who needed this grief? Try to do something nice, and all these kids can do is complain.* I knew I was setting myself up as victim, which is always a self-defeating role for a teacher, but why did these kids have to spoil things when a teacher is trying to do good?

Then Carol, still wearing her dark, heavy sweatshirt in our sweltering, end-of-June classroom, walked over and touched my arm. "Those are good oatmeal cookies." She actually smiled, this child who I hadn't seen smile all year. Carol smiled and she said, "Could I have another one?"

She gave me the gift of empathy and compassion. And now, reflecting on this incident so many years later, I think maybe I did teach her something after all. I couldn't enter it on her permanent record card—or mine. The data collectors couldn't graph it. Carol's gesture won't appear on any chart of world-class skills or on any test certifying teacher proficiency. But can anyone doubt that Carol made essential progress that year?

I insist that Carol had to learn to smile before she could learn to read. Certainly she had to learn to smile and to be able to put herself in someone else's shoes—even the shoes of a teacher—before she could have any hope for a satisfying and productive life.

But the corporate politicos, media pundits, and education entrepreneurs don't talk about social responsibility; they don't talk about compassion, about caring, about creativity, curiosity, initiative, self-reliance, or a myriad of other qualities that we need to nurture in our students. Certainly it's way past time to ask the Standardistos: Where's the test for compassion? For honesty? For curiosity? For moral commitment?

In "Self-Reliance," Ralph Waldo Emerson tells us that character teaches above our wills, that "virtue or vice emit a breath at every moment." This is scary stuff. If we take Emerson to heart and believe that with every breath teachers send out rays of virtue or vice, then why aren't we more worried about the character of the people running our schools than about finding a test that will show us if students in Alaska are ahead of those in Vermont in apostrophe acquisition?

Some astronomers say the universe can't be any older than ten billion years. Others say it can't be younger than twenty billion years. In *The End of Science*, John Horgan points out that debate over the Hubble constant offers an obvious lesson: Even when performing a seemingly straightforward calculation, cosmologists must make various assumptions that can influence their results; they must interpret their data. Horgan points out that acquiring more data about our cosmos won't resolve the issues. "Our ability to describe the universe with simple, elegant models stems in large part from our lack of data, our ignorance. The more clearly we can see the universe in all its glorious detail, the more difficult it will be for us to explain with a simple theory how it came to be that way."

There's a great moral here for teachers. Like all teachers, I have often felt overwhelmed by the constraints of the official systems, guidelines, and checklists. There is always the tension of balancing the required checklists with giving support to vulnerable children, which, surely, must be our most important function.

"Charles can be a little strange," his special education teacher warned me. That turned out to be an understatement. At age eleven, Charles was three years older than most of the kids in my third grade class into which he mainstreamed. Conferences with his mother, social worker, and psychologist revealed a long history of abuse, emotional upheaval, and retarded development.

Charles was on his best behavior for weeks, insisting everything was "very interesting." Even so, Charles couldn't help revealing his distress when I read aloud. Whenever I sat down with a new book—several times a day—the other children happily crowded around. Not Charles. He'd move to a far corner, scowling and twisting his body into strange shapes. To make sure I understood his discontent, Charles made chirping noises as I read. The other children and I developed a profound ability to ignore weird chirping noises.

The pressure of trying to be on his best behavior finally got to Charles and he vomited. Then he exclaimed, "I'm just a weirdo," and burst into tears. One by one, his classmates, who up to then had been polite but distant, rushed to his side, assuring him that everybody vomits. We had a class sharing of vomit experiences.

The next day Charles appeared in class with a large poster he'd drawn of me and the words, "I love this class very much." On the poster he had carefully printed the name of every child in our class. He'd asked his special ed teacher for help because, in his words, "Names are important. I need to get them right."

Of interest and speculation, this incident brought an end to

Charles' chirping, and he even began making suggestions of books for me to read aloud.

Charles began to read independently. I watched him read *Rumpelstiltskin* sixteen days in a row and then I stopped counting. Frank Smith reminds us that when a child persists in the same activity, when he reads the same book over and over, he isn't wasting time or trying to get out of "real" work; instead, he is learning what he needs to learn from that book. Over time, I watched Charles use *Rumpelstiltskin*, with its safe, familiar pages, as a warm-up. He'd read it quickly, move it to the edge of his desk, and then start in on a new book.

I won't pretend that teaching Charles was easy; but as he wiggled his way into the heart and soul of our classroom, I found it harder and harder to face up to his very real limitations. In May, Charles suggested that he might stay in my class another year and become my aide. "I know where everything is," he told me. I jumped at the idea. So did his special ed teacher. Charles had done so well. Just think what we could do in another year.

Reality hit us in the face when Charles' mother sent in a note, asking us to talk to her prepubescent son about sex. We had to face the fact that Charles was twelve years old—and growing fast. As much as I wanted him to, he couldn't stay in third grade.

During the last week of school I asked the children to choose their favorite book of the year and write about it—as a memento of third grade. Charles was immediately enthusiastic. "I know which one I want!" he exclaimed.

I thought to myself, "Yep, I know too."

But of course Charles surprised me again and chose *The Ugly Duckling*, a beautiful picture book I'd never noticed him reading. He had it hidden in the back of other volumes on one of the bookshelves. And Charles, who had never written more than six sentences about anything all year, wrote nine pages. He said he was going to send his report to the newspaper because he wanted everybody in the world to know about *The Ugly Duckling*. And this is how Charles began his commentary: *The ugly duckling found out it is okay to be different. . . .*

Let us all go down on our knees to this event. Surely this is a message that is just as important for the Standardistos as it was for one little boy and his teacher.

In point of fact, Barbara did poorly on the standardized reading test administered at the end of the year; Charles's scores showed good progress in reading for a third grader but placed him far behind his chronological level. I take such numbers seriously, but I remember that failure on a given measure signifies only what was measured. Only what Standardistos chose to measure. In judging my own worth as a teacher, I insist on additional criteria. Yes, I want teachers to be smart and conscientious and very knowledgeable. But this is just the bare beginning.

I don't give a fig whether or not teachers are accorded professional, national board status or any other bells and whistles. What is important to know about teachers is that they are people who don't ignore tears, teachers who stop for vomit. The teaching profession must be a nurturing one. Teachers who persist and triumph must be nurturers. "Drill and practice" have a bad name these days. But maybe we should consider resurrecting them, returning them to their rightful dignity. To that end, I have a modest little list of things to practice:

- Practice being helpful.
- Practice saying "Thank you."
- Practice saying "I'm sorry."
- Practice listening.
- Practice patience.
- Practice taking a deep breath, counting to five, letting it out, and smiling afterward.
- Practice reading riddles aloud.

"Don't use rotted names," warned Wallace Stevens. Just because a word has five syllables doesn't mean it's worth anything. The great words of teaching are of one syllable: read, write, teach, learn, work, skill, care, help, hope, trust, faith, love.

And the greatest of these is, of course, love.

Standing in the "Tragic Gap" Between What is and What Might Be—In School. That's What I Do Every Day.[1]

Kirsten Olson

I f you take learning seriously—as seriously as you take bodily wellness, a whole heart, the ability to feel peaceful—most American schools are pretty depressing places. I spend a lot of time in them every week. As a school consultant, I work with the whole strata of them—some of the most challenged, chronically under-performing public school systems in the country that are not making Annual Yearly Progress and are likely to be closed; and also some very high status, high achievement institutions, where very schooled up kids go to climb the attainment ladder, and where the reproduction of social, cultural and cognitive privilege is at the center.

Regardless of the school setting, or the class of folk it serves, there is a constant. Everyone is bored. There is abundant, overwhelming boredom among students: "Name the five common elements of fairy tales and find exact examples in the story and copy them below." There is boredom among teachers: "How many times do I have to tell you to do that? Just do the procedure and we can all get out of here." There is boredom and disengagement among school leaders and administrators, whom I am charged to aid, enliven, and inspire. "As a teacher, she's not worth putting much effort into. Let's just get through the year and hope it doesn't show on the test scores."

The boredom shows. Oh yeah, you know it does. In America, we have one of the highest high school dropout rates among industrialized nations in the world (meaning, we don't look very good in relation to our peers). In my hometown, Boston, the high school dropout rate among urban kids of color is so chronic and appalling (over 65 percent for young adults of color and other minorities) that if it were any other institution, the consequence of such failure would be that we would shut its doors tomorrow. (In Massachusetts, "Dropping out is like committing social and economic suicide," someone recently said. Here, an advanced degree is necessary to work at Starbucks.) When you ask kids how they actually feel about school, as I did when writing a recent book, they say things like, "No one noticed if I was there or not." "I slept a lot and the teachers just let me." "I wish I could do more interesting work." In a huge national sample of American high school students, one in three say they have almost no interaction with teachers in most of their classes, and two out of three say they are bored in class every day. [2] Add this to the fact that for many kids school is scary, unfriendly, and atomizing, and you don't have to think very hard, or feel very deeply, to believe that school, as we currently do it, is a punitive, rigid, wasteful, and sometimes brutalizing place for kids (and adults) to spend eight hours a day, or fifteen thousand hours cumulatively in their K-12 lives. (I also teach in college and graduate school. Many will spend much more time in school.)

We are all schooled up, as Ivan Illich would say, and are so used to being bored and having our learning lives disrespected in school that for many people interned (interred?) there, disengagement *is* the chief characteristic of the institution. School is about being null, being numb, being checked out. Go, but don't put your whole self out. That's the trick. The qualities of profoundly diminished learning are invisible to many; they don't expect better. The boredom is normalized, the lack of respect for engaged learning, and each other, is not only commonplace, but in the air that adults and children breathe. "She isn't the brightest bulb on the tree," or "He's a big time trouble maker," I routinely hear adults say about seven-year-olds. "There's nothing we can do about the fact that Quandel doesn't read in the sixth grade," another teacher says wearily. The expectation that not much can change is the grinding millstone of daily life. Get used to it. That's just the way it is.

Although my own educational background—predictable and familiar to white, middle-class Americans—involved some conventional affronts and triumphs (think *The Breakfast Club*, but without Molly Ringwald), I also had an impression of uneasiness and wariness in school—an inchoate sense that you couldn't be real there, that to reveal one's true self in school was to be in great peril. Greenville Elementary School, in Wilmington, Delaware, primarily served white children of executives of the DuPont Company, and other aspiring American dreamers. I recall vociferously trying to please my first grade teacher, Mrs. Regina, a dour, cranky-faced matron, by inventing compliments—"That's a very nice dress you're wearing," I would say about the shapeless brown sack that hung on her—or smiling at her with peculiar intensity as we lined up carefully, compliantly, *one by one* to go to lunch. I never won her approval. Sourly, unwillingly, she placed me in the top reading group, which even at age six every kid in the class had figured out was the best one to be in. One fateful day, however, I misspelled "gallop" and was moved to the *second* highest reading group, from which I'm sure I didn't emerge for a long time. Even back then I felt there was something wrong here, that there was something deeply strange and superficial about this system. You were either smart or dumb—and kids were being classified (or were classifying themselves) almost before they could tie their shoes. Mistakes were shameful and your fault, and making mistakes meant you were stupid. We were figuring out early on to be very cautious and approval seeking, and to focus on always being right. (Learning theorists tell us, of course, that *you cannot learn* without making mistakes.) Underneath the need for caution, the matter-of-fact sorting of us by supposed ability, and the rituals of "good" school performance we were being taught to display, I felt a lot of anger and hostility from adults towards kids. Mrs. Regina, punitive and joyless, seemed to take pleasure in children not doing well. All was not right. I learned to be careful.

Despite Mrs. Regina, I was a voracious reader. I read my way around the elementary school library—every biography, although less than a dozen books out of hundreds were about women. (Dolly Madison and Florence Nightingale—how's that for intellectual modeling?) When I outgrew the elementary school library, a neighbor's mother took her daughter and me to a local town library several afternoons a week. For me, reading was pleasure; books were my friends, and my world, a place where adults could not enter and where children's thoughts, ideas and observations were important, and of equal weight to teachers. I loved books because they were real, they were straight—they didn't pander, and you could take them or leave them on your own terms. While I generally did well in school, I came to feel unmistakably, with an ever stronger sense, that one's real intellectual life took place outside of school—real things, important intellectual events that actually mattered, were realities far beyond the curriculum and hidden from the gaze of teachers. I was also learning not to expect to be taught the things I really wanted to know about in school: about sex, or racism, or the assassination of John Kennedy—those were topics I would have to find out about for myself. School was where pre-packaged, institutionalized knowledge was passed to quiescent, passive children, many of whom had hooded eyes and other thoughts. Few of us were there. Or at least I wasn't.

My parents seemed largely oblivious. My father, a competitive and hard-edged college professor and my mother, a fragile, conflicted woman of the 1950s, were highly educated in conventional ways. They provided me, and my brother and sister with lots of books, but didn't seem too concerned about the negative effects school might have on us. (I would say now that they didn't understand their own school wounds.) SRA basal reading programs—color coded file folders on the teacher's desk of canned reading material meted out in tiny teaspoons (no reading ahead, or you'd be punished!)—didn't attract my parents' attention. My poorly educated fifth grade math teacher was superciliously appraised by my father, an Ivy League engineer, as someone who ought to be selling shoes. When I brought home an art project in which I had cut out construction-paper figures of a teacher putting children into a pot to eat, my father thought this was wry and funny.

Quietly angry and resentful, I began to practice what Herb Kohl calls "not learning." [3] Thrashing against my father's ferocious, unkind efforts to teach me the multiplication tables with flash cards, I decided I wasn't ever going to be good at math. (Unfortunately, I've made good on that promise.) I became careful and choiceful about what I was going to learn in school, and how much effort I was going to expend. Although I figured out how to play the game, I was also highly aware of, and vigilant about, those subjects in which I wasn't skillful or didn't easily flourish. I avoided them; I simply stopped doing things I wasn't good at. I declined to take risks in areas where I was less fluent, or hadn't established my reputation as a "good" student. I learned very little about things. It took me years to understand my attitude of self-protection and vulnerability.

Students in school now, however, do not have the choices that those in my era had. They cannot practice not-learning easily. Downstairs right now my oldest son is studying for an Advanced Placement biology exam to be administered at the end of his junior year of high school. My son, who is articulate and grown up for sixteen, can voice his learning conundrum. He knows that much of the work he must do for this exam involves the lowest levels of thinking, according to a common taxonomy of learning. (The test is based almost entirely on memorization for information retrieval, and ability to comprehend basic structures of knowledge, classification and error-analysis.) The AP exam—on which my son's biology teacher has never failed to garner 4s or 5s for every student in the class—is the culmination of a year-long "killer" biology course, one that crams a year and a half of honors college biology into a single high school year. My son knows that in all likelihood he will never take another biology course again; he is interested in politics but has done acceptably well in science—thus the necessity of the AP course. ("You must show colleges you're challenging yourself to the maximum level," his guidance counselor told him repeatedly.) Hour after hour, week after week, he has ground his way through this course, taking Scantron multiple choice exams on the Krebs cycle, Mendelism, and hagfishes. He has been involved in learning exercises that *do not* mirror the higher-level thinking skills actually necessary for scientific research. In fact, many of the performance behaviors he must exhibit as a high-attainment, competitive, college-bound student involve a kind of "false learning"—memorizing, reciting, recalling, specifying, and matching—that is far from the goals of what learning theorists call metacognition, the ability to plan and set goals for oneself in one's own learning, and the ability to identify and understand why particular knowledge is important to us. My son, and many high schoolers like him, are in the belly of a beast—they are aware that this part of school is a game, but one that is very hard to opt out of. My son is privileged by virtue of social class and skin color. Millions of American high school students will never have the opportunity to experience the affronts of AP class work: the color of their skin, the place where they were born, their gender, or their profoundly sub-standard elementary and middle school educations mean they have been turned away from this kind of performance opportunity years ago. Current educational policy dictates that we are supposed to want all children to have the opportunity to take AP coursework. As a matter of equity, I understand this desire well. As a parent and an educator, however, I am wary, and deeply skeptical.

I believe my son will find a way to make a meaningful life for himself in spite of these experiences, and perhaps he may even work to change a system that exacts punishing wounds on many. He has been helped along the way by being able to see his dilemma in many dimensions. He understands the need for conventional academic success along with the falseness and playacting that accompanies it. The shallowness of most of his teachers' evaluations of him, and the ways in which his teachers are forced to assess him rapidly, incompletely, and as a commodity, because they too are ground under the wheel of attainment-oriented education, are also parts of a consciousness he can express. He has had moments of intellectual flight in school—writing a paper on the history of conflict between the Shiites, Kurds, and Suunis—and his political activities, many friendships, and other interests refresh and enliven him. He is still deeply alive, in spite of the difficulty and boredom of AP biology. He has, so far I think, been protected from thinking too little of himself and from losing interest in his own mind. This is protection every child should be offered. But they aren't.

In another setting, in urban Boston, I work with teachers and school leaders in a middle school that is chronically dysfunctional. Teachers are poorly educated and under-supervised. School leaders are involved in emotional triangulation with each other and focus too little on the well being of the school and its students. In this setting, students have been acculturated to intense boredom and routinization, and to an implicit bargain: they will be asked to do little, as long as they don't act up too much. For them school is a necessary but uncompelling routine for the day—like driving at thirty-five mph with the cruise control on—not very difficult, without much meaning, disconnected from most emotional or developmental realities, a genial show. Not surprisingly, given the correspondence principle of education (you get educated for the capitalist work you are to do based on your social class—95 percent of these students are poor, working class, and of color), classroom work here is a lot like a minimum wage job: undemanding, uninteresting, repetitive, with little opportunity for advancement. Beyond the fact that its students will be grotesquely under-prepared to go on to high school after graduating from this school (we know statistically that they will be most likely to drop out in ninth grade, when they make the transition to high school), these students are being acculturated to chronic boredom and a lack of meaning around learning. School isn't about anything very important, so you can give it half (or less) of your attention and still get by pretty much just fine. Students in this school are incredibly friendly, easy to engage in conversation, filled with light, energy, and passion as soon as you engage them in something that they want to talk about. But mostly they move silently, listlessly from class to class, punching the clock of instruction and eagerly waiting for the day to be over. No wonder they are likely to drop out.

What have I decided to do about the dilemmas I see, working in the American educational system every day? How do I resolve these awful conundrums for myself, someone who has been trained up to see, moment to moment, that participating in our educational system can be diminishing and punishing—and also economically critical? That education can (and sometimes does) offer the means of liberation and the scaffolding for criticality, while at the same time also actively reproduces inequality, internalized oppression, and deep personal displacement? That people are both lost and found in school?

I have worked, and I am working, to make these dilemmas more explicit. I try to write, teach, and speak specifically about practices in school that I think harm students every day, and not practice them myself. I try to counsel individuals and school systems with whom I consult to be aware of the consequences of their actions, that what they say to students, and how they construct learning, really matters. That education is "soul crafting," as Cornel West says.

I am radical, and radically critical, and yet I am also trying to learn to be forbearing, to be humble. I believe that the system of education we currently have in our country needs to be taken down to the ground and rebuilt, and that students and teachers need much, much greater choice and control in the systems in which they are forcibly educated. I encourage student activism, and acting up—everywhere. But at the same time I am patient. I know people are afraid, they find it hard to conceive of something else, some other way of doing education; they think it is "a lot of trouble to remake our educational system," as someone recently said to me. For about a decade I studied the thinking and careers of deschoolers who have come before this generation: John Holt, Ivan Illich, Paul Goodman—and note the disillusionment and withdrawal they ultimately experienced around reform of the system. They opted out—ultimately left altogether, concluded it couldn't be done. Recollecting John Holt at the end of his life, George Dennison described driving around New England with him. Holt was gravely ill and dying of cancer; Dennison was at the wheel. Holt looked out the car window at some picture of New England natural beauty and said, "It's all so beautiful. If only they wouldn't mess it up."

I don't want to get to that point. I don't want to believe that I see something in the world that other people don't, because I think that means one has essentially disconnected, or held oneself above other—poor, deluded—people who can't perceive the same things that you do. I think that's fundamentally a mistake. As daunting as it is to stay engaged with the educational system, I think we all participate in the same systems, we all support them or have been influenced by them in some way or another, and we all bear ongoing responsibility for doing something about them, even if the work is messy, upsetting, very slow going, two steps backward for every one step forward. Every time I have a powerful conversation with a student in a classroom, every time I see the fire in the eyes of sixth graders, every time I experience how a teacher or administrator can grow and become more kind, more wise, more interesting in their classroom arrangements, I am refreshed by the quickening heart of the world. My impatience, my own sense of being overwhelmed, my wish for the system to be different are the weapons I must use, I must harness in the work, to stay with it and just keep on going. "After the final no there comes a yes, and on that yes the future world depends," wrote Wallace Stevens, and that's what I'm going with.

Because the dysfunctions of school are a lot like any real problem in life. They aren't easily solved and they require a lot of discipline, hanging in there, and just staying in the work, even if it isn't very pretty or inspiring. Ultimately, I do see small pieces of progress, signs of hope, light dawning. Like Herb Kohl, another school reformer and social justice worker whom I deeply admire, I am a hopemonger. I believe in the capacity of humans to remake themselves and their worlds. The pace is often much too slow for me, but still I believe it and see it happen. Every day, I am refreshed by the quickening heart of the world.

Notes

1. Contemporary author and philosopher Parker Palmer describes standing in the "tragic gap" between the world as it currently is—and what it might be. This paradoxical, double-sightedness can be a source of alarm, discouragement, and cynicism, or a well of hopefulness, discipline, and persistence. As an educator, especially one who seeks alternatives to conventional schooling paradigms, we may stand in this tragic gap every day—sometimes, it may feel, at every moment!

2. 2006 High School Survey of Student Engagement (HSSSE), administered yearly at Indiana University. It surveys over seventy thousand American students every year. www.indiana.edu/~ceep/hssse/.

3. "Learning how to *not-learn* is an intellectual and social challenge; sometimes you have to work very hard at it. It consists of an active, often ingenious, wilful rejection of even the most compassionate and well-designed teaching...It was through insight into my own not-learning that I began to understand the inner world of students who chose to not-learn what I wanted to teach. Over the years I've come to side with them in their refusals to be molded by a hostile society and have come to look upon not-learning as positive and healthy in many situations." (Herb Kohl, "*I Won't Learn From You*," 1994)

A Life of Learning: Empowering, Trusting, Unschooling Children
Wendy Priesnitz

For the past forty years, I have had a vision of a world where children and young people are equal members of society; where children are liked, respected, trusted, and empowered to control their own lives and to make their decisions about learning and life. For the past thirty-five years, it has been both my passion and my work to give life to that vision. My vision challenges many closely-held assumptions about how we nurture, educate and live with the younger generation. It also, by necessity, challenges assumptions about economics, women's role, and many other aspects of life on this planet. Being a relentless challenger of those assumptions is the way that I contribute to fundamental, radical change that, true to the Latin origin of the word, digs at the root cause of what's wrong with how our society educates its young.

*****

Like most other people, my upbringing and my schooling in the 1950s and 60s taught me to accept what I was told by my parents, my teachers, and everyone else in my life. I did that well. I was the only child of working class parents living in a Canadian, mid-sized industrial city. My parents had waited out the Great Depression to get married, only to have difficulty conceiving, so they were forty-one and forty-eight when I was finally born. I was a good little girl who got good grades in school with little effort, thanks, I imagine, to fine test-taking skills, which were grounded in my strong reading and writing abilities. One of my early memories of school is of wondering when they were going to start teaching me the things I didn't know, rather than what I already knew. Many years later, I began to understand how, insidiously, school had reinforced my inadequacies and had left me with what I now called "learned incompetency" and a fear of not being able to do things "right" the first time.

Nobody in my family had gone to university and nobody suggested I go there either. My dream was to be an airline stewardess, as we called them then, but I had not been encouraged to go after my dreams. Instead, I was supposed to know my place. And, in my mother's mind, school was my place because teaching was a suitable job for a woman, and as I realized much later in life, it had once been her dream. So, as a relatively naive nineteen-year-old, I went to teachers' college. I was a good little girl there, too, and once again got good grades. I did especially well at lesson planning and bulletin board decorating. And, bolstered by my winning of public speaking awards in elementary school, I actually got quite excited about the prospect of standing in front of a class and filling those adoring and adorable little heads with important facts.

When I graduated, I got a job teaching working class kids in my old neighborhood. What disappointment and disillusionment to discover that I was spending most of my time yelling at ten-year-old boys to keep them from swinging from the lights and jumping out the windows! They were not interested in my carefully planned lessons and colorfully decorated bulletin boards. In fact, they didn't want to be there at all. And, I quickly realized, neither did I. So, contrary to everything I had been taught, I terminated my career as a school teacher.

Then I did what I should have done while I was attending teachers' college: I began my self-education. I started to think about how people learn, as well as what they need to learn and why—and what gets in the way of learning. As part of my research, I spent some time working at a daycare center.

Daycare centers were not prevalent in the early 1970s, but my developing feminism led me to believe they were crucial if society were to move beyond the nuclear family and its smothering hierarchy. I was astonished at how undervalued and underpaid the entirely female staff was, especially for work that was so stressful and so important. What uninspiring places the centers were. I am a questioner by nature and that experience stimulated a lot of questions: Why was our society apparently undervaluing this work? Was it because women were doing it? Or did we value the care of the next generation so little? Did caring for the next generation involve more than Kool-Aid and regimented "play" time? What is liberated about paying other women a minimal wage to look after our children so that we can have high paying careers? Why do women have to embrace the male model in order to challenge patriarchy? Is there a third way? And where do the children fit into all of this?

As for education, I decided that all those lessons I had so carefully memorized in teachers' college about how to motivate students to learn were absolute nonsense. I realized that people (those kids in school and the daycare, as well as myself) learn things better if they are not compelled and coerced; if they are given control over what, when, where, why and how they learn; and if they are trusted and respected. I realized that until schools get in the way, children do not need to be forced to learn, because curiosity about the world and how it works is a natural human trait. I realized that memorizing material for a test (which I had done so well in school) isn't real learning.

Fortunately, around the same time, I met and married a man who somehow intuitively knew all of this, although he hadn't articulated it before. In the early days of our relationship, Rolf and I spoke often about how and why we would not send our future children to school, not quite understanding what a monumental decision that was. While I took my first tentative steps towards believing in myself as a writer and change-maker, he and I started a family. When I was pregnant with our first daughter, Heidi, in 1972, I fought anger, frustration, and sometimes despair at the state of the world into which I would bring her. As it does for many women, motherhood was focusing my early political consciousness. It was helping me understand how the choices I make in my personal life are linked to those I make on a larger scale. Propelled by a desire to create a better world for our children, we decided that Heidi and her sister, Melanie, who was born eighteen months later, would grow up not only absent from school, but unfettered by many of the assumptions people make about children's subordinate place in the world. Rolf and I began to create a life that would affirm the rights of all members of our family.

With that, I embarked on my life's work to advocate for a child's right to be raised and educated with respect and without the "isms"— sexism, racism, classism, ageism, consumerism, and other elitist or destructive social influences.

Then, in 1976, when the girls were ages three and four, Rolf and I started the home-based business that remains a vital part of our lives and my work to this day. With a small credit card advance, we launched a company that would publish both books and magazines, beginning with *Natural Life*, and would allow us both to stay at home with our daughters. We were in our mid-twenties, with no training or experience in the media world. He was a plumber and I was an unemployed teacher/fledgling writer. But we had the panache of youth and we knew from experience that there was a need for information and inspiration to help people question the status quo and the conventional, consumer-oriented ways that were damaging our earth. In those days, questioning the status quo meant joining the back-to-the-land movement, growing one's own food, and learning about non-conventional methods of parenting. So that is what those first few issues of *Natural Life* were about, with articles about how to plant cabbages, have a home birth, and construct a wash bucket bass fiddle.

Our home business was, itself, a deliberately alternative economic, social, and environmental choice. But little did I know that the experience would have ramifications far beyond the value of putting food on our family's table—or that it would teach me to challenge my assumptions about economics, education and food production, about what is truly important in life. Since my business education was self-directed, it also provided me with a living model of the sort of life-based learning experience I was beginning to envision for children—one that involved a combination of motivation, hands-on experience, questioning, mentor seeking, reading, error making and correction, and discussion. (It also provided me with the ability and the impetus—a decade later—to create The Home Business Network, which would legitimize home business and help other women create careers for themselves while staying at home with their children.)

Along the way, my family and I lived a good life while being true to our principles, at least most of the time. Instead of writing advertising copy to sell breakfast cereal or press releases to "greenwash" the public images of various multinational corporations, or composing mind numbing speeches for well meaning politicians, I plugged away at semi-profitable alternative journalistic pursuits, using my talents and skills to create change. We walked or rode our bikes whenever possible. We recycled and reused long before it became chic. We grew some of our food and bought locally grown organic food when we could. We made our own clothes or purchased them with no concern for brand name labels (and a fierce desire to avoid advertising those labels on the outside of our clothing). We also made our own entertainment. And for our young daughters, we facilitated life-based, self-directed exploration instead of sending them to school.

By the late 1970s, I was feeling the need to reach out, to communicate with other families who were challenging the assumption that children must attend school, but there was no mechanism for that. So, using my editorial platform in *Natural Life* magazine, I went public with our family's educational choice. Soon, we were in contact with a few other like-minded families who were pioneering homeschooling. I found myself to be in demand for media interviews, endlessly explaining how children learn without being taught, that a self-directed education does not equate with poor socialization, and that non-academic does not necessarily mean anti-intellectual. My speaking out led directly to a couple of run-ins with school authorities who mistakenly assumed that their authority legally and ethically extended into our home. At that point, I realized there was a need to educate school boards and their employees about homeschooling law, to advocate on behalf of homeschoolers, and to more formally organize what was becoming a movement. So, I founded the Canadian Alliance of Home Schoolers (CAHS). It was a national network that provided both advice and credibility to homeschoolers, and that nurtured many of the provincial support and advocacy organizations that are in place today in Canada.

In those days, my thinking was developing apace, helped along by discussions with John Holt, who was kick-starting a parallel American movement and sought our publishing advice as he launched his *Growing Without Schooling* newsletter; and by many strong homeschooling mothers on both sides of the border. With the help of this growing network, I formulated a list of the questions I was most often asked and most curious about myself. I then contacted as many homeschooling families as I could find with the first Canadian homeschooling survey. This early research, which I published in 1989—as imprecise and unscientific as it was—put a face to the movement in Canada, allowed me to estimate the size of the homeschooling population, and provided the basis for future studies.

All the while, I struggled to reconcile my trust in children's ability to learn about the world unrestricted with the growing number of religious families who were choosing homeschooling in order to control how and what their children were exposed to. As uncomfortable as I was with enabling school-at-home, I felt that the small and fragile movement needed to support all motivations and styles.

Truth be told, in 1979 I had not yet fully slain the schooling dragon in my own mind. If I had, I might have given the Canadian Alliance of Home Schoolers a different name! After all, the learning experience that my family was living had nothing to do with school (except for a determined lack of it!) and it was more community- than home-centered. Nevertheless, when I wrote my first book on the subject, I gave it a confusing and oxymoronic name: *School Free—The Home Schooling Handbook*. I eventually came to understand that what we now popularly call "homeschooling" is not meeting its full potential—and in many instances, is becoming more like school and therefore less of a real alternative. But in those days homeschooling was not at all common, and I was trying to reach as broad a spectrum of readers as possible with the message that since public schools were not meeting children's needs, alternatives had to be created and supported.

I have since become more precise about my use of language to describe my vision, but that early "big picture" thinking led me to understand the need to reach out to people espousing other alternatives to public school. (I had already decided that the public school system was so broken it could not be fixed, so I never contemplated working for change within the system.) My work as editor of *Natural Life* connected me with many wonderful people and a few organizations that shared the holistic view that everything—including education— is woven into the fabric of life (a notion that I find somewhat lacking in many of today's progressive organizations, which often ignore public education's problems). One of those that inspired me in the 1970s was the School of Living, with its focus on organic agriculture, cooperatives and worker-owned businesses, appropriate technology, local self-reliance and, of course, self-education, which was, arguably, its core. (Jerry Mintz's AERO continues to function under the School of Living umbrella.) Ed Nagel's National Association for the Legal Support of Alternative Schools (which was an early legal advocate of homeschooling) was another part of my outreach, as was Education Otherwise in the UK.

Closer to home, the Ontario Association of Alternative and Independent Schools (OAAIS) attracted my attention and some of my time. In the same way that homeschooling was (and perhaps still is) an awkward member of the alternative education community, I was somewhat of an outsider on the OASIS board, which was mostly populated by middle-aged male representatives of religious schools who were seeking government funding for their institutions. Nevertheless, I ended up serving a term as president of the association in the late 1980s, in the interests of solidarity for alternatives to the warehouse model of public education.

Combining my love of writing and editing with my activism also resulted in more publishing endeavors, notably *Child's Play*, which I published from 1983 through 1992. *Child's Play*—first a newsletter and later a magazine—was a source of support, resources and inspiration for families interested in home-based learning, alternative schools, and natural parenting.

Over the years, as I found my writer's voice, became a broadcaster and conference presenter, and interacted with the media about home-based learning, I gained some insights—and strong opinions–about how our use of language can either reinforce the status quo or nudge change to happen. I began to understand how words like "teaching" and "schooling" imply that some people are doing things to other people, that people at the top are acting on those farther down the totem pole. I realized that our public education system reflects a paternalistic worldview, which puts Man at the top of the hierarchy, controlling everything underneath, including women, children, animals, and the earth's resources.

With my daughters growing up and leaving home, and the years passing more quickly, I began to wonder if the small, personal choices my family and I were making went far enough. I watched child poverty and the abuse of women and children grow to epidemic proportions globally, while social safety nets were being torn apart in the name of fiscal responsibility. Youth crime appeared to be increasing, fueled at least partially by the violence that surrounds us, in both real life and in the media. Indigenous peoples were still fighting for their basic rights. I saw logging companies continue to ravage forests, tobacco companies cynically buying their way out of responsibility for their deadly product, global warming wreaking havoc with world weather patterns, garbage dumps overflowing, nuclear power plants and oil tankers leaking, and toxic chemicals being found in mothers' milk. I saw schools being overtaken by bullies, standardized testing and "dropouts" who were shunned by their communities. This was in spite of decades of effort on the part of activists around the world.

My need to "do more" led me, in 1996, to accept an invitation to run for the leadership of the Green Party of Canada. Although I had no formal experience with politics, I remembered that, as the feminist slogan goes, the personal is political and many of the choices I had made in my life were most definitely political.

The Canadian Greens were only thirteen years old at the time, and I took on the daunting task of trying to build a truly progressive, grassroots alternative to the mainstream political parties. Unfortunately, I quickly learned that many in the tiny party wanted a party that was not a party, an organization that would not organize, and a leader who would not lead. Disillusioned with other political parties, they were understandably wary of anything that could be construed as a hierarchy or bureaucracy. To the party's disadvantage and my frustration, this translated into a distrust of initiative, which resulted in lack of action and in endless conflicts about structure and process.

Feeling virtually alone in my desire to build the party from the bottom up, and tired of butting my head against a wall of testosterone, I once again cut my losses and resigned, disillusioned by the party's lack of ability to walk its talk, in spite of some wonderful policies and dedicated people. I tried to write a book about the experience, but soon realized that the experience had taught me something important, in the same way my brief school teaching career had done: I had learned that only when we have truly rejected the top-down model of ideological change will we be able to concentrate on building sustainable alternatives.

And surprise, surprise, I realized that I had known the source of the problem—and hence the solution—all along! One of our most revered and supposedly democratic institutions uses the tool of compulsion to subject children to a standardized curriculum, molds them into obedient consumers and fits them into their places in the hierarchy, leaving few of them able to do anything except keep paddling. So I ended up back where I had started from—thinking and writing about children and how we can best equip them to save the world, or at least to live happily and productively in it. The green politics book I was trying to write quickly became *Challenging Assumptions in Education—from Institutionalized Education to a Learning Society*.

In 2002, I decided that the time was ripe to launch a magazine on the subject of what I was, by that time, unwillingly calling unschooling. We named it *Life Learning*, and the phrase quickly began to be used as a substitute for "unschooling" and "radical unschooling" by those who were, like me, uncomfortable with a term that was non-descriptive at best and negative at worst. The magazine, over its six years of publication (the economic downturn in 2008 prompted us to integrate it into *Natural Life* magazine), nurtured an international community of wonderful readers and writers who believe children learn best without coercion, and based on their own interests, motivations and timetables. I edited an anthology of essays from the magazine entitled *Life Learning: Lessons from the Educational Frontier*, and its website continues to be a place for the community to gather.

*****

Recently, a PhD student successfully defended her thesis entitled

Reflections on Homeschooling, Mothering and Social Change: The Life History of Wendy Priesnitz. However, neither my life nor my work in support of homeschooling, mothering, or social change is over! My mission for the next decade involves using traditional networking, social networking technologies and the printed word to continue to influence both parents and educators to support children and young people as they educate themselves about the world and rescue it from the mess this and previous generations have made of it.

Do What We Can
Carlo Ricci

My schooling was relatively uneventful; yet, when I think about it all the memories that come to mind are negative. Sadly, I cannot think of a single happy schooling memory. I lived for weekends and extended holidays. I was a hollow student. I would go through the motions and try to just get by, survive. I was very quiet and respectful, yet as well behaved as I was, I still remember getting in trouble, although very rarely. These few times were enough to keep me even more concerned and panicked and empty.

I had school friends and others in the schooling community and thought that we were inseparable, but the truth is that as soon as school let out, I would never see these people. Looking back, we clung to each other so closely because this was a way to survive—there is strength in numbers. Being within a group, others would leave us alone. In elementary school, I hung around with the "smarter" students. I was among them not because of my academic achievements, but because of my "pleasant" behavior.

While in a primary grade, I recall an incident where the principal had to come in and scold us for a reason I don't remember. The teacher was out of the room for this, but unbeknownst to me at the time, she was peeping in through the door. At one point I must have smiled (perhaps out of nervous fear, or maybe one of my classmates did something)—

for this I was called out and interrogated by my teacher. I made up a silly and unbelievable story about how I smiled because I recalled a joke that one of my relatives told me earlier. She asked what it was and I made something up and shared it with her. Again, I do not recall the contents of our conversation but the negative feelings are as vivid today as they were then. As I was telling her the tale I recall understanding how silly my words were even to me as they were leaving my lips. In the end, I was released and permitted to rejoin my classmates.

In April 2009, my daughters and I were watching a film titled *Matilda* where a school principal was portrayed as being a mean woman who dislikes children. She beat the children and walked around with a strap. I shared with my four- and six-year-old daughters that when I was younger children were strapped. They asked if I ever was. I told them that I was not, but that I did have my sideburns pulled on a number of occasions. I then shared with them that once I was walking single file with my classmates going from our class to the French class. I must have slipped out of line and whispered something to another classmate. For this my teacher (who was feared by all the students in the school and who I dreaded from the day I found out that she would be my teacher) came up behind me and pulled on my sideburns so hard that my eyes watered. My daughters hugged me.

Again, for me these incidents were rare and far between, but I have friends for whom this was a daily occurrence. One of my friends was cracked over the head with a guitar for talking while the teacher sang a Beatles song—it could even have been "Give Peace a Chance!" This same teacher was known for tracing with his finger the words on the front of the t-shirts that some of the young female students wore. When we reminisce about our negative schooling experiences, too many times they are shared with much bravado and laughter, but the truth is that there is nothing funny about abuse.

As I said earlier, although I hung around with the smarter students I was clearly not the brightest among them. Schools are breeding grounds for instilling competition among children, and in me, this resulted in wishing that I were the highest achiever and the best artist. I recall, in middle school, being among one of a few students whose painting was not worthy of being placed on the wall. Not being the best made me feel fearful and inadequate. As Holt poignantly points out in his book *How Children Fail*, being the best does not eliminate the fear, it just gives it a different manifestation. He writes simply that, "They fail because they are afraid, bored, and confused" (p. 5). Later in the same book he writes;

> These self-limiting and self-defeating strategies are dictated, above all else, by fear. For many years I have been asking myself why intelligent children act unintelligently at school. The simple answer is, "Because they're scared" (p. 92).

Unfortunately, I, like far too many of us, have many, many more negative experiences that I can share. When I was in elementary school, a much older student depantsed me in front of his friends; when I was in high school, after gym a student spit at me and the spit landed right around my lips—stories like these are remarkable not because they are rare but because so many, if not all of us, have experienced a version of abuse connected to our schooling experience. This is a sad truth. I have talked to many people about their schooling experiences and I have yet to find someone without a negative personal story. Some believe that overall their experience was a positive one, yet I truly believe that they believe that because they have never taken the time to think about how their schooling has changed, shaped and wounded them as a human being. It is important to note that, overall, I felt that I was liked by people in the schooling community; yet I still had my share of negative experiences. What about those who are targeted? Moreover, how can all of the pressures of the schooling mentality not fundamentally change us as human beings?

As a high school student my grades were too low to get into university. I went to college for a year and then reapplied to university and got in with my college grades. Even as a graduate student I could not choose what I wanted to learn. I had to focus on what my professors wanted me to read and to answer their questions. Everything I focus on now I have learned on my own and do not give any credit to my schooling. My schooling was an obstacle and a hindrance, not a help. Even now as a university faculty member I am still limited and controlled by schooling. In order to gain tenure and promotion, faculty needs to conform and comply. We need to publish in journals that the decision makers (far too many of whom, unfortunately, have been infected with the schooling mentality) believe are acceptable and in the form that they believe is acceptable. Schools offer a very limited and a narrow view of what is valuable, and if you disagree or do not fit that view you are failed and led to believe that the problem lies with you. Personally, I now know and understand that I am not the problem, but that schools are. In the end, when I did not conform to the dictates of schooling, I was failed; when I conformed, I was let in. Ultimately, and I share this not to be a braggart but to make a point, for all intents and purposes I completed my Master's and my PhD at one of the most "prestigious" universities in Canada and around the world in one year for each, while I was working full-time as a high school English teacher. I believe that this proves that my teachers had me all wrong and that no one knows a person's potential, nor can they predict their future.

Now what?

Having come to view schooling in the way that I have, I feel compelled to act. A favorite assignment given to teachers in training is to ask them how they got to the point of wanting to be a teacher, and the correct answer that they must provide is that they have always wanted to be a teacher as far back as they can remember. (I have had students tell me that when they deviated and were truthful, their professors either asked them to rewrite their life's story or gave them a low grade, or they were called on their "incorrect" response.) When I am at my most philosophical, I see where I am now as being more mysterious than clear. I am the first and still one of only a handful in my family to pursue higher schooling, and the only to have a Master's or a PhD. More importantly, among my family and lifelong friends I am the only one who has dedicated his life to challenging the oppressiveness of schooling—even many of the scholars that I cross paths with, while they fight to improve the status quo, do not see a real need to transform the system; they just want to reform it. I have since met and read many likeminded thinkers who continue to be a source of inspiration and support, for which I am grateful and thankful. I have to say that once people are exposed to this way of thinking about schooling they overwhelmingly appreciate and understand the position. In short, I feel that, really, I have been thrown into my lot in life and now what? What follows is an attempt for me to share some of what I have done to date to try to contribute to transforming the world.

Foremost, I need to say that I believe that we can all make a difference. If we transform how we think and act, then we are changing the world. We live in the world and are a part of it, so anything we do to change our local context results in a change in the world. In other words, by changing myself I am changing the world because I am in constant interaction with it—it's that simple. As such, the schooling mentality goes beyond schooling. It pervades the world we live in and so schooling is a symptom of a much larger problem. The problem is a holistic integrated one that requires a holistic integrated solution.

Consequently, given where I am today, what are some of the things I am doing to transform the world? First, my job allows me a powerful opportunity to interact with a large number of people who can also choose to become a part of the solution. As an associate professor at an education graduate studies program I interact with many researchers, administrators, and teachers. When I meet with these people formally or informally, I try to share and act in ways that are consistent with a more learner-centered, democratic vision. Whether it is in a classroom, conference, meeting, hiring committee, promotion committee, or what-have-you, I bring an unschooling, learner-centered, democratic voice to the table. Overall, I get a very positive response. The idea, as I see it, is not to impose our vision on others, but merely to expose and promote in very gentle but powerful ways. In my last class, and in many of my classes, students (male and female, younger and older) cry as they begin to embody the truth behind the message. I try to help create a respectful environment where people can grow in their own way. I challenge in practice and in theory notions of grading, competition, externally imposed curricula and other assumptions of the schooling mentality. When I first started working for my university I realized that there was a need for developing more formal recognitions of these visions and so I created five courses at the graduate level that now get taught on a regular basis. The courses are very well received and attended. When I teach, my courses fill up very quickly and there is often a waiting list. Students tell me that they wait up or set their alarms for midnight so that they can be among the first to register. Again, I am sharing, not to brag, but to make a point: this and what students share with me speaks volumes to the need for learner-centered, democratic visions.

Second, I realized that as an academic, there was no place to get formal recognition for research around unschooling and alternative learning. I founded and now edit an academic peer reviewed journal titled *The Journal of Unschooling and Alternative Learning* (JUAL). I chose the name carefully because I was looking for an acronym that had meaning and was memorable. JUAL is pronounced "jewel" and can metaphorically be seen as a jewel in the sense that it is precious and has healing powers. I have asked the university to help me track how many hits JUAL gets and two days ago they finally did. JUAL was accessed about two hundred times in two days, from the 8th to the 10th of April, 2009. In addition, I make all of my writing available online for free and have used web technology such as YouTube to help get the message out. I created a YouTube unschooling channel that has reached a large audience and has the potential of reaching an even larger one. I also get a lot of emails about JUAL, the unschooling channel, and my writing from people all over the world. In part, I am hoping that these places can be hubs where people can congregate and can use them as starting points. I have, indeed, been told that this is the case. Making these spaces free makes them easier to access and that, I believe, is key.

Third, volunteering is also an important part of what I do. For example, I volunteer for the Ontario Federation of Teaching Parents (OFTP). They are an organization that helps people who wish to homeschool. I field many calls for them and have had to help schoolers and non-schoolers alike navigate the system. I have met with superintendents and principals, and do whatever else I can to help people who seek me out. Furthermore, I was an affiant for a court case challenging high stakes standardized testing that was introduced into Ontario. In addition, I attend many speaking engagements and do whatever I can to help get the message out. I have appeared in newspapers, on television, and radio. I believe that every bit helps and the more bits the better. I have talked to young and old, parents, professionals, and anyone who expresses an interest.

Fourth, the most personal impact I can make is through my own children. The greatest testament that I have is aspiring to live a learner-centered, democratic life with my children. I believe that children are among the last acceptably (by society) oppressed groups and my children have shown me how capable young people are once we learn to trust them. My research into what children have done throughout history and in the present and my travels continue to support the implementation of a learner-centered, democratic lifestyle—the successes go far beyond my own personal experiences and are there for anyone who is willing to look. Sometimes, if we focus on only our context we miss a broader and richer set of evidence that shows how capable young people are. Much of the research done around children takes place in schools or within a world that supports the schooling mentality, and thus we conclude that this is how children are. I have come to believe that this is not how children are, but how oppressed children are—which is very different. Given the chance and given respect, children can reach heights beyond all of our beliefs and expectations.

In conclusion, it is my hope that through our combined efforts many more people will be thrown into situations where they can live their lives in learner-centered, democratic conditions where they can be trusted and respected to unfold. As Holt writes in *Escape from Childhood: The Needs and Rights of Children*, "The point is not to worry about what is possible but to do what we can."

Memories of Barrie
Tim Seldin

I attended the Barrie School, a large independent alternative school in Washington, DC. Barrie was founded by my mother, Frances Littman Seldin, and its organization reflected a blend of her background in Montessori and progressive education, as well as her many years of working in large (and apparently also very progressive, loosely structured) residential camps in New York State.

The school began in 1932 with thirteen preschool children, then tripled in size when my mother purchased the buildings, land, and Montessori school founded by the Alexander Graham Bell family on his estate in Washington. In 1935, the school moved again, to a larger seventeen acre estate in the northern corner of the city, where it grew to an enrollment of five hundred students or so, two-year-olds to twelfth graders. We later moved to the school's present site, a forty-five acre farm about ten miles north of Washington, in 1975.

Barrie was established as a humanistic progressive school. It was not officially called a Montessori school, both because my mother saw herself as being eclectic in her educational philosophy, and also because, by the 1930s, Montessori had all but disappeared as an official movement in the United States. With no source for teacher training or most Montessori materials, we had to train our staff in-house and prepare our own hands on learning materials.

Barrie served two main communities: the large, and often very liberal, international community that has always flourished in the Washington, D.C. area, and the small, but growing, middle class black and Asian communities.

From the beginning, Barrie was considered a maverick within the elitist independent school community; our educational philosophy was different and my mother insisted that we stand firm on some of the most explosive social issues of our time—racial and religious discrimination, social elitism, and women's rights. The school was well integrated long before most other schools in the community, and brought together an interesting mélange of families from many different cultures and walks of life. Financial aid was a major part of the school's budget.

I entered Barrie in 1948 when I turned two. I grew up there, never going to another school, except for a few years when I lived in France. I graduated from Barrie's high school in 1963 as the top half of our class of two seniors.

A typical day as a young child at Barrie began, for many of us, before day break when our parents dropped us off at school on their way to work. In my case, my mother's work was at the school, but, like many of the teachers and staff, she was there by about seven o'clock winter, spring, summer, and fall. We went to Barrie year-round, often six days a week, because the school was open on Saturdays as well.

Like so many children who attend nontraditional alternative schools, Barrie was our second home. Many of the parents worked downtown and typically could not leave work until after five. We certainly were nothing like a day-care center, but parents knew that we would be fine until they arrived. Barrie prided itself on being a family-friendly school; working families appreciated its extended day and summer programs.

We thought of the extended Barrie community of teachers, parents, and staff as our second family. As the founder's kid, I was often asked to talk about Barrie, but every one of my friends would speak to visitors about the school with affection and conviction. When people asked us if we liked being at Barrie, we acted as if the question was odd. "Sure! How could anyone *not* love it here? The teachers are our friends, the stuff we learn is cool. It's interesting, and the other kids are like my brothers and sisters. It's a family. You feel really close to everyone."

My day as a little kid at Barrie began when I arrived, in my classroom. We would go to the kitchen and beg Edith, the cook, to make us pancakes, or we'd stay in our classroom and scoop ourselves bowls of cereal from a small bin, adding milk from small pitchers kept in a small refrigerator. Kids would drift in with their parents every so often. For the next few hours, we would help set up the classroom, go out to the greenhouse or to the garden to cut flowers to put in the little vases on each table, or we would work on cleaning the environment. The odd thing about Montessori is that kids typically really learn to enjoy doing "chores," except we didn't call them that, and no one made us do them. The young ones (a three-year-old might look young to a seasoned four- or five-year-old in a typical Montessori class) didn't start that way. We would have to show them, and remind them, and often we would even clean up after them. Eventually they got it. The rules are simple: If you use it, put it away when you're done. Don't disturb the peace indoors. Be kind to others. Find something to do that you enjoy, and don't hurt anyone. We would cut up fruit and vegetables for snack, make bread with our teacher or make ourselves little scones, squeeze oranges for juice, and take care of the class garden and animals.

Boy, were there animals! Barrie had twenty-five horses, give or take, and over the years, an assortment of ducks, chickens, geese, peacocks, sheep, llamas, turkeys, and of course school dogs and cats who spent most of their time around the classrooms. Looking back on things, I am amazed that the dogs behaved so well all those years. I don't remember any fights, and little barking.

Our day was spent moving from one freely chosen task to another. We might paint, or go down to the edge of the woods to explore a rotten log, or work in the garden. The class, like all Montessori inspired schools, had all sorts of learning materials, which we thought of more or less as toys. I don't remember anyone teaching me to read, but one day I could. Sometimes our teachers gathered a few of us for a lesson, and sometimes we asked for them.

In Montessori, children work with hands-on learning materials that make abstract concepts clear and concrete. This carefully prepared and sequenced collection of concrete apparatus allows kids to develop a clear inner image of concepts in mathematics, such as how big a thousand is, what we mean when we refer to the "hundreds" column, and what is taking place when we divide one number by another. This approach always made sense to me. Even now I have a sort of muscular memory. I can close my eyes and see math processes work themselves out in my head.

A typical math exercise that I've seen four- or five-year-olds play out looks something like this: Two children begin to work together to construct and solve a mathematical problem. No one assigns this work to them, they choose it freely. Using sets of number cards, each decides how many units, tens, hundreds, and thousands will be in his addend. The cards showing the units one to nine are printed in green, the cards showing the numbers from ten to ninety are printed in blue, the hundreds from one hundred to nine hundred are printed with red ink, and the cards showing the numbers one thousand to nine thousand are printed in green again, because they represent units of thousands.

As the two boys construct their numbers, they decide how many units they want, find the card showing that quantity, and place it at the upper right-hand corner of their work space. Next they go to the bank, a central collection of golden bead material, and gather the number of unit beads that corresponds with the number card selected. This process is repeated with the tens, hundreds, and thousands.

The two addends are combined in the process we call addition. Beginning with the units, the children count the combined quantities to determine the result of adding the two together. If the result is nine or less, they simply find the large number card that represents the answer. If the addition has resulted in a quantity of ten beads or more, the children stop at the count of ten and carry these unit beads to the bank to exchange them for a ten-bar: ten units equals one unit of ten. This process is repeated with the tens, hundreds, and thousands.

Many people have heard that Montessori kids are exceptionally neat and organized. That part never took root in me terribly well. I must have certainly had some level of ADD, and generally found myself great at seeing the big picture or figuring things out, but fairly useless at organizing the details of a big project. I found other, more talented kids to work with.

The days involved a great balance of art, music, drama, cooking, woodworking, and practical life around the school. We learned to lay bricks, build horse fences, and work in the school greenhouses.

By the end of a typical day as a preschool or elementary kid at Barrie, I had probably completed twenty to thirty different activities.

Among all the days that I spent at Barrie, one stands out as the most vivid. It was May of 1954, the end of our fourth-grade year in which our teacher, Hazel Small, had gotten us so excited about Greek and Egyptian mythology that we could barely talk about anything else. She arranged for a special experience to tie our study of the Iliad and Odyssey together. We left Fern Place early in the morning and drove to Annapolis, where waiting for us in the water was a replica of an ancient longboat with fifteen burly men at the oars. It was as if our dreams had come to life. We were ushered aboard and cast off for a day under the bright sun pulling at the oars beside these wonderful sailors. With Miss Small's guidance, we watched how the waves affected our progress and experienced a delightful rest from our labor when the wind set the sails.

It took almost no effort to imagine ourselves aboard an ancient ship, off to a fantastic adventure. Late in the afternoon, we pulled up on a sandy beach and unpacked a dinner right out of the *Iliad*: a roast of lamb, which we rubbed with garlic, herbs, and olive oil and set upon a spit over the coals. As the sun set, we ate our feast slowly with spring onions, pita bread, grapes, honey, and feta cheese, and we drank grape juice from leather wine skins. As we sat by the fire, Miss Small stood beside us, dressed in a beautiful white cotton robe with a full hood that framed her face in the firelight, playing the role of an ancient story teller.

As she softly recounted the familiar words of the *Odyssey*, we felt a direct and powerful connection with the far distant past. Don't tell me that history is not alive! I've sailed a long ship across wine dark seas and sat at the foot of Homer's daughter and heard her tell the tales of great men and women, gods and goddess.

That moment in my life, and others just like it, will stay with me always. At Barrie, learning was more than repetition of facts. It was an adventure that sparked my imagination and set in motion a quest for knowledge that has become an intrinsic component of the adult that I am today.

Barrie's pastoral setting was by deliberate design. My mother was deeply committed to outdoor living and environmental issues. We spent forty years as a "country" school in the city, moving further and further uptown as urbanization began to invade the school's island of tranquility. The Layhill Road property in Silver Spring was purchased in 1956.

During the late 1950s, all of us in the Upper School spent one day a week at the Layhill Road campus, clearing the trees, digging the lake, and transforming the old farm into what it is today. We had a strong sense of ownership and pride in the trees that we planted, the fences that we built, and the buildings that we painted. My mother's plans to build a new school on the Layhill Road campus, were, unfortunately, not realized before her sudden death in 1971.

A few years before this, as a graduate student of education and psychology, I had become fascinated with Barrie on a professional level and joined the staff in 1968. When my mother died, the Board of Trustees asked that I continue her work as Headmaster. I served in that position until 1993, when I stepped down to serve as President of the Montessori Foundation.

My mother's death led us to finally make the move from Fern Place. As we prepared to build on Layhill Road, the State of Maryland imposed a sewer moratorium, and we could not complete our entire construction project. We had no choice but to temporarily close the Upper School. During that same period, we completed the transition to a formal Montessori curriculum, which enriched everything that we had learned from our first forty years. We were able to reopen the Upper School in 1982.

From what Zoë Readhead, the Headmistress of Summerhill School, told me, Barrie would have qualified as a democratic school. We sure never thought about it in those terms.

Kids had as much authority as parents and teachers, and everything was done by consensus, within the ground rules that over-arched the entire school (what we called a Blueprint). Remember, we studied what we wanted most of the time, we traveled all around town and overseas, we interviewed people for information, wrote our own textbooks, and most often learned in Socratic seminars or by doing.

The school was basically run at three levels: the class (or House), the division, and the community. The classes, like many Montessori schools, were basically an empowered community of independent children who were well behaved and frankly, quite bright.

One difference is that we went to school in some really neat old mansions, with very good furniture, so running around inside was not okay. On the other hand, we gardened, fed the twenty-five horses three hundred sixty-five days a year, helped the mechanics fix the twenty-five school buses and tractor, and on and on.

Few students got into any trouble except for smoking on campus, which we were not supposed to do, but did anyway. I don't remember any real punishments, although the worst (and best) thing was to have to spend the day with Nettie, the school nurse. She was a fascinating character, and most of the students loved to listen to stories of her childhood. If we did do something annoying to others, we were just busted, scolded, and fined. Kids were the primary enforcers of the ground rules.

Classes made major decisions for themselves and resolved conflicts. Since very little was done as a whole group, this was a daily routine, but did not have a lot to do other than simple tasks.

In the Upper School (grades seven to twelve), we set the courses that would be offered each term to a very large extent at the weekly division meetings. Not everything was up for grabs, but much of it was. We needed to have a learning plan in lots of different areas from elementary through high school: including history, geography, economics, psychology, sociology, technology and industry, architecture, mathematics and higher math, the biological and physical sciences, philosophy, literature of all types, creative writing, expository writing, research skills, storytelling, myth, theater, and music, art, and dance appreciation and creation. All this plus Latin and a second language from age five through high school. We also handled almost everything to do with Upper School admissions and hiring new teachers and staff.

We did not worry about grades until high school, and even then did not take them seriously. We followed the Dalton Laboratory Plan (a Montessori inspired contract system that allows students to move at their own pace to a large degree), and worked through courses at our own pace, retaking exams until we passed at an 80 percent or higher level. We graded or evaluated one another's work and understanding of what we were studying.

At the monthly Community Meetings all students, teachers, parents, and administrators were invited to gather. At that age level we had no real power, but the administration listened to us and responded to our concerns, questions, and recommendations. They also asked us to consider most, but not all, major issues before they made the final decision. There was a commitment that neither the administration nor the board would make a policy or decision not supported by our core values set forth in a traditional document called our "blueprint."

Someday I should really write all this up. It certainly was not perfect, and Barrie seems to be very different today. But I loved it like it was my extended family, and I miss being part of that community every day.

I served as headmaster at Barrie for twenty-two years. Over time the school became well-known within the large community of Montessori schools around the world, and it evolved into an educational laboratory, with its own teacher education program, university connection, publishing house, magazine, and seminars for school leaders. In 1993, my last year at Barrie, more than three thousand principals and teachers came for stays ranging from a day to several weeks of observation or practicum field study.

I was elected to the board of the American Montessori Society in 1978, and over the years I worked with many schools that were struggling, often due to issues of ineffective school leadership or poor governance. I felt that Barrie reflected a model of excellence and a community that promoted a sense of connection and empowerment, and I saw that its model could be translated to other schools all over the world.

So, after twenty-five years at Barrie I decided that I could best serve the larger community of schools by developing an organization to provide tangible assistance. In 1992 I organized the Montessori Foundation, which is an international resource center to the many thousands of Montessori schools around the world. We publish journals, organize conferences, consult with schools, run live and online courses for Montessori teachers and school leaders, encourage schools to work together at the local and state levels, and provide many networking services. Through our membership arm, the International Montessori Council, we accredit schools and provide an even broader level of mentorship and support.

A Moment in Time
Herb Snitzer

Edith Hamilton, the Greek scholar, once remarked that "leisure and the pursuit of knowledge, the connection was inevitable—to a Greek." The Greek word for leisure was *schole*, what we now call school, but leisure is a far cry from what we demand of children these days.

Educating a child for a future world is an awe-inspiring experience. Teachers are not prophets, nor do we have crystal balls to see what tomorrow holds for us, let alone for the many children to whom we extend our knowledge, and with whom we exchange ideas and share in discovery.

One hundred years ago, early union leaders were able to get child labor laws passed, getting many children out of the factories and replaced by adult workers making adult salaries. But what of the kids replaced? What was the culture to do with thousands of uneducated children? Make schooling compulsory and structure schools as if they were assembly lines; pass the "raw materials" through a series of graded exercises and eventually produce an "educated" person. Educated? Perhaps. Trained? Indeed! One hundred years ago we made a crucial mistake, and today we only continue to make that same mistake.

It was against this growing rigidity in education practice, here and in European countries, that a small number of brave and determined educators began to appear on the education scene. To begin with, Homer Lane instituted a program teaching responsibility through self-government at The Ford Republic School in Detroit, but perhaps the most famous of these educators was Alexander Sutherland Neill. Neill was the founder and first head of The Summerhill School, in Leiston, Suffolk, England, a school now headed by his daughter, Zoe Readhead.

Neill was my mentor and a close friend for the last thirteen years of his life (I first met him when he was seventy-seven and I was twenty-eight). He also wrote the introduction to my 1972 book, *Today Is for Children, Numbers Can Wait*, and is the single most important person in my life, because he was able to show me ways of living that were integrated, holistic, and caring.

It was Neill's 1959 book, *Summerhill, A Radical Approach to Child-Rearing*, that set the tone of the Free School Movement of the 60s and 70s, giving others the direction and strength to start free schools throughout the United States and elsewhere.

I first met Neill in November, 1961, when I visited Summerhill as an interested parent. At that time, I was working as a photo-journalist for many of the national magazines and other photographic outlets. I recall our first meeting as though it were yesterday. I was waiting in a room with pretty beat up furniture, cigarette butts on the floor, and a few busted windows, when a gray-haired, tall, older man, walked in and stuck out his hand; "Hello, I'm Neill, what brings you here?" I was startled by the direct, yet overwhelming warmth of his voice. We chatted for five minutes or so, at which time he said, "Feel free to walk about, I need to get back to my math class," and out he marched. I was captivated. I stayed at Summerhill for a few more days, and before leaving, I asked Neill if he would be open to my returning to do a visual documentation of the school. He was open to the idea and so were the children, whose permission I also needed.

Returning to the United States, I called Nat Hentoff, a friend and fellow journalist, and asked him for the name of an editor who might be interested in the project. This lead me to the Macmillan Company, and a contract was given to me by Emile Capouya: enough money—in those days—for me to return to Summerhill for the fall of 1962 and produce a series of photographs and conversations, which were published in my book, *Summerhill, A Loving World* (1964).

After I, again, returned to the States, I called, at Neill's request, Alvin Bronstein, the head of The Summerhill Society—a New York-based organization trying to start a free school, which they never did. Alvin and his wife and I became friends, and were determined to start a school patterned after Summerhill. By the late summer of 1963, in a small town called Lewis, New York, in the Adirondack Mountains, sixty miles from the Canadian border, we were able to do so.

The Lewis-Wadhams School was established to carry on the ideas and principles of Homer Lane and A.S. Neill, and I had come to a major fork in the road. Was I to continue my blossoming photographic career? Or was I going to commit myself to alternative education? Was I going to leave New York City, and all that I had accomplished, to move to the Adirondack Mountains and begin a new life? We opened the school with six children and a staff of two teachers, and I traveled back and forth between Lewis and New York City, completing photography assignments for *Life*, and other national magazines and record companies. All this income went into the school, keeping it alive as best we could. It was such a heady time for all of us. At the end of the first year, our director, Wilf Blakeley, returned to England, and I was privileged to take his place (a position I held for the next twelve years). Alvin went on to become head of the National Prison Project of the ACLU and moved to Jackson, Mississippi, in the middle of the civil rights movement; his wife stayed at Lewis-Wadhams, and eventually, she and I married, keeping the school alive until 1976, when it closed its doors for good. In 1964 we met a young, idealistic teacher, Jerry Mintz, who came and worked at Lewis-Wadhams before going off to start his own school and founding the Alternative Education Resource Organization.

Through all the events and happenings of 1963 and 1964, Lewis-Wadhams held firm to the principles of Lane and Neill, even when we were lambasted by self-proclaimed New York City radicals for not becoming institutionally politicized. Individually, over the years, we had staff members who were socialists, communists, conscientious objectors, feminists, and once, an under-cover CIA agent (or so we suspected). But we didn't let our personal views corrupt our major focus: we were there to support children in their steady (or not so steady) growth into young adulthood. We were determined that our personal failings not intrude upon the lives of the children; the school was not going to be an excuse to cop-out on *adult* responsibilities.

Children did not have to show up for scheduled classes; the teachers did.

Teachers and students were not allowed to use drugs of any kind and if they did, they had two chances to change before being expelled by the entire community. Young adult teachers were viewed as mentors, friends, with whom one shared confidences; and through the years the school prospered and grew in population, and for the most part, the children with whom I stay in touch have grown into sensitive adults with families of their own.

The one over-riding remembrance (and there are many) is the workload we all experienced. Twenty-four hours a day, seven days a week, seventy-five children were given the opportunity to run and play and question. It was beautiful and exhausting, simply hard work, and for us adults, it produced a need to get away, not only in the summer months, when the school was closed, but during the school year; weekends in New York City or Montreal, or a day in Plattsburgh.

We did not have a multi-racial/multi-ethnic student body or faculty representation, despite my efforts to do so. I spent a lot of my time away from Lewis-Wadhams, lecturing at colleges or wherever people gathered to know more about freedom for children, how it works, the results that occurred, and how the kids functioned in the "bigger world." I was always conscious of the fact that we had very few inquiries from African-American parents, and when a child was admitted, he or she stayed briefly, the major parental comment being that they had hoped there would be more black children. The irony, for me, was that I contacted the ABC Foundation in Boston—a foundation committed to financially supporting lower-income kids in private schools—but the director told me point blank he was interested in getting "his kids" into Exeter or Andover, then into Yale or Harvard. In effect, he wasn't interested in "experimental education." End of comment and contact.

What I have seen over the years is that when it comes to education, black families are just as conservative as white families, and just as interested in "climbing the ladder of success." I agree that freedom has its limits, and discipline and hard work are involved with learning, but I walk another path when training replaces educating. Can children be educated as well as trained for a world yet unknown, in which they will eventually take their place? There is a vast difference between someone who is educated and someone who is primarily trained to fulfill a societal function. I am not suggesting that one can be both trained and educated. From what I now see in college curricula, one can graduate from college without taking one course in ethics, philosophy, comparative religion, or American History. There seem to be too many teachers and institutions caught up in the training game.

Today we hear and read sustaining cries for vast educational change, for new technologies, Charter schools and a myriad of innovative approaches all bringing to education a cure for the ailing patient. My position in the educational scheme of things is to state quietly (and not so quietly at times) that all the words, all the new systems, all the educational paraphernalia will not change the basic problems of education. Nor will they change the ills of a society that places higher value on those who are trained rather than on those who are educated. If we want trained people, then develop training schools with curriculum similar to what we once had in those schools for kids who were not going on to college, who knew they wanted to be mechanics, plasterers, painters, etc.

The obvious question, then, hangs out there: what do I mean by being educated? I mean exposing children to areas of enlightenment that encompass all cultures, not just Euro-centric sensibilities. Art, music, history, science, religion, philosophy—these would be the areas of investigation, not in a rote manner, but as living, breathing, vital programs, taught by both left and right of center teachers whose agenda is one of education and not indoctrination. Why do we need to bail out the banks? What would happen if they did go out of business? What would it mean to have a single payer health plan? Which presidents held slaves? Does religion help or hurt in the understanding of mystical experiences? The questions are limitless. Sadly, though, there is very little of this kind of inquiry going on at the high school or college levels. Go to college, then get a graduate degree, specialize and don't get too concerned about the bigger picture.

The Lewis-Wadhams School was more interested in educating its student population. We did all we could to question almost everything, including the very systems we were living under. Does having freedom make one a better person? Not teaching a young person to read until they are ready—is that fair to the child? To this question, I am interestingly more of a mind to disagree with my position of many years ago. Today I believe it is more worthwhile for young people to know how to read at a very young age, and then to turn that child loose on Google or any and all libraries around the world. A glaring statistic relating to the incarcerated population shows that 75 percent are illiterate. So it seems to make sense to teach children to read and to make sure that *all* children read before they do anything else, and if it takes two, three, four years for them to learn how, then so be it. We constantly questioned, and continued to question everything we were not in agreement with. They were wonderful times when we were confronted by a ten-year-old or a sixteen-year-old because they felt comfortable to challenge in ways that were constructive.

The school remained a vital alternative education institution for thirteen years, finally closing its doors in July, 1976. Personally, this was a painful time because I did all I could to keep the school open. The rising costs of almost everything just did us in and we had no financial reserves; we were a tuition-driven institution, our faculty receiving little salaries, no retirement or pension plan, and no medical fallback. We were also getting older and the energy needed to sustain an open society was not in evidence. It took us a year to finally call it quits and it was a sad day.

Since then, I have lived in Portland, Maine (briefly), then moved to Cambridge, Massachusetts, where I worked on the Polaroid Education Project for a few years, teaching at The Art Institute of Boston on a part-time basis and returning to my first love, photo-journalism. In 1992, I moved to St. Petersburg, Florida, where I am currently living. I have remarried and am making art, writing, and keeping myself abreast of education issues. I am also working on my memoirs, and my photographs are beginning to be collected by museums and private folks, which pleases me a great deal. An old friend of mine once said, "Herb, you just have to outlast everyone." I am doing my best; I turned seventy-six this past November.

The Second Coming, Sort Of
Len Solo

Sometimes a personal journey mirrors the movement of the larger society; it can also be a lamp that throws light on that history. At the risk of seeming immodest, I think my history with innovative and alternative schools, starting in the 1960s, is a metaphor for that time in education.

In 1969, Stan Barondes and I established the Teacher Drop-Out Center (TDOC). Our center was initially located in the School of Education at the University of Massachusetts in Amherst, where the Dean, Dwight Allen, had created a loose, informal climate that supported experimentation by doctoral students and faculty.

Stan and I had been high school teachers who had become disenchanted with the intolerance toward change in the public schools in the area where we taught, just northwest of New York City. We cared about developing high quality curriculum, about the kids, and about linking the two into an electric unity. We talked *with* students, we tried to explore significant moral and intellectual ideas that we and the students were engaged with, we experimented with moving away from lectures by breaking classes into smaller groups and trying hands-on activities and projects. This was in the middle-to-late 1960s, and we both got into trouble with our administrators.

So, we dropped out of teaching, sensing that there were others like us yearning to create good learning environments for students. This was about the time that Herb Kohl published an influential article in the *New York Review of Books* about the kind of work he was doing with kids in his class in Harlem.[1] We thought there must be places for people like us to teach, and our vague idea in establishing TDOC was to find them. Simultaneously, we hoped to develop a list of people who were, like us, looking for such good schools in which to teach. We thought we could serve as a kind of marriage service—matching specific people with specific schools.

We began to look for good schools. Early on, I contacted John Holt in Boston. John had published *How Children Fail*, which became quite popular, and he was invited to speak all over the country. In his travels, he had come across a number of good schools and had begun to compile a list of them. When we contacted these schools for information, the people we spoke to referred us to others, and within a few months, we had put together an annotated list of about two hundred schools.

Most of these were fairly new, small, private, alternative schools. They were modeled after Summerhill, the British Infant Schools that flourished in the fifties and sixties, and Montessori schools. There were Waldorf schools, farm schools, storefront schools, free schools, open schools, community schools, urban academies, parent cooperatives, schools-without-walls and schools-within-schools; each school was different, and they all held a wide variety of beliefs and practices, sometimes conflicting. What they had in common, though, was a fierce dedication to being student-centered, to teachers working closely with kids, to personalizing learning, and being communities of learners.

Compared to the schools I had attended growing up, in rural southwestern Pennsylvania, these schools seemed like they were from another universe. My experience was the K-8 Catholic school taught by nuns who were mostly concerned with teaching religion and rooting out evil—including the use of paddles and hands that slapped often—and the public high school that had, at most, two teachers who had anything memorable to teach us. These were schools where we sat at bolted-down desks for six hours a day; where teachers talked at us, not with us; where the curriculum was go-from-page-one-to-the-end-of-the-textbook, memorize "important" facts, plus do constant worksheets; where it was rare to discuss an idea or to read an interesting book or to do an exciting activity; and where students, staff, and parents had absolutely no say in how things were organized and run.

(As an aside, I should note that because school was so dull and so easy, my friends and I went to high school about half of the time. With the other half, we explored the world: went on camping trips without adults; trapped; went hiking, biking, walking and hitchhiking; played pool; played baseball and football; and just hung out together.)

The alternative schools we found were all over, though most were clustered in or near New York City, northern New Jersey, Cambridge/ Boston, Philadelphia, Seattle, Berkeley, and San Francisco. Though most were on the East and West coasts, there were also a number in St. Paul/Minneapolis, Chicago, East Lansing and connected (directly or indirectly) to colleges and universities. There were still others sprinkled around the country, though there were not many in the South or the Southwest.

We discovered a world of excitement in these "new" schools—an excitement generated by a closeness between adults and students in environments where teachers were given the freedom and the responsibility to try out their ideas. We soon found that the number of these schools was growing monthly. By the middle 1970s, our list had expanded to over three thousand innovative and alternative schools, though we had not verified the quality of a number of them.

When we had developed our initial list in 1969 and early 1970, we mailed out information to schools about TDOC and asked them to list their open positions with us. We began a modest newsletter that profiled schools and announced our services.

The Teacher Drop-Out Center quickly became widely known. Newspapers and magazines wrote about us and we appeared on radio and TV programs. We were deluged with letters from teachers who wanted information about alternative schools. Most of these letters were long and detailed, telling stories of teachers' struggles to try out new ideas in their classrooms and the bureaucracies that stifled them. We served as a sort of match-maker for a few months, connecting teachers and schools, but the sheer volume of teachers looking for good schools forced us to abandon these efforts.

We began to list the positions in our newsletter and charge a small fee for it, since we were graduate students with no incomes and families to support. We also published articles about alternative schools: about how they were structured, how they worked, how teachers taught, how they solved legal problems, who their students were, and other, similar issues, such as materials, books, and resources for teachers and schools. Soon, we were receiving and publishing articles from teachers, administrators, parents, students, and people like John Holt and Jonathan Kozol.

Indeed, it was a time when a number of educational writers became famous and most of them became our friends. These included the previously mentioned John Holt, Herb Kohl, and Jonathan Kozol, but also included George Dennison, Paul Goodman, Bea and Ron Gross, Neil Postman and Nat Hentoff.

This was a heady time for Stan and me, a time of great educational excitement: everything that was part of the traditional, accepted educational system was being questioned and confronted. Why should we all teach the same things? Why does curriculum have to be standardized? Can't there be high standards without standardization? Are there ways to teach reading besides using basals? Shouldn't schools personalize learning? Why do kids have to sit in rows and be talked at by an adult standing in front of the room or sitting behind a desk? Can the style of teaching be matched to the student's style of learning? Is it possible to have classrooms where students work cooperatively using materials and projects? How can curriculum be integrated? Does school have to occur in a building? Are there alternatives to testing and grading since these tend to degrade students? Who can be teachers? What should be studied? Should the range of subject matter be traditionally thin and narrow or could it be infinitely expansive and deep, as is the world? Should children be required to attend school and classes? Can students be involved in school decision-making? Can parents be equal to administrators and teachers in making decisions? Is it possible to meld these alternative schools into some sort of national movement to change all of education?

Of course, this questioning was happening in the midst of *The Crisis in the Classroom* and *The Greening of America*, and while much of it focused on pedagogical issues, some school reformers confronted the sociological functions of traditional education: making children loyal and well-functioning members of society, while serving as sorting institutions.

The Teacher Drop-Out Center was right in the middle of this new energy around the re-thinking of schooling. At the time, our activity seemed to mirror the Progressive School Movement, from the 1890s through 1930s, and it was exciting to discover the books and schools of that movement, and to recognize the parallels between us. In some ways, we saw our movement in the 1960s and 1970s as the second coming of these progressive schools, but in hindsight, it is clear to me that we were more like a mini-second coming. In the 60s and 70s, some people spoke about an "alternative school movement," but since it affected no more than 1 to 2 percent of the student population and lasted for only twelve to fifteen years at that level, it was not really a movement.

Nonetheless, our center helped to organize conferences about alternative schools, and these were, inevitably, informal, quite different from the traditional conference of present-a-paper, with one or two responders, and a question-and-answer session. Our conferences were more like fairs, with face-painting, music, home-cooked meals, "new" games, interactive talks and community-type meetings that involved adults and students. In addition to this opportunity for low-key networking, we also helped individuals and groups to establish new alternative schools.

Unknown to us, while we were founding TDOC on the East Coast, a similar group was forming on the West Coast. They called themselves the New Schools Exchange and they began to publish a newsletter similar to ours, but more "professional" looking. We were literally mirroring each other's activities. We made contact with the people at NSE in the early 70s, but we never really worked together.

By the middle 1970s, there were at least a dozen small, alternative school journals and newsletters being published around the country. Each of these publications became a local center of information and activism about alternative schools. Except for *TDOC, NSE Newsletter* and *Changing Schools* (out of the University of Indiana), these publications were short-lived, as were many of the schools themselves.

The schools from that time died out fairly quickly for many reasons—lack of money, poor implementation of ideas, weak leadership, starry-eyed teachers, political pressures and the like. My own sense, based on first-hand knowledge, was that a significant number of the alternative schools were not very good.

The good schools—for example, the Cambridge Alternative Public School, in Massachusetts; Dave Lehman's Community School in Ithaca, NY; Herb Snitzer's Lewis-Wadhams School in mid-New York state; Margaret Skutch's Early Learning Center in Stamford, CT; and the Free School in Albany, NY—were very good indeed. Once you saw them, you would not want to send your child anywhere else.[2]

In 1971, I moved to New Jersey to start and run a teacher education program at Stockton State College, a few miles west of Atlantic City. Simultaneously, I established the Atlantic County New School, a K-8, multi-graded, open classroom school, loosely connected to the college, which I initially started for my own children. I also directed a state-wide network of public and private alternative schools during the early to mid-1970s.

Alternative public schools were established early on. That's where the children were and that's where the possibility of sustained funding was. People felt the power of ideas from the private alternatives and wanted similar kinds of schools in the public sector. Obviously, then, alternative public schools sprang up in the same areas where there were private ones: in and around New York City, Cambridge/Boston, Seattle, Philadelphia, Berkeley, St. Paul/Minneapolis, and San Francisco.

By the mid-70s, with funding from the federal Department of Education, a number of these cities had established a network of alternative schools. Most prominent were those in Berkeley, San Francisco, St. Paul/Minneapolis and Seattle. Even smaller cities like Cambridge, MA, and Montclair, NJ, developed a system of choice as the basis for their public schools. The concept of neighborhood schools was abolished and in its place parents could choose from a variety of different kinds of schools.

Like the private schools, these public alternatives were incredibly varied: open schools with multi-graded classrooms, Montessori schools, free schools, schools-without-walls, fundamental or back-to-basics schools, E. D. Hirsch core knowledge schools, schools-within-schools and the like. There were traditional schools where one or two teachers were trying out new ideas, in the same way that Herb Kohl had done a few years earlier. Some, like the Angier School in Newton,

MA, developed an open classroom sequence along with the traditional set of graded classrooms under the leadership of Roland Barth, who a few years later founded the Principals' Center at the Harvard Graduate School of Education, along with myself and a few other area principals helping him.

But there were differences between the private and public alternative schools. The latter were mostly small schools, but were still larger than most private ones. The fervor and radicalism lessened and changed, though groups in urban areas seized the opportunity to assert community control over schools in their neighborhoods. Oceanhill-Brownsville in NYC became famous as parents struggled with the Board of Education and the American Federation of Teachers for control of their schools, and this sort of effort occurred in many cities. In Washington, D.C., for example, TDOC was instrumental in helping groups of parents gain control of the Adams School, as well as find a principal and number of teachers. Next door, we worked with the Morgan district as it became community controlled and chose Ken Haskins as its principal.

By the mid-70s, cities began using alternative schools as "magnets" to help desegregate their public schools, and these schools—supported by federal, state, and local funds—spread rapidly.[3] Thousands of magnet schools grew up all over the country in cities large and small: in Boston, MA; Hartford, CT; Chicago, IL; and Rochester, NY, for example.

Massachusetts established a very strong racial balance law, which financially supported the development of a system of "controlled choice," and magnet schools became a way for districts to achieve racial balance. A parent could choose whatever public school s/he wanted in a district, regardless of neighborhood, just as long as there was space and racial balance was maintained. Free transportation was provided. Cambridge was the first district to establish this controlled choice system in the early 1980s and it is still in operation now. Actually, the plan was based on the city-wide Cambridge Alternative Public School (CAPS), founded by a group of parents in 1972, before the concept of magnets existed. I became principal of CAPS in 1974, and it evolved into the Graham & Parks Alternative Public School in 1981.[4] Each of the K-8 schools in the district was encouraged to become a "magnet," to distinguish itself in some way, and many did. As a result, there are now three open classroom schools, a two-way bilingual school, an E. D. Hirsch school, a Montessori school, and an inclusion school for parents to choose from, in addition to several traditional schools that are evolving distinct identities. Almost a dozen other districts in the state have established similar controlled choice programs.

There was an ominous appropriation of alternative schools in many public school districts, which was the establishment of "alternative" schools for "special" students. Kids who caused problems, potential or actual drop-outs, and special needs students were isolated off into separate, "alternative" programs. This practice became so pervasive that the word "alternative" is now understood by most public school educators to mean these "special" schools for these "special" groups of students.

This, to me, is a profound co-option and perversion of the entire notion of alternative schools. It is a perversion of what I see as one of the main goals of many such schools: to have a group of students—balanced by race, gender, social-economic backgrounds, styles of learning, and age—learning together; to have a good school for all kinds of children.

The starting point for learning in a democracy has to be a balanced, heterogeneous group of students. From here, a school can begin to grapple with other structures: how to get these diverse children to work together; how to establish curriculum that actively engages children and adults in significant moral, intellectual, and ethical issues as well as in basic skills and concepts; how to work out decision-making processes that involve everyone connected to the school—staff, students, and parents; and how to establish teaching and learning practices that are consistent with democratic ideals.

This is exactly what happened in the 1960s and 1970s, and it's this questioning and grappling with ideas, practices, and structures that led to the establishment of alternative schools.

Notes

1. Herb later expanded this piece and it was published as *36 Children*.

2. For those readers who would like to learn more about what a school was like during that time, I'd recommend George Dennison's

The Lives of Children, probably the best book from that period. It tells the story of a small alternative school in NYC. Actually, it is the story of a John Dewey/Paul Goodman inspired teacher and the kids he taught. For those who want a wider view of what was happening with these new schools then, I'd recommend Allen Graubard's *Free the Children: Radical Reform and the Free School Movement* (1973).

3. This was another turn in the continuing use of alternative public schools for reasons other than educational; from their beginnings, alternative schools were political.

4. For a detailed look at the school and why it worked so well, see my *Making an Extraordinary School: The Work of Ordinary People* (PublishAmerica, 2009).

Educating For Human Greatness: A Higher Vision of Teaching, Thinking, And Learning
Lynn Stoddard

Kim Peek memorizes phone books of cities large and small. If he's been there and you tell him a name, he will tell you the phone number and address. Or you tell him the phone number and he will tell you the name and address. He reads other books with his left eye scanning down the left page while his right eye scans down the right page. His brain combines the information to make sense of it.

Tony DeBlois is blind and autistic. If you tell him the name of a musical composition by Chopin, Beethoven, Bach, Rachmaninoff or any other classical or modern composer, he will play it completely, and flawlessly, on the piano. I am an eye (and an ear) witness of a demonstration in which some musical skeptics challenged Tony with pieces they thought he couldn't possibly know. He soon made believers of all of them. If Tony has heard it, he can play it perfectly, without practice. Tony also writes his own pieces, music and lyrics, and sings beautifully in a deep baritone voice, even though it is hard for him to converse in complete sentences.

There are some amazing people who can add a long column of four- or five-digit numerals in their heads faster than you can do it with a calculator, others who produce amazing pieces of art, and still others who can fix anything that is broken. As I write this chapter, forty-seven-year-old Susan Boyle has captured the hearts of the world by singing "I Dreamed a Dream" in an incredibly beautiful voice on the *Britain's Got Talent* television show.

Why am I telling you about these incredible people? Because after over fifty years as an educator, I've become convinced that our society vastly underestimates human potential. Our school systems, public and private, reflect this low view of people, often with a valiant effort to standardize, and make students alike in knowledge and skills. What would happen if we started to see, in every person, a set of remarkable gifts and talents to be developed? What would happen if, instead of trying to make people alike, we started to nurture positive human diversity? How large is the ocean of undeveloped talent in America? And how much of that undeveloped talent resides in our huge prison population? What would you be like if your school system had placed talent development at the top of its priorities?

Educating for Human Greatness is a framework for redesigning education around a higher estimate of human potential. It was started as a result of some unusual experiences I had while on active duty in public schools and has since been refined and expanded by a group of distinguished educator practitioners. The framework is a totally different, higher vision of teaching, thinking and learning. Because many people have the conventional mind-set about what schools are for, I feel it will be helpful to relate some of the experiences I had that led to this "higher vision."

Challenging the Conventional Mind-Set

My journey into the diverse world of "alternative education" officially started with a position paper I wrote for the Utah Association for Supervision and Curriculum Development (ASCD) in 1973. At the time, our country was in the middle of an education reform movement called "Back to Basics." I had just finished a term as President of Utah ASCD and was still on the Board of Directors as the immediate past president. In our meetings there was much discussion about Back to Basics and what was happening to public education because of it. I proposed that our group should prepare a position paper that would set forth our views. I should have known better. I was selected to write the paper and present it to the Board for approval.

This became a turning point in my career as an educator. Up until this event, I had taught fifth and sixth graders in the public school system for ten years and was then in my thirteenth year as an elementary school principal.

The Back to Basics movement was energized by a very popular book by Rudolph Flesch, *Why Johnny Can't Read*, and some radical ideas of B.F. Skinner, a psychologist who maintained that you could shape human behavior with "positive reinforcements." Flesch said that children couldn't read because they didn't know how to use phonics to unlock words. The ideas of Flesch and Skinner became a strange marriage that caused a flurry of excitement and anticipation that children could be taught how to read at younger and younger ages. "Teach your baby how to read" became a slogan for the cultural elite who wanted to brag that their children could read sooner than the neighbor's. Schools were being pressured to drop everything and use Flesch's reading program to teach reading and Skinner's methods to shape behavior.

Now picture this. Our country was enamored with the idea that we should go "back to basics," centered in phonetic reading instruction in elementary schools. Along comes the Utah Association for Supervision and Curriculum Development with my position paper titled "Learning to Read Should NOT be the Primary Purpose of Elementary Education." Wow! Can you imagine any stance that would be more in opposition to the prevailing mood of the country? When everyone was concentrating on reading, Utah ASCD asserts that it is the wrong focus!

My position paper started with this quote by the eminent English philosopher, John Locke:

This much for learning to read,

which let him never be driven to.
Cheat him into it if you can,
but make it not a business for him.
'Tis better it be a year later before he can read
than that he should this way
get an aversion to learning.

The following are more excerpts from my position paper, approved by the Board of Directors. Keep in mind that this was 1973 and compare it with what has been happening in recent years. Does history repeat itself?

> The great majority of people in our country believe that the primary mission of the elementary school is to teach children how to read. This belief is traditional, long standing and deeply embedded. To propose any other notion will likely bring a deluge of protest—yet the ASCD Board of Directors feels so much damage is being done because of this belief that we must speak out and do what we can to help people re-examine their beliefs and establish some new priorities for elementary education.

The position paper goes on to tell what happens to children when we make reading the main "business" of schooling: "Self-esteem is damaged, children learn a false concept—that the only way to gain knowledge is through reading—and overemphasis on reading delays or cripples the development of the ability to inquire and to reason."

History Repeats

One recent commercial reading program is called "Reading First." It is a program that insists that children need more phonics to help them unlock words. It uses a system called DIBELS in which children are supposed to learn how to pronounce nonsense syllables phonetically. Much time is spent drilling students on the nonsense syllables. It appears that Rudolph Flesch, like Elvis, may not be dead after all.

Now I'm not going to argue the role of phonics in helping children learn how to read except to say that my experience confirms what the noted linguist, Frank Smith, says about it; "Children don't learn reading from phonics, they learn phonics from reading." In other words, it is the act of reading that instills the ability to recognize similarities in word construction and words that "sound" alike. The "sounds" of individual letters of the alphabet are not a factor because phonetic "sounds" are always a blend of the sounds of two or more letters together, not single letters alone. "Sounds" are not a factor, or else how do you explain that deaf people learn how to read all the time?

The problem with commercial programs that make reading a business for children is that they often ignore individual differences and destroy curiosity. In my position paper for ASCD, I mentioned three major issues that we should be concerned about:

1. How can we maintain and build upon the natural zest for learning which children have when they start school?
2. How can we help children develop a repertoire of skills for locating and learning information, creating and extending information, communicating ideas and solving problems?
3. How can we help children develop their unique, individual identities, talents and interests?

These three concerns became the danger signals for making reading the main business of elementary education. In the position paper we outlined three priorities that we felt were more important than children learning how to read in elementary school:

1. Help children develop their inquiring, creative minds.
2. Help children develop individual talents, identity and feelings of worth as members of the human family.
3. Help children develop powers of expression and communication.

The position paper attracted a lot of attention. Thousands of copies were printed and distributed. The Rudolph Flesch and B.F. Skinner devotees challenged the Utah ASCD Board of Directors to a debate in which the Flesch/Skinner people would defend the proposition that the main business of elementary school is phonetic reading and behavior modification. The ASCD Board of Directors would show that there are other things, those listed above, that are more important than learning how to read, but that reading would be a natural outcome.

A time and place were set and the debate occurred before a large gathering of people. For my part of the debate, I showed a filmstrip I had prepared that showed the damage of making reading a business for children. I called the filmstrip "Children on the Roof," and it started with a narrator mimicking the famous film star who played the part of Tevye:

> "Children on the roof—sounds crazy huh? But here in the big red schoolhouse you might say that every one of us is a child on the roof, trying to scratch out a pleasant, simple tune without breaking our necks.

> Why do we stay up there? How do we keep our balance? I'll tell you in one word, *tradition!* In the big red schoolhouse we must keep basic skills uppermost in our minds so we will not lose our balance."

In the filmstrip I tried to show that elementary education does not—cannot—change because of *tradition*. Our society has a mind-set about what schools are for. Every time the system tries to respond to new research, something pulls us back—in this case, Back to Basics as manifested in the Flesch phonics book.

The Back to Basics movement appeared at the exact time that a new way to teach literacy was being investigated. It was called "whole language" because it showed that basic skills could best be learned in context—as a natural process of actually using them in the process of investigating and interacting about the environment. In other words, reading, writing, and arithmetic could best be learned while actually reading, writing and doing math—for genuine, not contrived, reasons—while doing and talking about actual, hands-on investigations.

There were many teachers, including myself, who were beginning to feel that the whole language approach had great merit. Subjects of the curriculum could best be taught and learned as integrated skills while actually using them, rather than as separate, isolated disciplines taught before they were needed. This became most clear to me when I found that students learned how to spell best when they wanted to learn to spell the words they needed in writing their own stories. Having all students study a standard list of words each week for a test on Friday no longer made sense to me. Whenever a student didn't know how to spell a word while writing, I would have her come to me with this question, "Is this how you spell _____?" I would either agree, or write the word for the child, who would then use it on their paper and place it in a personal, self-made notebook for future reference in case it was needed again.

The main difference between learning how to spell by studying from a list or learning while writing, has to do with where the child stores the word in his or her memory. When words are learned from a list to pass the test on Friday, they are placed in short term memory. After the test, the words are often forgotten because the purpose for learning them was to pass a test. I found that children better retained words they learned for use in writing.

Reading, Writing and Math as Tools

To illustrate a point, I must tell a story of how I taught reading in elementary school. I had a typical class of fifth and sixth graders whose reading levels ranged from a beginning level to eleventh grade ability. The district reading supervisors recommended teaching reading in three groups divided by ability. I tried it several times and could never feel comfortable with it. Our small school did not have a library, but we had access to the county public library through a loan program. Once a month I would go to the library and pick up three large bundles of one hundred books wrapped in waterproof canvas. The books, both fact and fiction, covered a wide range of topics and reading difficulty.

On the special day, when it was time to open the bundles of books, I would take out each one, hold it up, express enthusiasm for it, and see if anyone in my class would be interested in reading it. Invariably, several hands would go up. At the end of the book opening ceremony children would be invited to select a book to read for an hour. We would often take some time for children to tell about the book they were reading. To solve the problem of never having enough time for this, children were invited to write a short book review on a 4x6 inch file card and put it in the card file, especially if they found a book that was exciting to them. The file was always available for children to read the reviews of their classmates to help them find a new book to read. Students soon discovered that it was important to write legibly so others could read their reviews. In addition to this, I would read a chapter from *The Adventures of Tom Sawyer* or another classic book every day after lunch.

This is how I taught reading, and part of how I taught writing. After one year, I checked achievement test scores and compared them with the previous year; the students had improved, on average, three grade levels in reading ability.

I'm telling this story to show that students will learn to read and write better when reading and writing are taught as a *means* to an end, as a way to gain and share wonderful knowledge and information. In my book *Educating for Human Greatness*, I also relate how a great first grade teacher, Beth Moore, taught beginning reading by inviting students to label their original pieces of art. At the same time students were learning to read, they were also growing in the powers of imagination. The first words to read were their own!

I believe mathematics can also be taught more effectively as a tool of inquiry—by inviting children to observe and investigate their environment—through counting, weighing, measuring and comparing objects and events. An alert teacher can always find ways to use math as a tool—rather than as a goal—to help students find genuine problems to pursue.

Back to the Future

Before going on, perhaps I should tell you that after the great debate, a new ASCD President asked me to stop distributing the infamous position paper because it was no longer the position of Utah ASCD. The Back to Basics Movement had carried the day. The whole-language way of learning literacy was smothered by *tradition!* Because most people in our culture felt they had learned to read from phonics, they endorsed Back to Basics as the wave of the future.

Now, fast forward ten years. I was having a summer "retreat" with the teachers of Hill Field Elementary School, where I was principal. Near the end of our meetings a teacher said, "We need to find a better way than Back-to-School Night to get acquainted with parents and learn of their needs for their children. We need to meet with each child's parents one-on-one to get acquainted and set goals." The traditional Back-to-School Night had consisted of a meeting with all the parents coming and hearing the teacher tell what s/he would try to accomplish during the year and how the parents could help.

To make a long story short, the PTA helped us set up one-on-one meetings with teachers and each child's parents. We asked the parents to come prepared to answer three questions:

1. What would you like the school to help you accomplish for your child this year?
2. What are this child's special needs, interests, talents and abilities that we should keep in mind?
3. How can we work together to accomplish your needs?

We also developed two different priority surveys for parents to indicate their most important needs for the education of their children.

The practice of holding get-acquainted interviews and conducting priority surveys at the beginning of each school year became very popular. These measures provided valuable information for what we should be doing. Each year, as we compiled the results of the priority surveys, an amazing picture began to emerge. In interviews with thousands of parents, over several years, teachers were surprised to learn of three needs that parents felt were more important to them than the need to have a child achieve in reading, writing, and arithmetic. First, parents wanted us to respect children as individuals, to pay attention to each child's special needs, and to help youngsters develop their unique talents and abilities. Second, they wanted children to increase in curiosity and passion for knowledge—they wanted children to "fall in love with learning." And third, parents wanted teachers to help children learn how to express themselves, communicate and get along. The priorities were so consistent with nearly every parent; we surmised that these may be the core needs of people in every culture—the need to know who we are and what we can become (identity), the need for knowledge (inquiry), and the need for respect and love (interaction). This finding led to a new, key concept of the Educating for Human

Greatness model—*basic skills, reading, writing, and math, should not be viewed as goals, but as a tools to help students grow in identity, inquiry, and interaction.*

A New Goal and Higher Purpose for Education

The get-acquainted, goal-setting meetings that teachers had with parents at the beginning of each school year had an amazing effect. A relationship was established that lasted the whole year. Teachers and parents became good friends and developed a full, working partnership. They started inventing strategies for helping students grow in Identity, Inquiry, and Interaction. There is not room in this chapter to elaborate on three strategies that were significant—the School Post Office to develop reading and writing skills, the "Shining Stars" talent-development program, and the "Great Brain Project" for developing student inquiry. Suffice it to say that the strategies were a huge factor in establishing fantastic parental support and involvement.

During these years of joyful education, there were two powerful forces that influenced us. One force was a great deterrent, the other a significant stimulus. In 1983 the U.S. Department of Education declared our nation to be at risk because our schools were failing to produce students who were competitive with other countries. The famous "Nation at Risk Report" set off another round of so-called "reforms" similar to Back to Basics, but with one major difference: student learning in reading, writing, and mathematics would be standardized. Subject matter specialists decided what all students should know and be able to do at each grade level, and standardized achievement tests would be given to make sure it was happening. Intense pressure was applied on teachers to teach the prescribed content at each grade level.

The other force that influenced us was the need in Davis County, Utah for larger jails, and more of them. Two jails in our county were enlarged and another, enormous one, was built while we were engaged in Educating for Human Greatness. We learned that jails all over the country were overcrowded, and we asked ourselves, what is wrong in our society that there are so many lawbreakers? If schools were to emphasize talent development, would it make a difference?

We have now arrived at the crux of the Educating for Human Greatness philosophy. It all hinges on these critical concepts:

Unlike conventional education, student achievement in curriculum is *not* the primary goal. The top priority is talent development, creativity, and the power of inquiry and respectful communication, qualities that are most likely to result in contributive behavior.

What, then, is curriculum for? A wide range of subject matter content is used as a *tool* to help students grow in the dimensions of human greatness. A different kind of assessment and accountability tool is used—not to measure student uniformity, but to assess the development of PHD—positive human diversity.

The Educating for Human Greatness Alliance

Fast forward again to the present day. There is a growing group of over two hundred distinguished educators, parents, and researchers who have discovered the value of Educating for Human Greatness. They are working to share it as a comprehensive framework for communities to use to make public education fit their special needs. These people have given of their time, means, and knowledge to refine and expand the framework. If you want to learn more about it, with the possibility of joining to help us redesign public education, please contact the author (lstrd@yahoo.com) or visit the Human Greatness Ning (definegreat.ning.com).

The World Becomes What You Teach: Education for a Peaceful, Sustainable, And Humane World
Zoe Weil

I grew up in an upper middle class home in Manhattan and attended the Nightingale-Bamford School from first through twelfth grade. Nightingale was and is a small, rigorously academic, college-preparatory girls' school with a reputation for high achievement and scholastic excellence. A couple of years before I graduated from Nightingale, the valedictorian and salutatorian at Princeton University were Nightingale graduates, and when you consider the fact that Nightingale's graduating classes in those years ranged between twenty-five and thirty students, this is rather extraordinary.

When I got to college in 1983, I was amazed that I was suddenly receiving A's in English, having rarely gotten above a B+ on an English assignment at Nightingale. I was very well prepared, at least in writing. All this sounds good, the ideal education that everyone, not just the privileged, should have. But I have come to believe that by failing to identify a high enough purpose for the education it provides, even Nightingale—purported to deliver one of the best educations money can buy—ultimately fails at the great opportunity schooling can and should offer our children and the world.

Such criticism could easily sound like the whiny, spoiled voice of the overindulged. Hundreds of five-year-olds compete to get into Nightingale every year, each one's family willing to pay an extraordinary amount of money for this elite education. How can I possibly think that this form of education is anything less than ideal? I was fortunate enough to attend Nightingale and to have had the preparation that got me into an Ivy League college, so why do I now consider the form of education I received so far from what I have wanted for my own child?

Here's an anecdote that may help to explain my frustration. In my mid-twenties, my then boyfriend, now husband, and I were walking in a park in Philadelphia that had several plaques dedicated to the revolutionary war. After reading one, I awkwardly asked him what the difference was between the revolutionary war and the Civil War. He was dumbfounded.

Of course I had learned about American Revolution and the Civil War at Nightingale! I'd taken lots of history tests and did well on them; Nightingale had not failed to teach American History. But for me, history classes were so unbearably boring, filled with names and dates of battles and dull texts, and I used every opportunity to ask to be excused to go to the bathroom for a moment or two of sanity. In the end, all those A's and B's in history meant little. I hadn't learned. I'd memorized, regurgitated, and quickly forgotten.

It's an absurdity that someone in her mid-twenties, who received the education I had, would not know the difference between these two wars, and I certainly don't think that it's Nightingale's fault that I didn't retain this information. Somehow, though, my teachers failed to inspire me to convert the facts they had me memorize into lasting knowledge about aspects of my country's history that would be meaningful, useful, relevant, and *worth* retaining. While I knew I should be embarrassed by my question, I discovered that I was much more curious about the purpose of all that memorization that didn't stick. Why hadn't I remembered it? What was it all for?

Another anecdote: There were four reading groups in first grade. There were a couple of children in the "second-grade readers" group, who were the most advanced; a few "Pathfinders," who knew how to read but not well enough to be with the second graders; a large group of "Pixies," who were not yet readers but who were bright; and a final group that was called "Dwarves." Imagine that. By second grade, these names, or should I say this name-calling, had been replaced by A and B groups for all subjects other than music, art, and dance. I remember wondering in elementary school how "B" students lived with themselves; how they endured what must have felt like daily humiliation. No obvious or strong value was attached to other qualities, talents, and skills, so no matter how funny, fun, friendly, athletic, imaginative, artistic, or simply good and kind a girl was, we were all ultimately judged and ranked by our ability to do well academically. The very fact that I wondered how "B" students lived with themselves shows how deeply I had internalized the belief that self worth depends upon being smart and getting good grades. Apparently school was for success, and success was narrowly defined by good grades, which led to good colleges, which led to lucrative and respectable careers.

By fifth grade, we were not just taking tests, but also exams, and I became physically ill the morning of my first exam at ten years old. This was a recurring state for the next seven years. School was less a place to learn, and more a source of fear about daily academic performances. For these I was rarely fully prepared because I was uninterested in most of the required books and textbooks, or in the lectures from our teachers, and simply tried to get by with good enough grades. The ubiquitous comment from my father reading my report card, "As long as you did your best," drove the knife of self recrimination deeper, as I could count the times on one hand that I actually did my best in school. School rarely inspired my best. That was not what it was for.

Although I didn't much like Nightingale, I took it on faith that it was about as good as schools get. I never expected that one day my own field would be education, or that I would write this essay saying that even Nightingale wasn't good enough, not just for me, but for almost all Nightingale graduates and a world that needs more from us than preparation for elite colleges and high-powered careers. It would take me a while, however, to realize this and to develop a different vision of education, one that seeks to answer the question "what is school for?" with something more worthy of our children's imaginations, hopes, and intelligence.

In my early twenties I was hired as a teacher and naturalist at a wildlife rehabilitation and nature center. I spent much of that year teaching in a variety of South Jersey schools and to groups of students who came for field trips to our center. One small group stood out, and twenty-four years later I still remember the children I taught that morning. They were homeschoolers.

When I heard that a group of homeschooled children had arrived, I approached them full of judgment. I thought they would be weird, socially inept, and uneducated. I was in for a surprise. They were the most engaged, patient, creative, curious, compassionate, interesting group of kids I'd yet to teach. It was my first clue that our country's approach to schooling might itself be problematic. If children without school were this terrific, what was it about school that was dumbing down the rest of them?

After a year at the nature center, I went to graduate school. Looking for a summer job between my first and second years in a master's program, I applied to teach several week-long summer courses for seventh and eighth graders at the University of Pennsylvania. One of my courses, on Animal Protection, was the second most popular of the sixty offered that summer, and I watched in amazement as my students made new choices because of what they were learning. One boy became an activist overnight. I had taught about product testing on animals on Wednesday (in which household and personal care products are dripped into the eyes of conscious rabbits, smeared onto the abraded skin of animals, and force-fed to them in quantities that kill), and Thursday morning he came into class with homemade leaflets about animal testing that he handed to passersby on a Philadelphia street corner during lunch.

I had found my life's work.

Since then I have been teaching about the interconnected issues of human rights, environmental preservation, animal protection, and culture in hundreds of secondary schools and numerous colleges, to tens of thousands of students. I have brought pressing issues of our time to classrooms in an effort to provide young people with the information and inspiration to participate in creating positive change. Many have started or joined school activist clubs, made healthy new choices, and gone on to careers that contribute to a more just society. I have come to

believe that this kind of education—what we call humane education—
has enormous power not only to positively influence our daily decisions
but also to inspire active participation in the creation of a better world.

After several years as a humane educator, I began to identify certain
components that comprise quality humane education. These include:

1. Providing accurate information about the great challenges of our
   time so that students have the knowledge to make healthy,
   humane, and sustainable choices
2. Fostering the three Cs of curiosity, creativity, and critical thinking
   so students have the tools to create more just and restorative
   systems
3. Instilling the three Rs of reverence, respect, and responsibility so
   students have the motivation to face challenges enthusiastically
   and with commitment
4. Offering positive choices and the tools for problem solving so
   students become conscious choicemakers and engaged
   solutionaries for a peaceful, sustainable, and humane world for all

Because I have taught in so many kinds of schools, I have had the
opportunity to witness a range of school cultures and approaches. I
have taught in wealthy suburban public schools and inner city ghetto
public schools, at Christian schools and Jewish schools, boarding
schools and military academies, democratic schools and schools for
"juvenile delinquents" and runaways.

There have been a few schools—far too few—I have loved. They are
places where students are deeply engaged; where inspired and inspiring
teachers clearly care about the kids as individuals and the kids care
about each other and their teachers; where the grounds and buildings
are conducive to learning and health, and where the atmosphere exudes
enthusiasm, happiness, and creativity.

There have also been places that have surprised me in both positive
and negative ways. I appreciated the good manners of the students at a
particular Catholic girls' school, but couldn't get the girls to participate
at all. They just sat politely with hands folded on their desks and
listened but wouldn't engage with questions. Their curiosity and their
voices seemed blunted. At one of the most prestigious private schools

in Philadelphia's Main Line suburbs, where I expected intelligent questions from well-behaved students, a group of boys in the back of the assembly snickered and made rude comments. Conversely, at a school for kids who'd been kicked out of numerous other schools, I experienced some of the most profound moments of my career as several students, who cared deeply about what I taught, wanted to create change for others despite the dire circumstances of their own lives. And at a military academy, where my own stereotypes led me to expect at least a bit of hostility towards the "progressive" issues I was teaching about, I had one of the most curious, respectful, and intelligent Q & A sessions I'd ever experienced, from boys who saluted me as I walked on their campus.

I have come to believe that there is no one ideal school for all children. Free schools work well for some, while Montessori for others. Much of what my son received at his Waldorf-inspired elementary school was extraordinary, but Waldorf isn't the best choice for all. Project-based learning is great, but not everyone does well with it. Homeschooling, while an excellent choice for many, is impractical for lots of families. And at my recent thirtieth high school reunion, when I asked my classmates if they thought they had received a good education at Nightingale, most of them said yes. One woman, who was the valedictorian of our class, had had a wonderful experience at Nightingale and she adored our history teacher—one of the teachers whose class I sought to flee at every opportunity due to boredom.

So while I have developed very strong opinions about schooling, teaching styles, grades, rote learning, standardized testing, bells, textbooks, teacher training, current standard curricula, disconnected subject matter, and much more, my strongest beliefs about education—and my current life's mission—revolves not around what kind of school is best, but rather around the question I have continued to come back to ever since Nightingale: *what is schooling for?* While I don't believe there is a specific kind of school or pedagogical structure that is best for all children, I do believe that there should be agreement on the actual purpose of schooling, and that this overarching purpose should drive the curricula, approaches, projects, and teaching in all schools.

We must shift the goal of education from producing graduates prepared for jobs—whether as factory workers, farmers, business people, scientists, etc.—to nurturing a generation of graduates who have the motivation and skills to create healthy and humane factories; life-sustaining and sustainable forms of farming; humane, environmentally-friendly, and just businesses; scientific discoveries that are grounded in ethics and that lead to inventions that contribute to the well being of all, and so on.

If the purpose of all schooling everywhere becomes to prepare learners for their important roles in creating healthy, just, humane systems—whether in healthcare, politics, business, construction, transportation, energy, food-production, or law—we will see a rapid and remarkable shift away from unsustainable, cruel, unjust, and destructive systems towards ones in which we can all thrive.

Imagine if instead of acquiring the capacity to read and write so that we have skills we need for future jobs, we learned that reading and writing were our tools for lifelong learning so that we could contribute to spreading a message of peace, restoration, beauty, joy, and health through those future jobs. Imagine if instead of plodding through irrelevant word problems in math, we addressed real world concerns using computation to solve actual challenges, not simply to determine when trains leaving at different times will meet on arbitrary tracks. Imagine if history had nothing at all to do with memorizing names and dates, but everything to do with understanding our behavior, psychology, social dynamics, and past choices in order to create systems of governance, politics, economics, conflict resolution, and diplomacy that pave the way for peaceful and just societies. Imagine if science courses utilized the knowledge of equations and theories to launch students toward the incredible process of discovery and invention for a healthier world.

Imagine if learners studied food or clothing or electronics as interdisciplinary subjects, examining current systems of production that are unsafe and unjust and exploring and creating those that are sustainable and humane, using and developing greater competency in the core skills of verbal and computational literacy, research, critical and creative thinking, and problem solving. Imagine if humane education were offered to every child, in age appropriate ways, from kindergarten through college. Imagine the world these children would create.

I have seen what happens when students are offered humane

education. They become empowered to create change, to choose wisely and compassionately, and to do the most good and the least harm to themselves, other people, animals, and the environment (what I call the MOGO—most good—principle). They know they can and must contribute to a better world through whatever jobs or careers they pursue. They are not apathetic. They become agents of their lives, rather than passive recipients of the status quo. They make a difference.

Unfortunately, humane education is still relatively rare in schools. A few months ago I spoke at the National Honors Society induction at my son's high school. I had the audience analyze a conventional T-shirt, asking what the positive and negative effects of this ubiquitous piece of clothing might be on ourselves, other people, other species, and ecosystems. When we examine something as common as a T-shirt, we discover that it may have contributed to child slavery, pesticide contamination of water and soil, sweatshop labor, significant fossil fuel use, animal testing of toxic fabric dyes, and more. After the talk, one of the inductees told a friend that it made her so angry that they'd never been taught any of this before. "We should have been learning this since kindergarten!" she exclaimed.

I couldn't agree more.

I co-founded the Institute for Humane Education (IHE) to train people to be humane educators and to promote humane education so that it would become as ubiquitous as T-shirts. At IHE we are working to build momentum for this shift in schooling's purpose while we also offer training and resources—in the form of everything from free, downloadable humane education activities for educators, to workshops, to online courses, to a distance-learning M.Ed. and certificate program in humane education—to put legs on this vision.

Given all the grave problems we face, we must change dangerous and destructive systems into ones that are healthy, just, and restorative, and this will only be possible when teachers prepare their students for their critical roles as ethical choicemakers and enthusiastic changemakers. This is what school should be for.

Afterword

After reading the fantastic journeys of this disparate group of educational visionaries, one is compelled to ask: what is the commonality that drove them with such passion to such heights? We cannot exactly say it was the times, as their careers started anywhere from the 1950s to the 1990s. It has to be something deeper, more significant. Of course there is no definitive answer and we leave it to the reader to try to ferret that out. But from my point of view the commonality is an intensely human reaction from individuals who were all able to sense that something was very unhealthy for children, very inhumane, in the traditional schooling environments that they encountered. Perhaps there were others who found themselves successful in that system, or who—even though they disliked it, even though they could sense something was wrong—couldn't imagine there could be a different approach. The people who have told their stories in this book were the whistle blowers, the courageous thinkers and doers who dared to try to change things.

I have had the good fortune of personally knowing most of the authors whose tales are recorded here. So I was surprised and pleased to find, upon reading their stories, that there was a lot that I hadn't known about them. It was like fitting together some previously lost pieces of a puzzle, only to find that it opened up to a much bigger puzzle, the solution of which will finally change our system of education to one that will meet children's real needs.

When Carlo Ricci approached me with the idea of doing this book I was struck by the brilliance and simplicity of its concept. We have worked well as a team in putting this volume together, though I'm not sure that we understand yet what we have tapped. It is our fervent hope that our project will push us further toward an education revolution that will better meet all of our needs.

Jerry Mintz

Further Reading

Alternative Education Resource Organization
www.educationevolution.org

Turning Points Suggested Reading List
www.educationvisionaries.com

Democratic Education
www.democraticeducation.com

Contact

Alternative Education Resource Organization
417 Roslyn Road
Roslyn Heights, NY 11577-2620

info@educationrevolution.org
alternativeeducation@gmail.com

(800) 769-4171
(516) 621-2195